AF796674

SEE & DRAW

drawing from observation

KARL V. LARSEN

Davis Publications, Inc. Worcester, Massachusetts

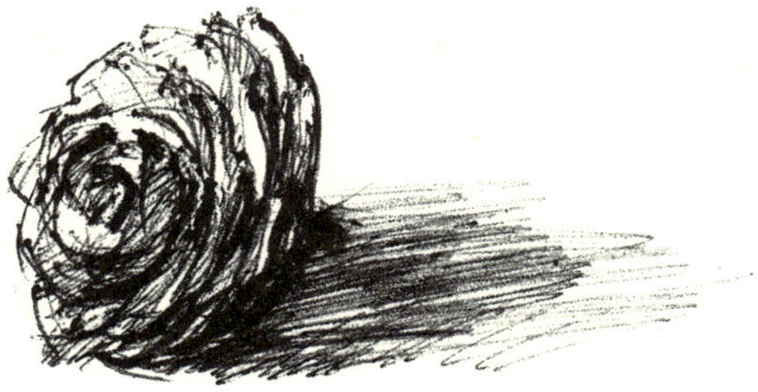

Copyright 1993
Davis Publications, Inc.
Worcester, Massachusetts, U.S.A.

All rights reserved. No part of this publication may be reproduced or transmitted in any form or by any means, electronic or mechanical, including photocopying, recording, or any storage and retrieval system now known or to be invented, except by a reviewer who wishes to quote brief passages in connection with a review written for inclusion in a magazine, newspaper or broadcast.

Library of Congress Catalog Card Number: 91-73904
ISBN: 87192-242-8
10 9 8 7 6 5 4 3 2 1

Se og Tegn
Grundbog i iagttagelsestegning

Originally published in Danish by Lindhardt and Ringhof Publishers, Copenhagen, Denmark. © 1988 Karl V. Larsen

Printed in the United States of America
Type Design: Nancy Dutting

Cover design: Paola Di Stefano

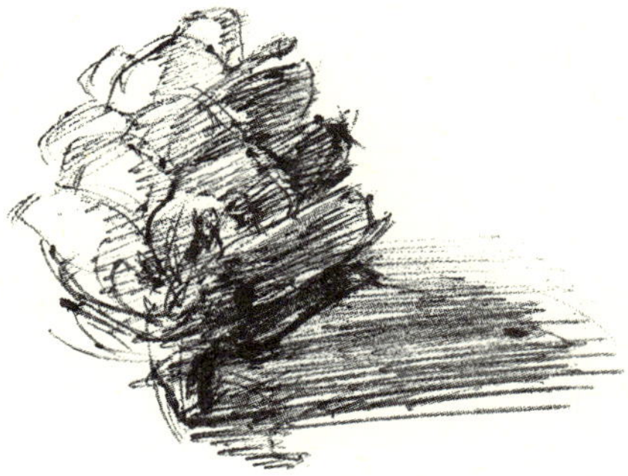

Contents

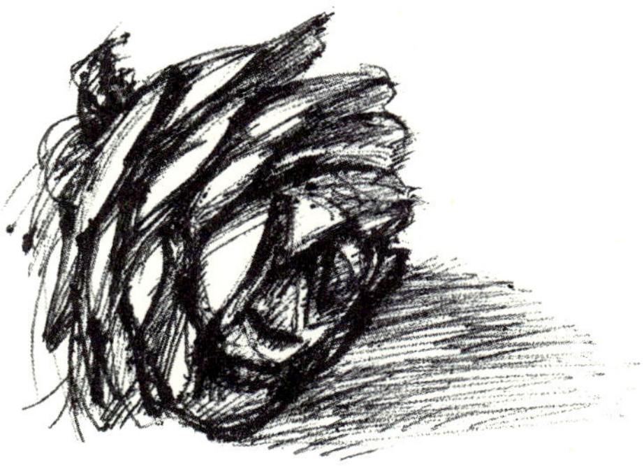

Drawing and coloring are the fundamentals of art.
Draw not only with your pen but also with
what you have in your head.

Cennino di Drea Cennini
Libro dell'Arte, circa 1400

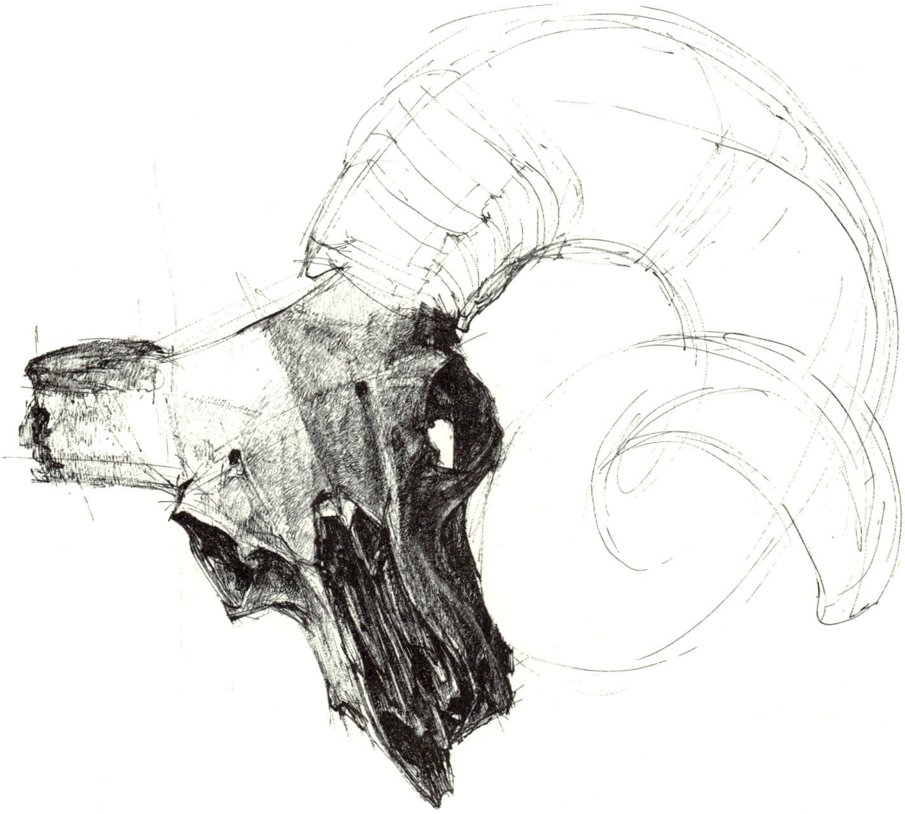

Introduction

There is a widespread belief that the primary goal of "classic art" and, later, "naturalism" was to imitate nature in art through realism or, more correctly, the illusion of realism.

But, taken too literally, this view could lead to a misinterpretation of the facts and so to misunderstanding. The truth is that painting, drawing and sculpture have rules and goals that have nothing to do with nature. Nature is and always will be an inexhaustible source of inspiration. However, artists have always been analytical about how best to include such inspiration in their art.

The "ideal" classical form, first seen in Greek and Roman art and, later, in Renaissance masterpieces, demonstrates this. Form in both cases is very clearly the refined result of intellectual and philosophic thought—the essence of a thorough study of nature.

Throughout the seventeenth century, these ideals of form became the natural basis for education in the art academies and schools of visual arts being established at the time in all the leading capitals of Europe. However, in the twentieth century, the value of this kind of educational philosophy has been severely criticized.

There have been several periods of history in which accepted ideals have been thrown out and then, after a few years, quietly re-examined and reinstated. Some predict that this will happen in the case of traditionalist art teaching. But, until then, it is mostly in schools with an "applied art" point of view that the concept of "classical drawing and design" survives.

Now, close to the end of the century there are signs that a more general interest in the old "academic approach" is awakening. I shall be very pleased if this book can help in any way to further this development.

As you will see, there is nothing nebulous about how I propose to help the tradition of "academic drawing education" gain momentum. Over the years, I have read many books on the subject of drawing instruction. I found none that I could recommend to others or that I could use in my own teaching. So, I decided to write my own. They all, I might add, have the same shortcoming. They describe how to draw but then neglect to include drawings that are directly related to the text. Instead, they substitute innumerable works by world famous artists that, at best, have only vague reference to the lessons being taught. Admittedly, there is some merit in exposing students to examples of the best art humankind has created, yet forcing beginners to constantly compare their own first works to those of the masters can have a paralyzing effect, sometimes to the point where a disillusioned student may decide to give up.

Therefore, I have chosen an approach in which first priority is given to the concerns of the student. Making use of my thirty-five years of experience as an artist specializing in drawing, twenty-five years of which I have spent teaching basic drawing (both subject and figure drawing), I have thought it best to organize my book into a logical sequence of lessons and to keep the text short and readable. Because my observations indicate that a real understanding of drawing first occurs when one sees and is moved by drawings on paper, I have taken considerable time to choose detailed drawings and sketches of my own that I think best illustrate points of instruction.

I would be dishonest if I stated that by using this book anyone, even an unprepared person, could learn to draw. The book provides information and inspiration, but this in itself is not enough. Drawing requires practice, experience and much diligence to achieve good results. But, there should be numerous opportunities for the interested student to spend many fruitful hours absorbing the techniques and sharpening the skills described here.

Especially in the beginning, it is important to develop a critical attitude toward one's own work. Don't go on to the next lesson until you are satisfied with your work on the present one. You are sure to be pleased and surprised at how generously this kind of self-discipline and application can be rewarded.

Karl V. Larsen

Drawing Supplies You Will Need

We all want good results and for that we need good tools. However, drawing tools do not have to be expensive. Reasonably priced supplies and equipment are not difficult to obtain. Here is all you need to work through the drawing activities in this book.

A Drawing Board: A good drawing board is an excellent investment, but there is no need to purchase an expensive one. A smooth-surfaced sheet of three-ply plywood large enough to accommodate an 18″ × 24″ (46 × 61 cm) sheet of drawing paper will do just as well.

Paper: You need not purchase first quality drawing paper when less expensive paper is often excellent to draw on. You can often save money by buying loose sheets of any of the following in a stationary store or the school supply section of a department store: high grade newsprint (preferably rough on one side, smooth on the other); a twenty-five percent cotton bond typing paper; or any paper of a quality similar to cartridge paper which has a rough side suitable for drawing.

Pens: There are many different pens and pencils available. Start with the simplest: a fine line marker or a ball-point pen capable of producing an uninterrupted black line. Such pens have an unexpected advantage—they don't let you hide your drawing mistakes as you might be tempted to do when working in pencil or charcoal which is more easily erased. Erasing is a bad habit generally, but especially so for the beginner who should be able to analyze his or her mistakes and learn from them. Pencils and India ink pens are excellent drawing tools but they should not be used until you have had considerable drawing experience. In my own classes at the School of Applied Arts in Denmark, erasers are not permitted and only ball-point pens are allowed.

When I enrolled as a student in this same school some forty years ago, my teacher was the well-known artist, Victor Isbrand. It is his method of teaching drawing that I have adapted for use in this book. It was important to him that any approach to making art be broad and focused on excellence. He had no patience with superficiality. He postulated that there was more to being an artist than just mastering its techniques. By working hard and energetically one can obviously improve one's skills but, he suggested, art is so profound that, no matter how hard one works at it, there is always something more to learn. It is because of this combination of enthusiasm and humbleness which permeated Victor Isbrand's philosophy of art education that his teaching has become an inspiration for me.

My purpose in this book is to give a broad introduction to drawing rather than a closely focused one. I have avoided the details of perspective and composition and completely dispensed with any discussion of color. This is not because these aspects of art are not important but because beginners can easily become confused and lose enthusiasm when confronted with too many concepts all at the same time. For those inspired to seek further and deeper involvement, there are many excellent books that deal with more advanced aspects of drawing than those explored here. Such books are widely available in local libraries and book stores.

There are many roads to success in drawing, and there are any number of tools and supplies by which to obtain good results. But, in terms of the lessons outlined in this book and your own capabilities at this point, the most rapid progress will be made by those who stay with basic papers and easy-to-use pens recommended earlier which will more than adequately accommodate the needs of even the most advanced drawing activities outlined in this book.

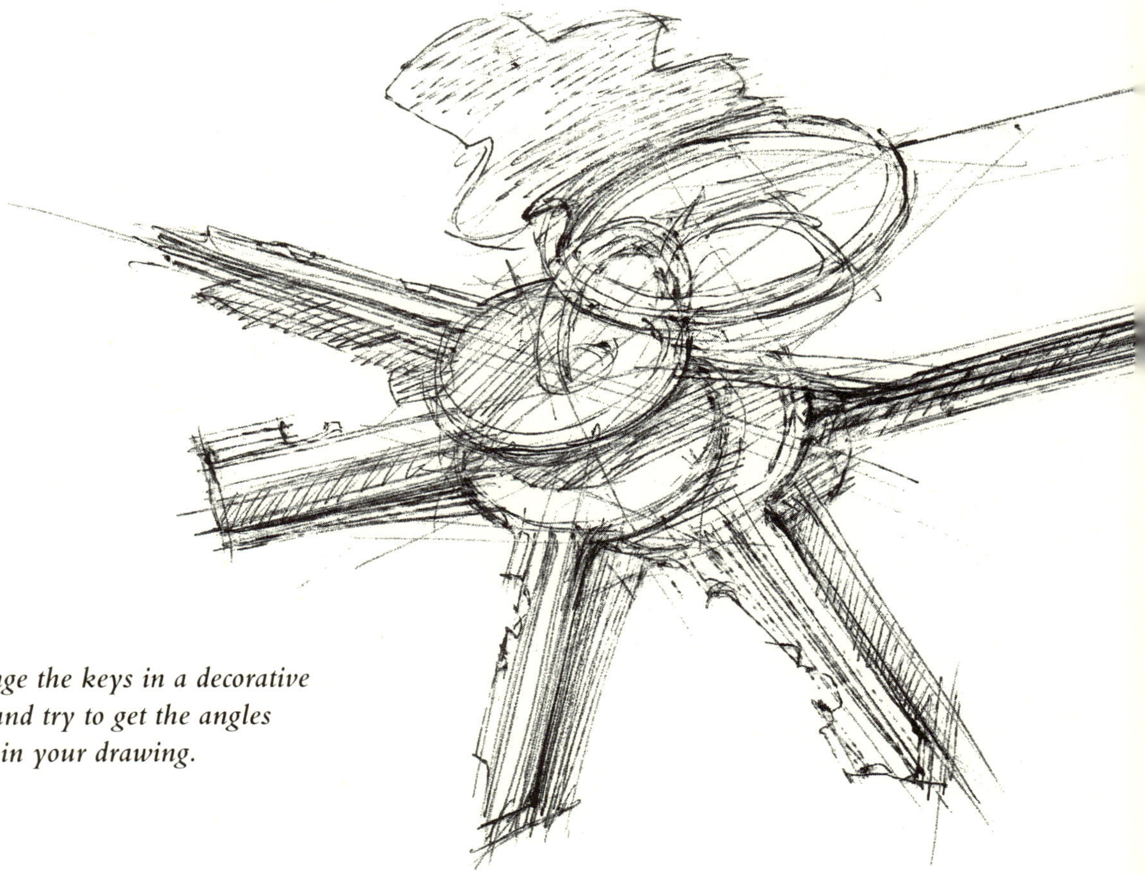

Arrange the keys in a decorative way and try to get the angles exact in your drawing.

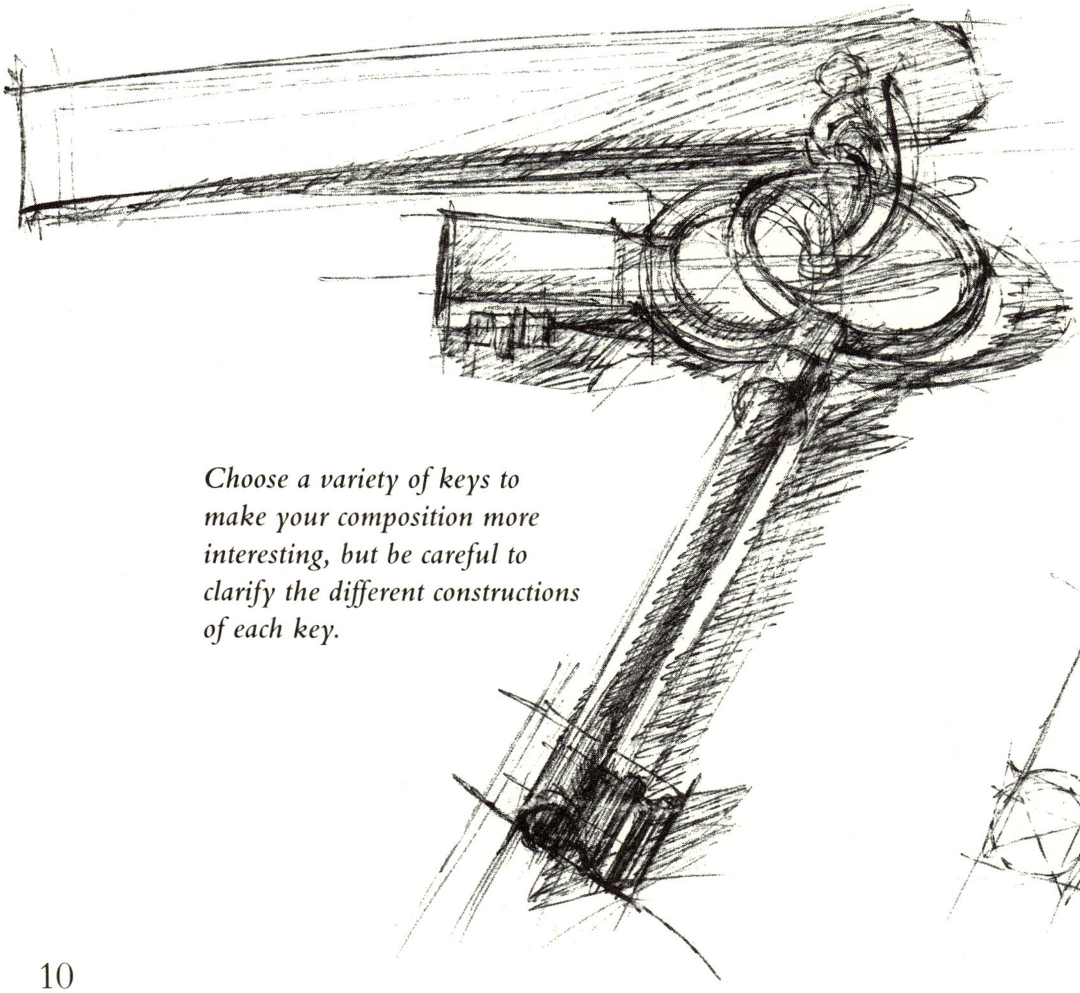

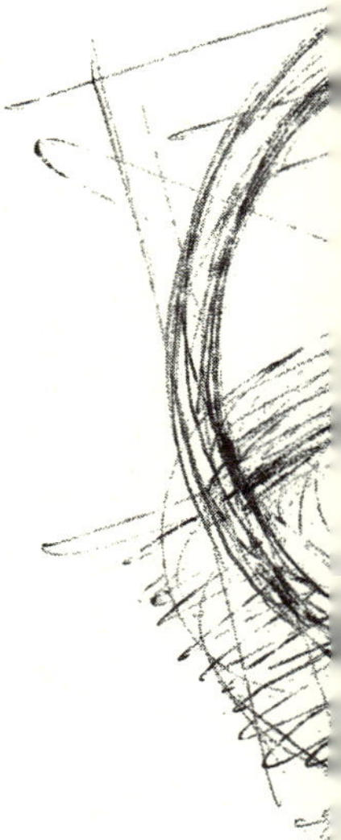

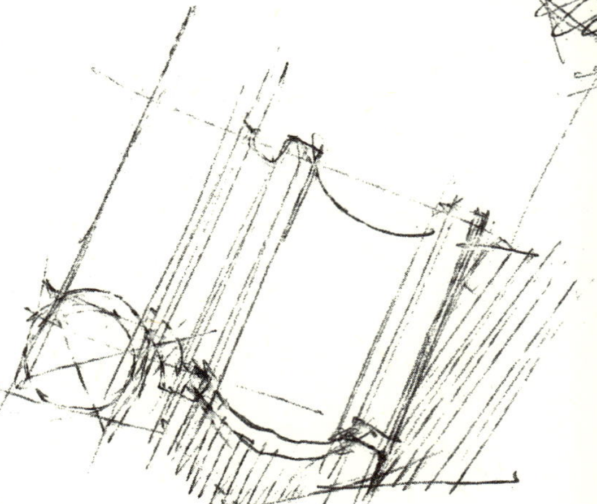

Choose a variety of keys to make your composition more interesting, but be careful to clarify the different constructions of each key.

LESSON 1

Drawing Useful Objects

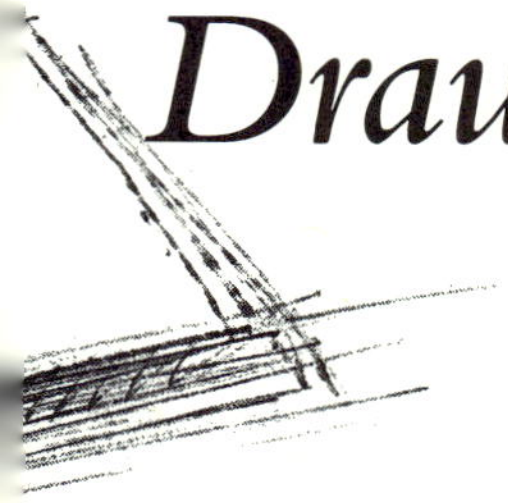

It's wise to choose simple everyday objects as models for your first drawings. A bunch of keys, for example, is visually uncomplicated and readily available—the kind of subject matter that challenges but does not confuse the beginner. To heighten concentration it's best to isolate the keys from any kind of visual distraction.

Take a piece of cardboard and fold it once. Place it as a continuation of your drawing board so that it lies in the middle of your line of vision. Place the keys on the white cardboard and study them carefully. The white cardboard helps eliminate any distractions from your surroundings and restricts the picture plane. The picture plane, with its horizontal and vertical points, is the imagined or constructed plane that we transfer to the paper.

Look for the angles of the different types of keys that have similar horizontal and vertical points. Place the keys carefully. Where you see ovals, circles or ellipses, draw a square in perspective, deep into the picture plane. To find the middle of the squares, make a cross by drawing lines from opposite corners. Connect these middle points with the middle lines of the keys. It is now possible for you to draw the keys.

Circles in perspective appear either as oval, ellipses or straight lines. Circles are difficult to draw, especially when they become ellipses because of foreshortening. Your first attempts will usually look awkward, but don't give up. Sketch the squares systematically and make the ellipses taut.

You'll quickly discover that there are four points where the ellipse is longest and has the greatest tension. By applying this knowledge and continuing sketching, you'll soon have good results.

Let me reiterate my enthusiasm for your use of the ball-point pen in completing this and the lessons that follow. Because its line is so thin, can't be erased and can't be obscured by blurred lines and soft shading, you can't help but be confronted by your mistakes and so have an excellent opportunity to correct them in your next drawing. Another suggestion: don't draw small, and you will have a better overview of your work.

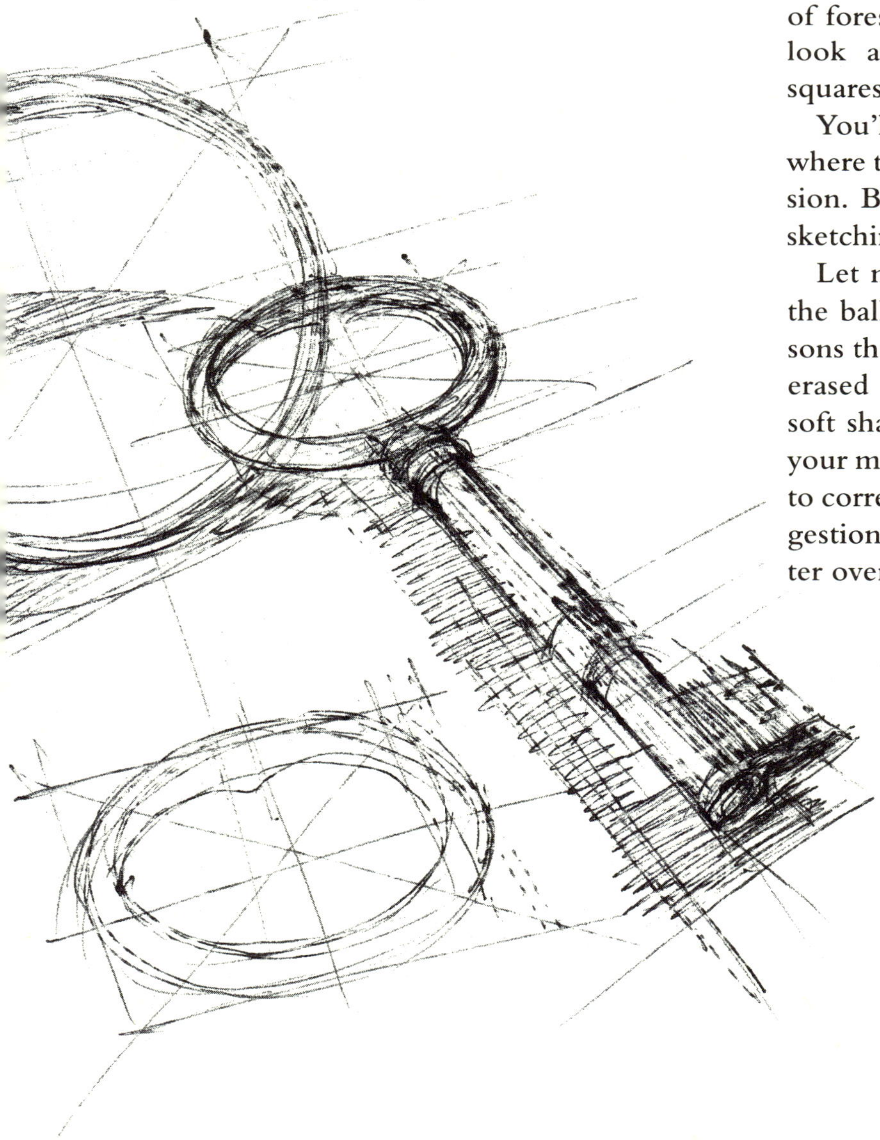

Draw the squares or rectangles in perspective as a guide to placing the key and key ring correctly in the picture plane.

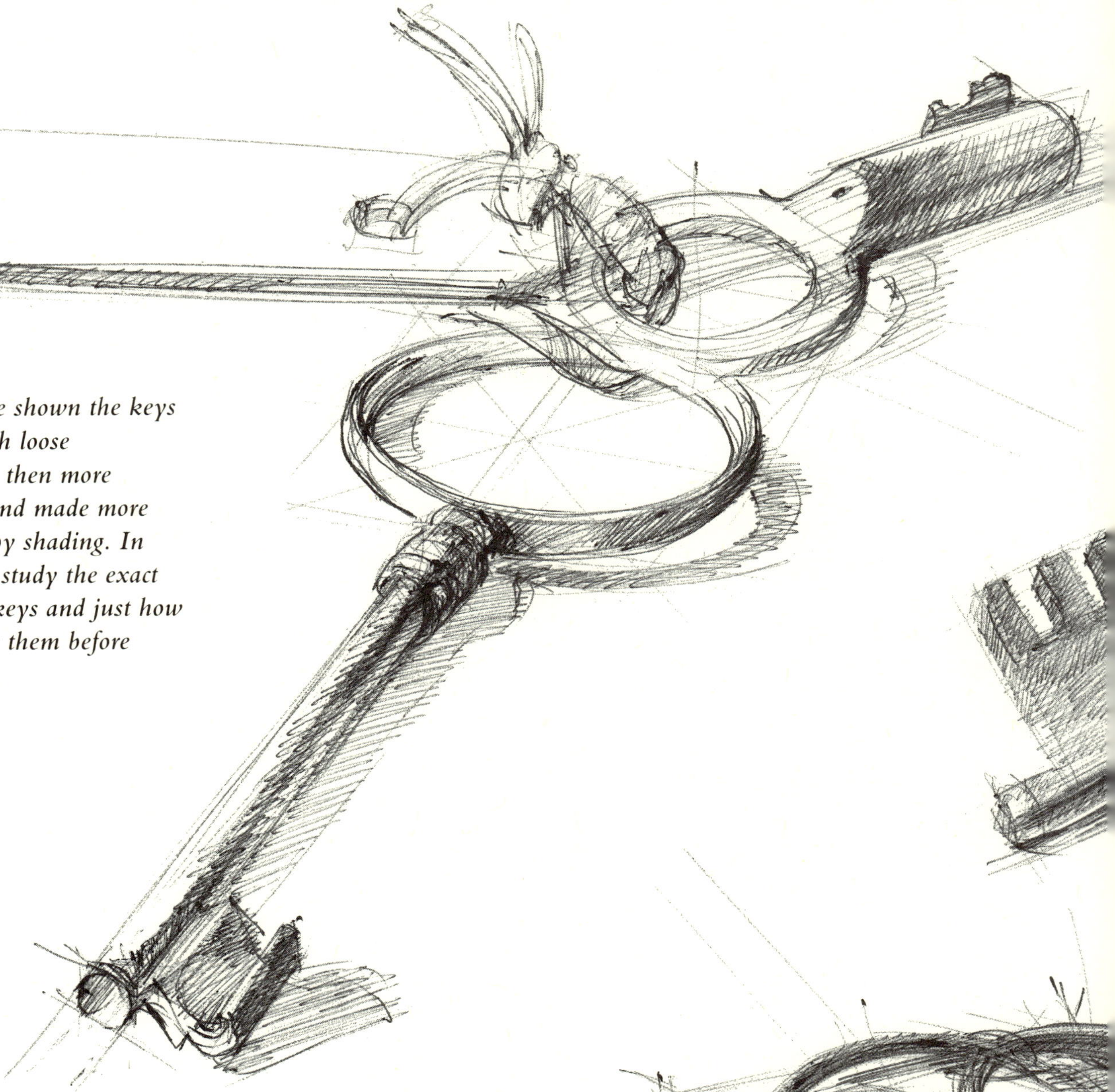

On this page I have shown the keys first sketched in with loose exploratory strokes, then more carefully executed and made more three-dimensional by shading. In your own drawing, study the exact construction of the keys and just how the light falls across them before shading.

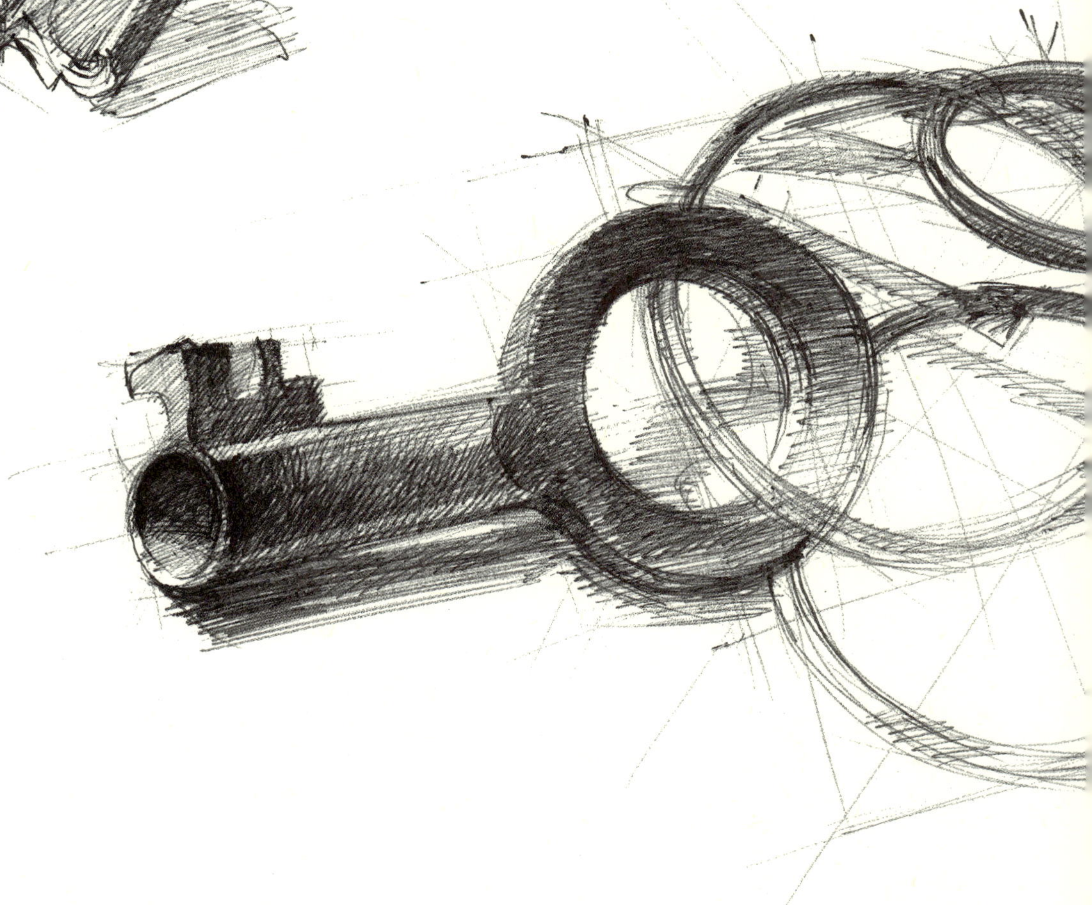

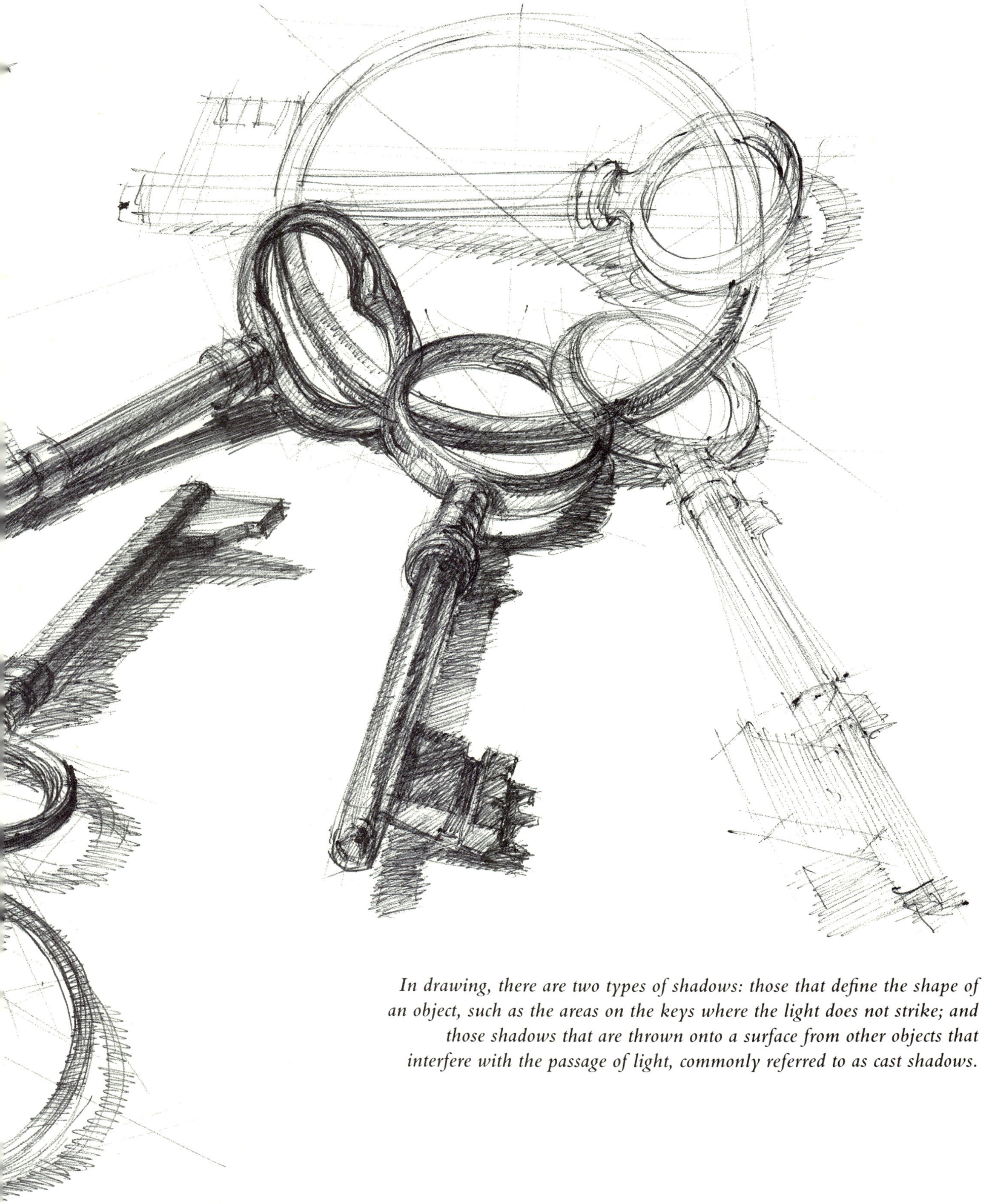

In drawing, there are two types of shadows: those that define the shape of an object, such as the areas on the keys where the light does not strike; and those shadows that are thrown onto a surface from other objects that interfere with the passage of light, commonly referred to as cast shadows.

A good object to draw is an open compass. Be careful to establish the thickness of each part correctly.

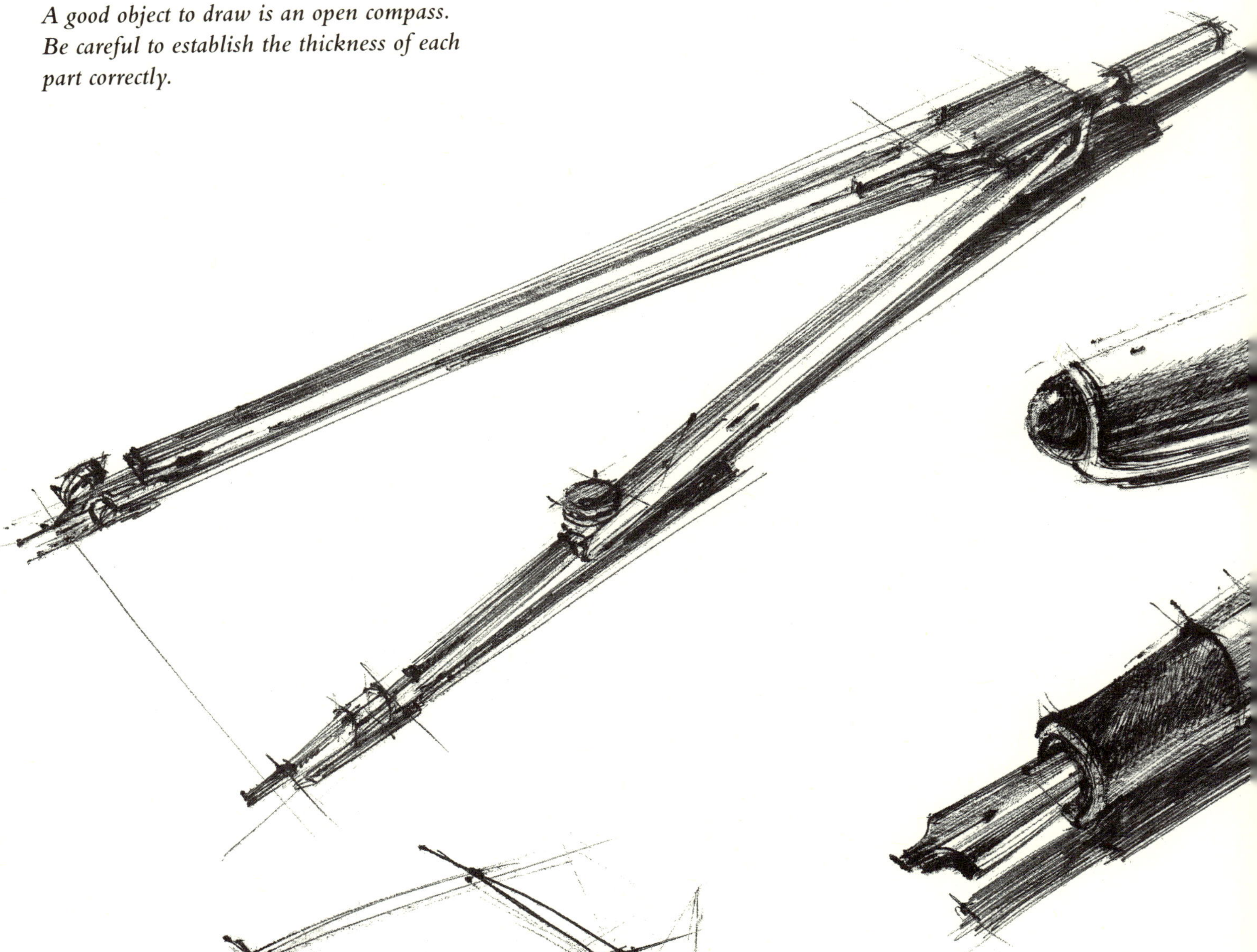

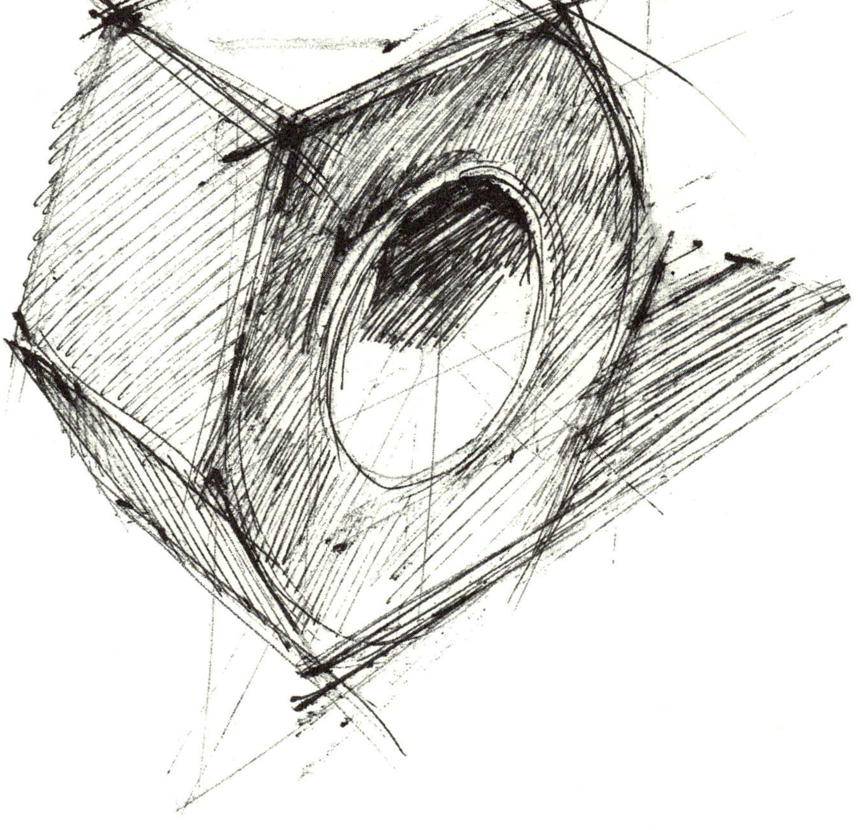

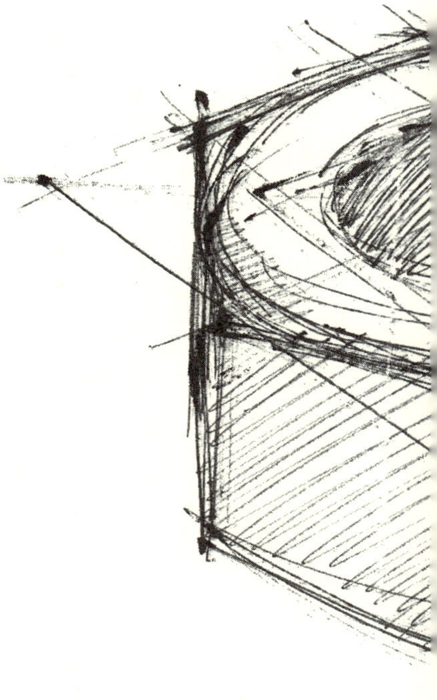

Try drawing an old-fashioned fountain pen. Your shading should follow the form to emphasize the cylindrical shape. Sharp contrasts of light and dark are needed to give the feeling of metal.

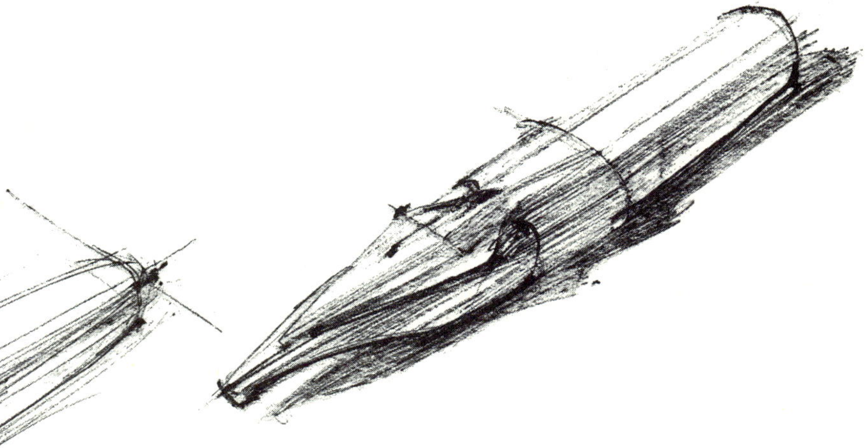

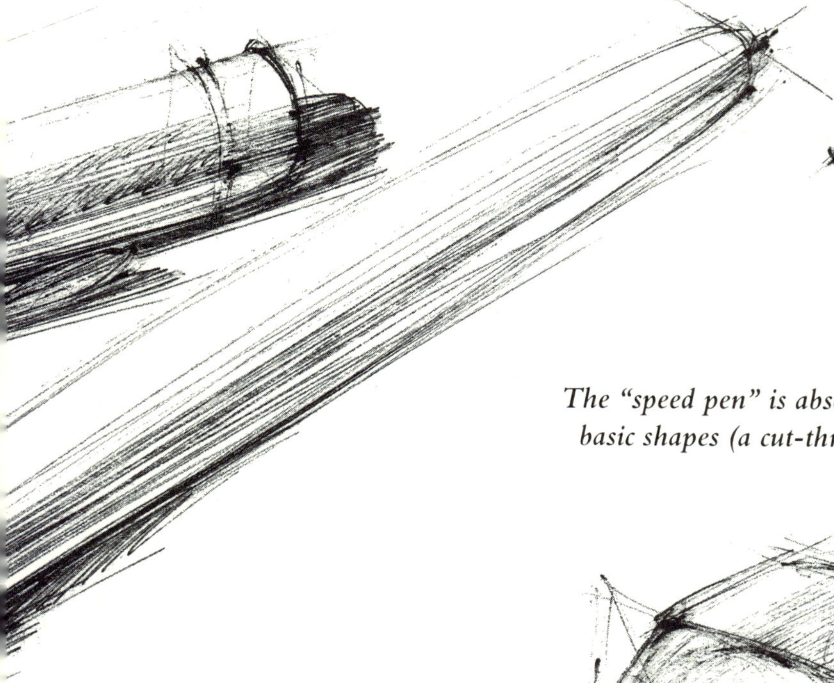

The "speed pen" is absorbing to draw because its construction is made up of basic shapes (a cut-through cylinder and three-edged pyramid). It is also a manageable object for the novice to undertake.

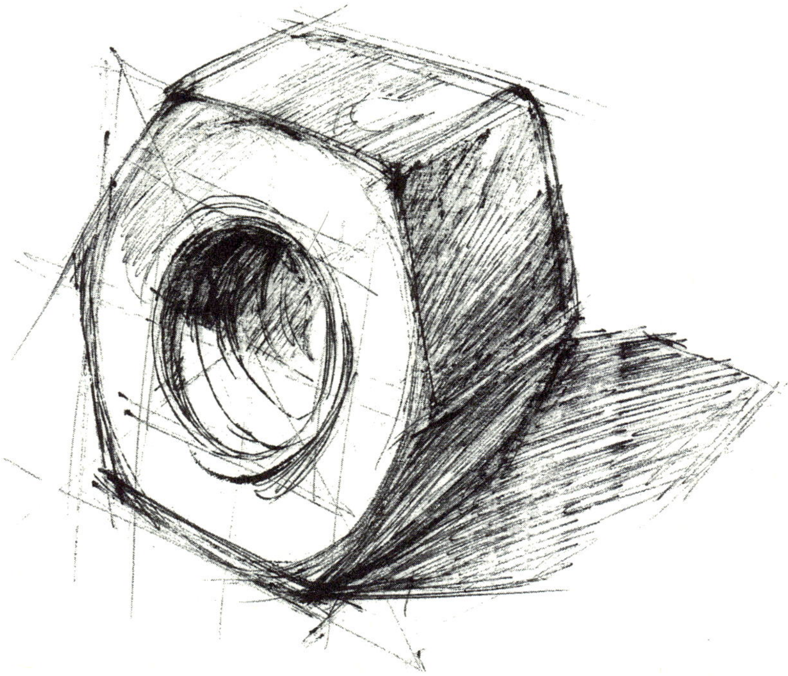

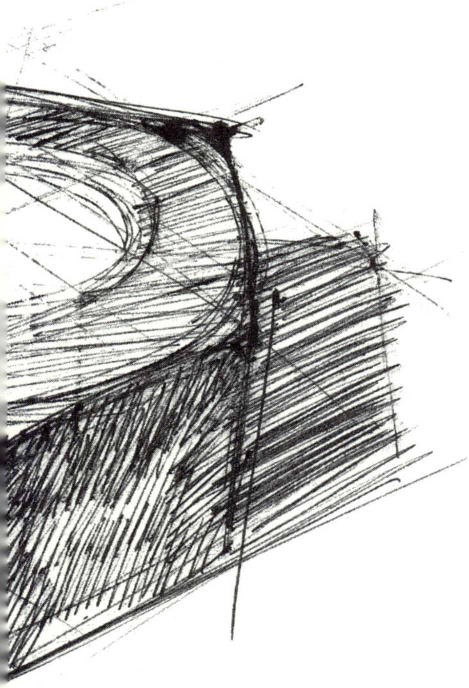

When drawing a faceted object like the nut you see here, start with a square. Draw a circle within it. Make a cross in the square and draw six tangents extending out to the circle. Add depth and repeat the tangents. Create the center hole by first drawing a square and then a circle within it.

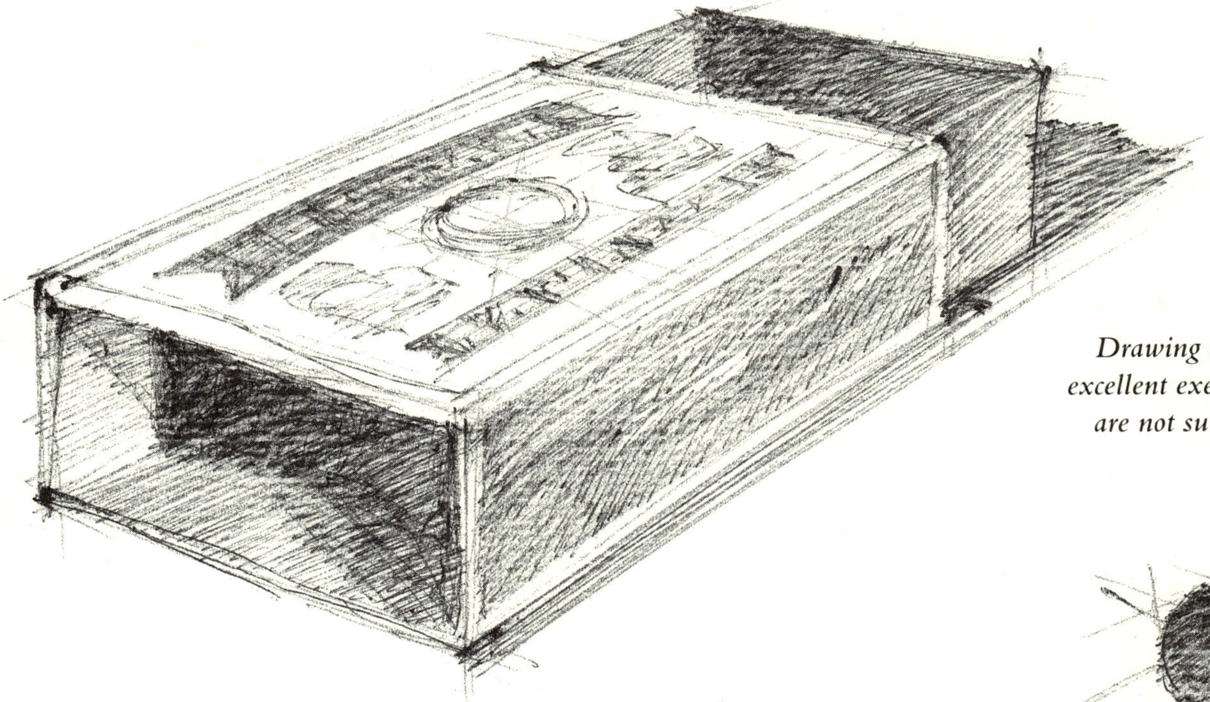

Drawing a box of matches is an excellent exercise, especially if you are not sure about the concept of perspective.

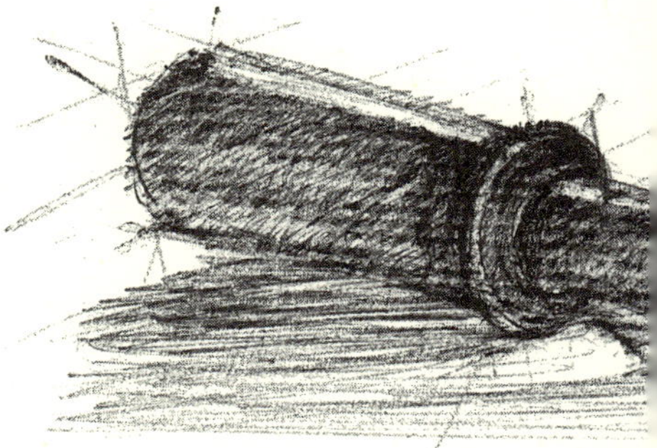

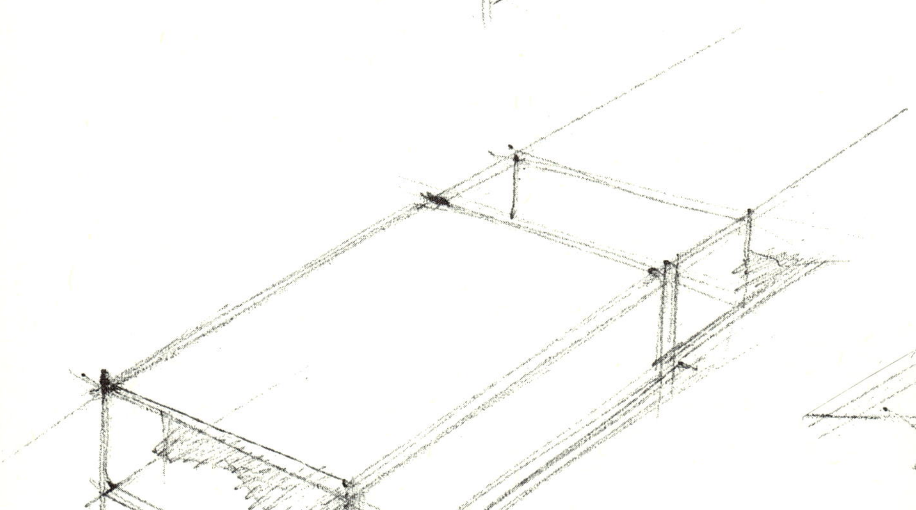

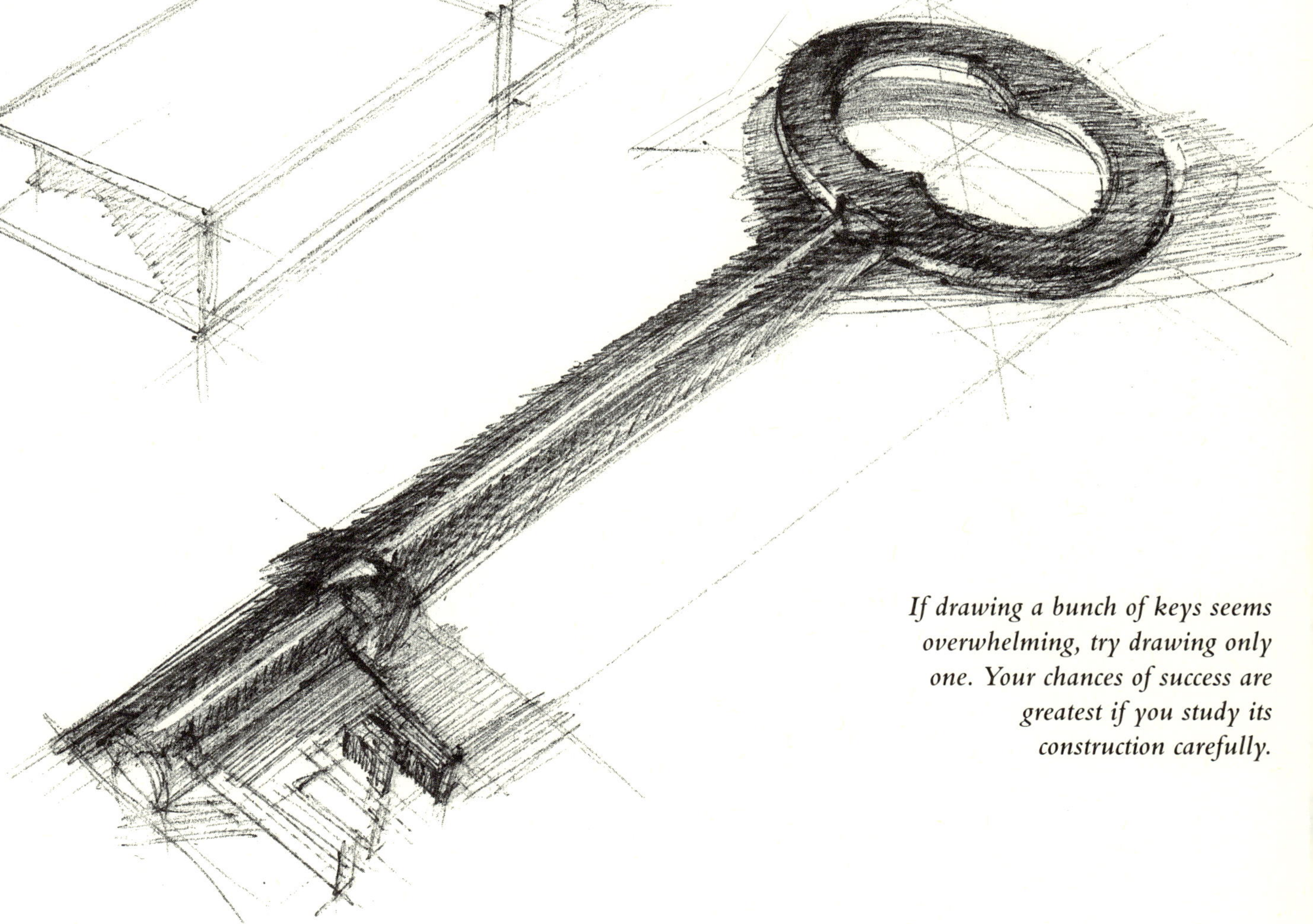

If drawing a bunch of keys seems overwhelming, try drawing only one. Your chances of success are greatest if you study its construction carefully.

Something as elegant as this old clock key (Baroque, 18th century) with its beautifully turned wooden handle might be difficult to find. But try to locate something interesting to draw, preferably made up of several basic forms—ball, cylinder, cube.

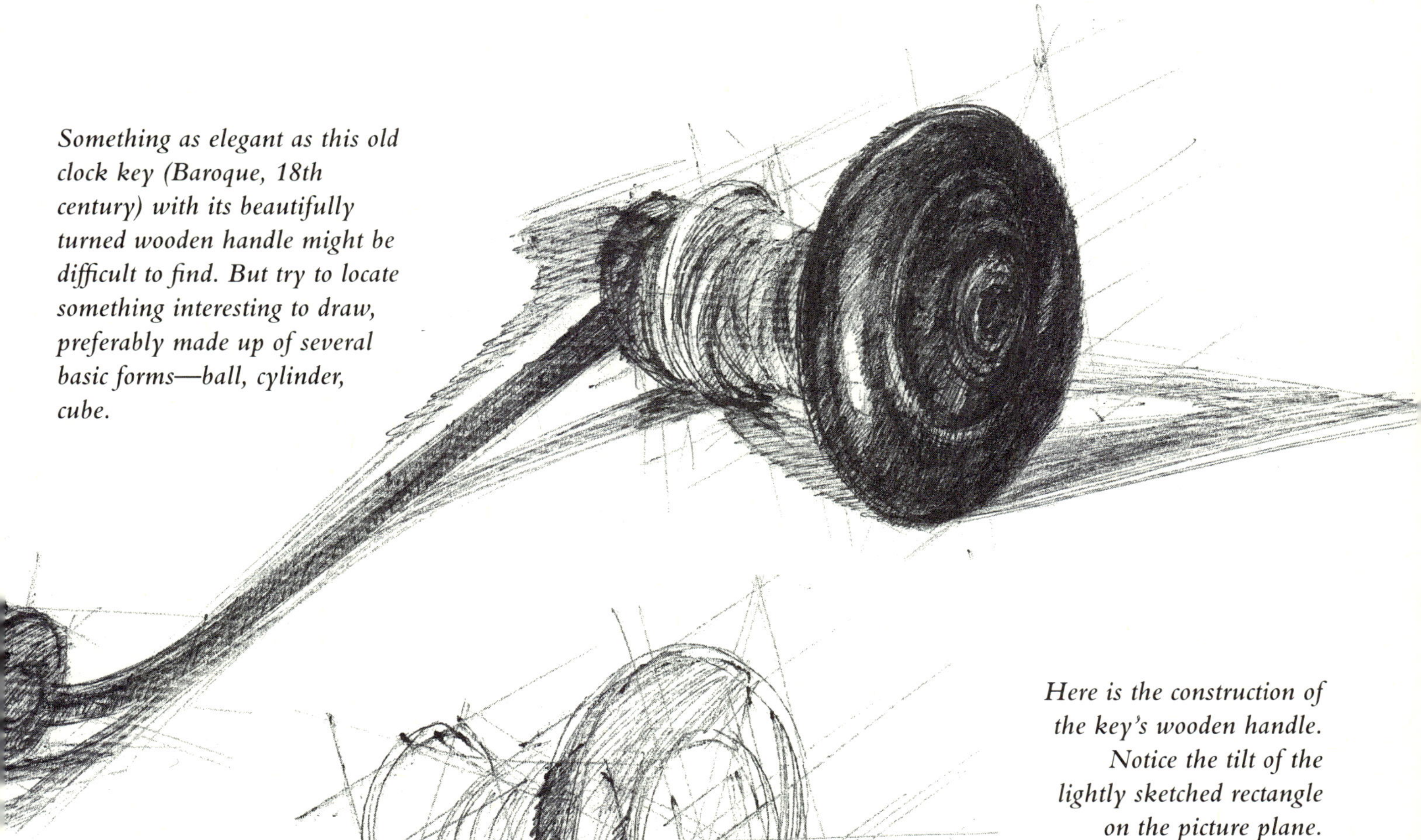

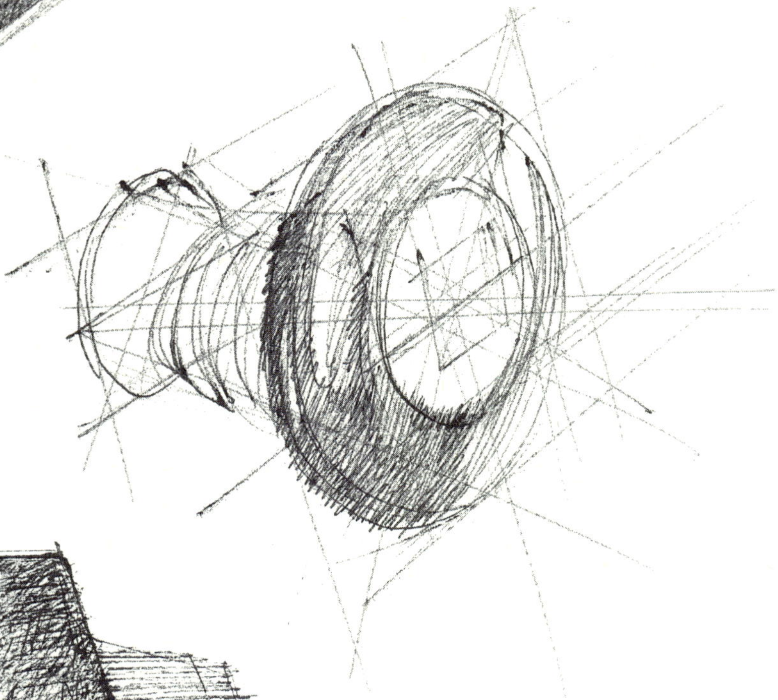

Here is the construction of the key's wooden handle. Notice the tilt of the lightly sketched rectangle on the picture plane.

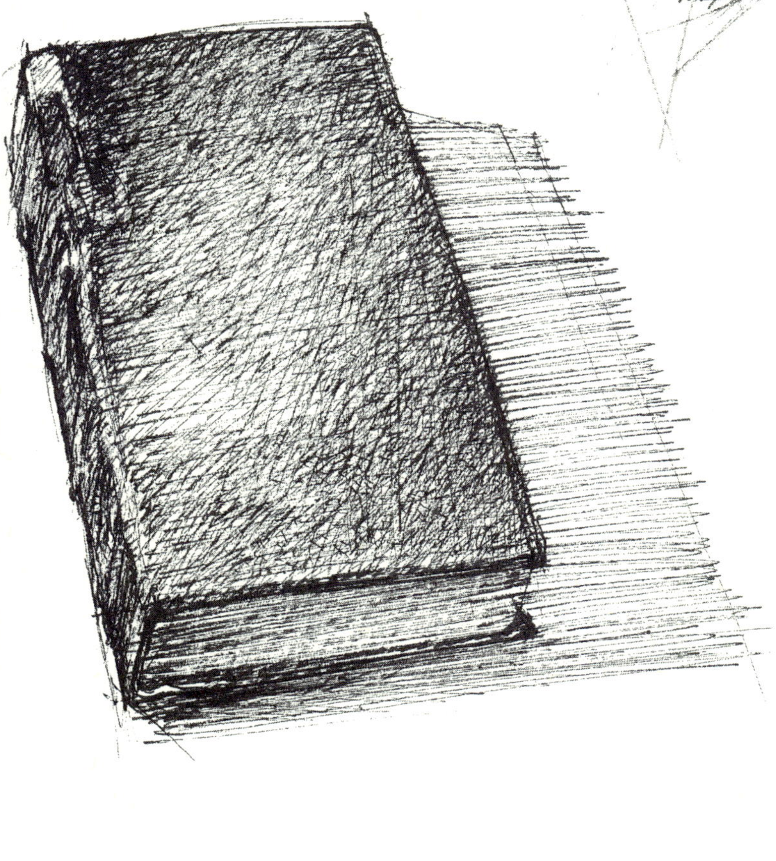

The basic form of this old book is identical to that of the box of matches. Shadows rendered so as to draw attention to its warped and worn-out appearance make it visually more interesting.

Old door handles made of bone and wood are good things to draw because they give us the opportunity to contrast the appearance of different materials. Here, for example, we can appreciate the shininess of brass and the lustre of mother-of-pearl in the surfaces of the same handle.

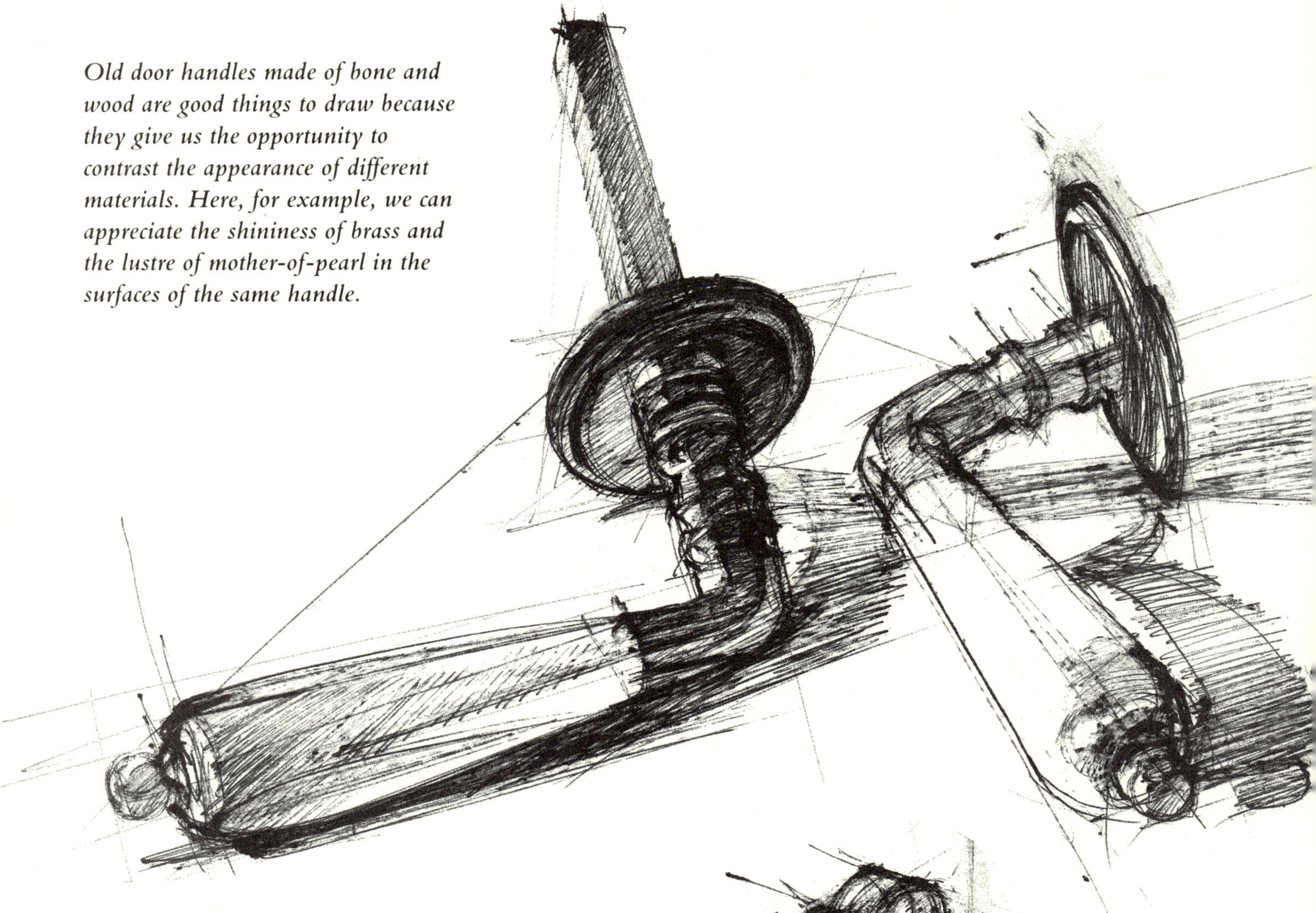

To draw a faucet is an exciting but also demanding project. Start with the handle. First sketch a square, make a cross within it and make six spokes.

Draw curves to create the faucet's true appearance, all the time adjusting for the slant created by the foreshortening, and adding depth.

As you sketch the faucet itself in perspective, remember that it sits perpendicular to the handle. Use cast shadow to give the illusion of three dimensions.

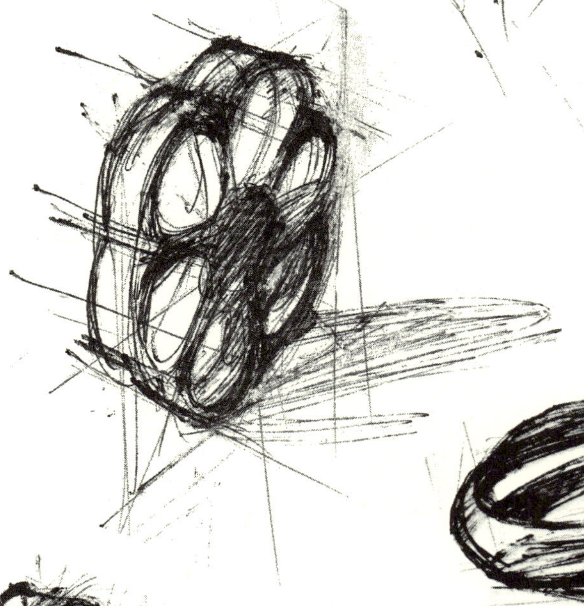

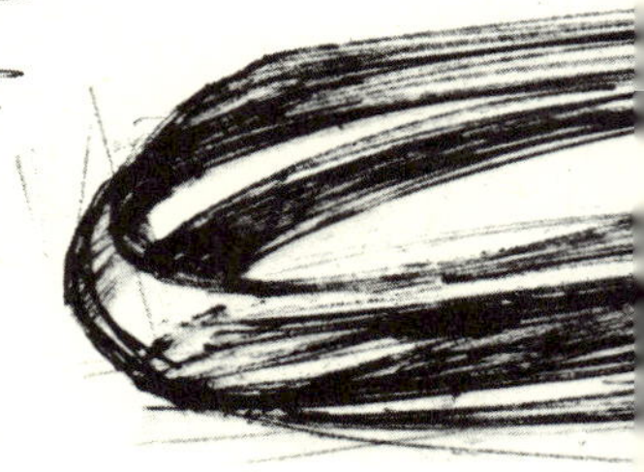

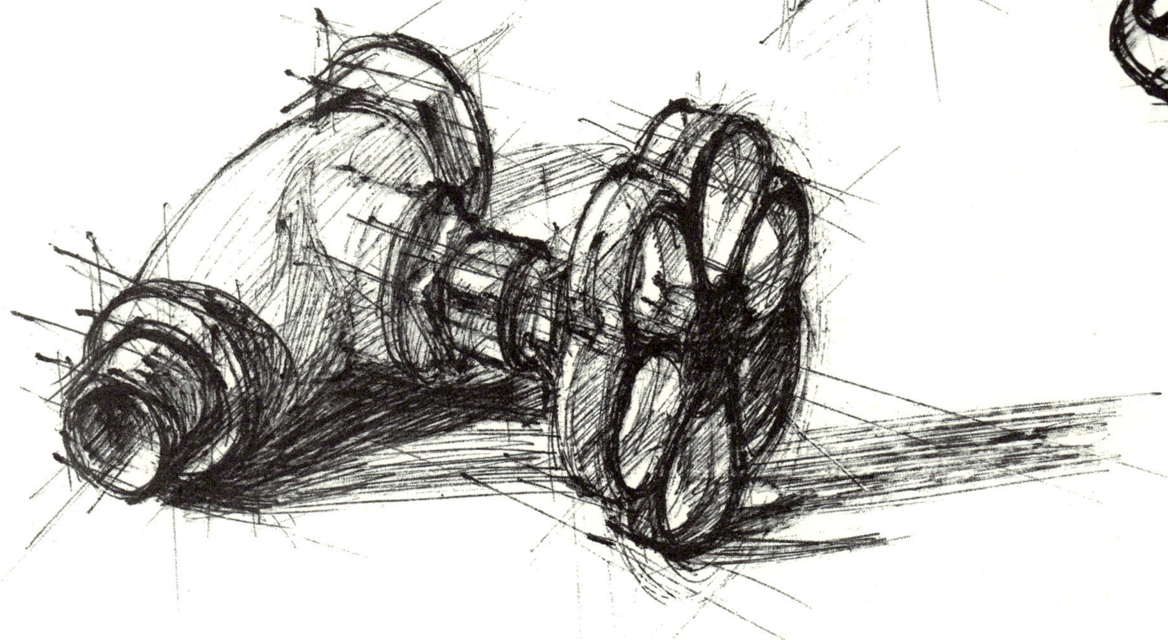

Here is another challenging object—a handshower. To draw it successfully, study it carefully. Take a good look, for instance, at the twist of the circle and how it continues into the handle before you put pen to paper.

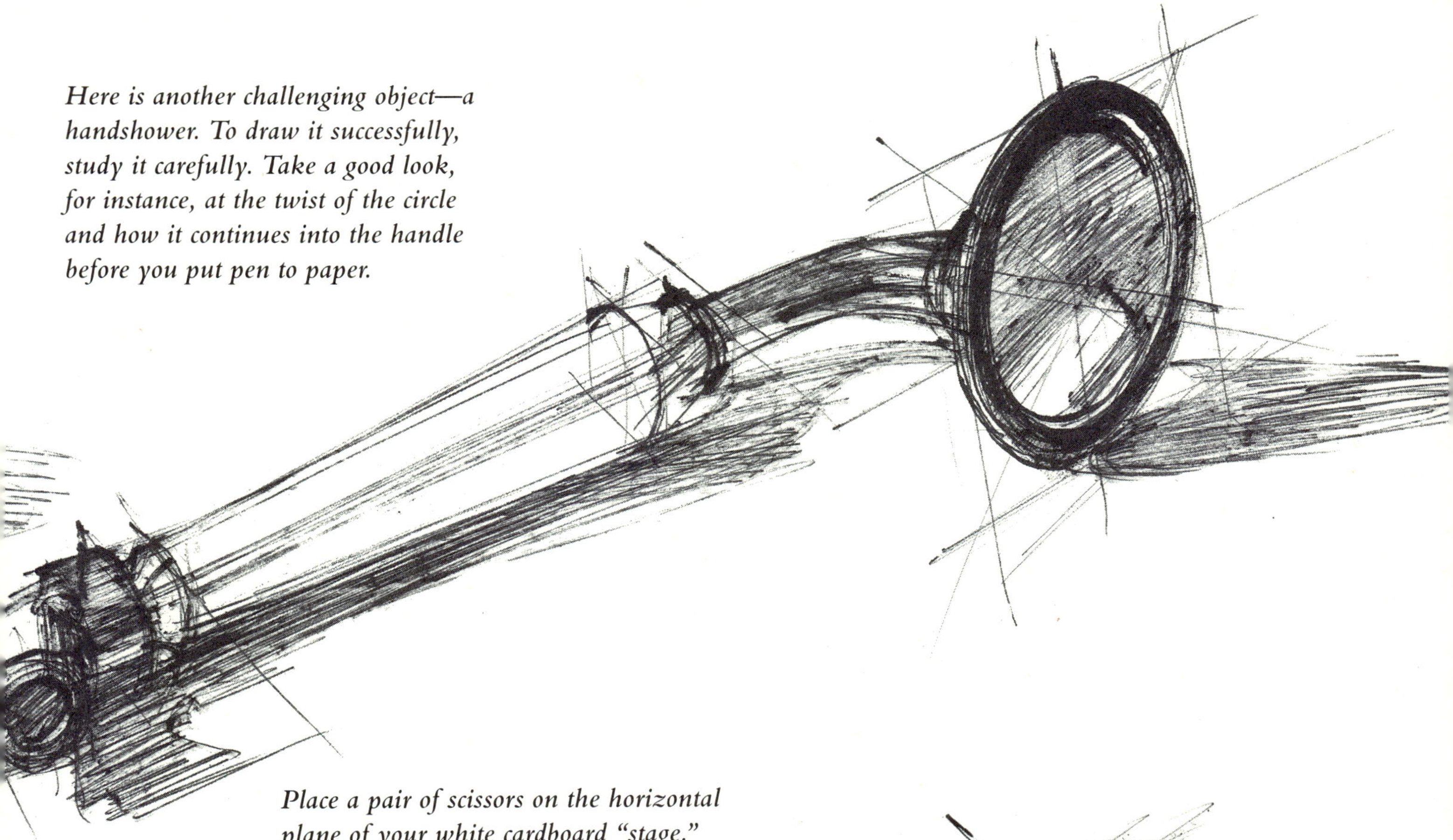

Place a pair of scissors on the horizontal plane of your white cardboard "stage." Make sure you have a strong light source. Note that the two handles are not the same. Bring your drawing to life with your use of cast shadow.

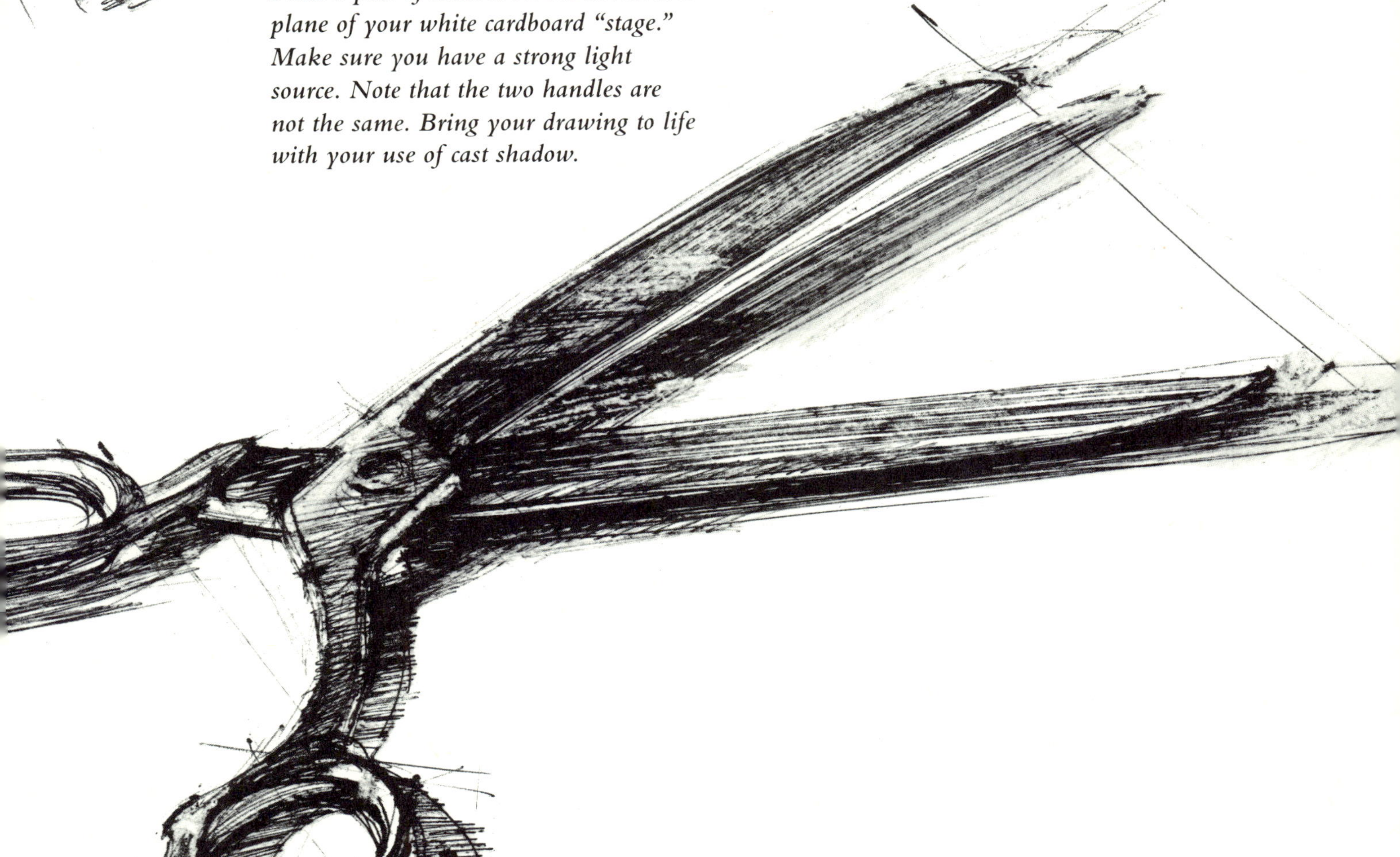

LESSON 2

Drawing Commonplace Objects

Object drawing, as will be clearly seen in the following pages, is an extensive subject that never fails to challenge the artist whether or not the drawing task at hand is rudimentary or extremely demanding. Of course, the more exacting the subject, the more you'll notice mistakes and shortcomings in your drawing. It's important, therefore, that the earlier and less complicated exercises, let's call them "etudes," be drawn and redrawn several times until they are completely understood.

In this lesson we will take on tasks that are broader in concept and much more demanding than those you have attempted thus far. It is only reasonable then to expect that you may experience difficulties. But don't despair even if the results of your efforts don't live up to your expectations. When you run into a problem, don't keep reworking your drawing, it will only get more black. Instead, start fresh.

Never discard a drawing even though you might consider it unsuccessful. Every drawing has qualities that can only be evaluated in time. Organize a portfolio, use it to file your drawings, good or bad. Date each piece so that you have an accurate record of the intermediate stages of your development. Looking back, you might be pleasantly surprised at your progress.

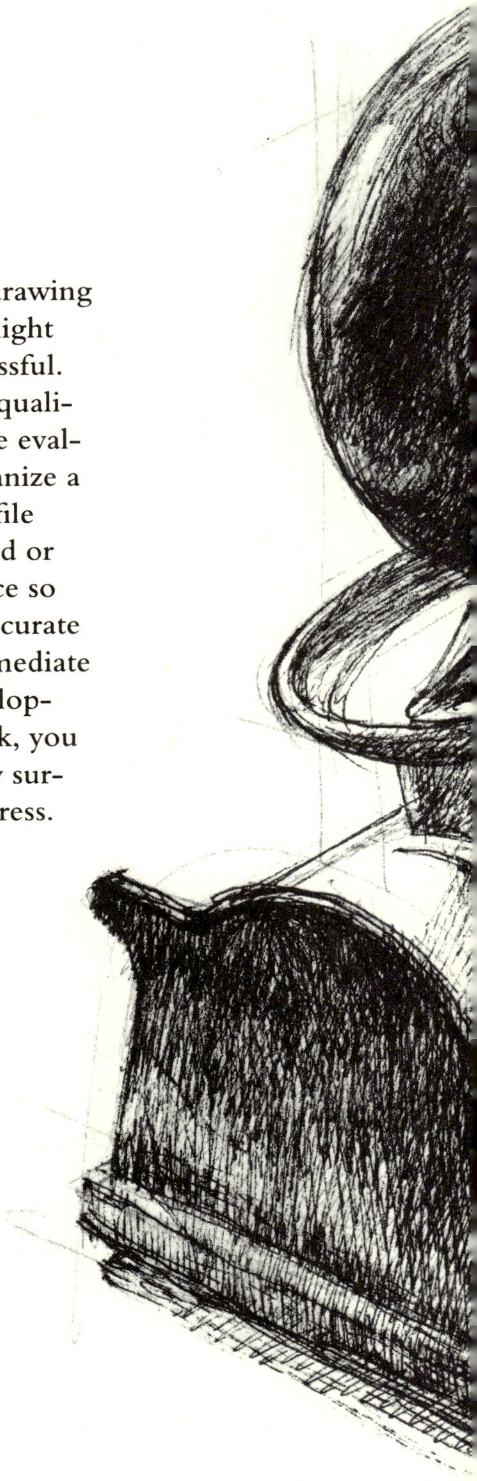

Two irons from the middle of the nineteenth century. One was heated by charcoal.

In drawing each of the irons, I have tried to bring out its scupltural form. Black and heavy, difficult to handle, these two objects out of the past are impressive in their massiveness. Emphasizing the visual plane on which each is firmly planted injects energy into their relationship.

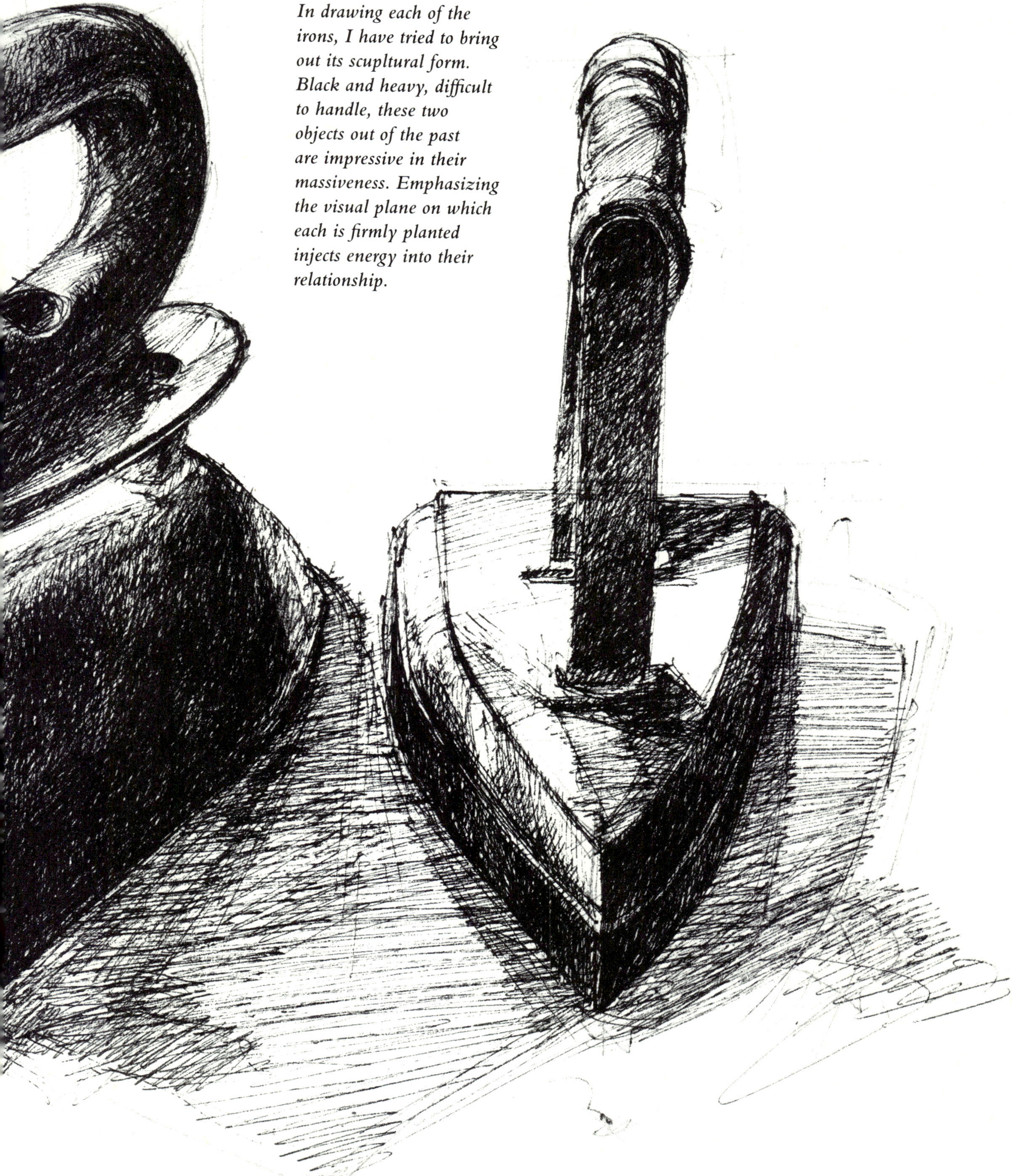

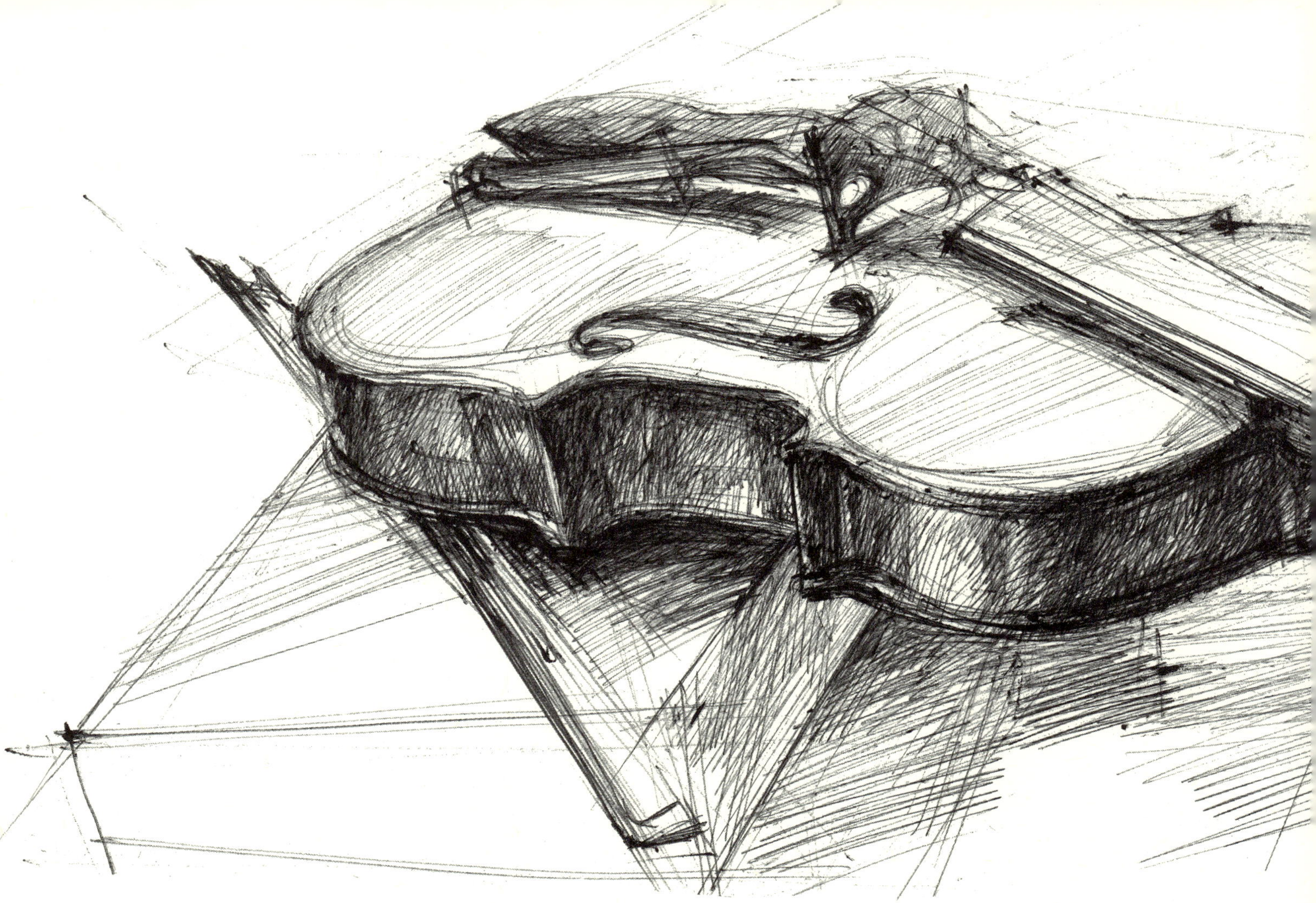

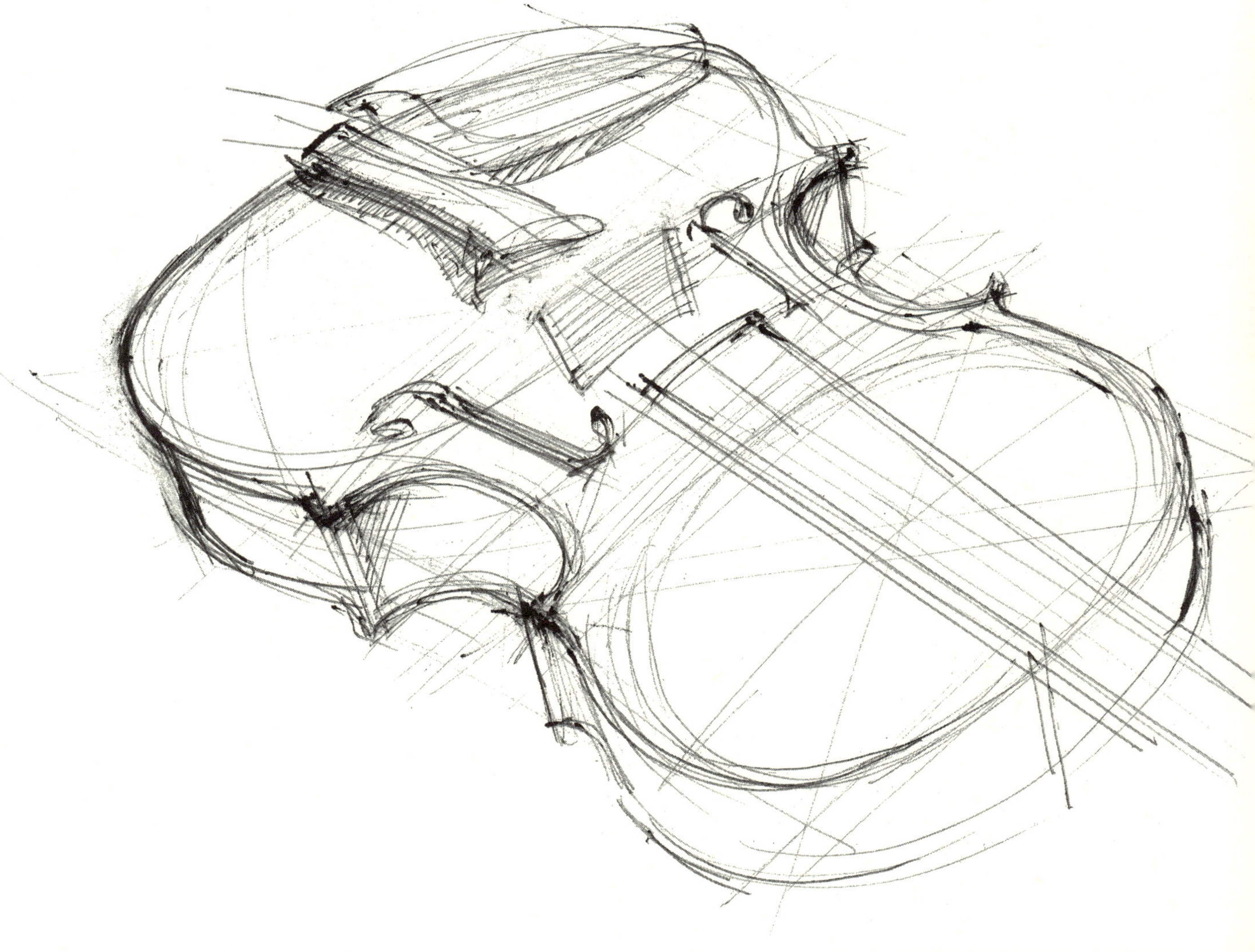

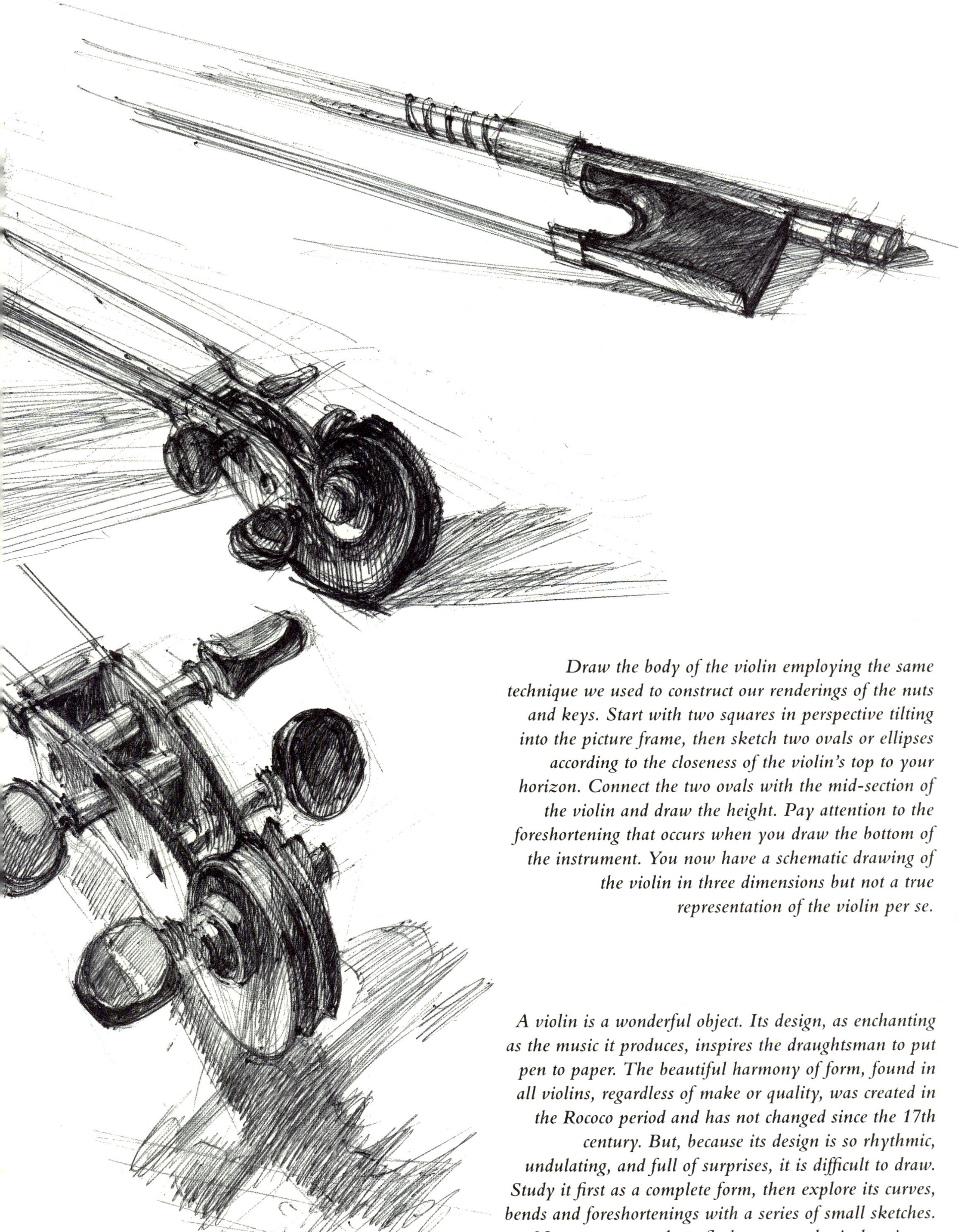

Draw the body of the violin employing the same technique we used to construct our renderings of the nuts and keys. Start with two squares in perspective tilting into the picture frame, then sketch two ovals or ellipses according to the closeness of the violin's top to your horizon. Connect the two ovals with the mid-section of the violin and draw the height. Pay attention to the foreshortening that occurs when you draw the bottom of the instrument. You now have a schematic drawing of the violin in three dimensions but not a true representation of the violin per se.

A violin is a wonderful object. Its design, as enchanting as the music it produces, inspires the draughtsman to put pen to paper. The beautiful harmony of form, found in all violins, regardless of make or quality, was created in the Rococo period and has not changed since the 17th century. But, because its design is so rhythmic, undulating, and full of surprises, it is difficult to draw. Study it first as a complete form, then explore its curves, bends and foreshortenings with a series of small sketches. Now you are ready to flesh out your basic drawing to capture the full beauty of this remarkable instrument.

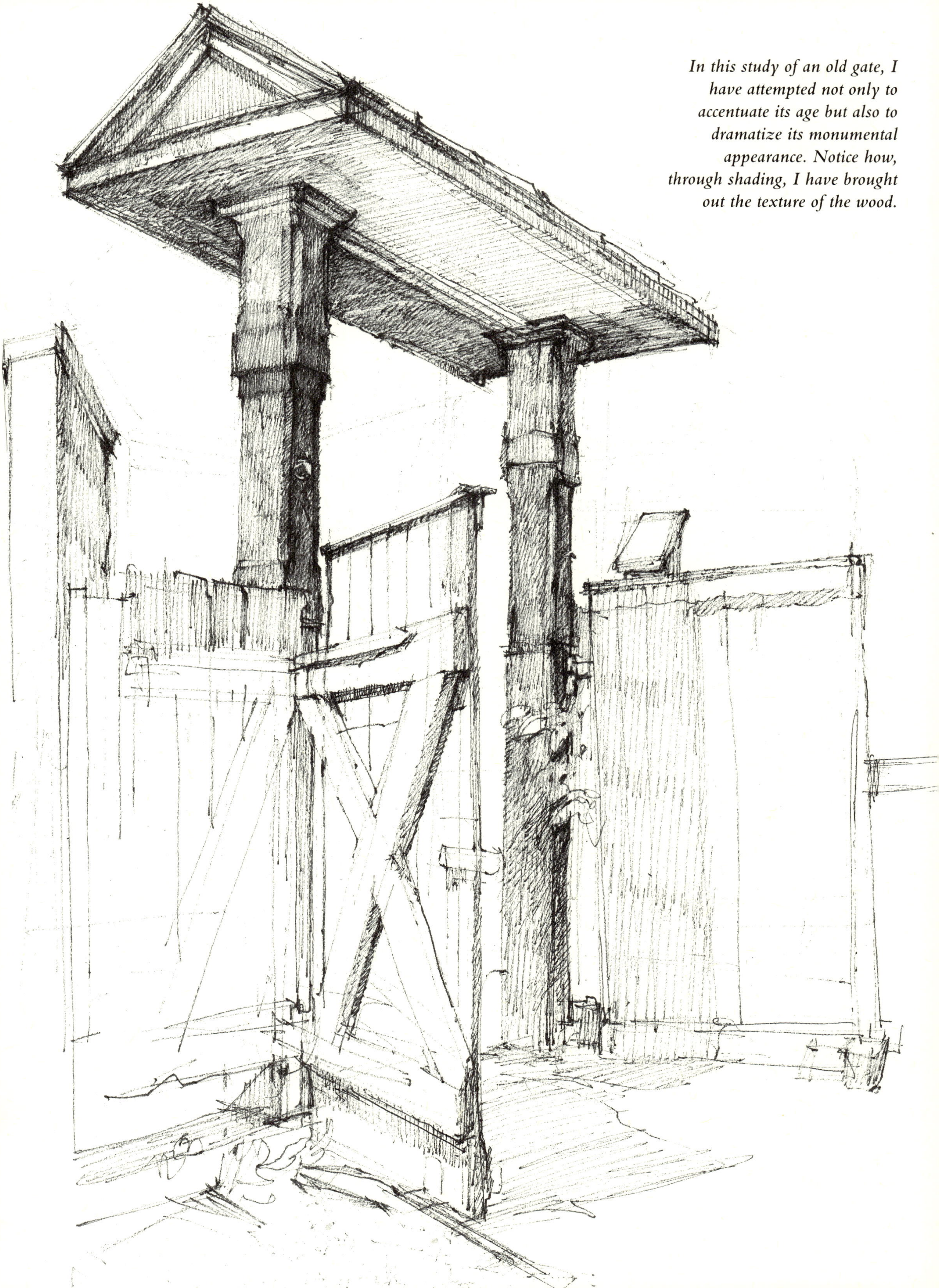

In this study of an old gate, I have attempted not only to accentuate its age but also to dramatize its monumental appearance. Notice how, through shading, I have brought out the texture of the wood.

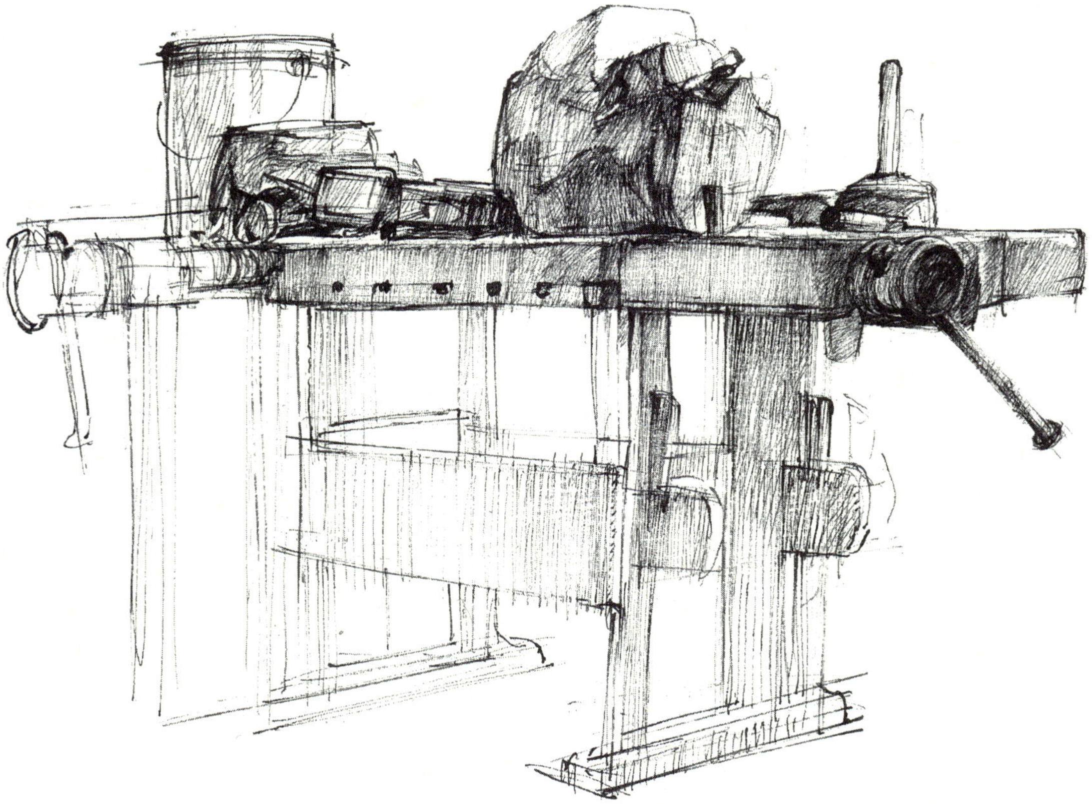

Notice the perpendicular shading that emphasizes the upright quality of this old workbench. Its skinny legs, the long handles of the bench screws, the slender grip of the mallet, and the perpendicular feeling of the paint can all contribute to the drawing's sense of verticality.

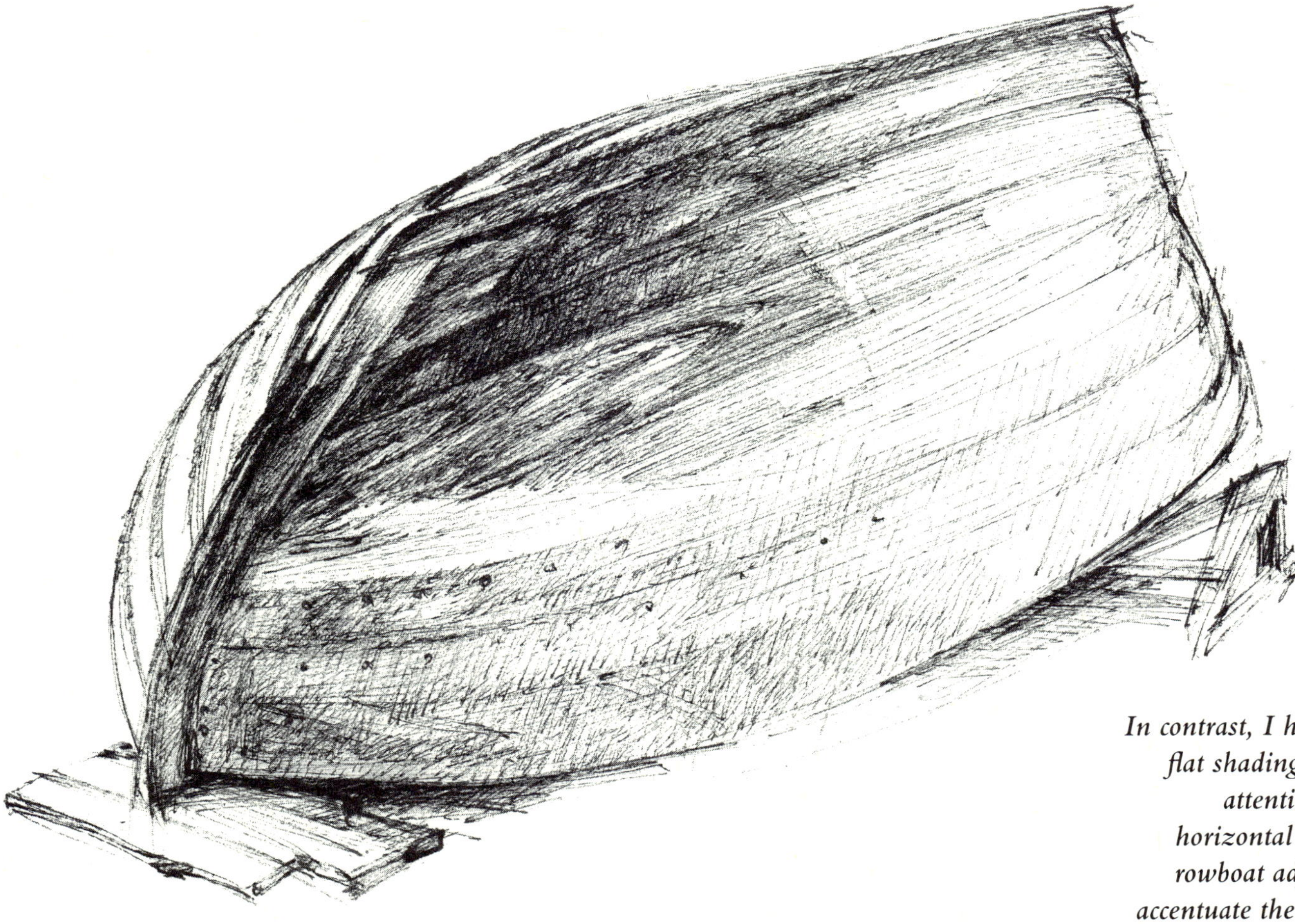

In contrast, I have used flat shading to draw attention to the horizontal line of a rowboat adjusted to accentuate the rounded form of its old curved planks.

Both these object drawings from the harbor are preliminary sketches, not final drawings. This is why the surroundings are not clearly defined. It is interesting to note, however, that the scale of the objects is enough to create perspective depth.

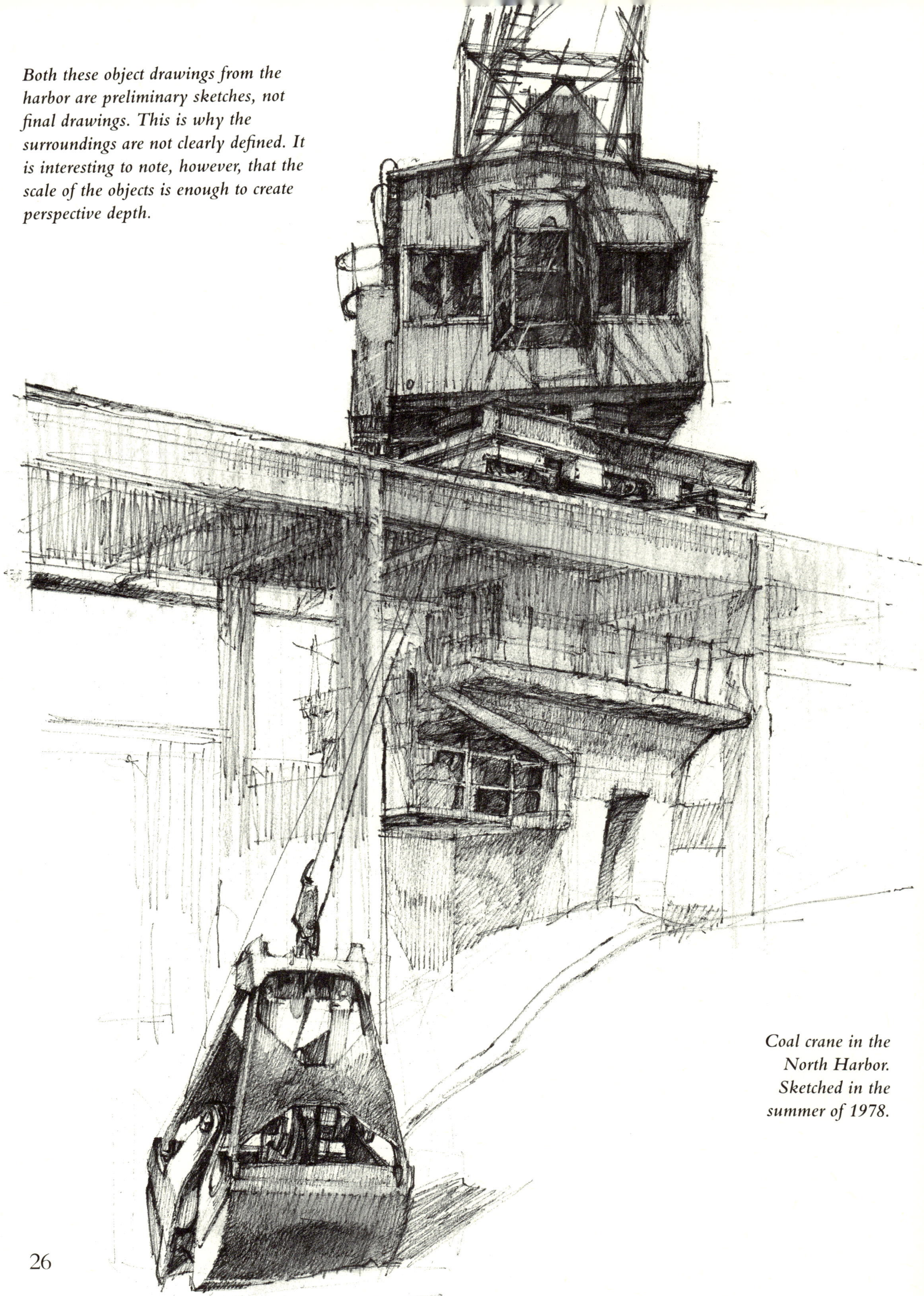

Coal crane in the North Harbor. Sketched in the summer of 1978.

Notice how, even though both drawings are diagonally composed, a sense of verticality is maintained through shading.

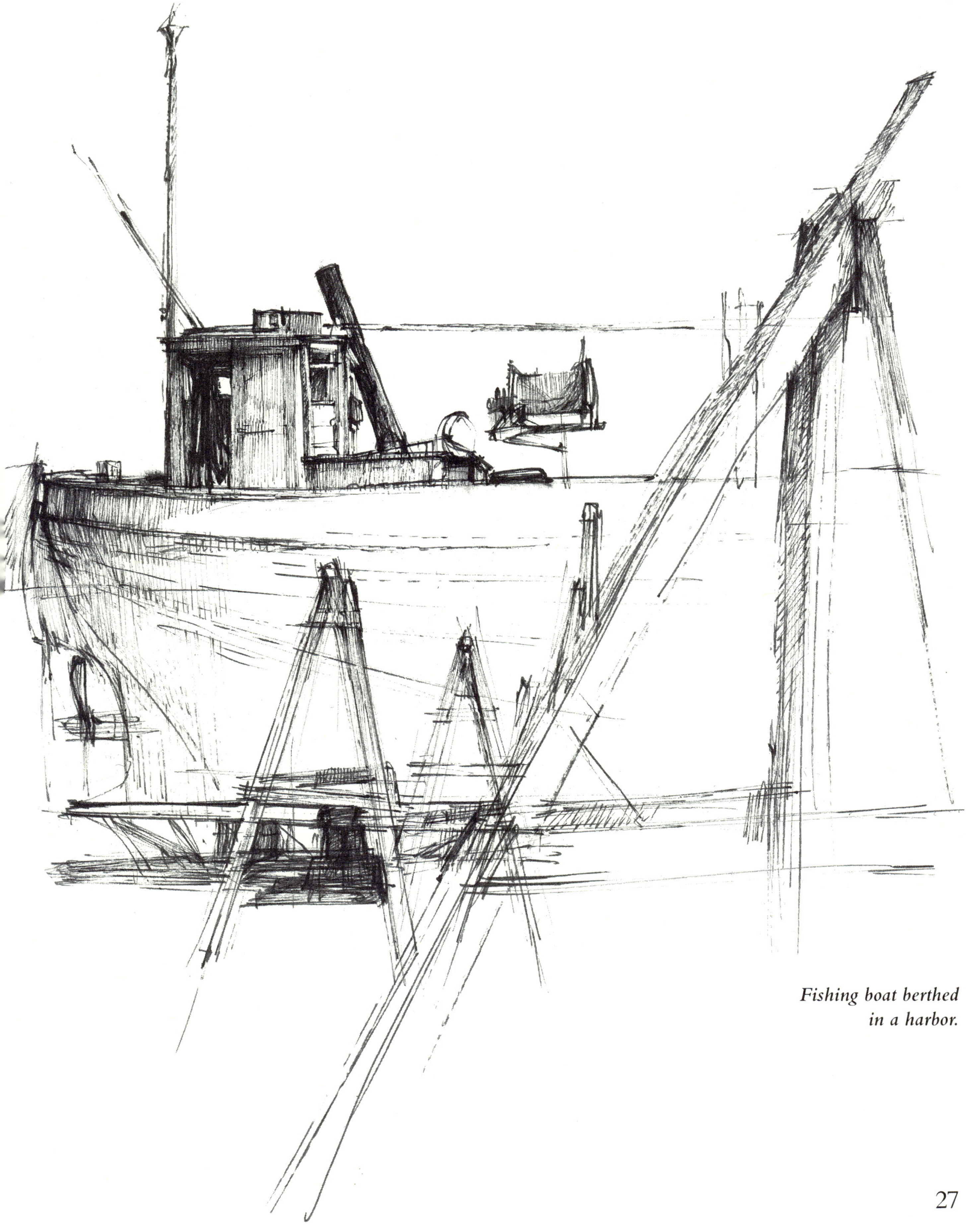

Fishing boat berthed in a harbor.

LESSON 3

Plants, Roots and Other Organic Materials

The first two lessons dealt with the kind of familiar human-made objects that surround us in our daily lives. Whether made by machine or by hand, they have one thing in common: they are all constructed. Now, we are going to draw subject matter that is *organic:* created by nature with little if any human influence. We will quickly discover that such nature-made materials have very different attributes from those which are constructed.

In nature, we find new rhythms that are different from those that we discovered in the world of constructed objects. The structure of plants, for example, depends on principles of growth; branches on trees are placed randomly, grasses grow to different heights. This "growth principle" is quite different from the design elements that govern the appearance of constructed objects. Please underscore the idea of "growth" in your notes as it is important and will be referred to again. It is necessary, too, to observe the "internal tension" that is the life force resident in everything that grows. One can capture its energy by always drawing from the inside out, following the contour, never working the other way around. Tighten the form. Don't be afraid of overdoing it, somehow one seldom does when drawing from nature. Emphasize the diagonal shifts and staggered rhythms that make nature so alive and dynamic, and your work will be dynamic, too.

A good exercise is to study the form of leaves and stems and then draw their outlines. If a leaf is twisted or if one passes under another, draw them as if they were transparent.

Knotty branches and the gnarled roots of old trees and large plants are good subjects for study. Defining the planes involved strengthens your ability to work analytically and constructively, while stressing the organic approach develops your ability to express the dynamic rhythms and inner tensions inherent in growing things.

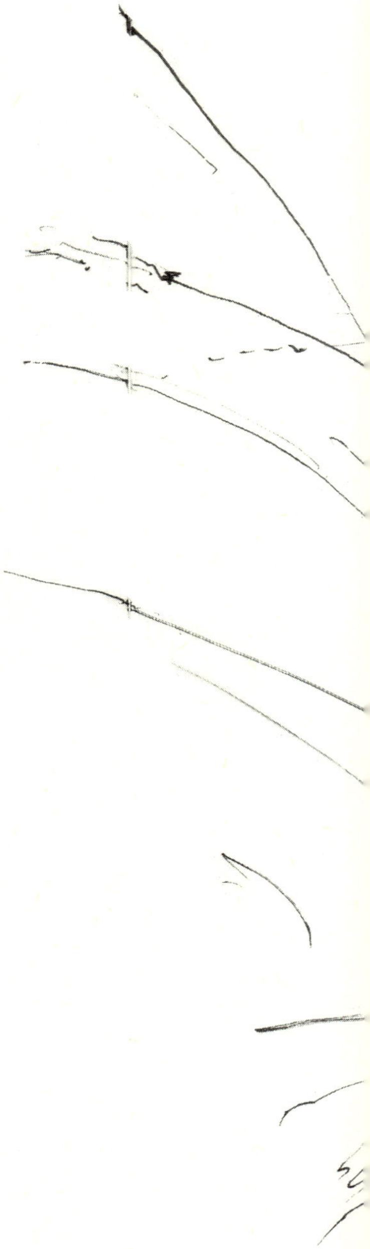

Highlighting the foreground creates in itself the effect of sunny, lush vegetation.

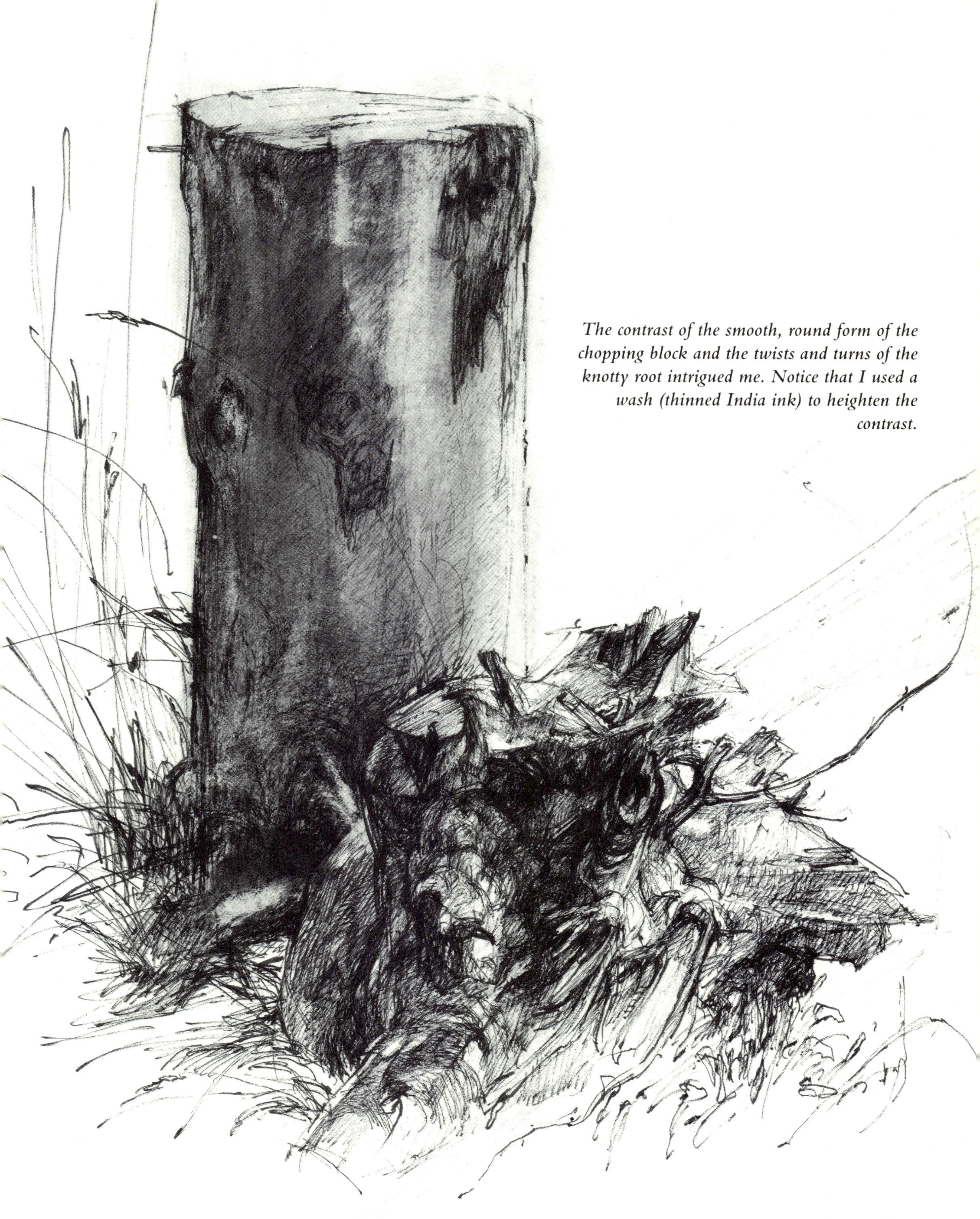

The contrast of the smooth, round form of the chopping block and the twists and turns of the knotty root intrigued me. Notice that I used a wash (thinned India ink) to heighten the contrast.

It's fun to draw the staggered rhythm of a fir cone. Studying its structure increases one's understanding of the basic organic principle of growth.

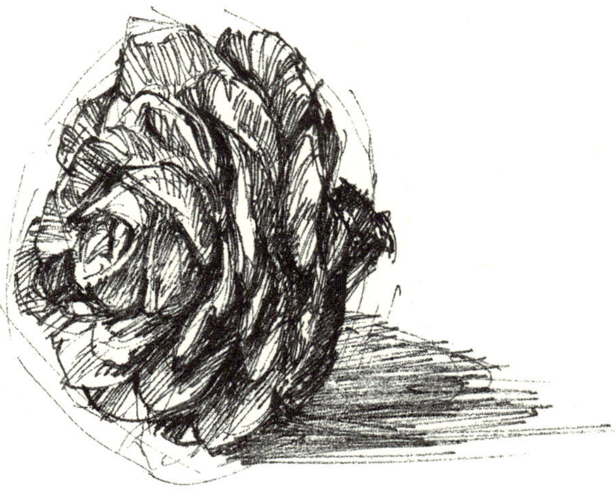

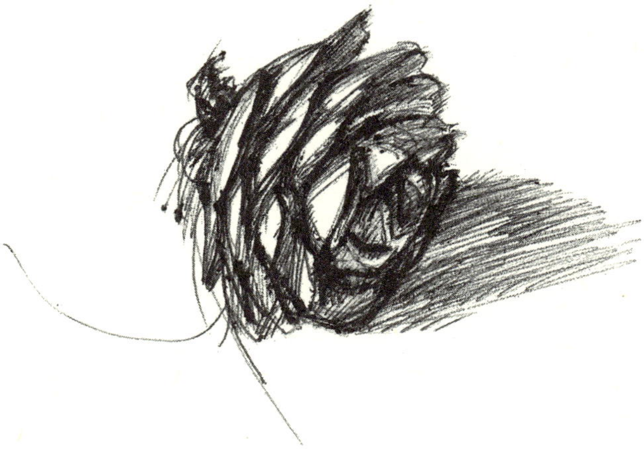

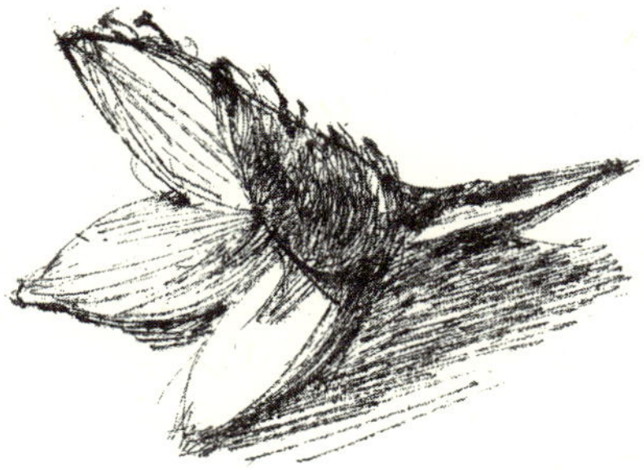

Observe the beautiful springiness of this little seed capsule. Spreading it open, you'll be surprised at the strength of its structure.

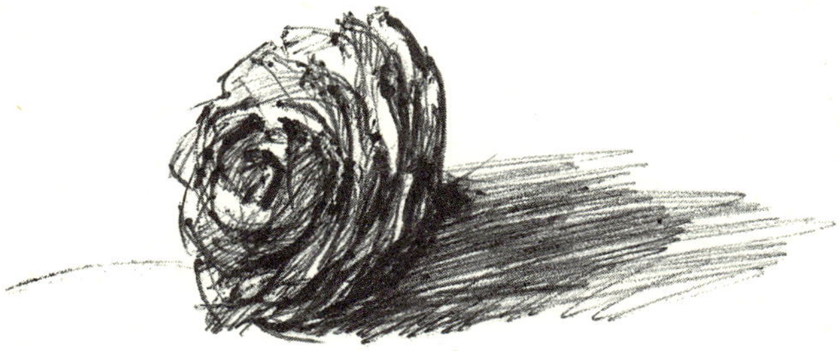

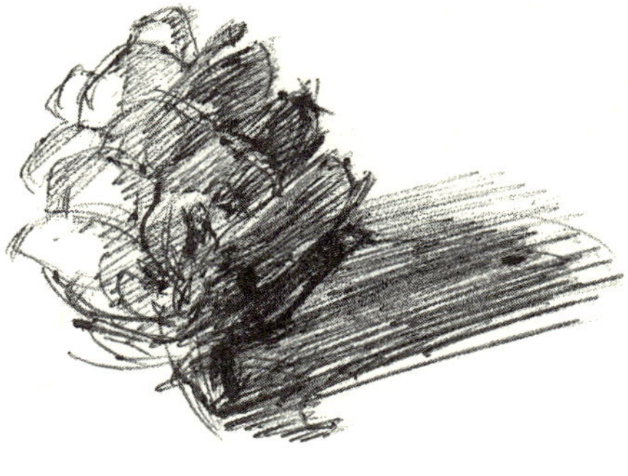

Starting from within, use long strokes to draw the leaves. Think of them as transparent where they bend and twist, and draw them that way. In my own drawings, I always begin with the stems and veins.

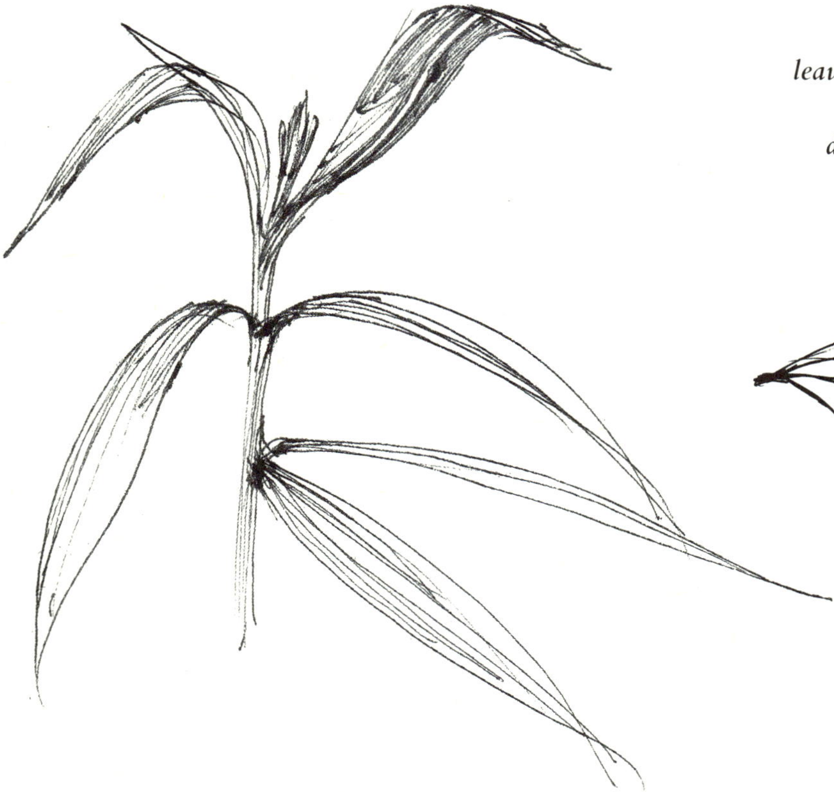

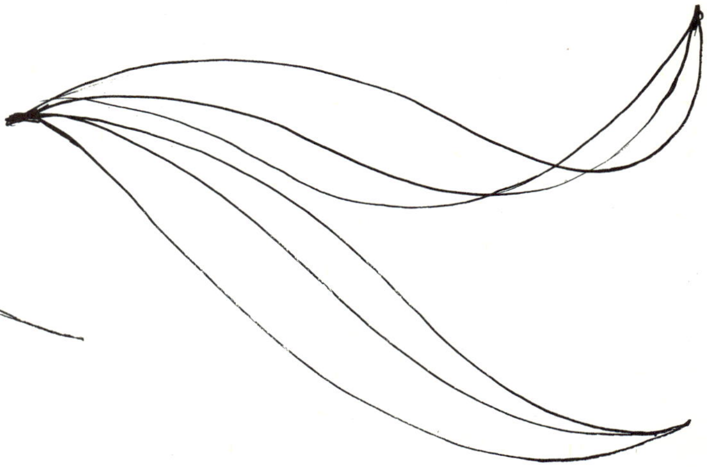

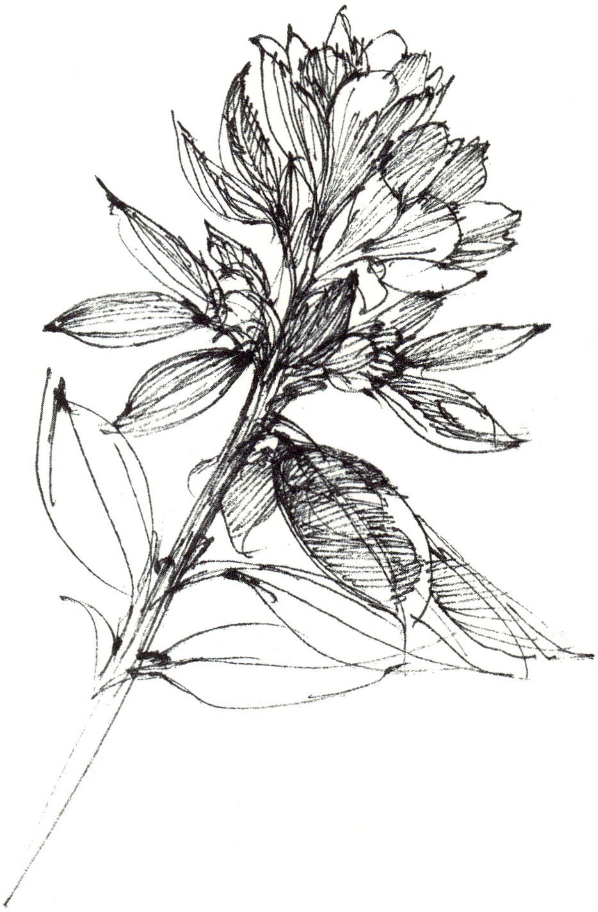

The same rules are applicable when drawing flowers. Stretch the petals and sepals to observe the structure. In your own drawing, create as much fullness as possible.

It's fascinating to visually explore the form of a tree branch. The many small warps and fissures that, at first, look arbitrary, now appear to be logically placed. Before you draw, concentrate on the overall shape; don't get lost in the details.

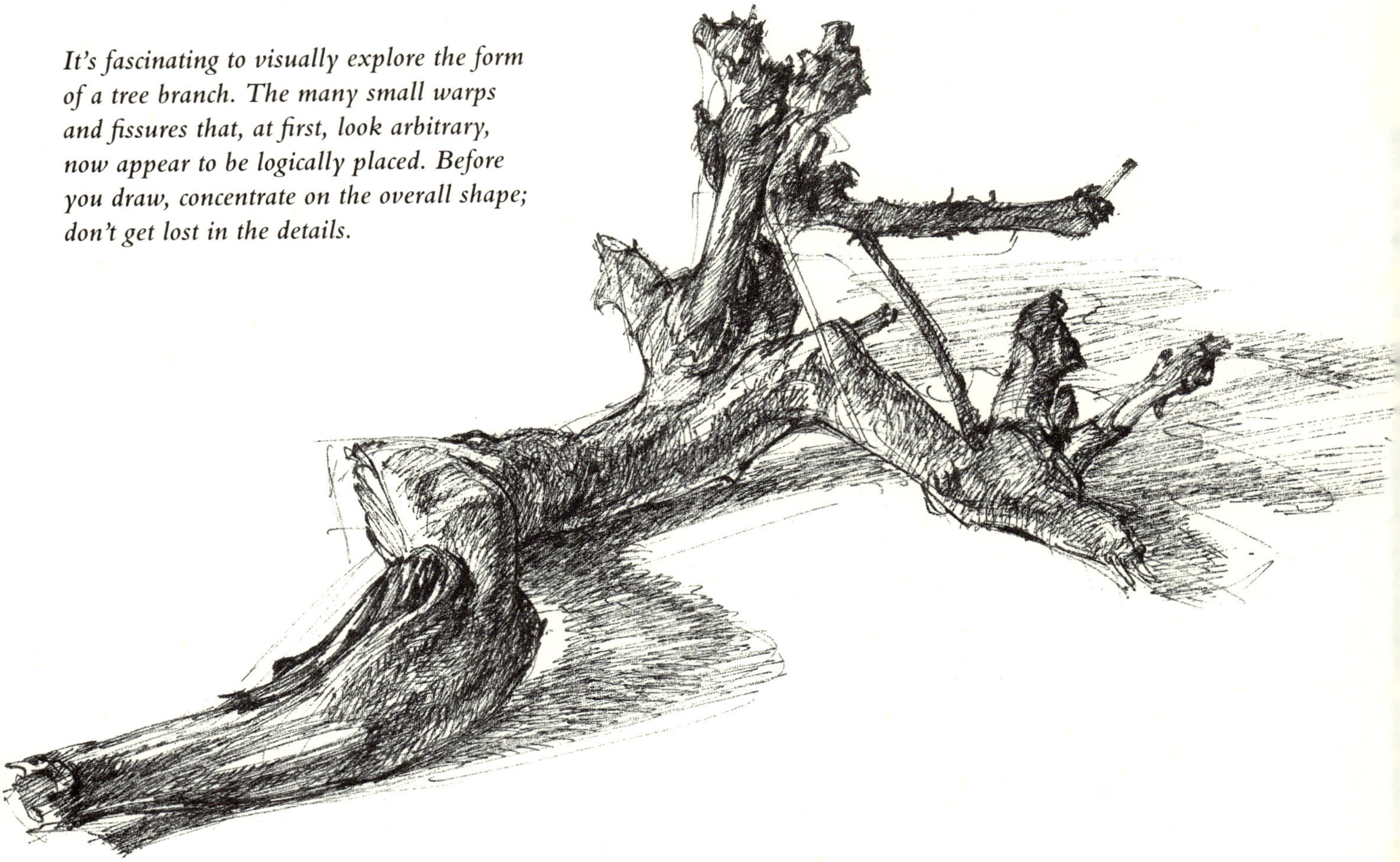

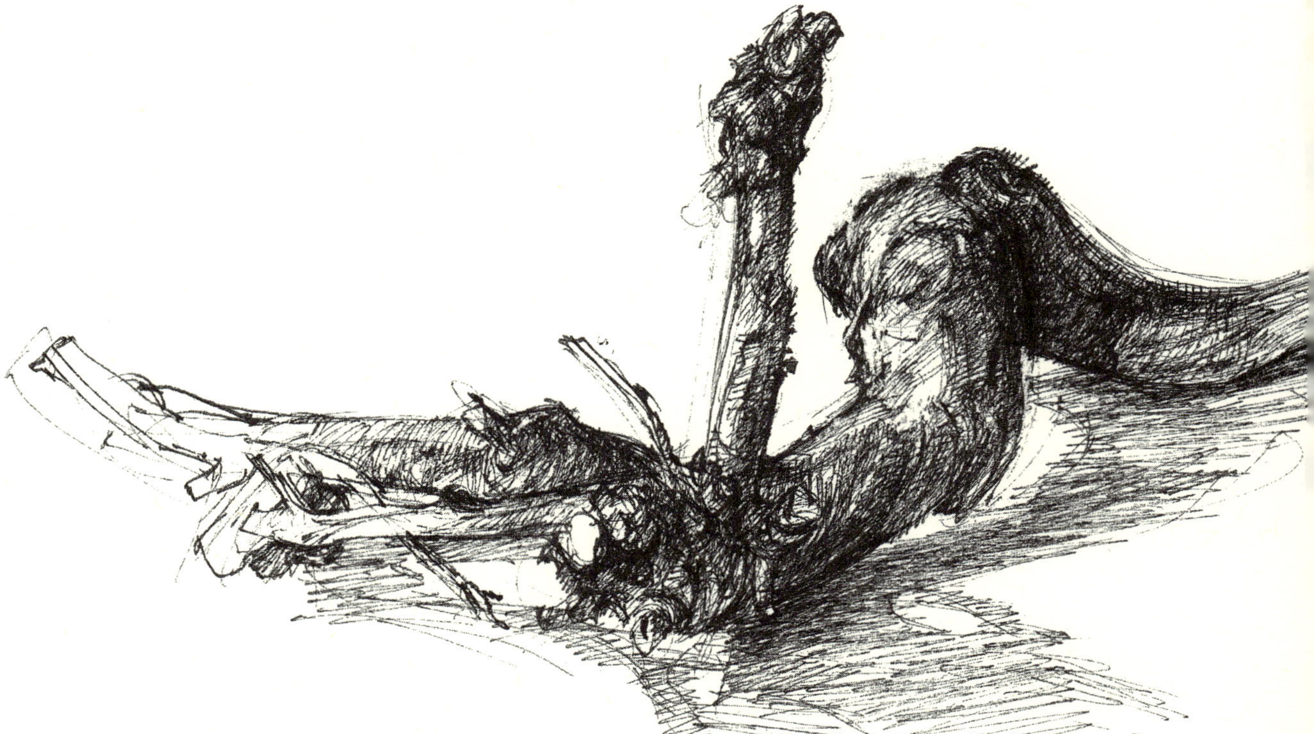

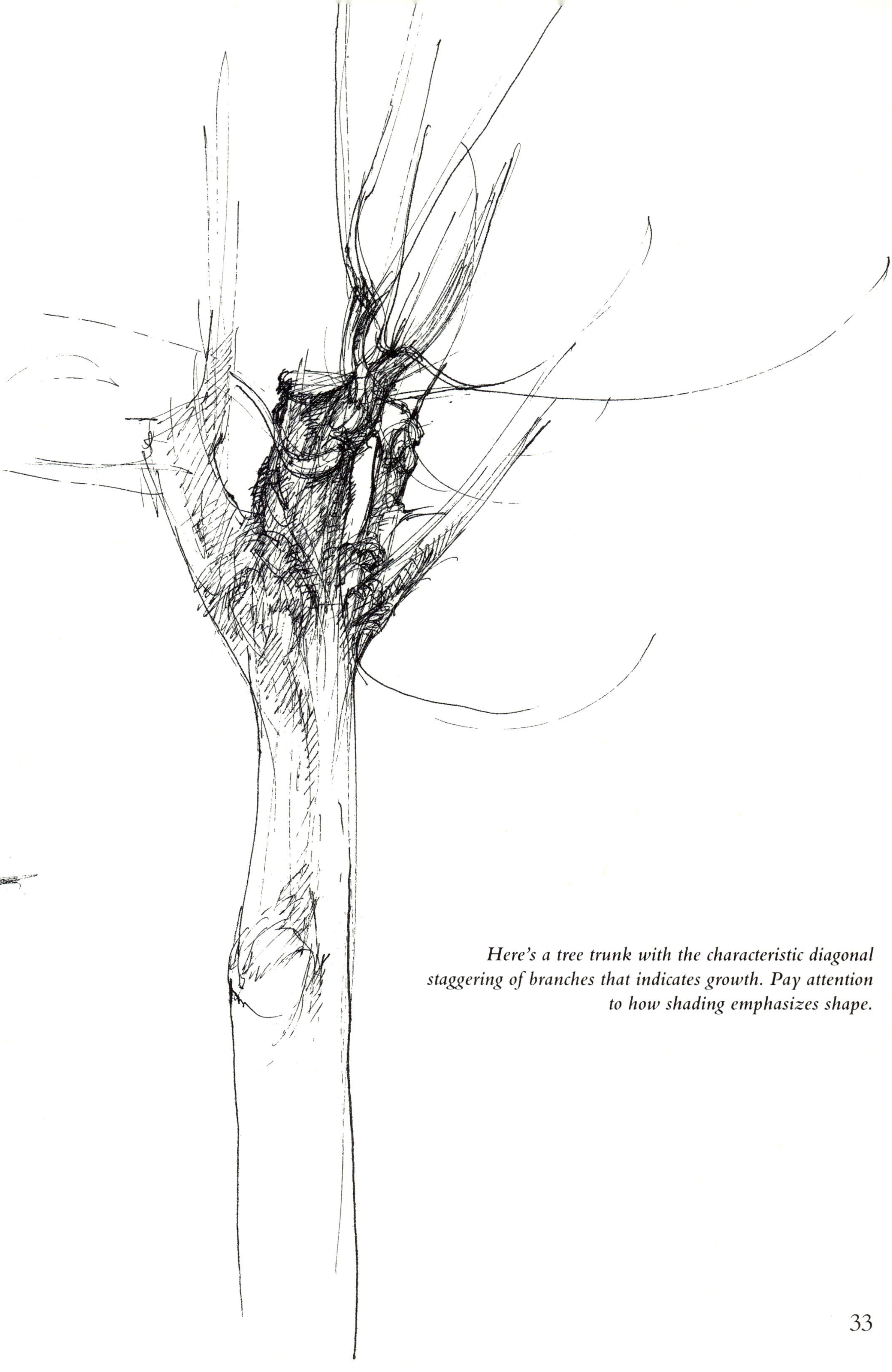

Here's a tree trunk with the characteristic diagonal staggering of branches that indicates growth. Pay attention to how shading emphasizes shape.

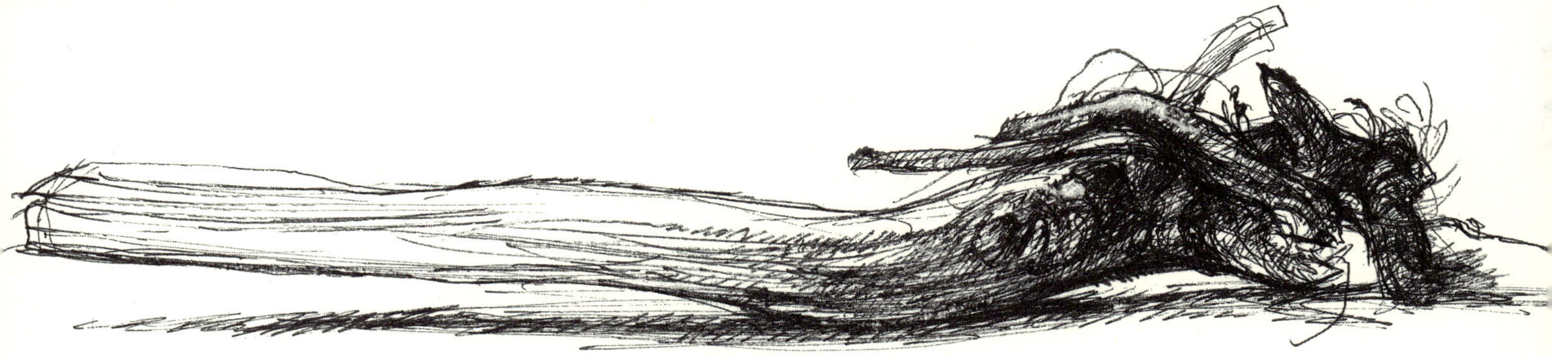

In this study, I have created contrast by first emphasizing the uninterrupted smoothness of a sapling's slender trunk, then making the drawing "explode" with detail where we first observe the delicate root.

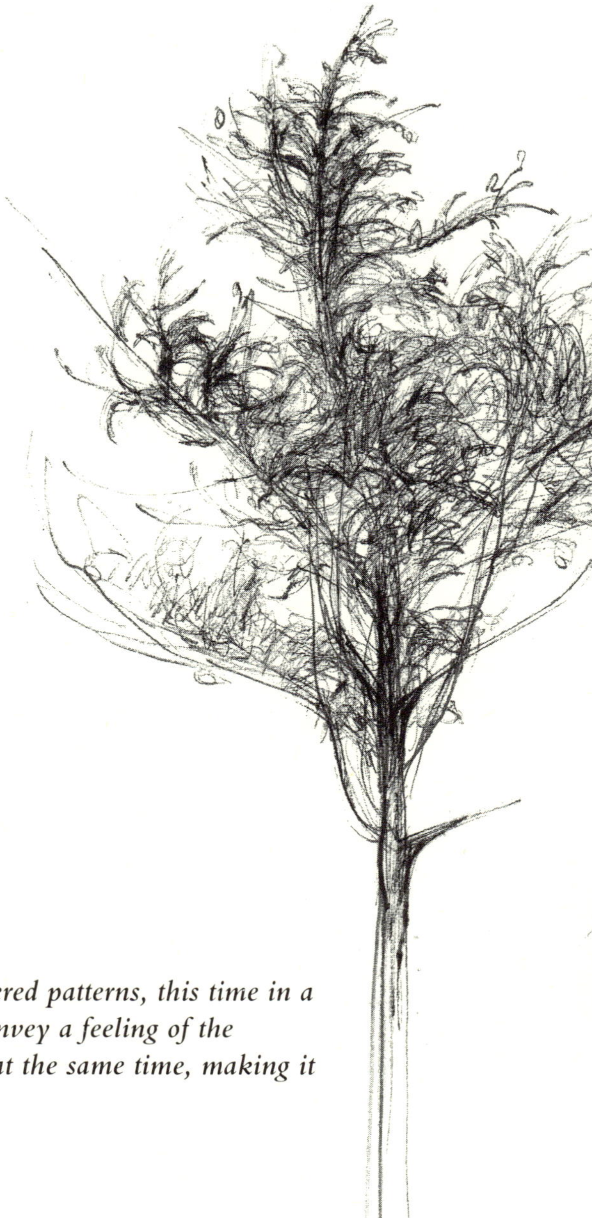

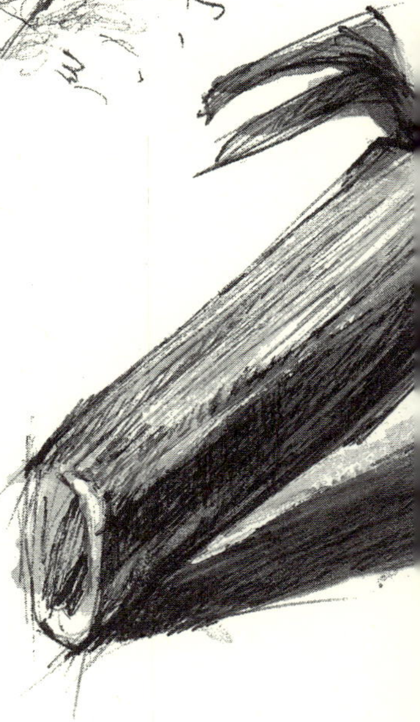

Again we observe another of nature's staggered patterns, this time in a rendering of a tree top. I've attempted to convey a feeling of the lightness and delicacy of the foliage while, at the same time, making it a part of the total composition.

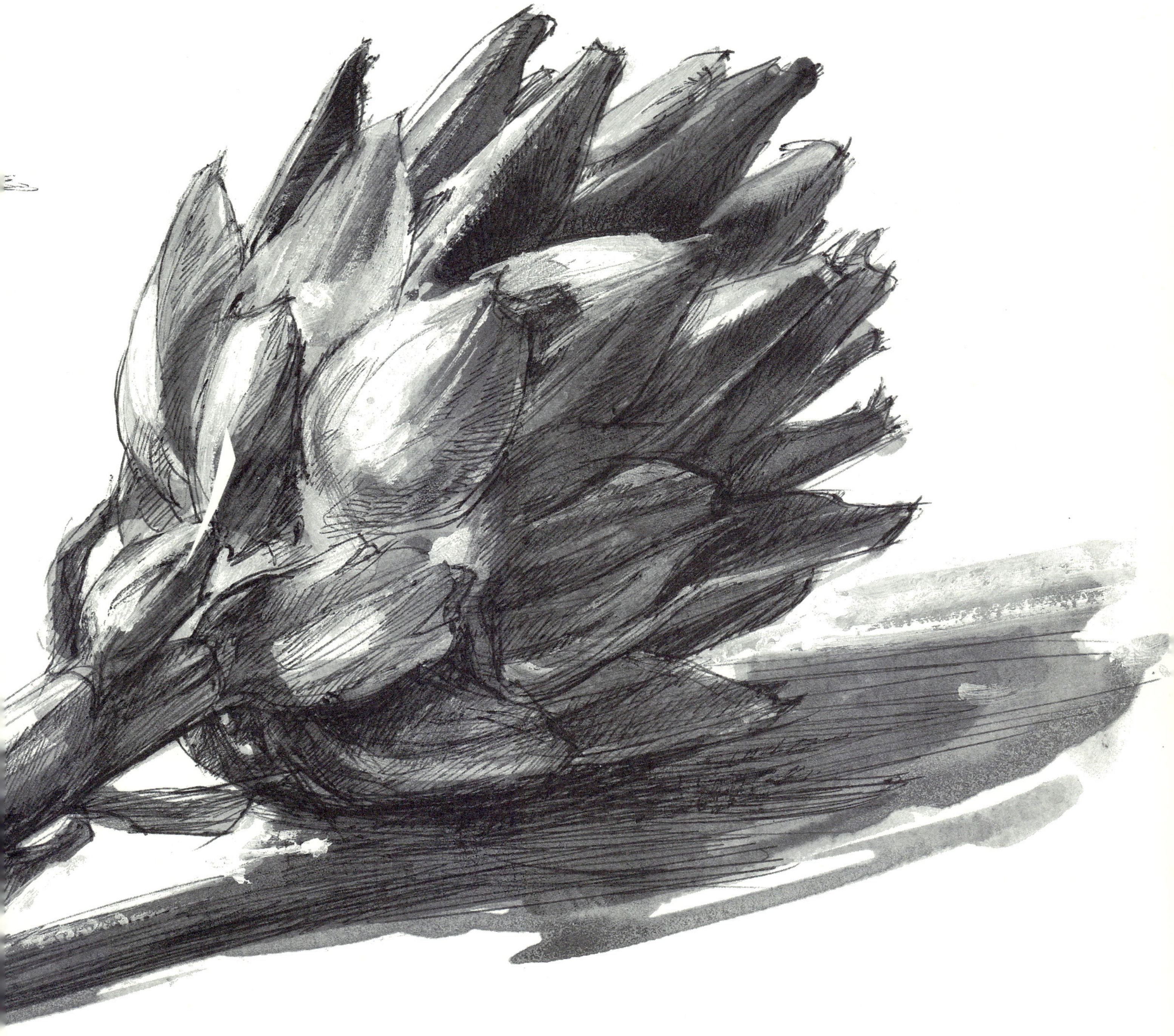

This big, rather coarse, artichoke is an excellent subject to tackle. My initial rendering was made by using a brush and thinned India ink. Details and more definition were supplied by an India ink pen. Note the staggering of the leaves that reminds one of the structure of the small fir cone (page 30).

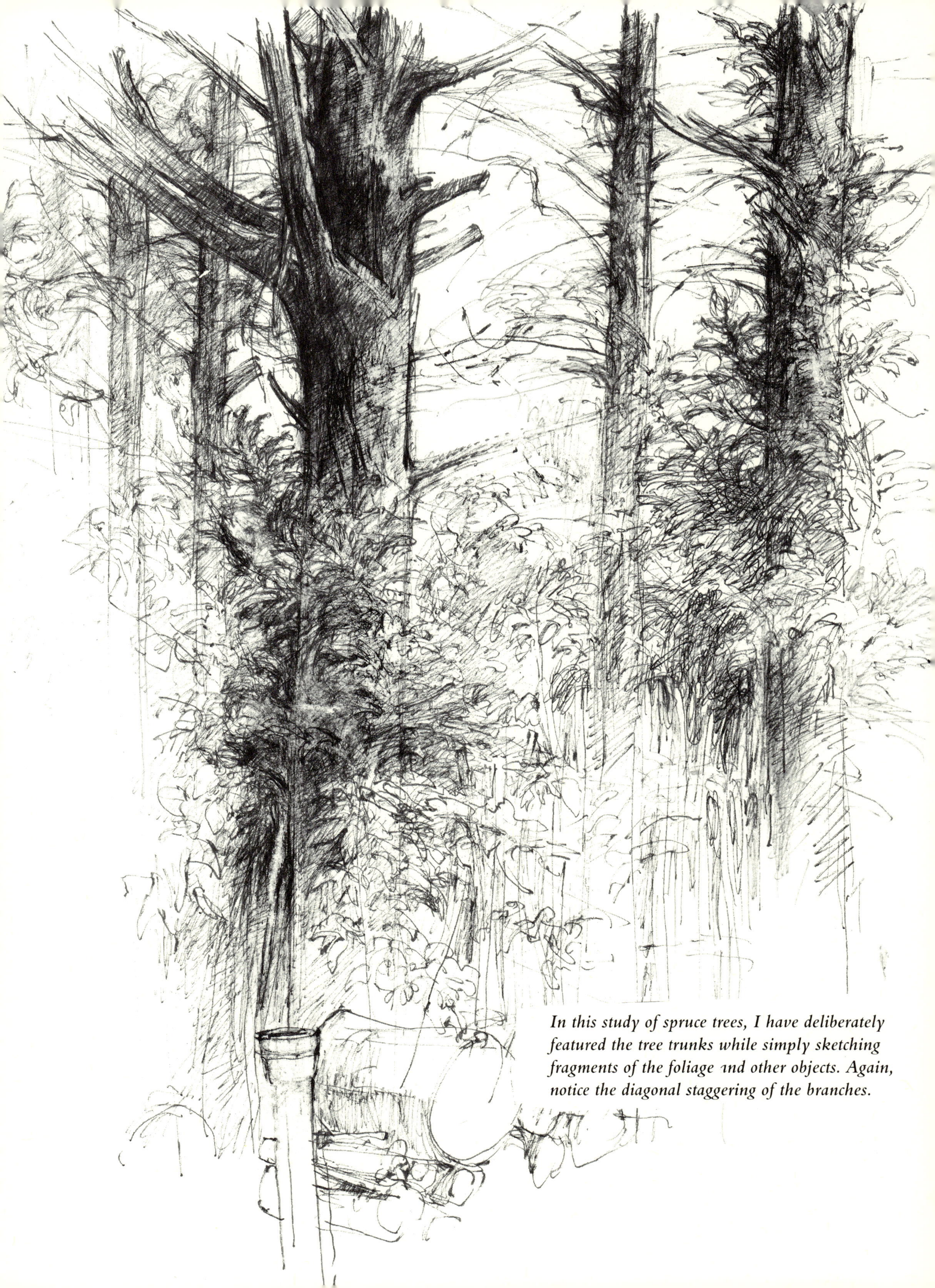

In this study of spruce trees, I have deliberately featured the tree trunks while simply sketching fragments of the foliage and other objects. Again, notice the diagonal staggering of the branches.

LESSON 4

Bushes and Trees

Organic subjects include everything living from plants, insects and fish to animals and people. The differences between organic and human-made objects are so fundamental that we need to be very aware of them.

That we are part of nature is a truism. Perhaps because of this, we are very much in tune with nature, accepting all that it represents as good and, with few exceptions, beautiful. Much of our basic thinking about what is acceptable in art, the principle of proportion, the golden section, for example, is grounded in our admiration of things natural. It's important to keep this in mind as we attempt a landscape or try our hand at drawing animals and people.

A concept that guides my own work reads like this, "the basic rhythms of the organic form are seldom in parallel order." When we realize that it's only very rarely that we see a plant or tree with stalks or branches "laterally reversed" rather than staggered diagonally, the usefulness of this concept to an artist interested in working from nature becomes abundantly apparent.

Once you understand this view of nature, its rhythms will begin to influence your work. There will be a feeling of "growth" in your drawings that is important for you to express. Here's something else to bear in mind when working with nature. It's easy to lose the image you have in mind when you are confronted with an overwhelming profusion of branches and tree tops. Look at them as a "mass" and start sketching in broad outline. Forget about trees as single units, it's better to break down the mass of foliage into light and dark areas. In such situations you must make a conscious effort not to get lost in a web of details; if this happens, you will find it impossible to create a completely satisfying drawing.

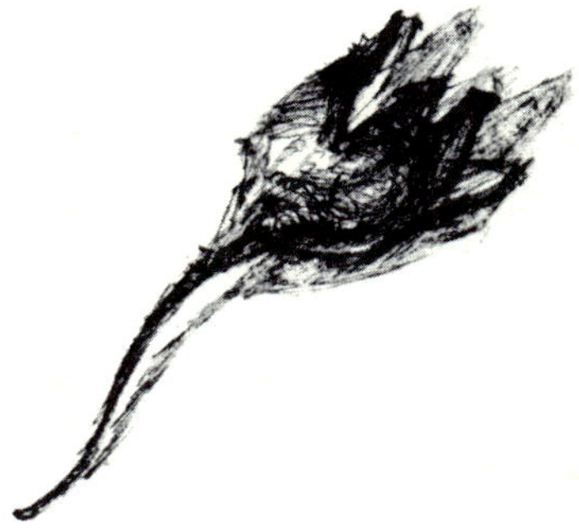

A study of a bud can be very absorbing. The closed form of this beautifully organized but tiny unit offers the artist many exciting possibilities.

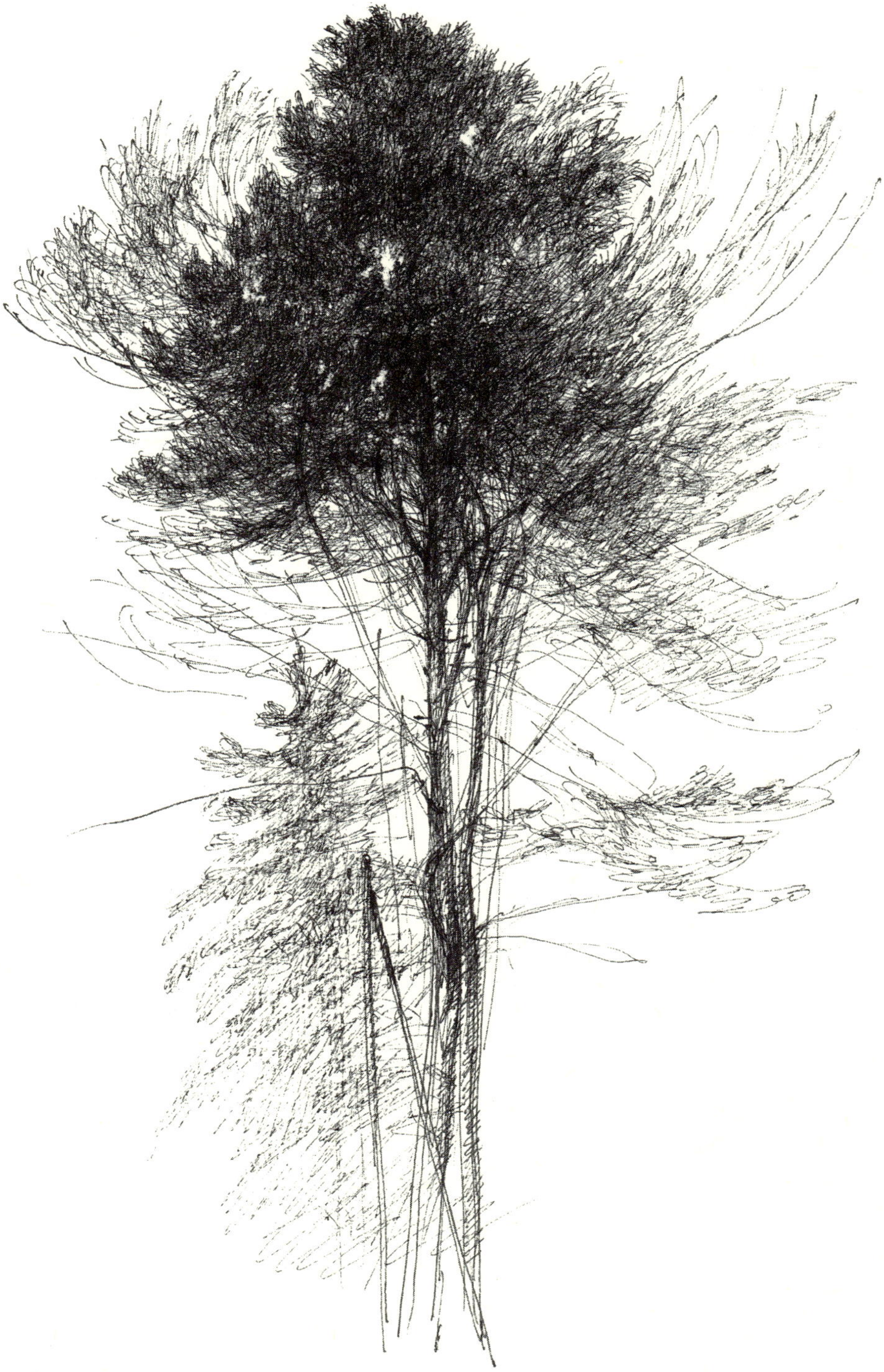

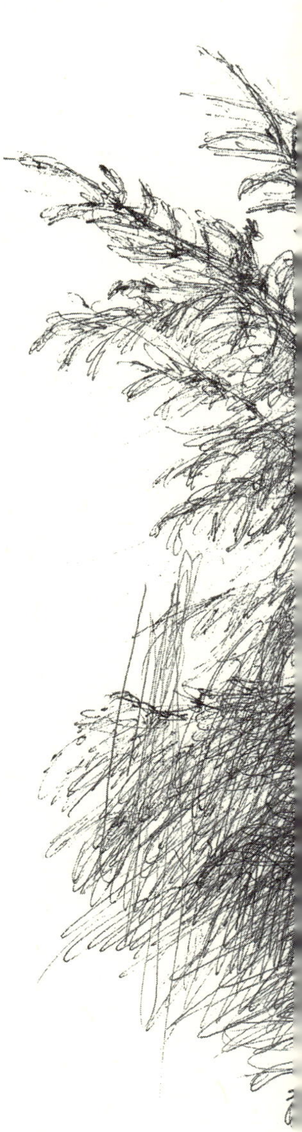

Because the mass of foliage crowding the upper reaches of the tree is so dense, we get the impression of an almost decorative flatness relieved only by the lively contrast of the sturdy top to the spidery branches lower down.

I have given these young fir trees character and created a feeling of forest space solely by playing light against shade rather than delineating detail. This technique is useful in dealing with any kind of tree.

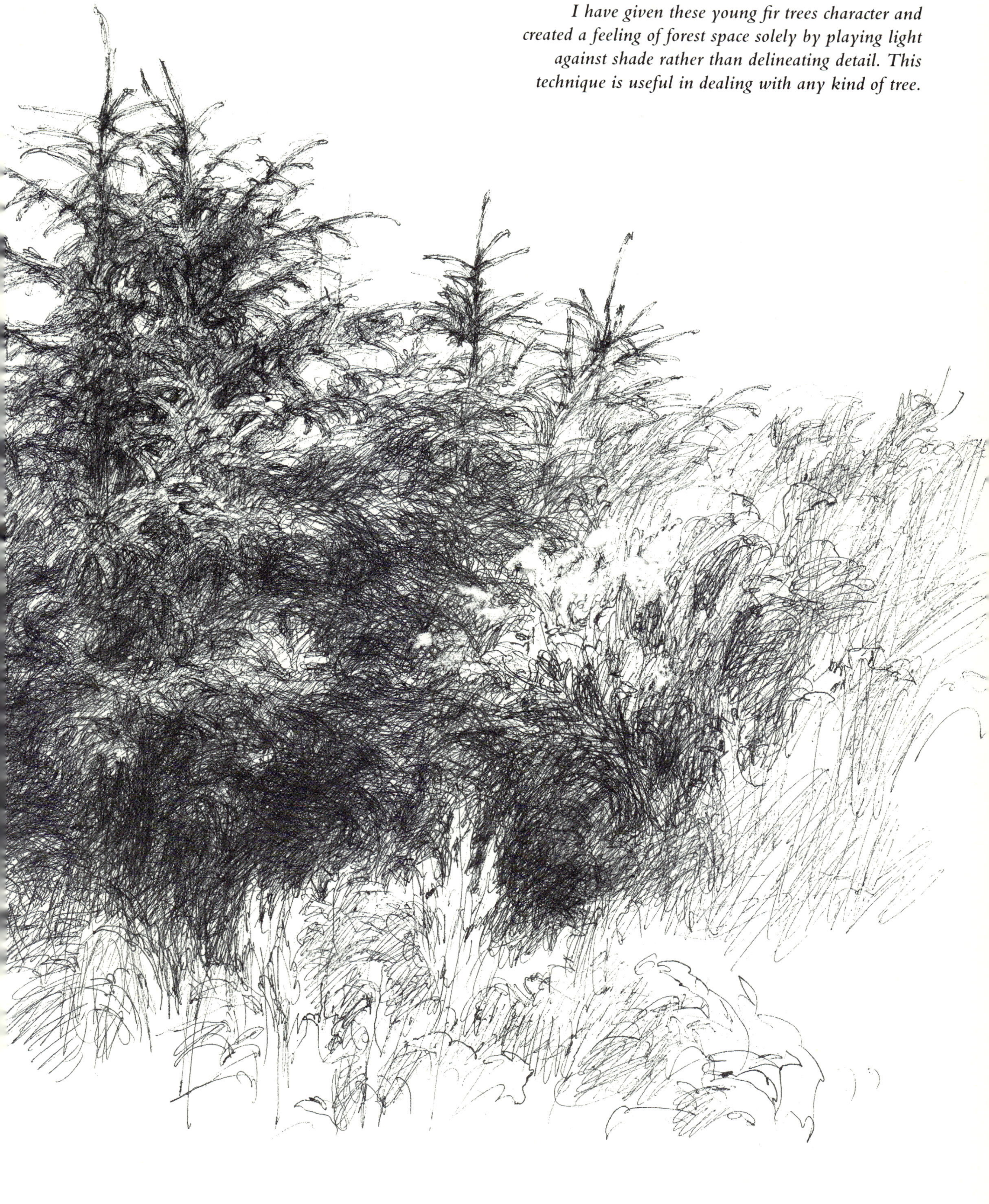

An alder is an exciting tree to draw because of the strong textures of the trunk and the dramatic thrust and twist of the branches. Each tree has its own personality that the sensitive artist seeks to capture in his or her drawings.

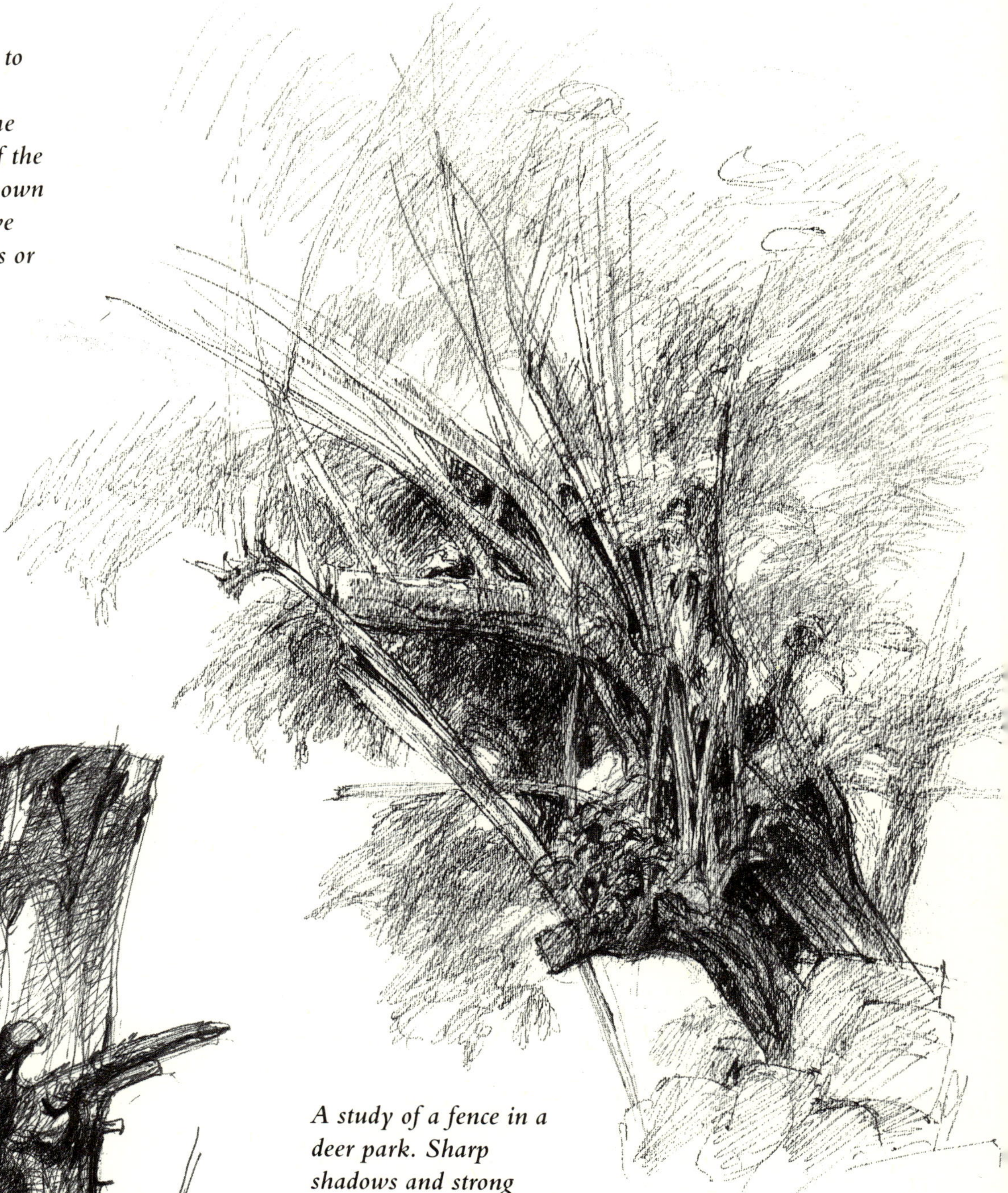

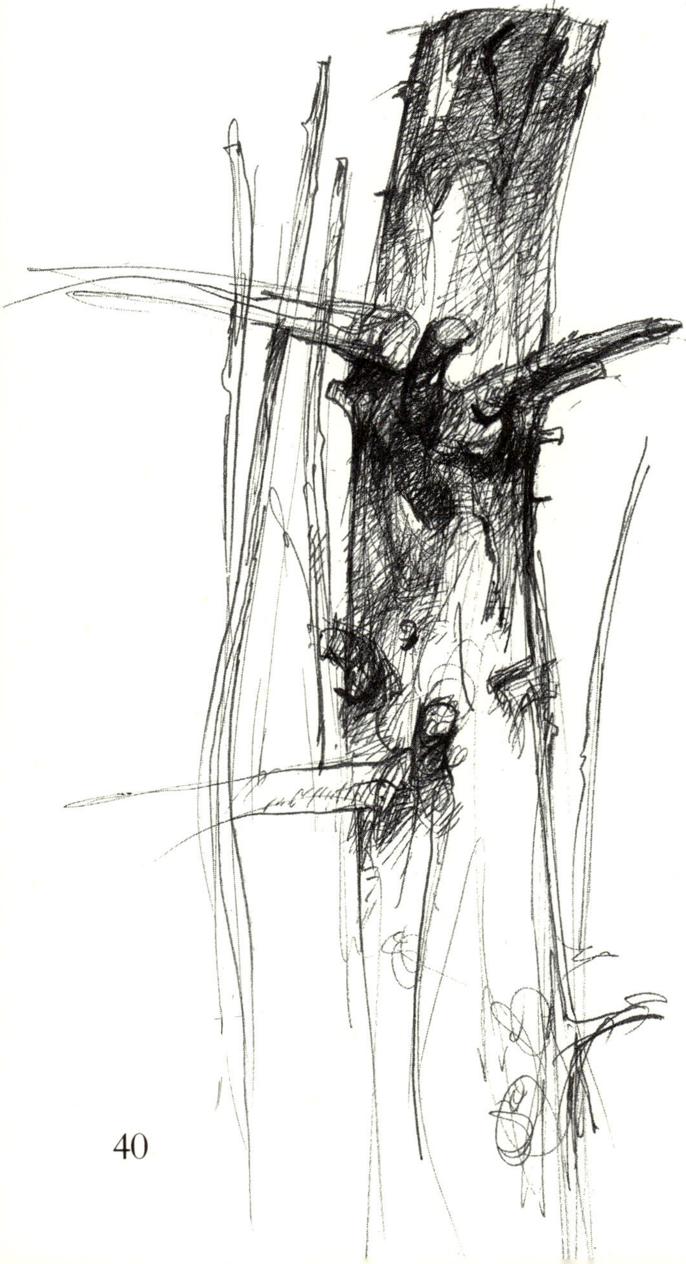

A study of a fence in a deer park. Sharp shadows and strong contrasts signal the approach of summer and warmth.

Trees are different from one another just as no two people are exactly alike. Draw a "portrait" of a tree. Express its special rhythm and character. Bring out the feeling of inner strength that empowered the original seedling to break through the crust of the earth.

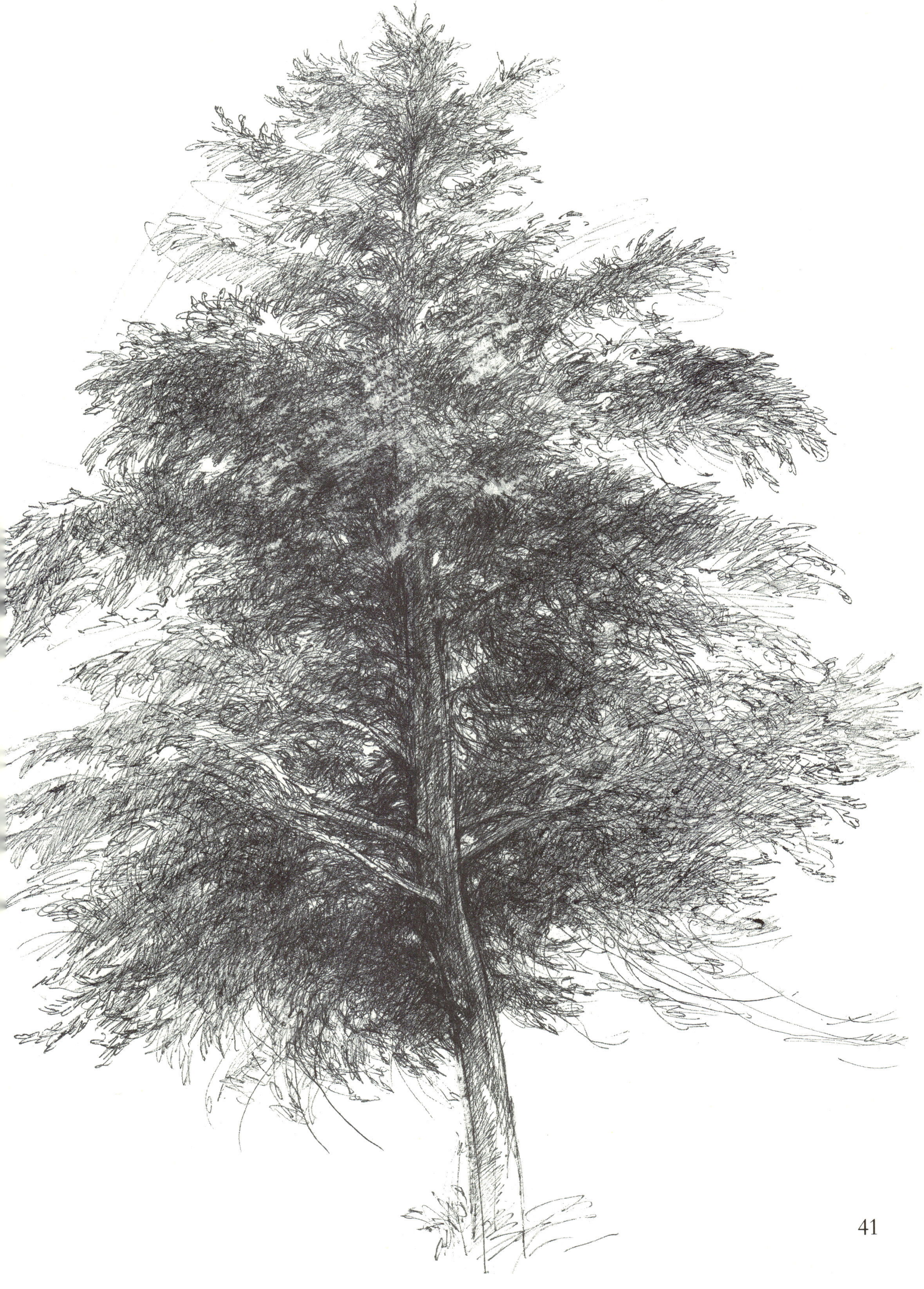

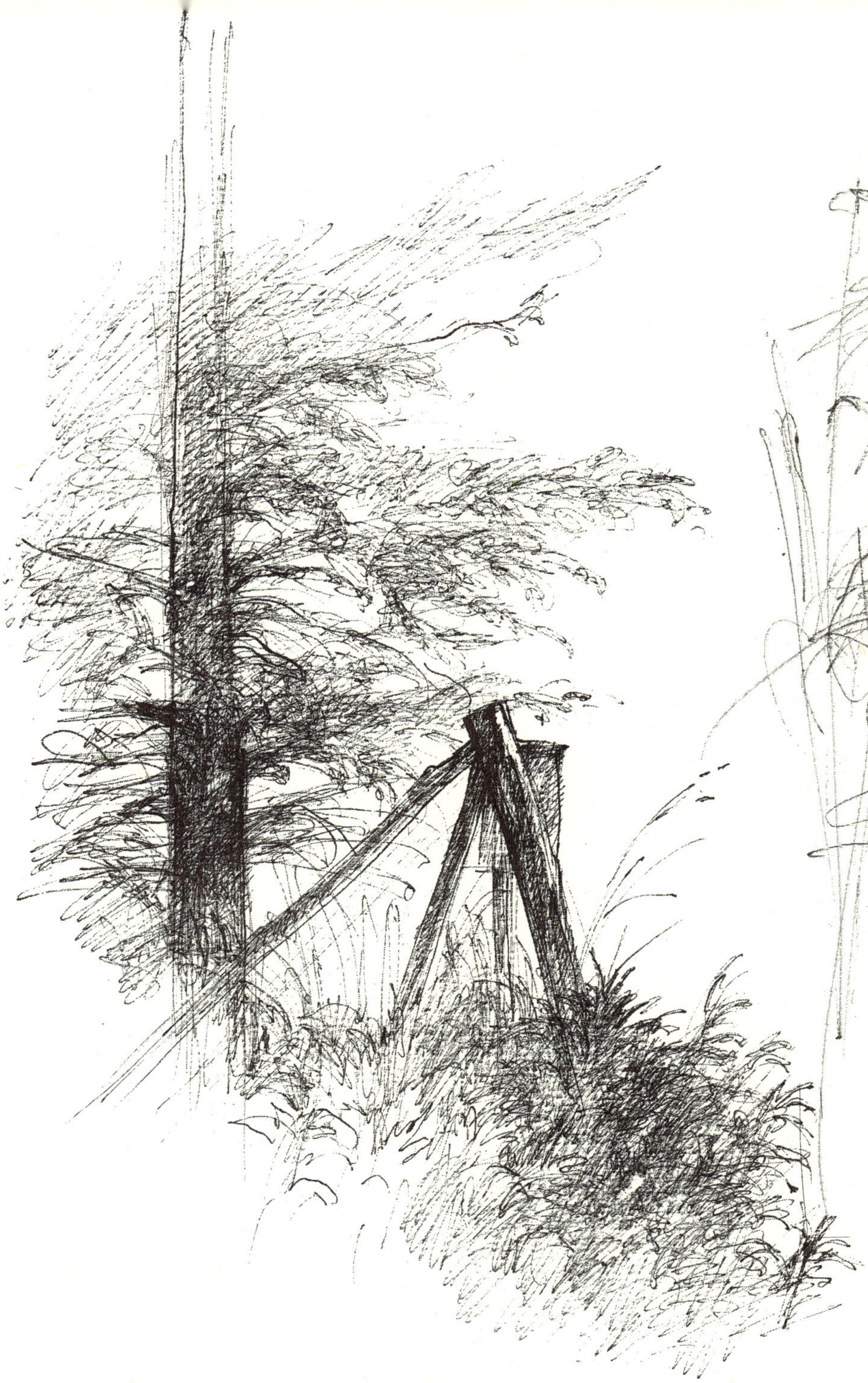

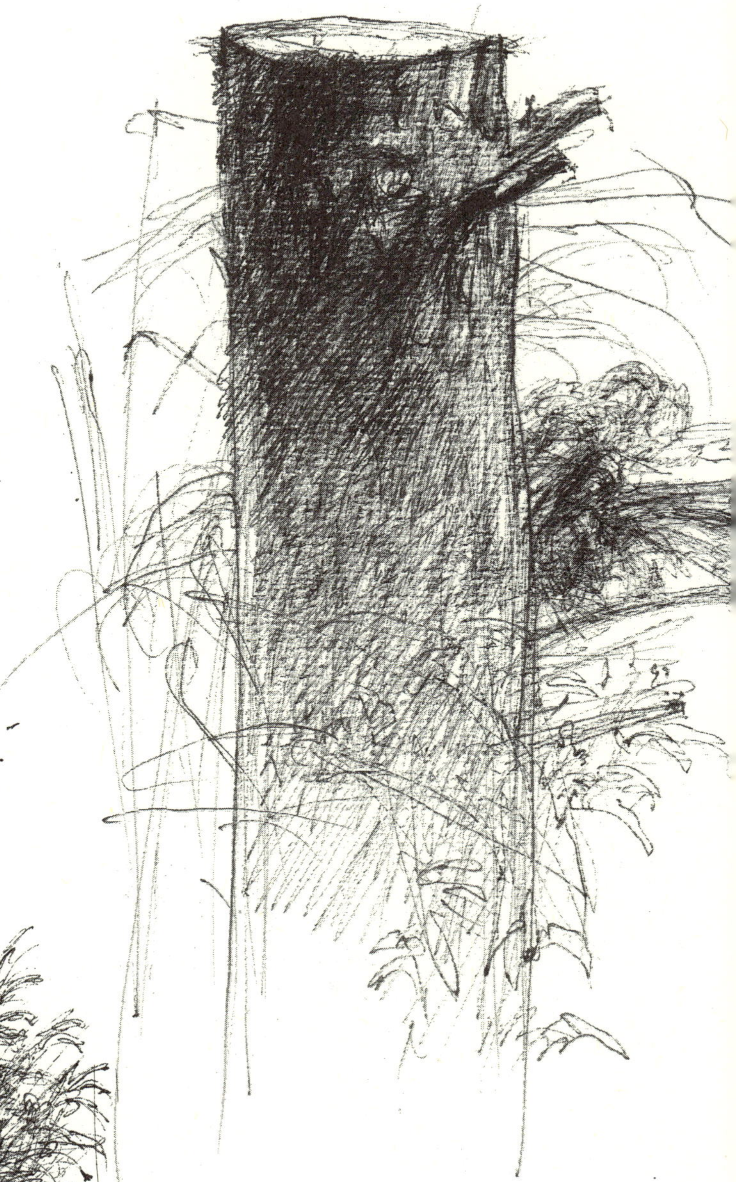

Although clearly two-dimensional, this drawing still expresses space.

Drawing is an intellectual pursuit. A drawing well thought through and expertly rendered can be so compelling as to be considered brilliant. This does not necessarily mean that it is a work of art. But for a drawing to be successful, even brilliant, the artist cannot sin against the canons of good practice and disregard the principles governing mastery of the picture plane. It's the dynamic use of line and the sensitive organization of black and whites on a flat surface, not illusionistic effects, that bring distinction to a drawing.

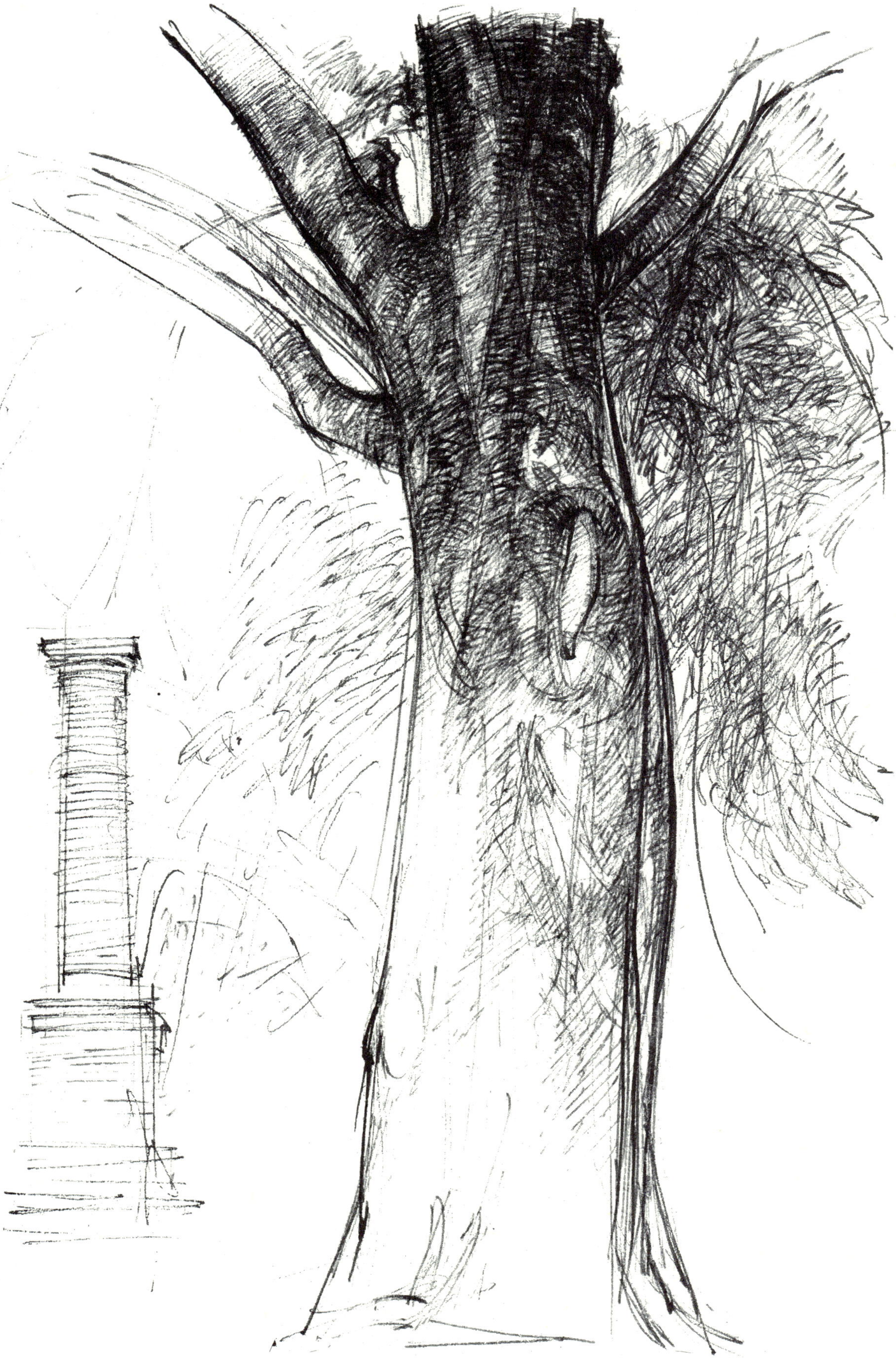

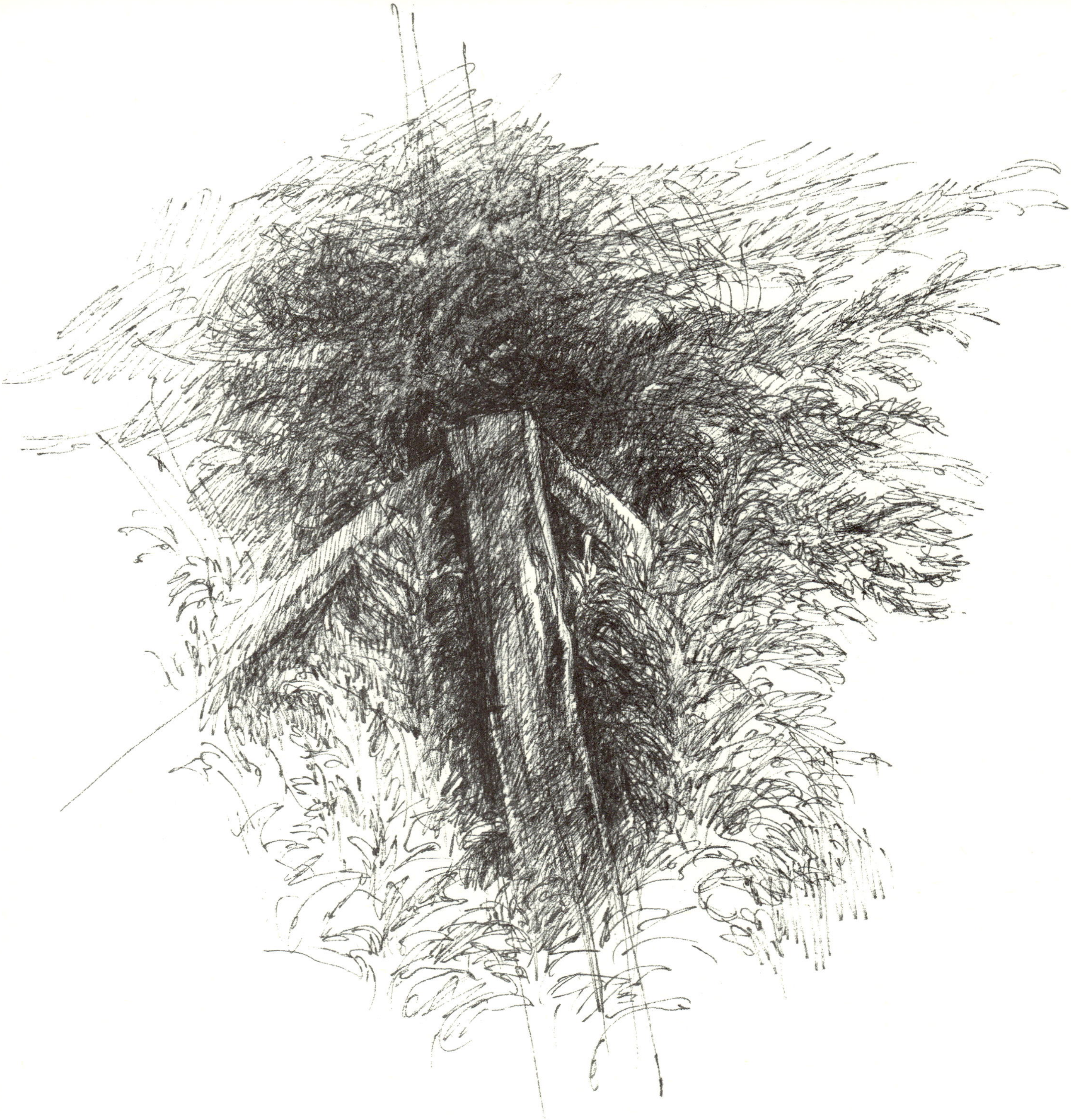

A fence post, overgrown with lush vegetation, presents the artist with an excellent opportunity to depict the rustic surface of the post while contrasting its visual qualities with those of the dense undergrowth around it. Even more important is the chance to capture the play of darks and near-darks within the foliage that are in contrast with the unrelenting sunshine of a summer's day.

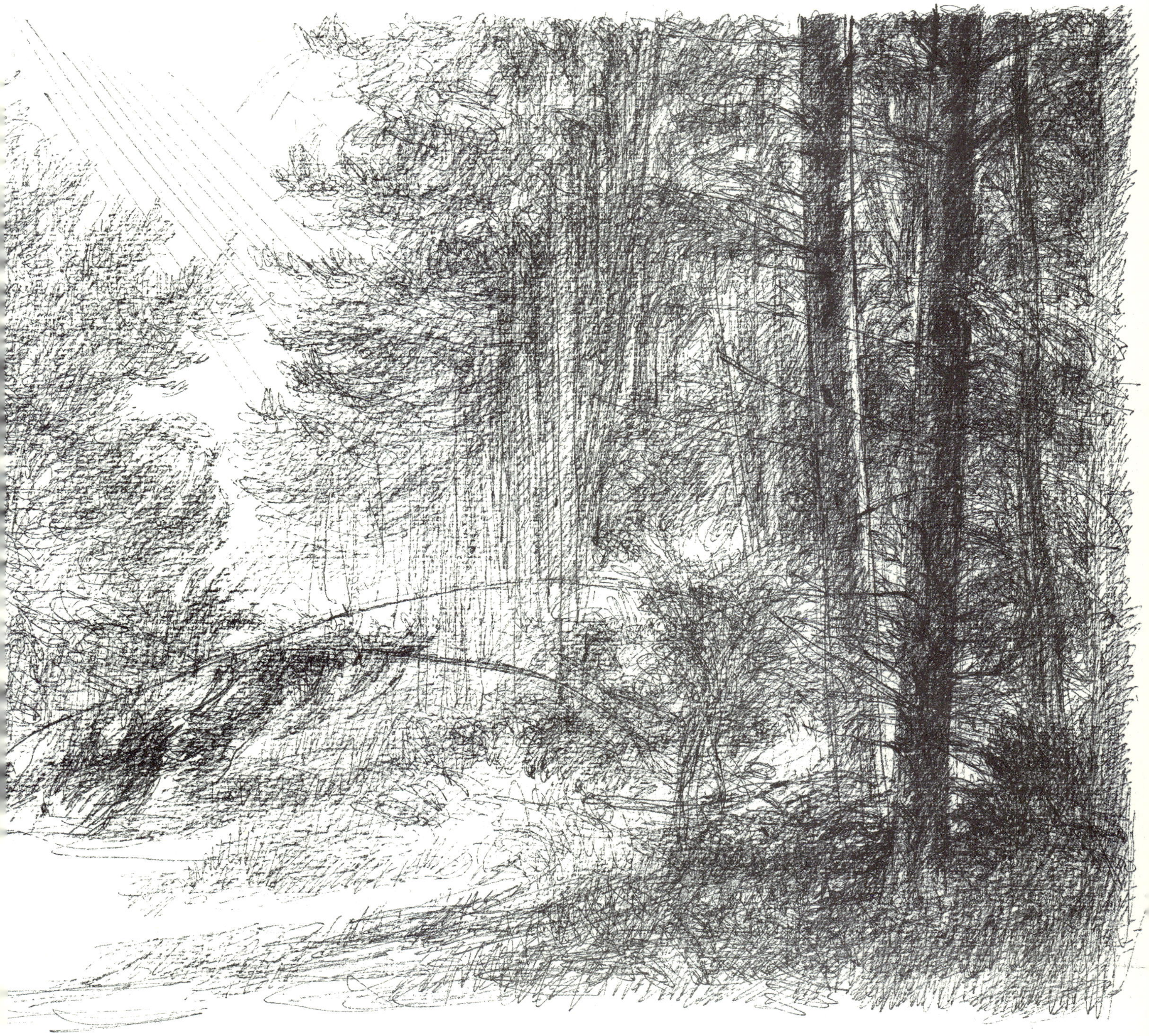

What's our first reaction to this drawing? Just a clearing in the forest with a couple of fallen trees in the foreground, one might say. But the more we look at it, the more we realize there is much more than that; there are graphic qualities and a feeling of the oppressive heat of intense sunshine. I know I have succeeded when viewers begin to see more in one of my drawings than what they perceived with a first look.

LESSON 5

Composition

Many painters have captured on canvas the natural beauty of the countryside, from pale green high forests with their straight beech trunks in early May to an expanse of hilly farmland on a sparkling, cold winter day. Some people say that this type of pictorial imagery is passé, that it belongs to history; but nature is always with us, just as open and just as beautiful now as it ever was. It is up to the individual to decide what it can bring to him or her.

We adapt the visual impressions we receive from nature to coincide with a personal point of view that might be quite different from that of others. The attitudes we form about certain subject matter may derive from the circumstances of our childhood. Have you ever wondered why some artists repeat the same motifs, often expressed in different guises, throughout their lives? Because art is so personal, it is important that we listen to ourselves when we attempt a landscape or a cityscape. Be loyal to your intentions. Don't let a fashion or fad dictate how you decide to express yourself. Throughout your life there will be experiences, images and events that "leave you cold" and others that make you glow with delight.

Spontaneity is of great importance in drawing but, just as important, is the kind of calm, level-headed planning that is necessary if the "geometry" of your drawing is to be effective. In this lesson, we will review the basic principles of composition that guide us in the construction of a drawing as well as explore other important fundamentals, such as the role of dynamics in personal expression, that together contribute to the success of a picture.

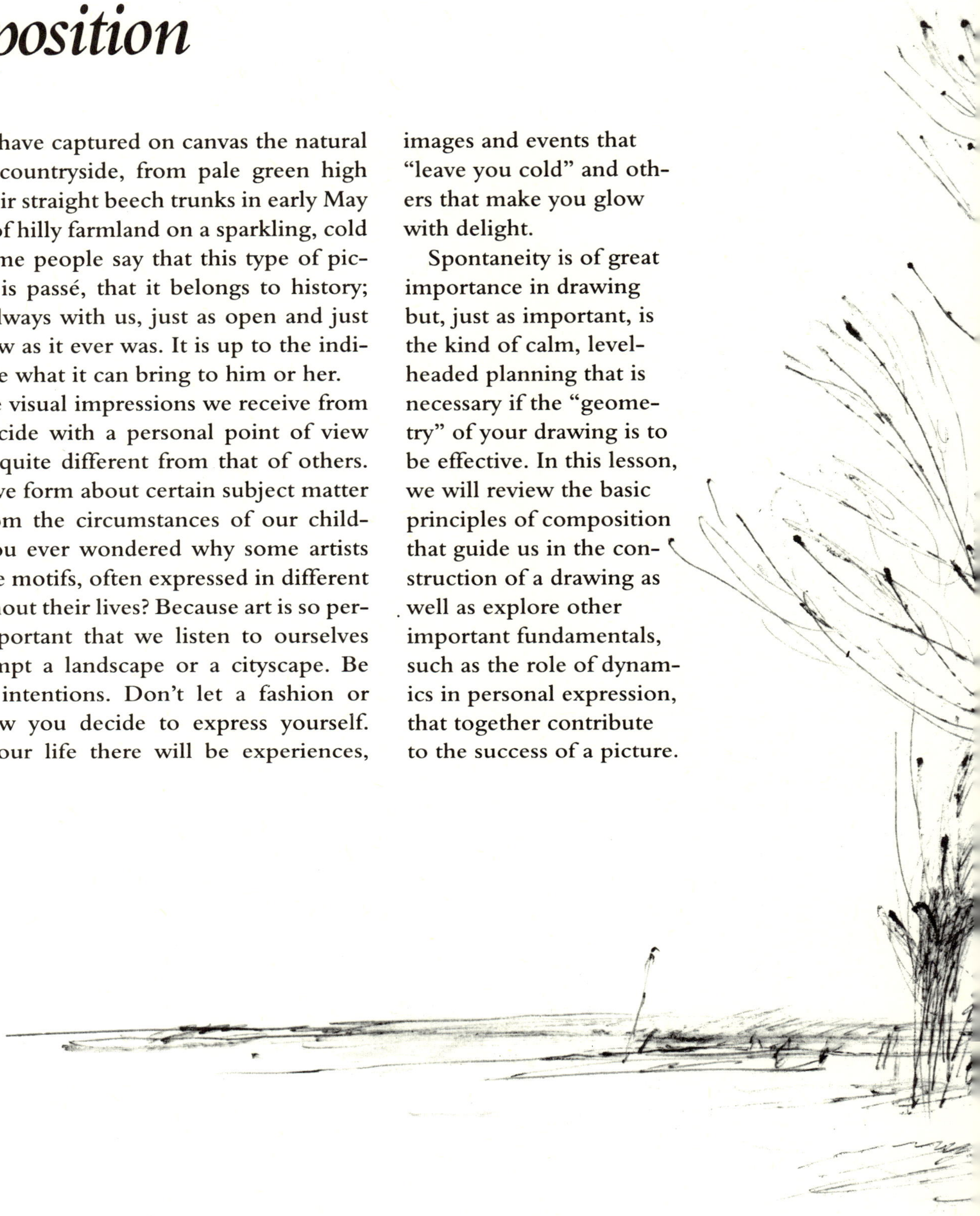

Busy with our own thoughts, the beauty of a country road bordered with pollard willow trees might not be immediately apparent to us. But, here, in a drawing that plays the massiveness of sturdy black trunks against a delicate filigree of thin branches, we cannot help but be taken with the elegance of nature.

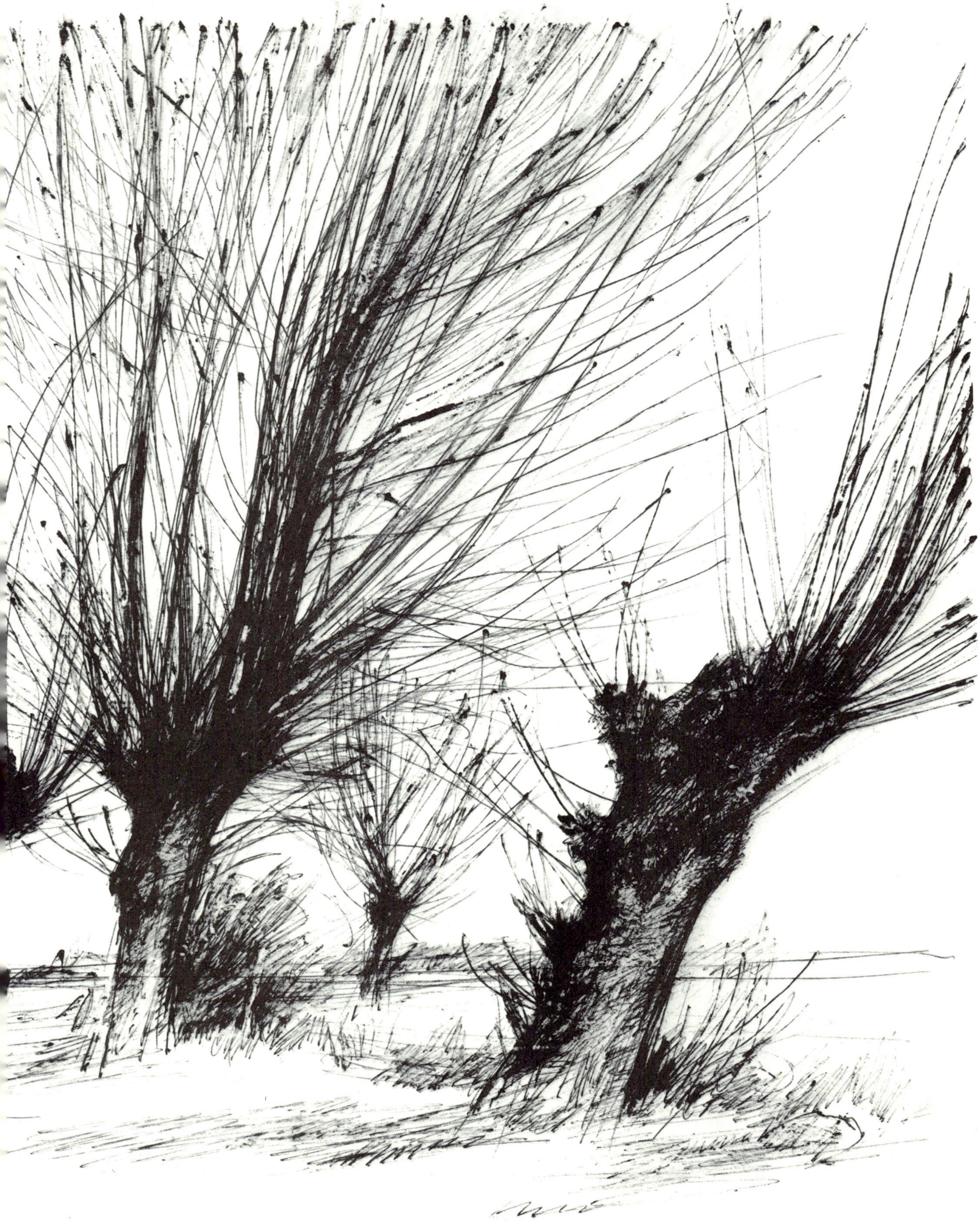

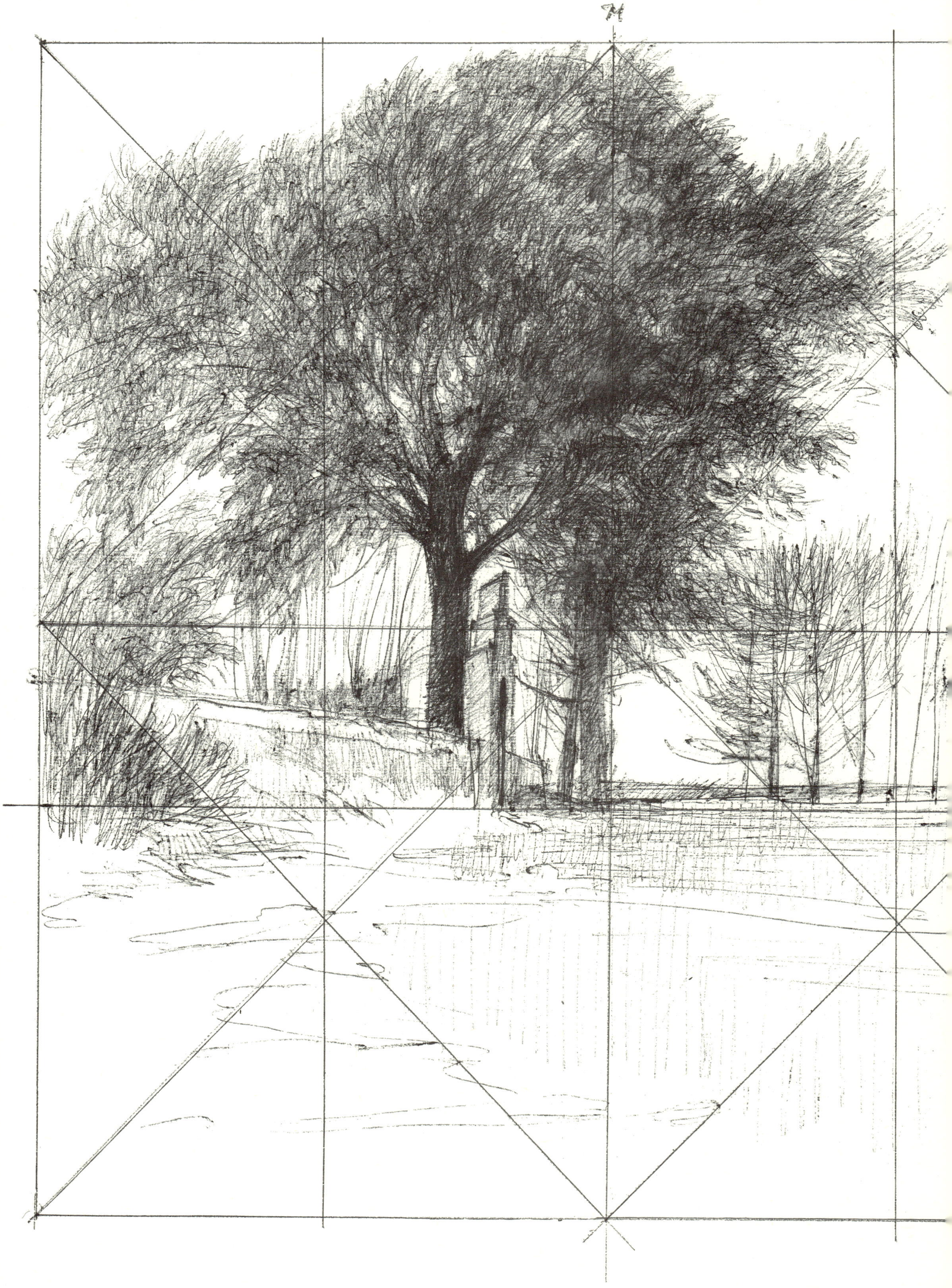

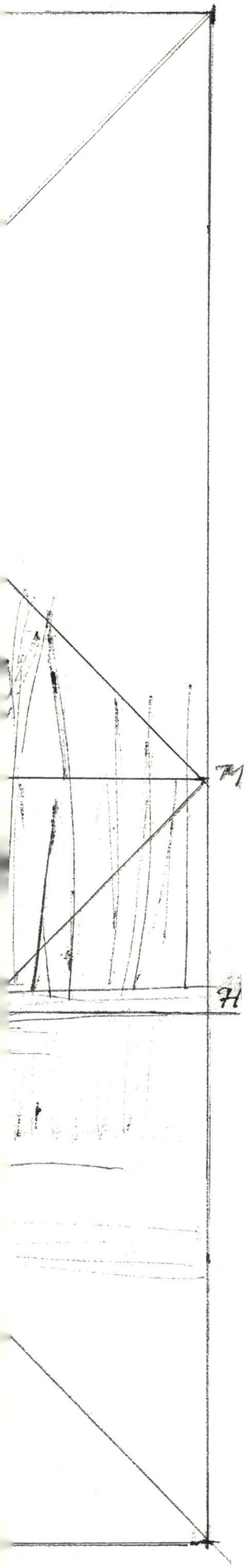

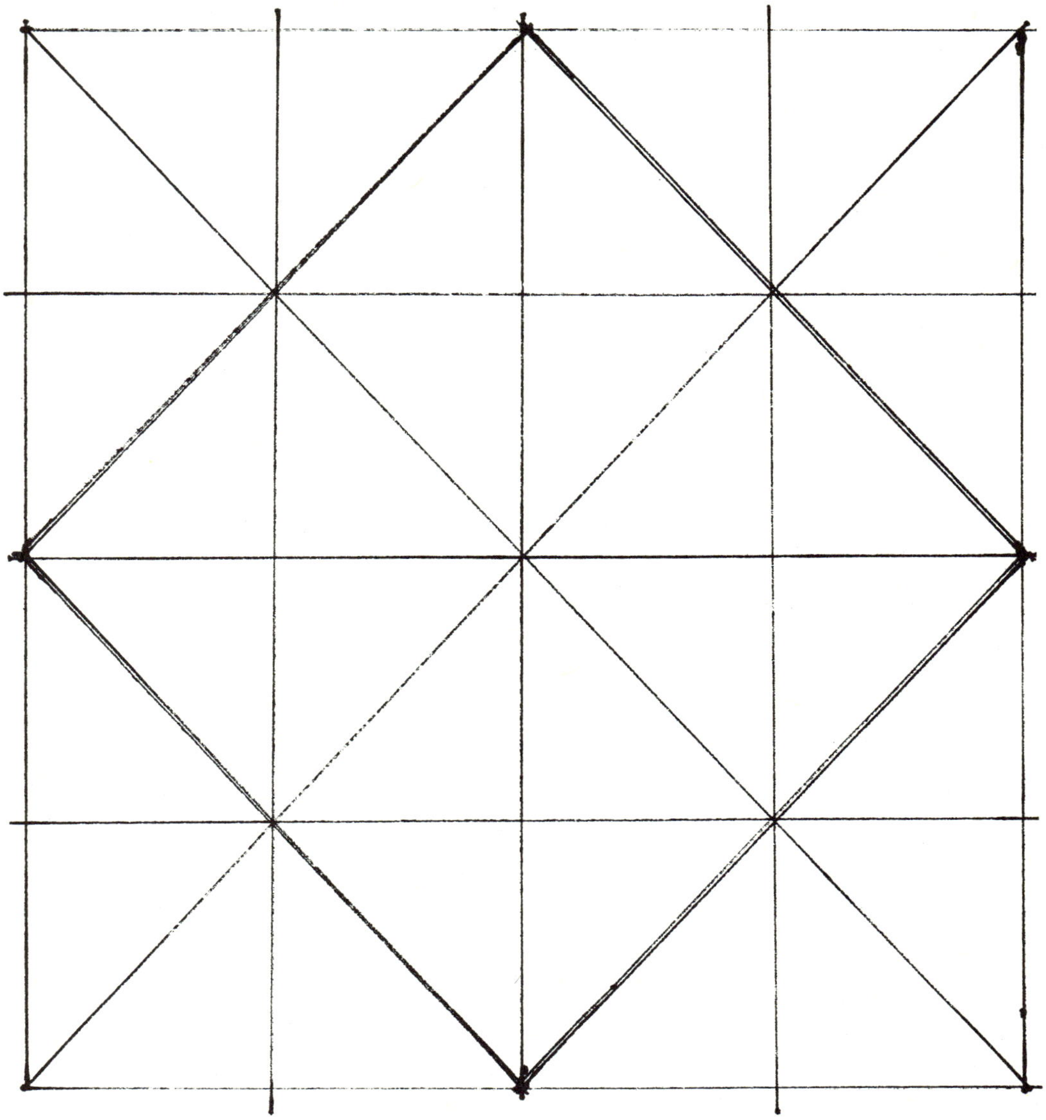

When you have decided on the size and format of a proposed composition, draw this simple diagram and fit your drawing into it. Its square grid of vertical, horizontal and diagonal lines will act as a guide to help strengthen your composition. Moving the subject matter to a new position while using the same grid for a second drawing often yields an even more striking image.

Here I've chosen to work with the same grid but adapted it to a rectangle. It acts as a kind of "safety net" to keep the central points of my composition in place and to establish a strong sense of the relationship of the baseline to diagonal and vertical thrusts. Notice the scaling of the group of trees according to the principle of the "golden section"—three to five, five to eight, etc. When you plan to proportion your composition in some such classic manner, it's best to outline its dimensions on your paper before you begin to draw the image you have in mind.

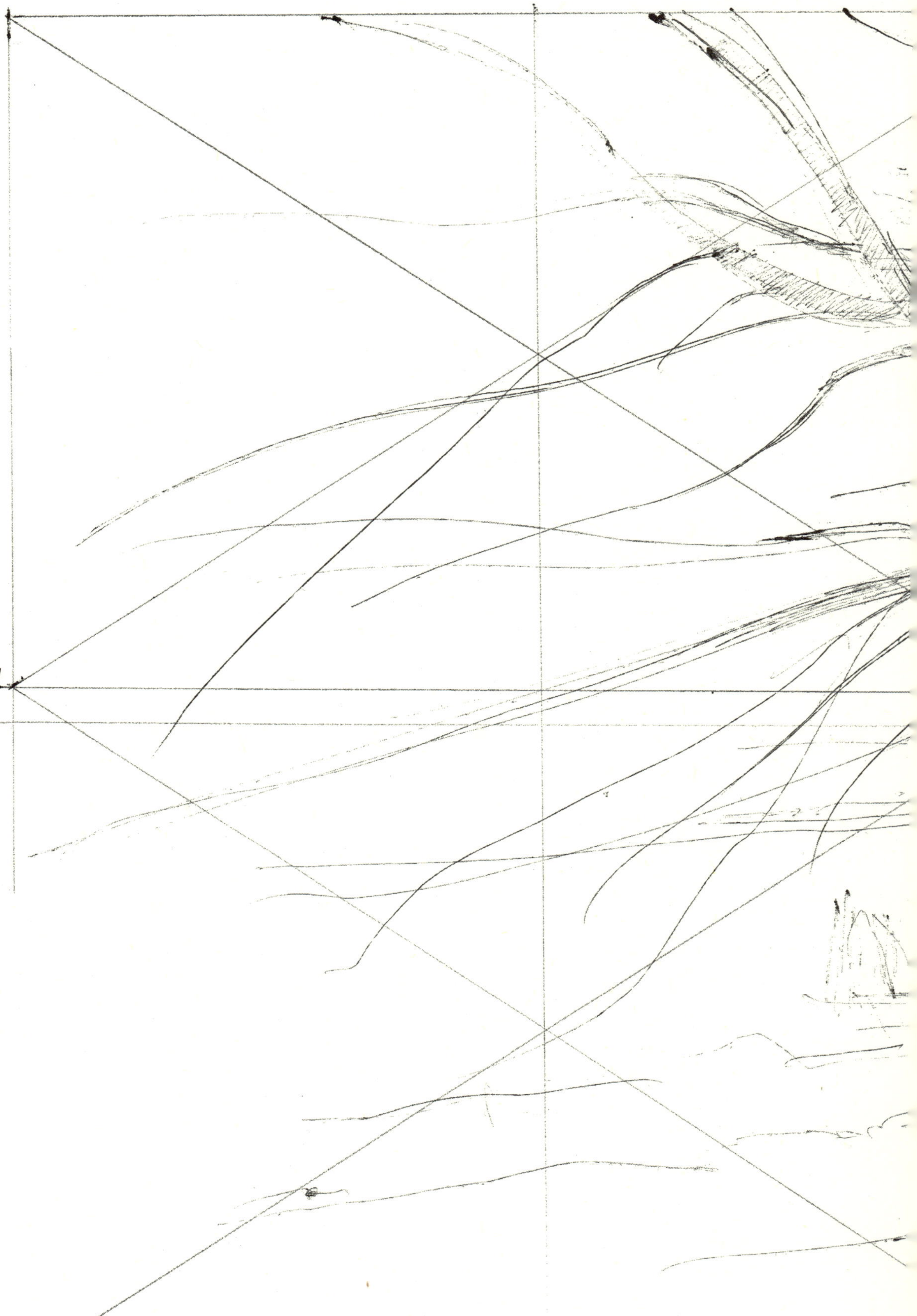

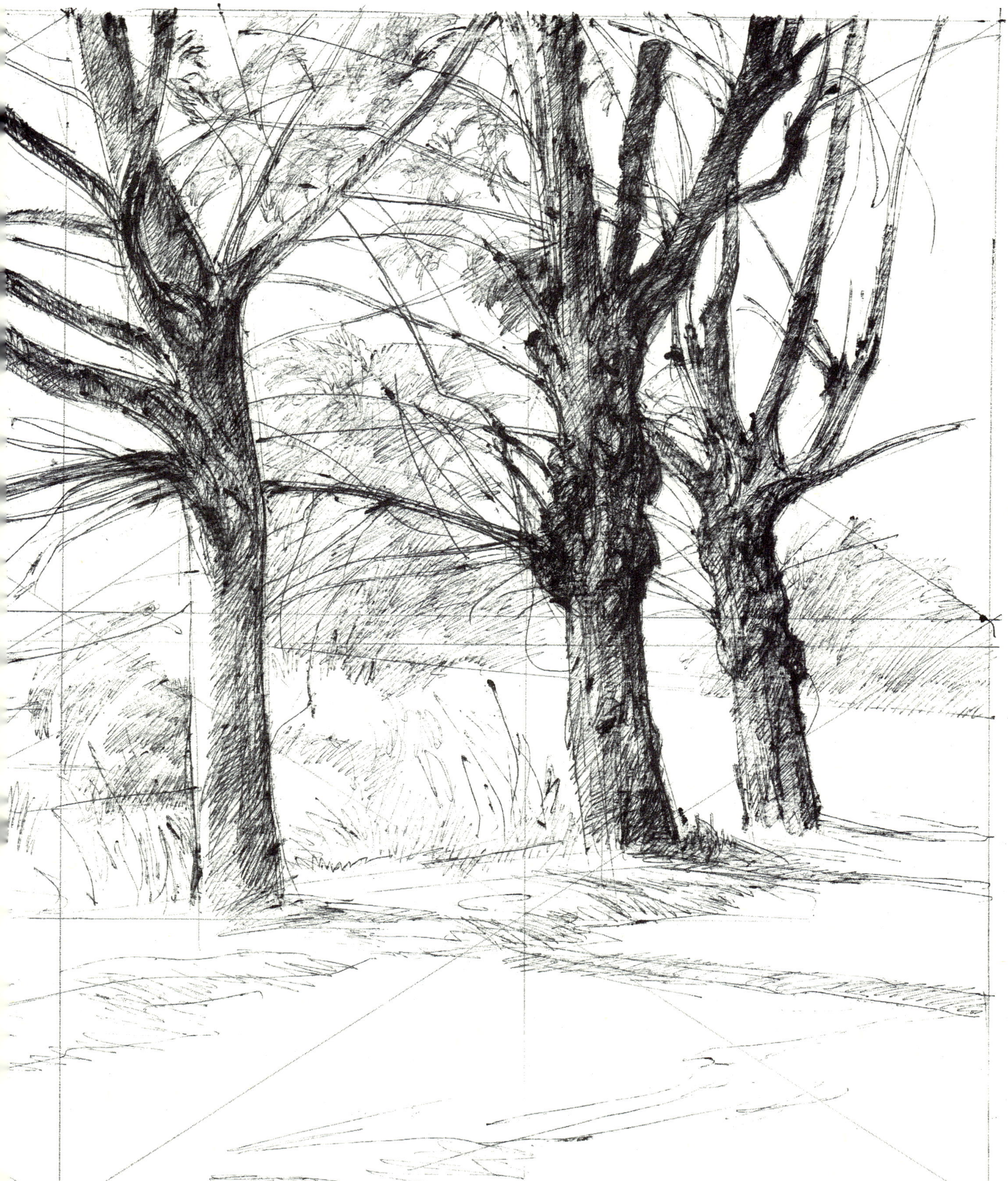

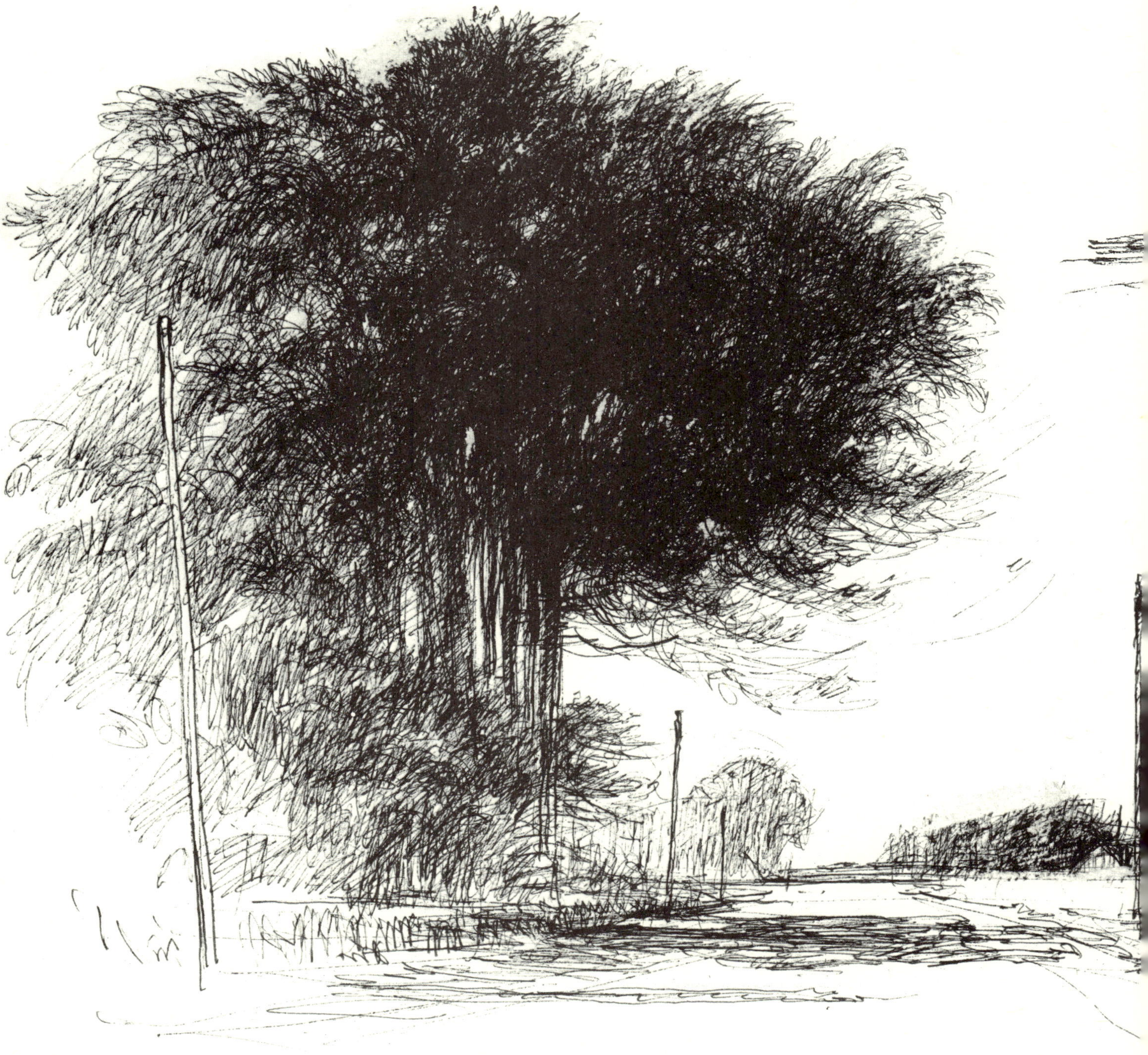

A country road on a summer's day has heavy cast shadows.

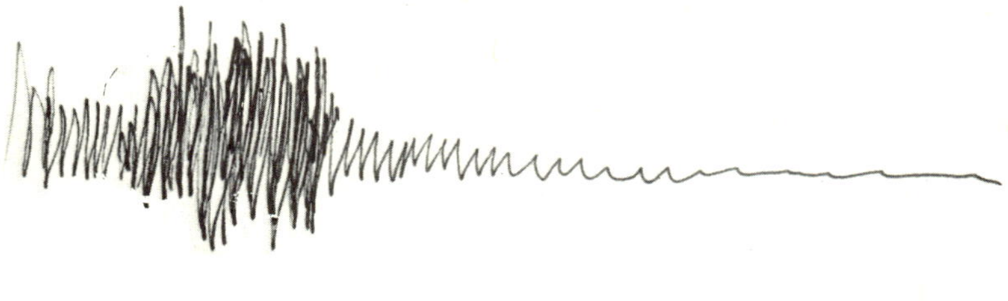

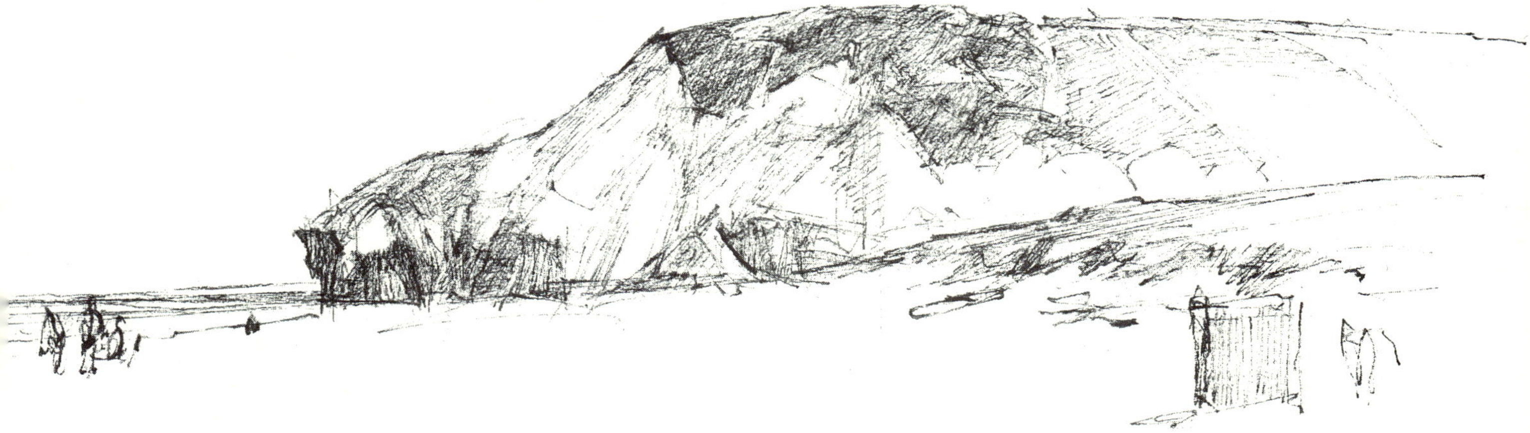

In this drawing, the white paper represents the beach, the people indicate the scale, and the image is constructed according to the proportions of the "golden section."

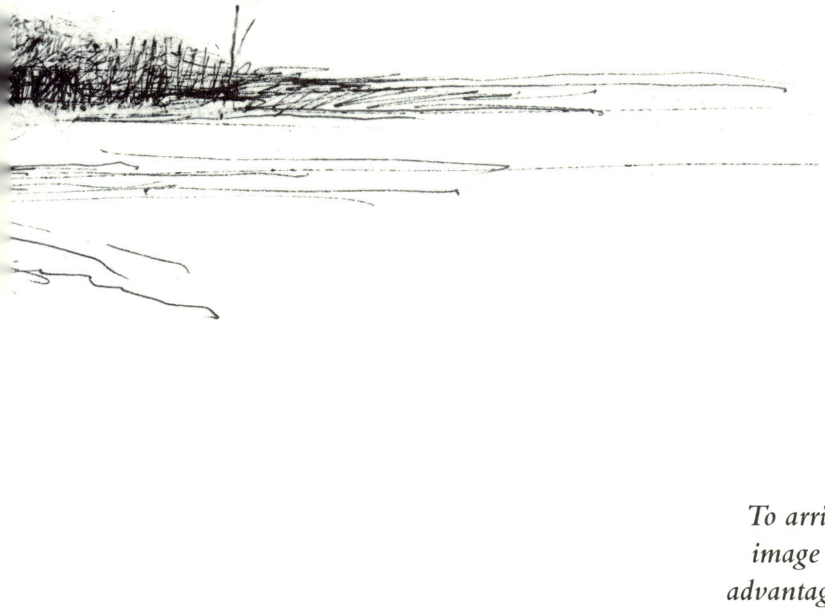

To arrive at a successful drawing, it is important to place the image on the paper so that it occupies the area of best visual advantage. While it must convey information, it must do so in a dynamic manner which I often enhance by adding contrasts of rhythm and color. Below the drawing I have often made a "diagram" in the hope that it will clarify the means by which I arrived at the final composition.

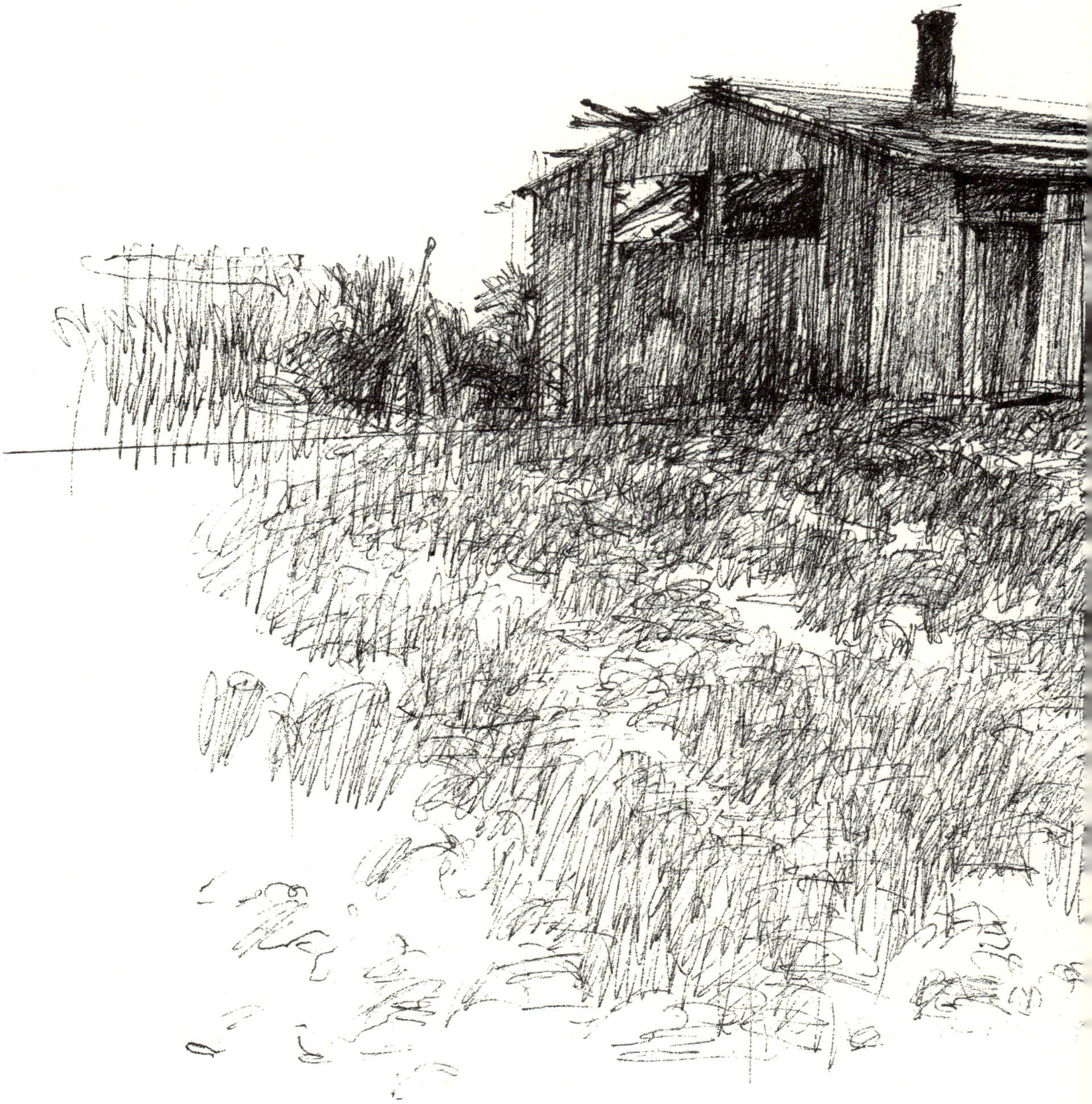

Abandoned railway station and run-down barn.

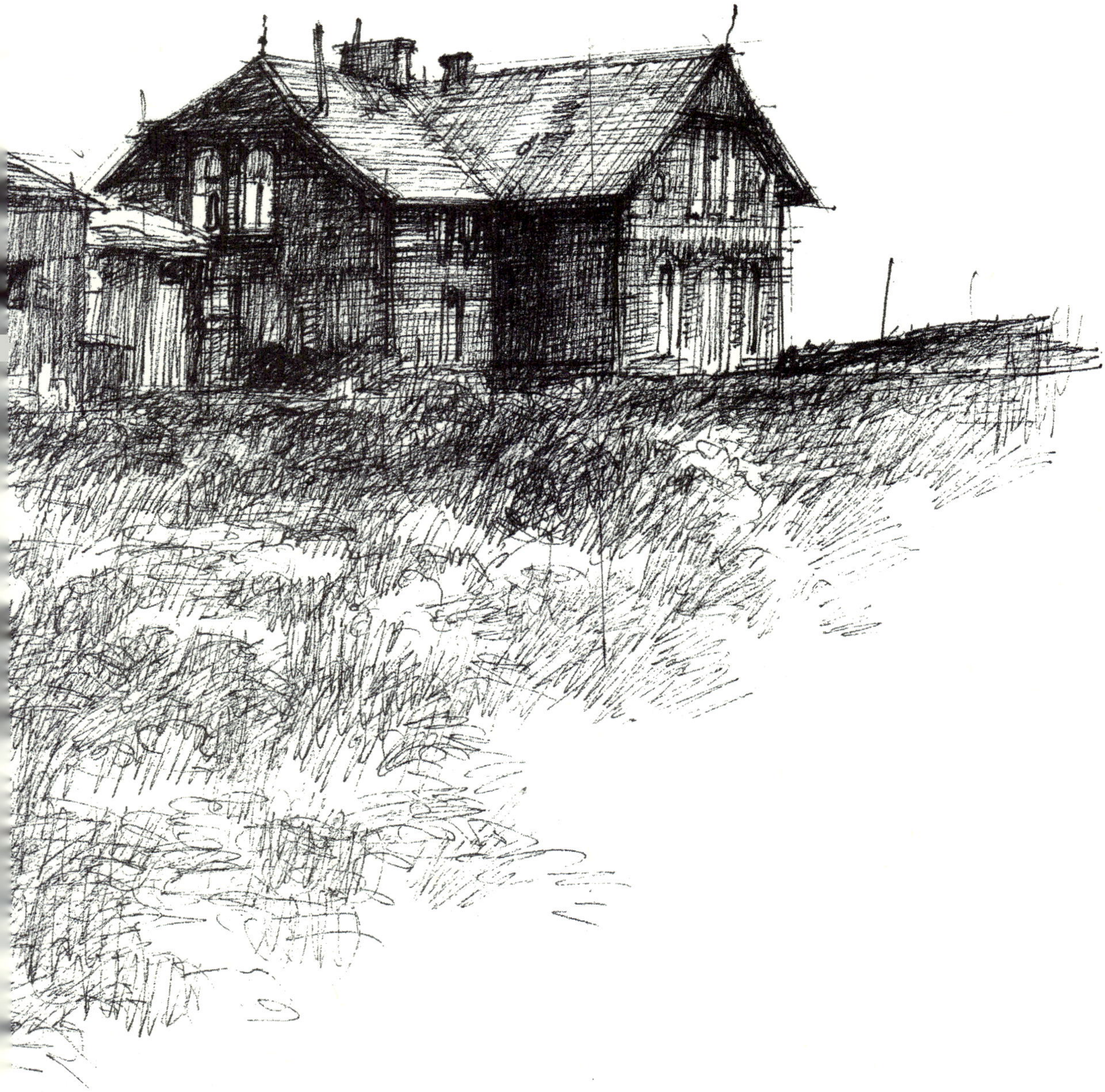

When composing a drawing it's important to identify the foreground, middleground and background. Sometimes, it's advantageous to have a deep foreground to provide a long lead-in to the primary image area. At other times, just the opposite approach produces the best effect.

In this drawing, a deep lead-in creates contrast between the wide expanse of lush, waving grass and the tightly grouped buildings. To heighten the effect, the dark of the almost silhouetted houses is also in contrast against the light of the foreground.

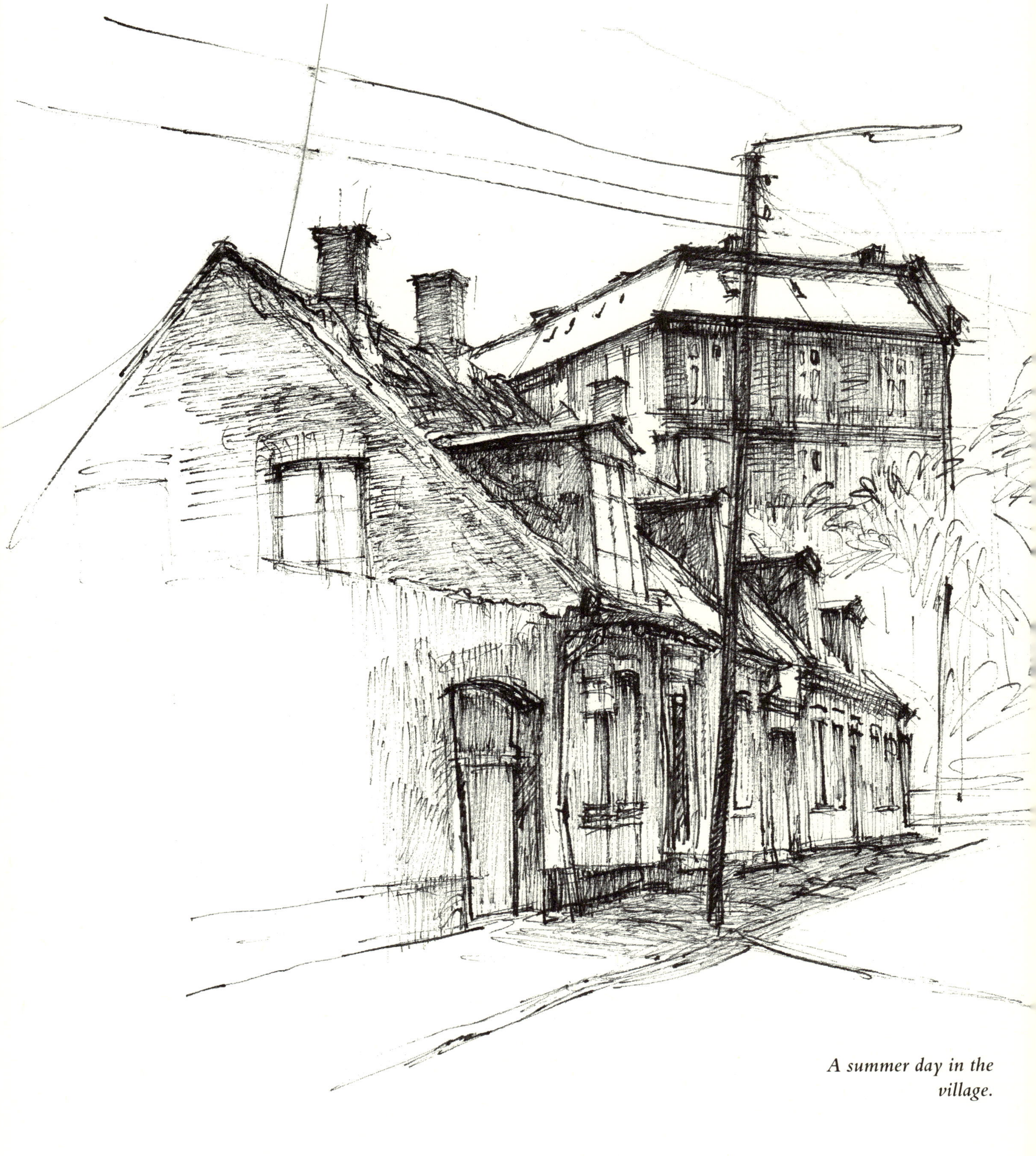

A summer day in the village.

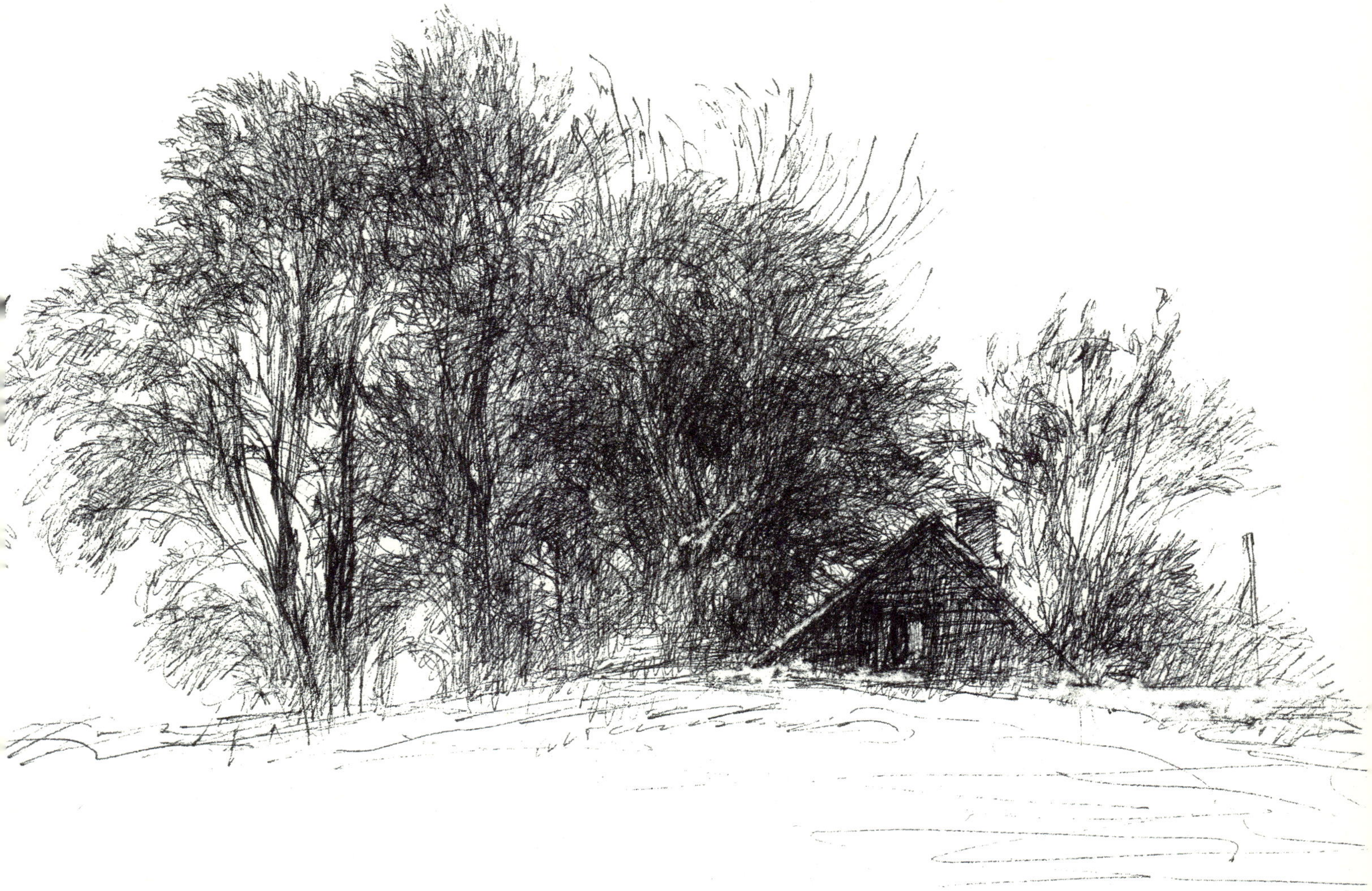

In both of these drawings, the middleground dominates. The composition focuses on what is most interesting—details of the brickwork, the crowns of the trees, and the simple outline of the drawings themselves.

To bring out the character of this old windmill and toolshed, I brushed on a water and India ink wash for the dark areas and used a pen to sketch in both the outline and the details. To establish the grey middle tones I diluted the wash.

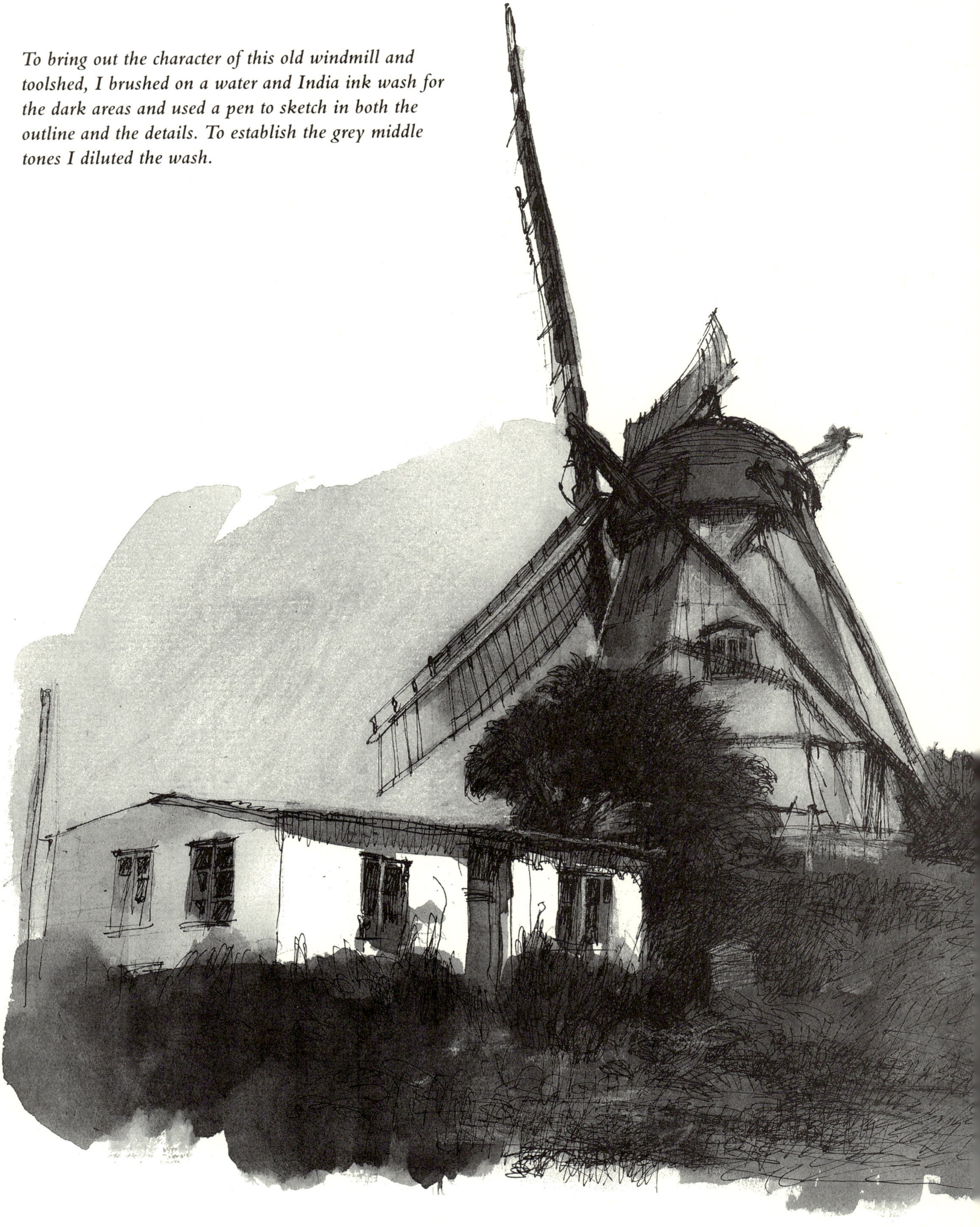

L E S S O N 6

Interiors and Exteriors

Museums are excellent sources of subject matter for those interested in drawing. The drawings in this lesson were made directly from exhibits on display at an open-air museum and farm collection of Copenhagen's National Museum in Denmark. Admittedly, finding and then getting permission to sketch the interiors of old farm buildings is difficult, but museums such as this one offer alternatives by allowing us to observe and draw the furnishings and interior architecture representative of the way farm folk lived years ago.

Whether you are drawing an interior or exterior scene, the placement of your image on the paper is extremely important. My advice is to work large, but if you see early on that your drawing is going to run over the edge of the paper or can't include everything you want it to, don't compromise, start over. Don't be tempted to make a line drawing first and then begin shading. It's better to work as much as possible on all aspects of your drawing simultaneously.

The main room of a farm house. The Danish Farm Collection, National Museum, Copenhagen.

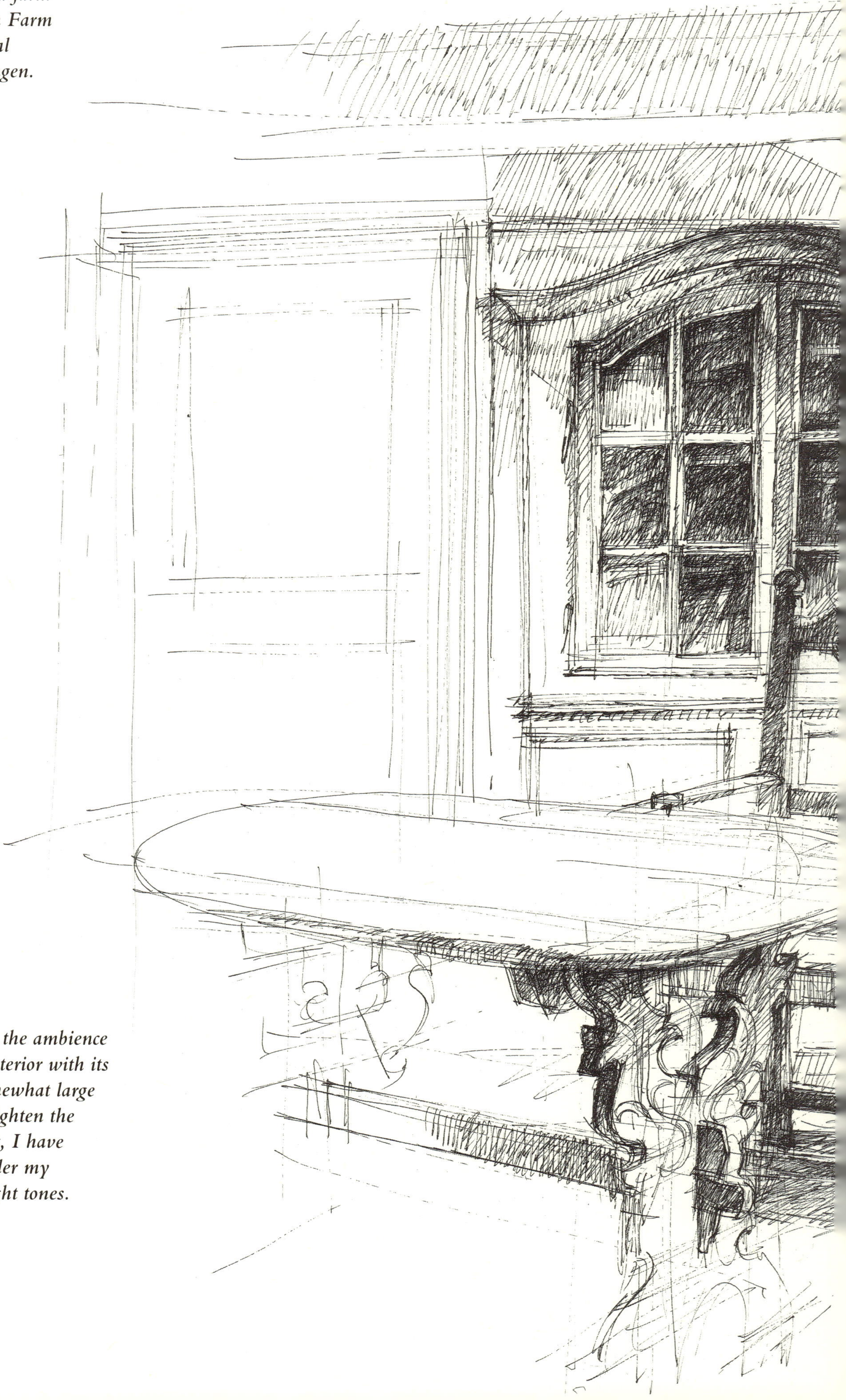

In order to capture the ambience of this charming interior with its blue walls and somewhat large windows which brighten the room with sunlight, I have taken pains to render my drawing in very light tones.

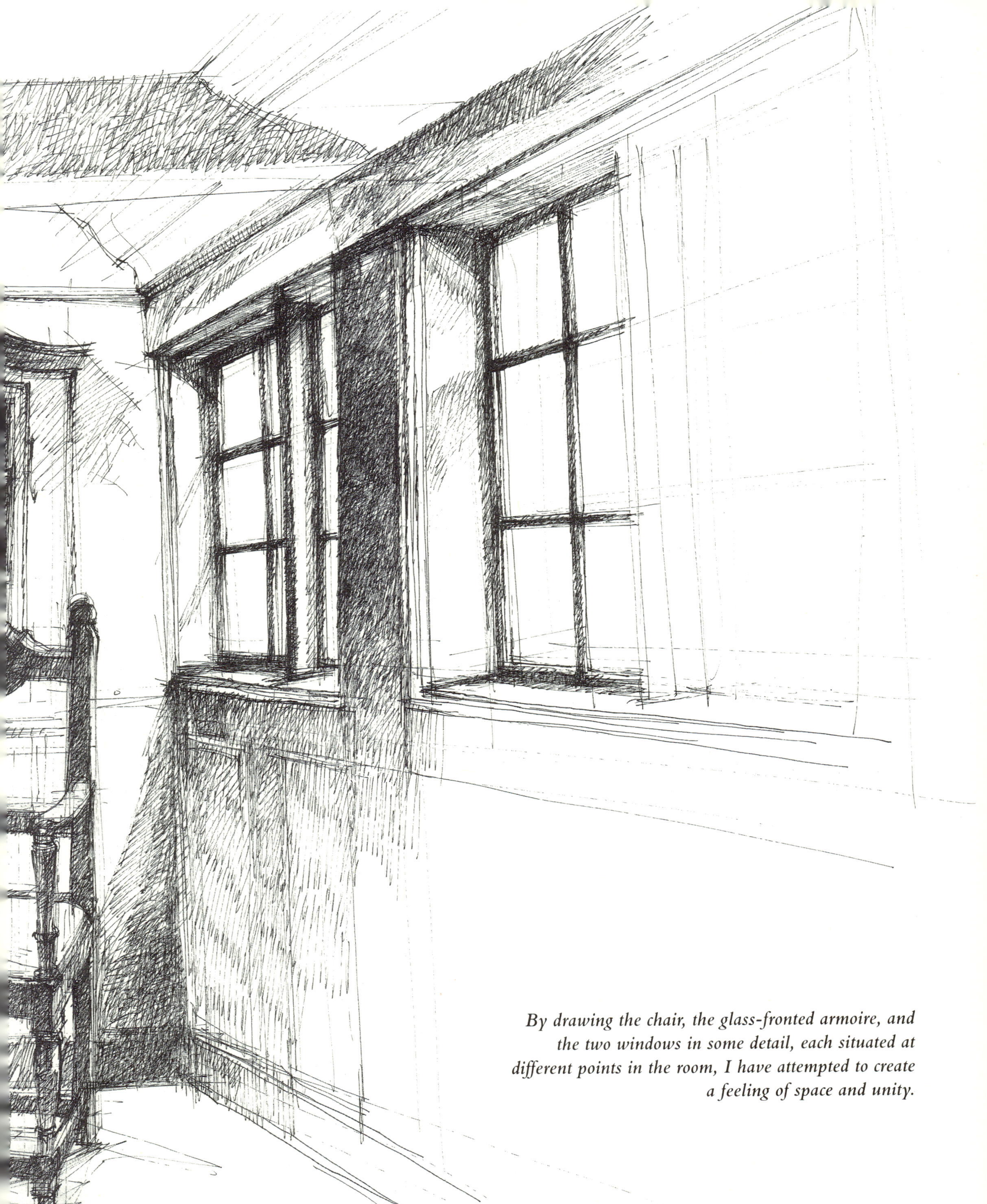

By drawing the chair, the glass-fronted armoire, and the two windows in some detail, each situated at different points in the room, I have attempted to create a feeling of space and unity.

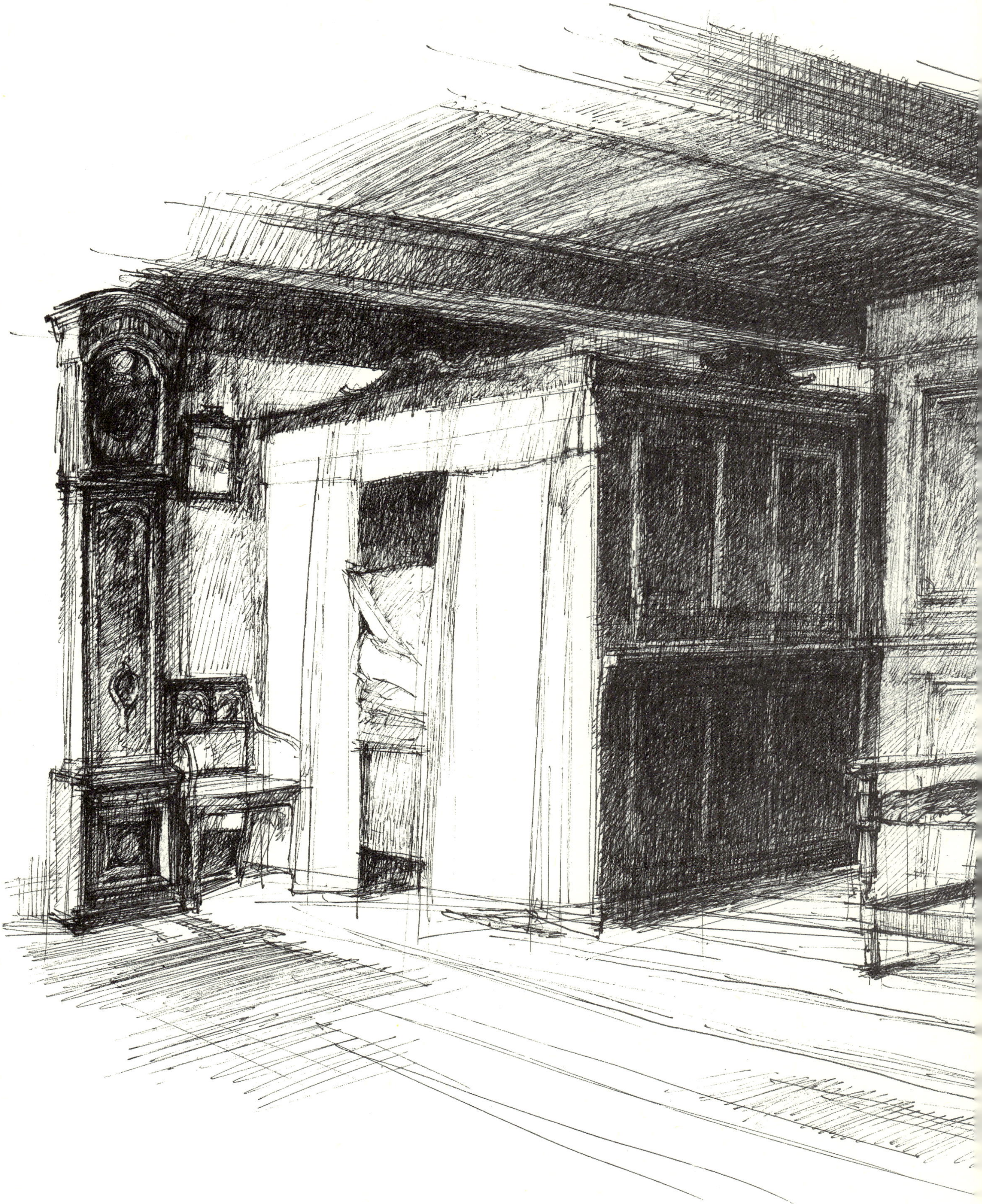

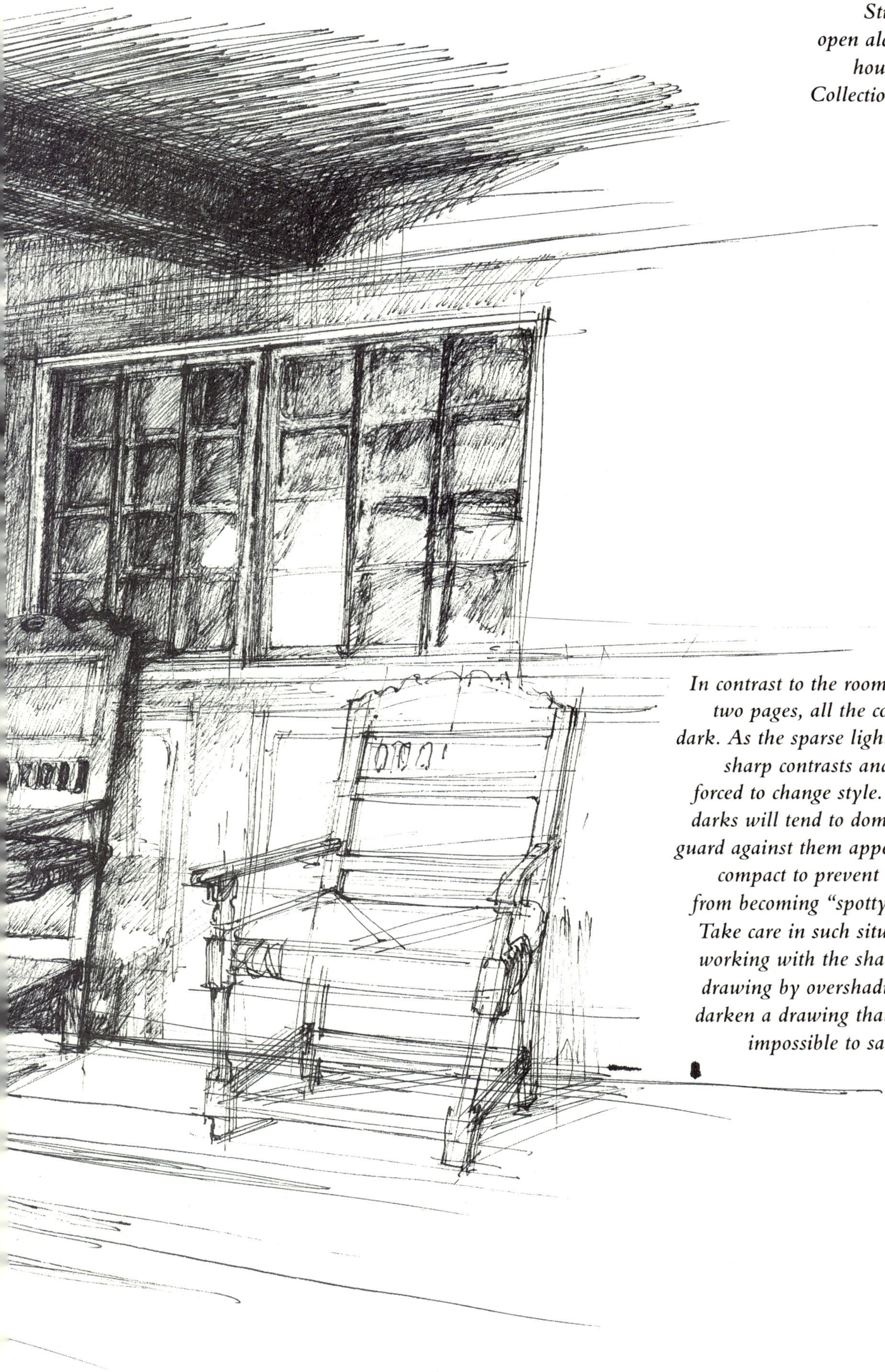

Study of a room with an open alcove in a Danish farm house. The Danish Farm Collection, National Museum, Copenhagen.

In contrast to the room illustrated on the last two pages, all the corners in this room are dark. As the sparse light in those areas creates sharp contrasts and dark shadows, I was forced to change style. In such instances, the darks will tend to dominate. The artist must guard against them appearing too isolated and compact to prevent his or her composition from becoming "spotty" and losing its unity. Take care in such situations. It's easy when working with the shadow areas to lose your drawing by overshading. It's not difficult to darken a drawing that's too light but almost impossible to save one that's too dark.

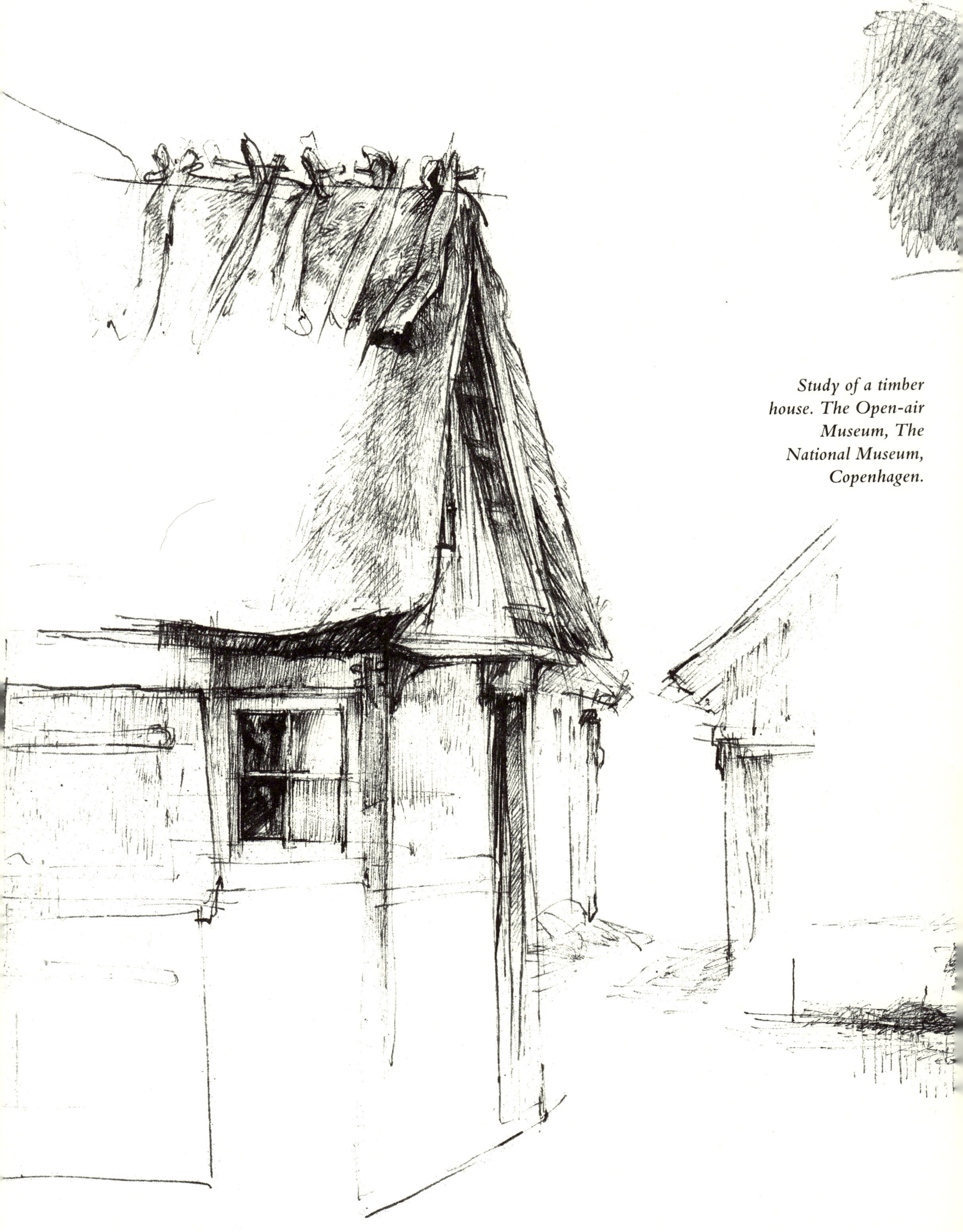

Study of a timber house. The Open-air Museum, The National Museum, Copenhagen.

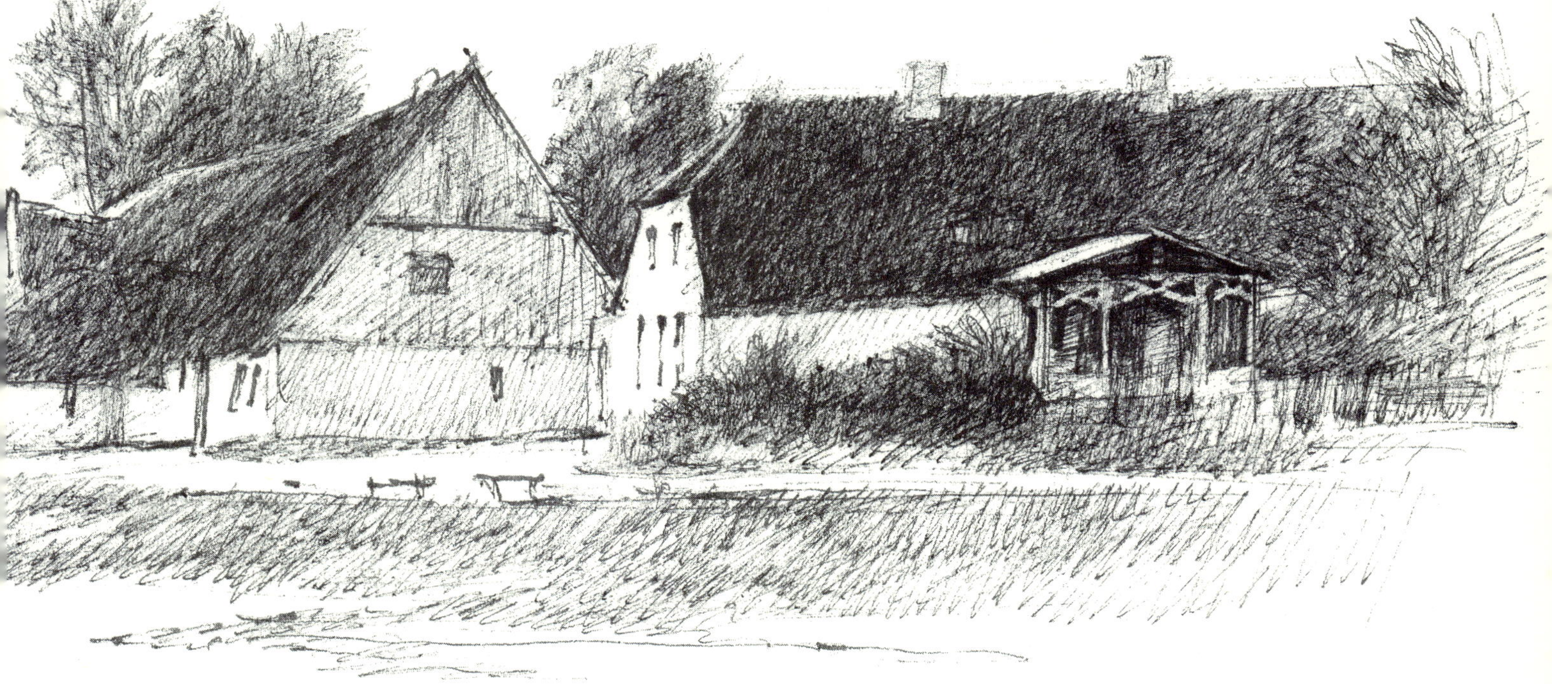

Now we're at the point where we should try our hand at "exteriors"—buildings, of course, but also fences, farm equipment and such that are all part of the landscape. Get close to buildings, so you can study detail—the construction of a thatched or tiled roof, window frames, lintels, shingling, etc. Pay attention to textural differences between different building materials and the crookedness of many old houses. You should also observe and sketch details of trees, bushes and other vegetation.

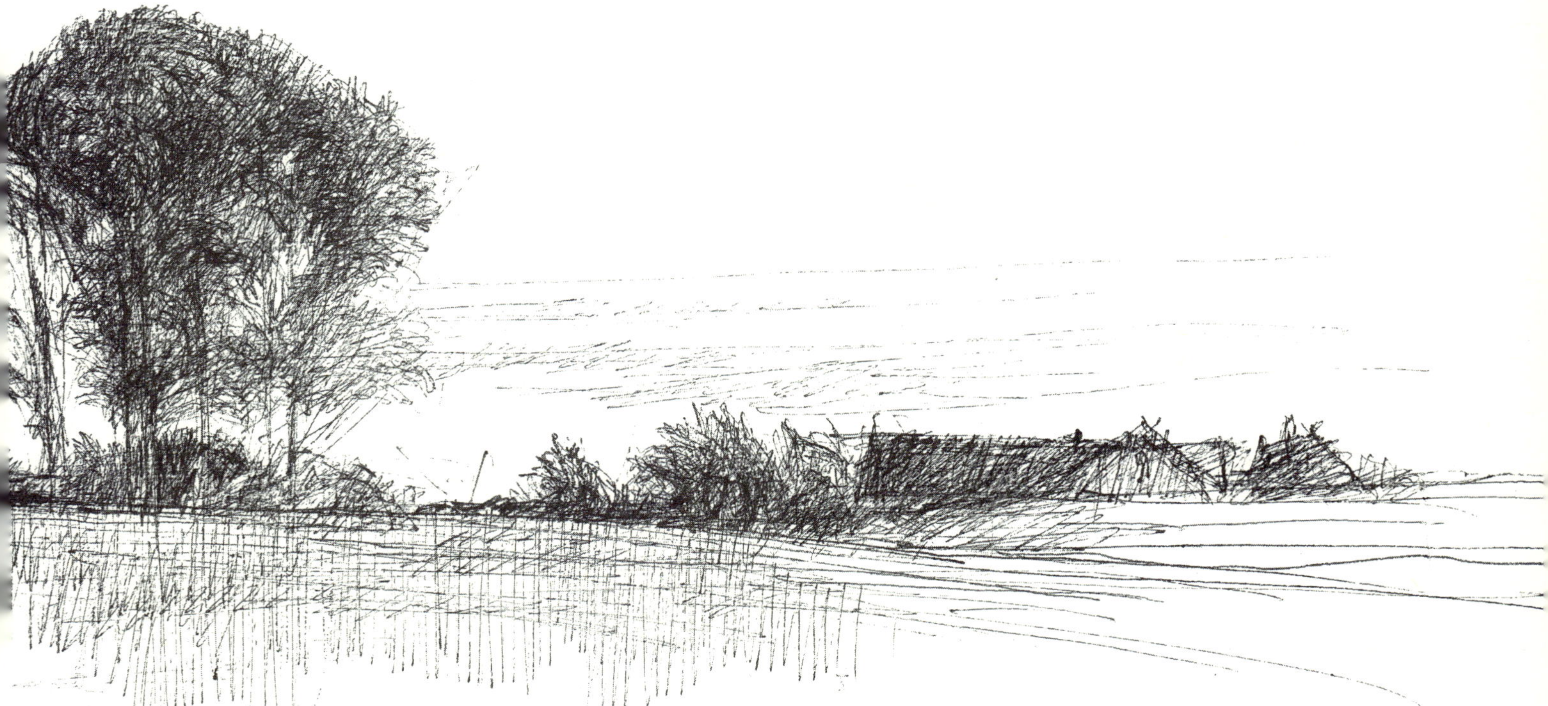

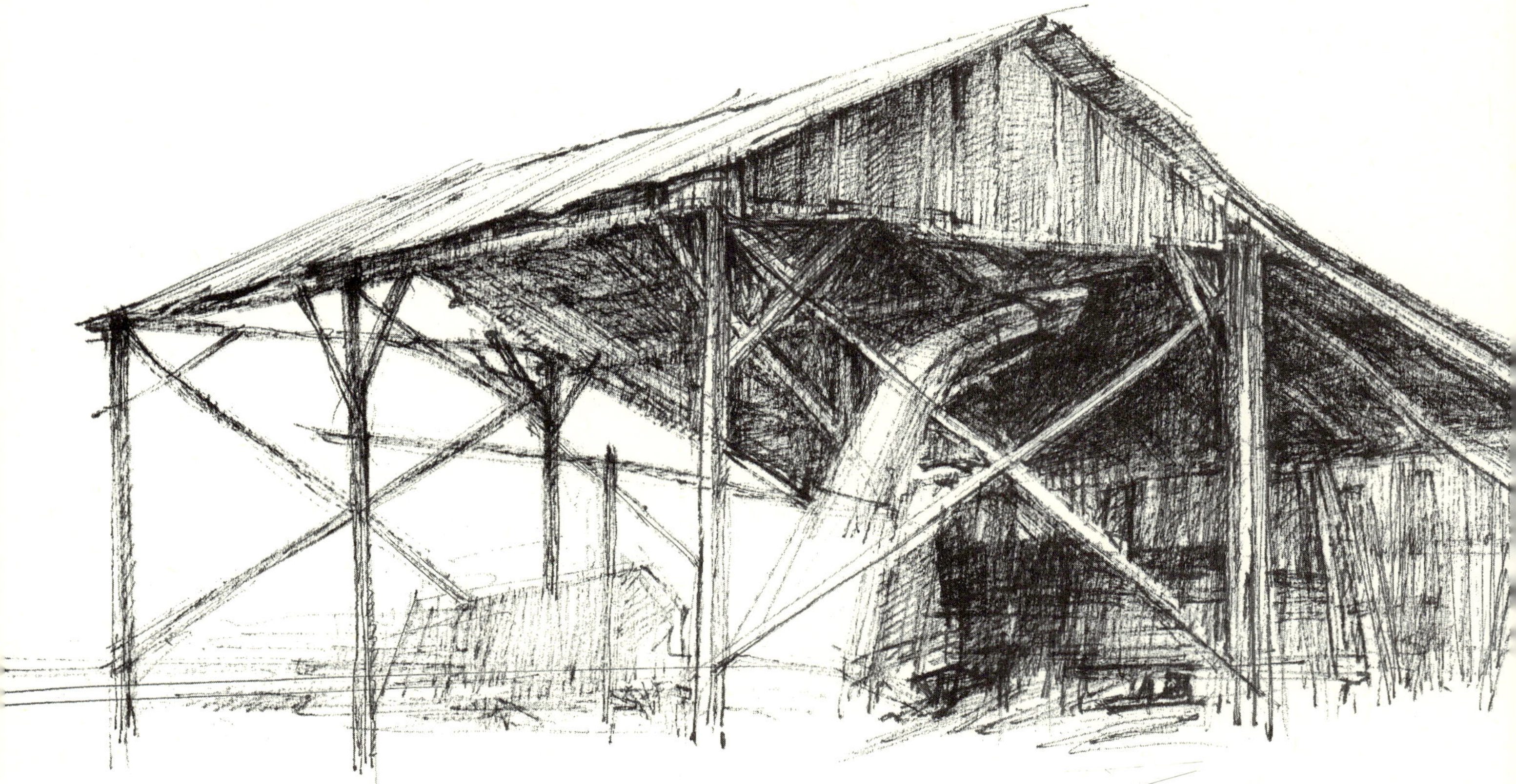

This open barn used in the summer for storing tools and farm equipment makes a good subject for a drawing of landscape architecture. Because of its interesting construction, it can be detached from its surroundings to stand on its own as the major focus of a satisfying composition. When choosing such a subject, it is wise to select one of interest to you so that you don't miss interesting details of the object and its surroundings.

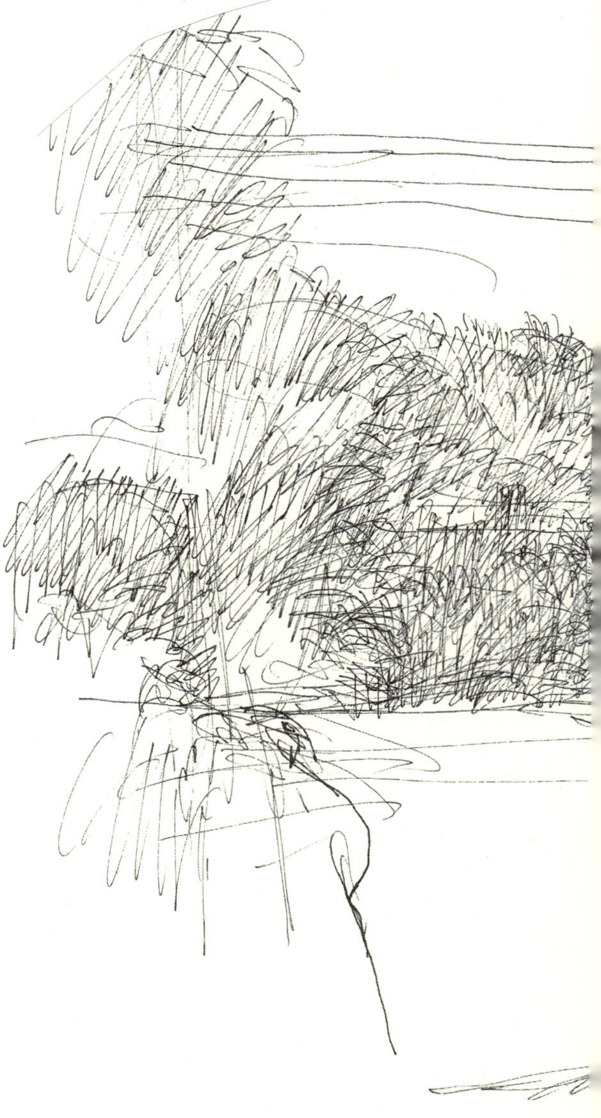

What adds energy to this drawing is the contrast between the fir tree that is firmly planted in the foreground and the row of telephone poles that disappears into the background. The poles remain identical in form as they diminish in size, thus providing the tension that activates this visual statement.

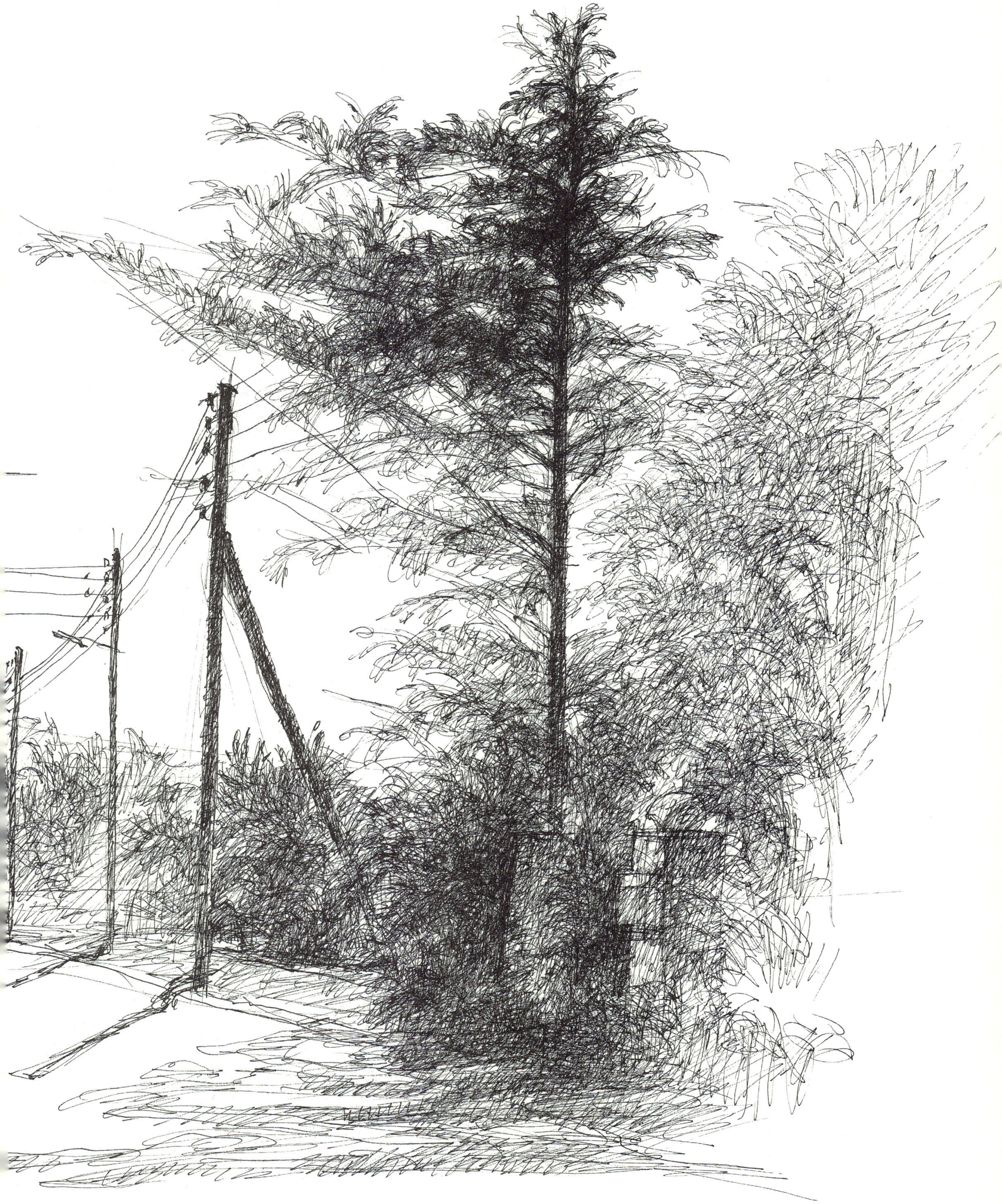

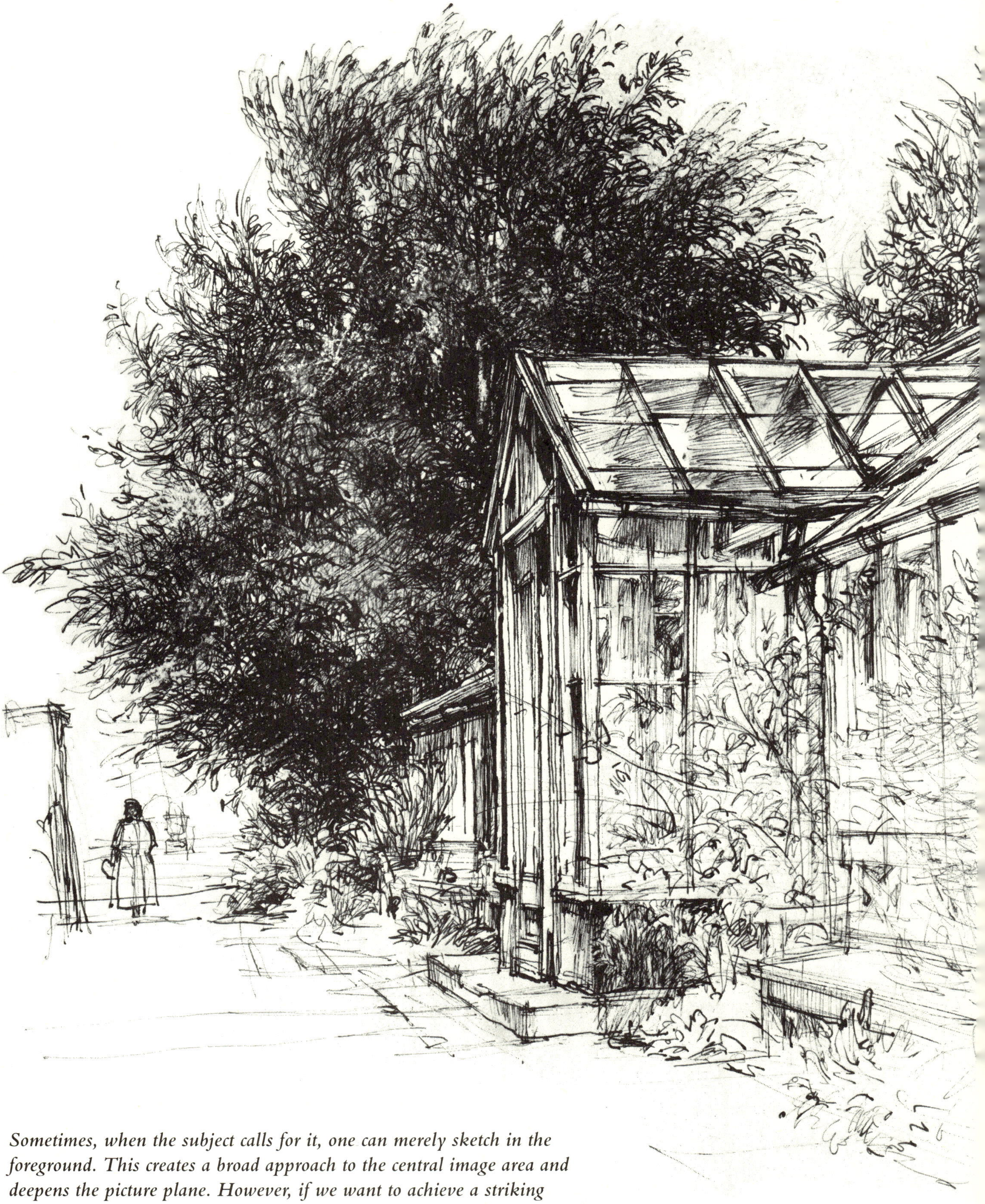

Sometimes, when the subject calls for it, one can merely sketch in the foreground. This creates a broad approach to the central image area and deepens the picture plane. However, if we want to achieve a striking effect, it is necessary to work the middleground in great detail, just as, in most cases, we would elaborate the foreground.

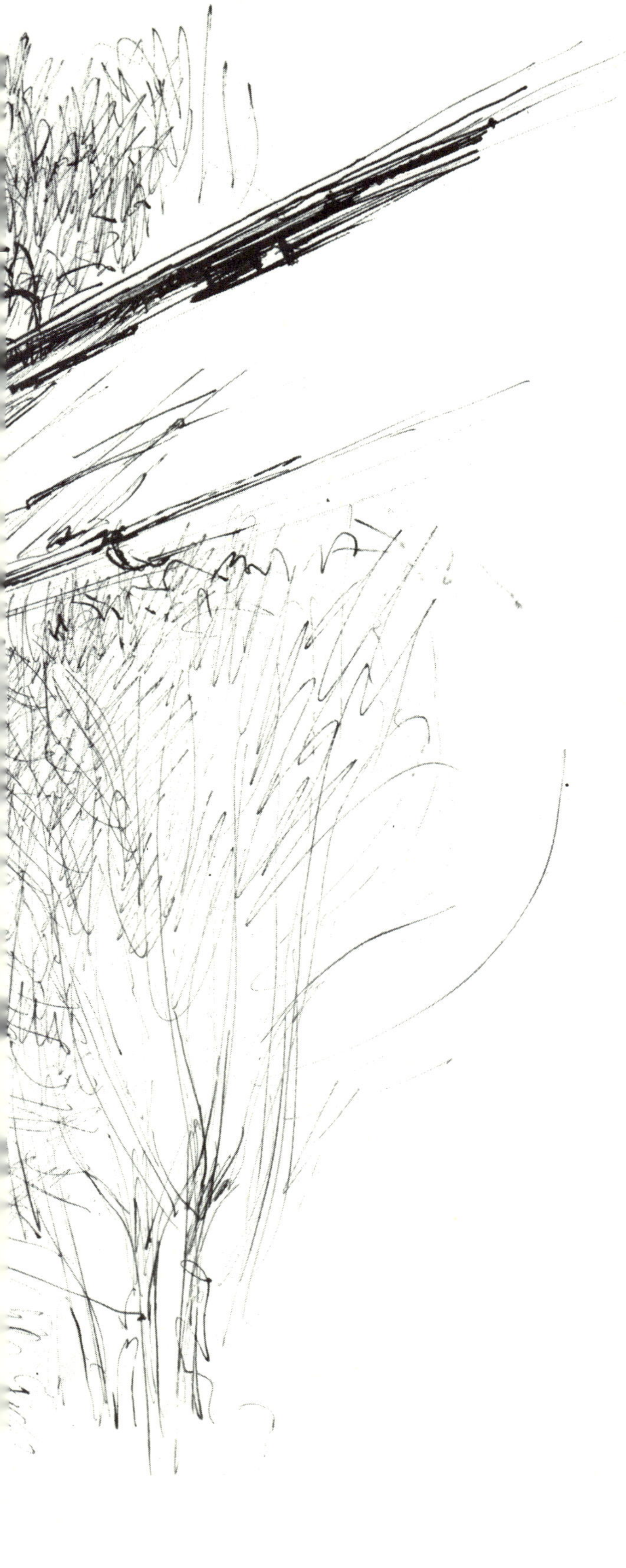

LESSON 7

Cityscapes

When starting a drawing of a cityscape, two things are important. First, how much of the actual scene will you include and what is it that immediately catches your interest? Second, be very clear about where your verticals and horizontals will be positioned. To be successful, a cityscape must not only convey visual information about the setting but also have vitality and substance. In short, it must have weight and texture and an attractive distribution of light and shadow to give it graphic quality.

Thus, it is important to take time to plan your composition, to choose the paper size that will best accommodate what you want to include, and to establish your angles of vision. This is the time, too, to think of priorities. What do you want to stress to convey your feelings about the subject matter? All parts of a drawing cannot have the same emphasis if it hopes to hold the viewer's interest—the eye must be stimulated more in some areas and less in others.

A clear distribution of your horizontals and verticals is the best framework upon which to build your drawing. This will help you keep track of the foreground, middleground and background. In most cases, the foreground should become a natural entry into the drawing with enough substance to anchor the composition to the paper. The middleground should be concerned with detail in contrast to the background which is best left diffuse. As in reality, our perception of images becomes more and more blurred as we experience them at further and further distances. It is said that Rembrandt when working on his etchings arrived at the qualities of the foregrounds, middlegrounds and backgrounds exclusively in the etching bath. He would first expose the foreground area of his copper to the acid and then gradually let the acid bite into the rest of the plate. This meant that the foreground stayed in the bath about one and a half times longer than the background. When printed the foreground appeared black and strong whereas the background, which had been in the bath for only a few minutes, printed light and bright.

It's important when drawing outdoors that you make sketches for reference later. These should not only include visual information reminiscent of written notes, but should also preserve the spontaneous pleasure one never fails to get from transforming a subject into a drawing. When you are both careful and observant, such sketches can be useful years later. I have drawings that I made 35 years ago that I still use for reference today.

Study drawing made in the summertime in the mid-1960s of the orphanage in Ryesgade, Copenhagen; since demolished.

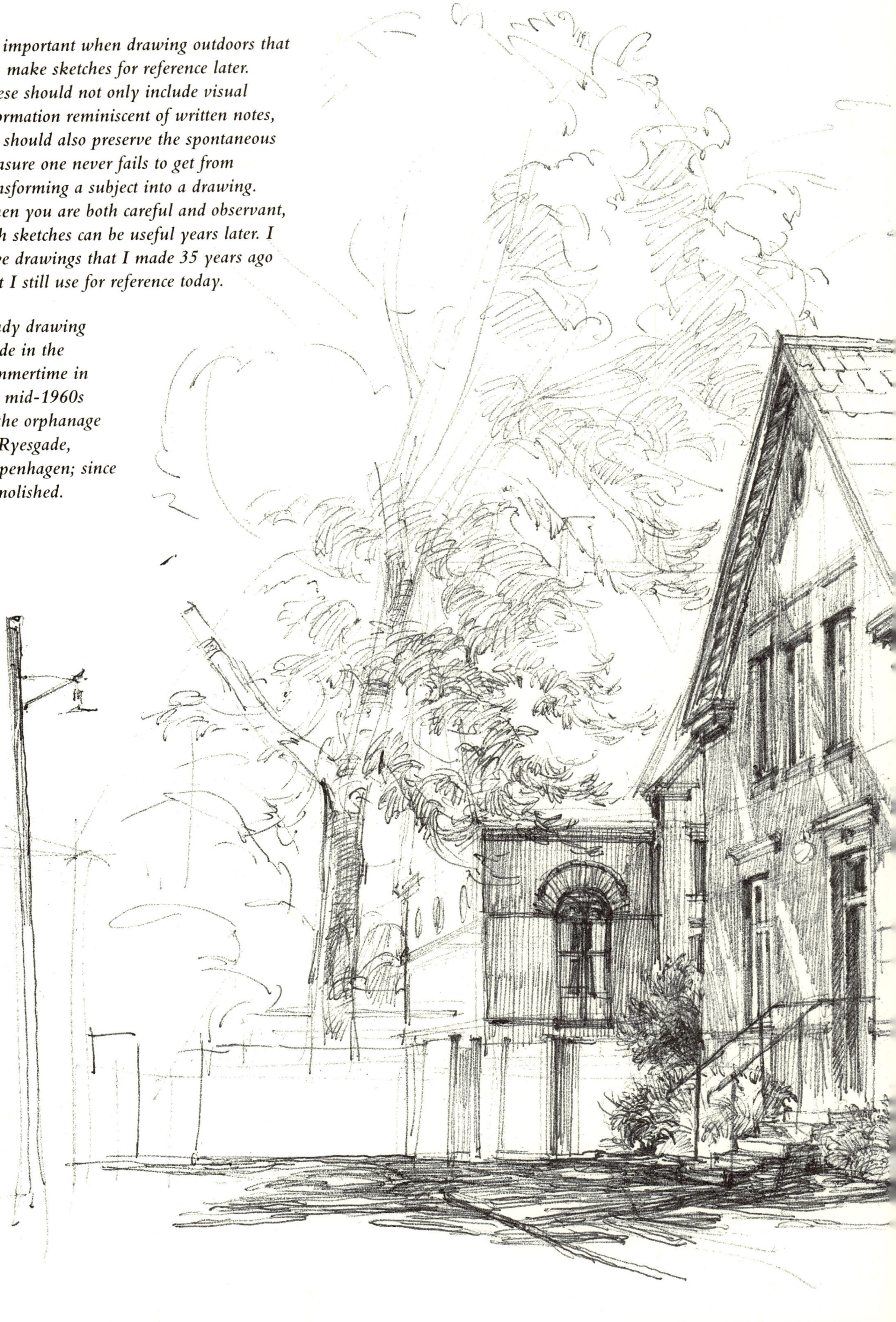

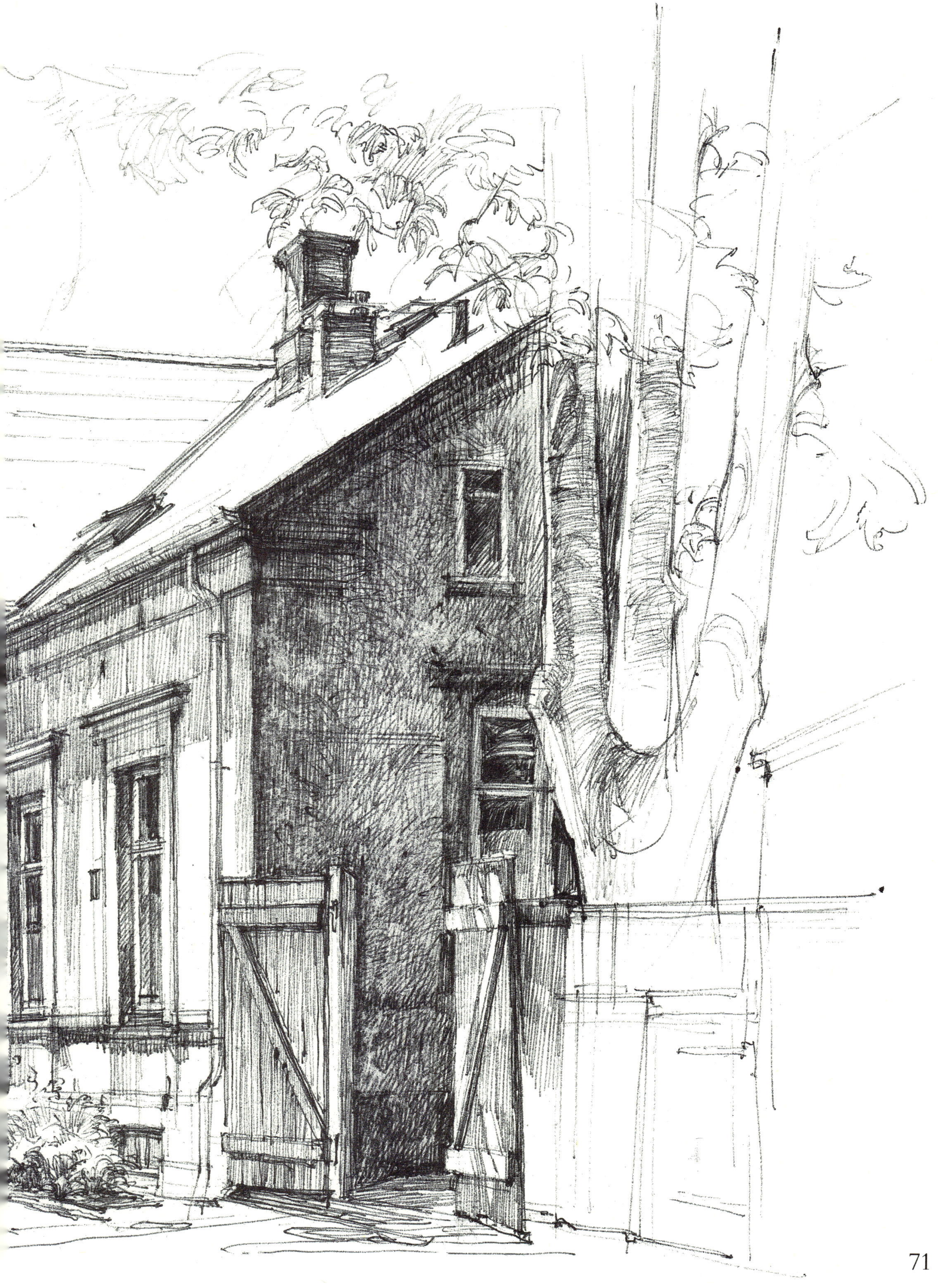

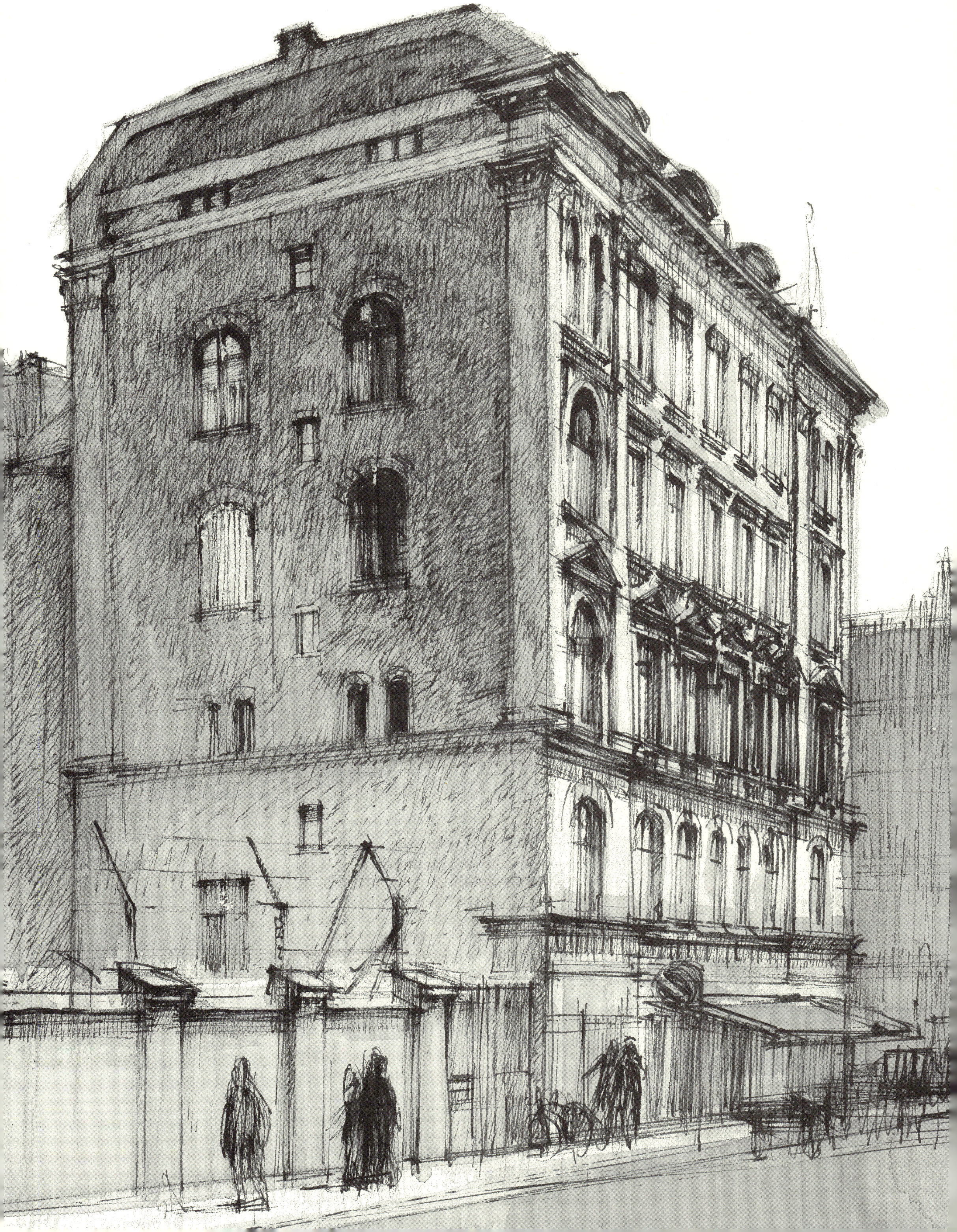

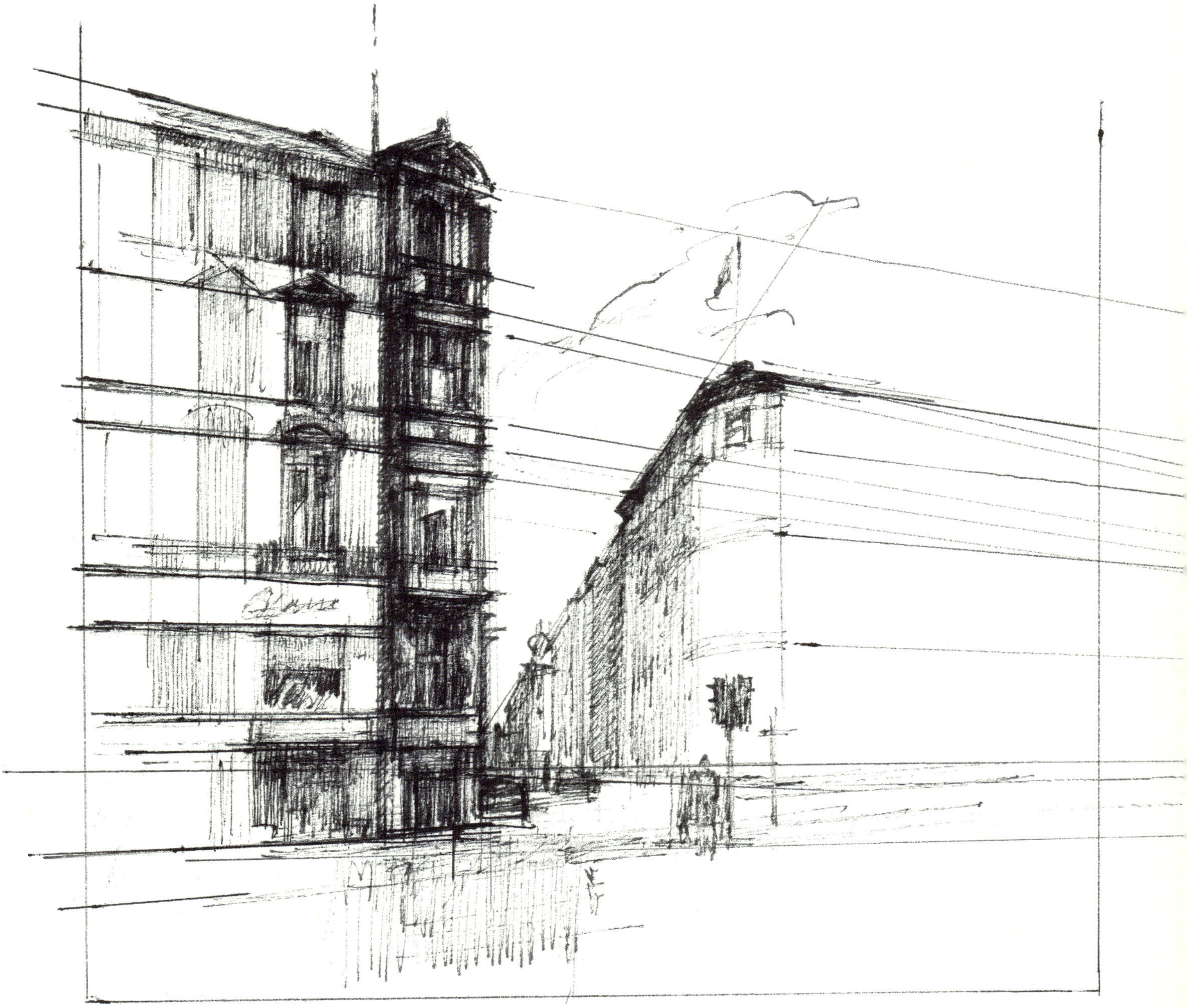

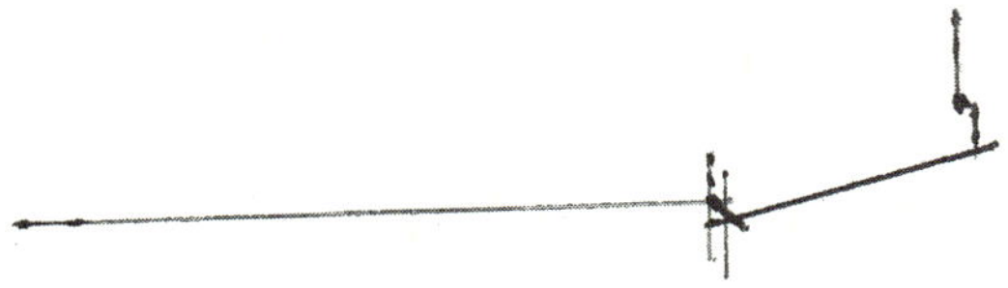

In the drawing on the left I used the wall as an introduction into the picture plane. I took a good deal of care drawing its details and textures with India ink; then made the effect even more graphic by using an India ink wash (India ink dissolved in distilled water). Such a wash creates a variety of gray tones that help to give a rendering of this type the weight and texture necessary to make it look convincing.

When starting a drawing, especially of houses or street scenes with many angles, it's essential to place your horizontals and verticals accurately. This provides the framework for an effectively executed rendering.

Waiting for the train in Northern Jutland in the early 1980s.

In this drawing of a Danish country railway station, the platform leads us into the picture. I let a 3-5 division of mass (the "golden section") influence the appearance of the station. This traditional approach resulted in a harmonious composition.

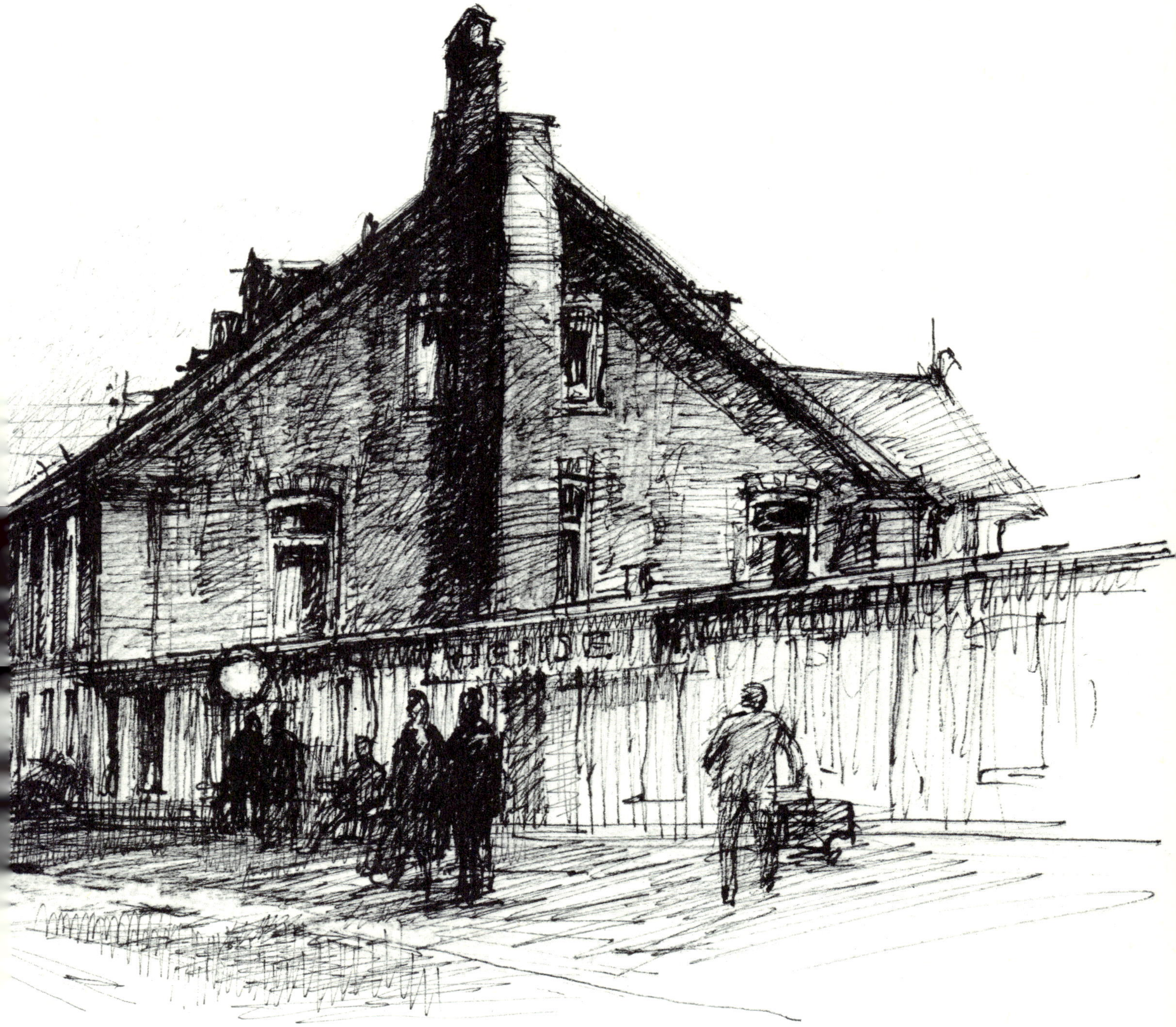

Here I've chosen to use an entirely different approach from the traditional by designing the picture space so that its dominant elements are pushed right up to the front of the foreground. As it is, the road work with its dark piles of earth and stones provides an excellent lead-in. As I mentioned earlier, it's a good rule to make the most of an element in the subject matter that catches your fancy. As a consequence, I've concentrated on the texture and general appearance of the house on the right, while being careful not to disturb the drawing's overall effect or make the composition lopsided.

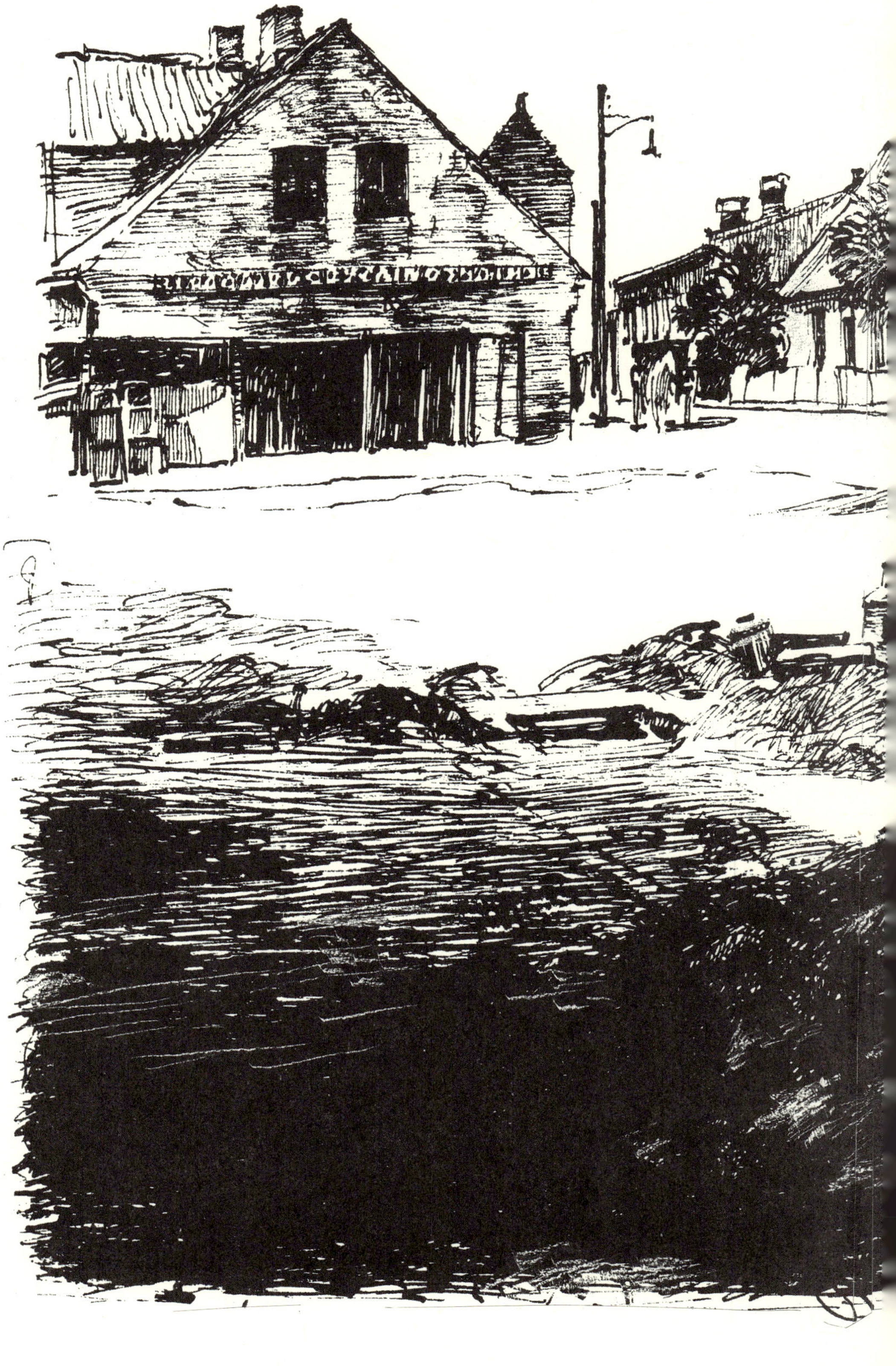

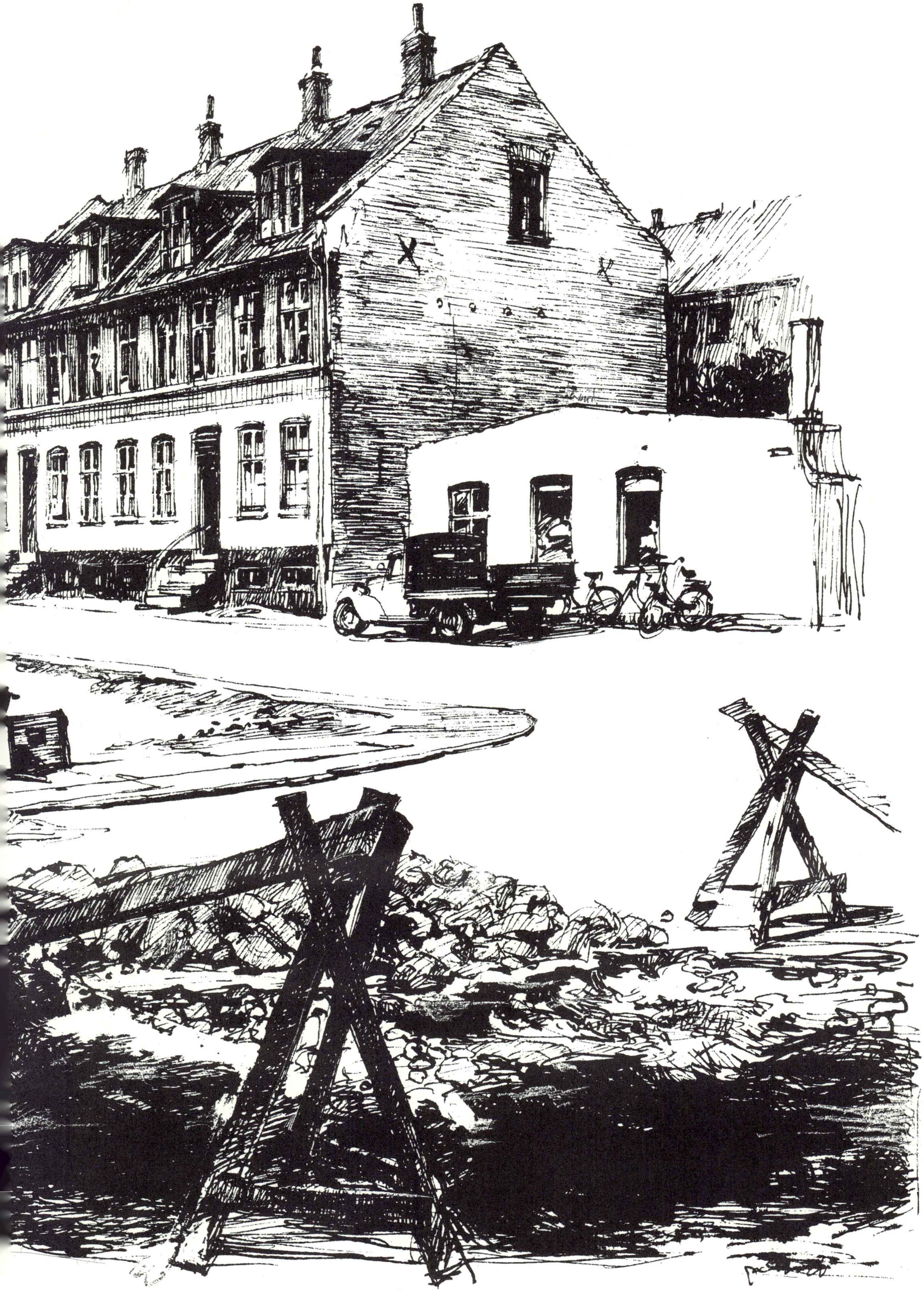

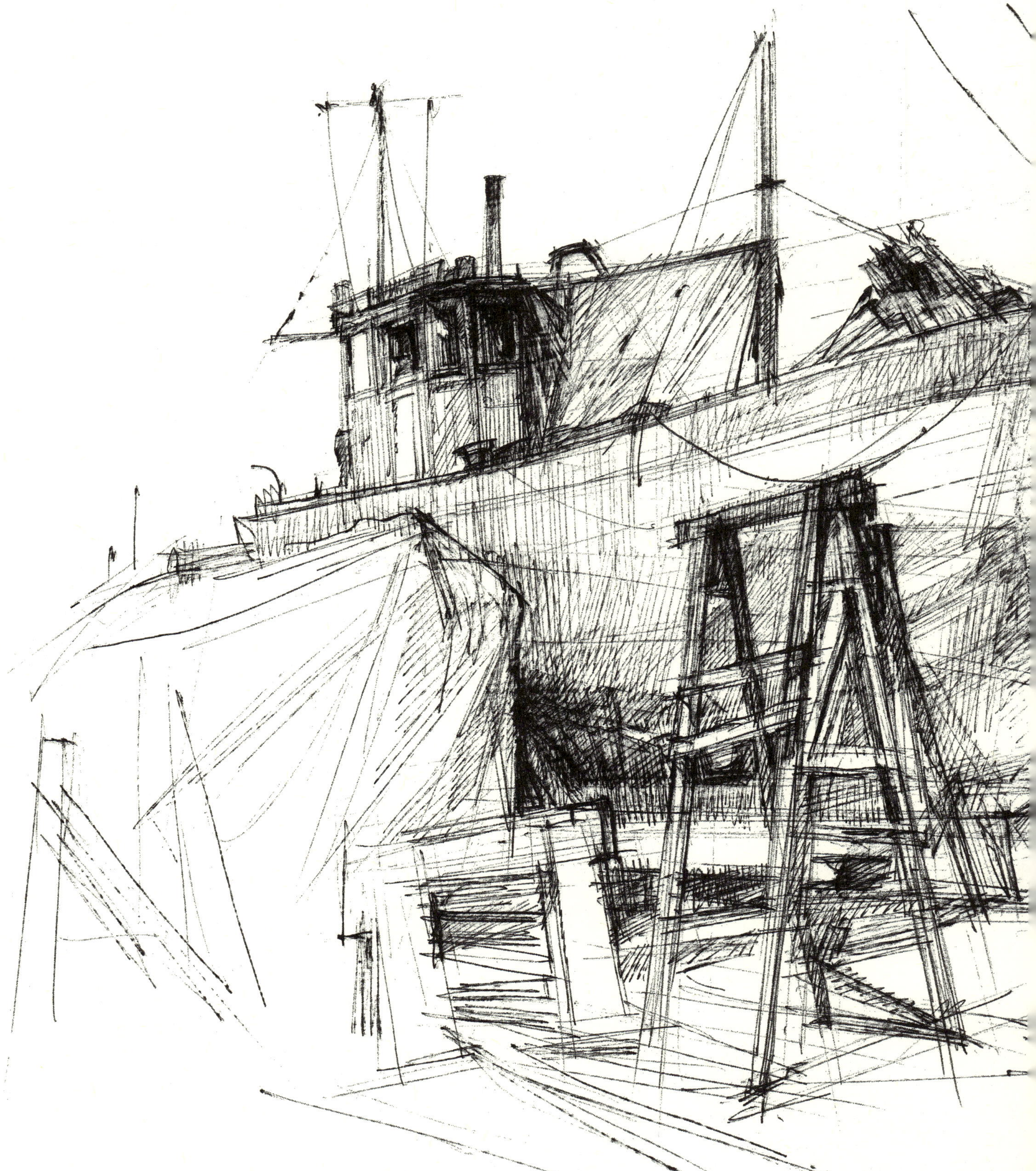

LESSON 8

Fishing Boats, Coaches, Cannon, etc.

A subtitle to this lesson might be "object drawing in large format." In principle, it shouldn't make any difference whether one is drawing a valve, a complicated mechanical thread, a coil of rope, or a big boat. But, because of the size of a boat, many of us are frightened by the prospect of drawing it.

Let's size up the problem. We have to admit that, if we have the knowledge and ability to draw keys, valves and nuts, the problem of drawing a boat is not insurmountable. Remember the first maxim—to extend the verticals and horizontals that determine how the mass of the object exists in space. Then make sure of the angles in relation to the picture plane.

Here are some other suggestions. Don't make the sketch of the boat, in this case a Danish cutter, too detailed at the start when you are still composing your drawing. Constantly keep the overall picture in mind. Place an object in the foreground, a ladder or a sawhorse, perhaps, that can be both a natural introduction to the whole drawing and an indication of the boat's much larger proportions. Now that you have established the basics, you can enjoy seeing your drawing come to life even though there are sure to be other minor problems to unravel along the way.

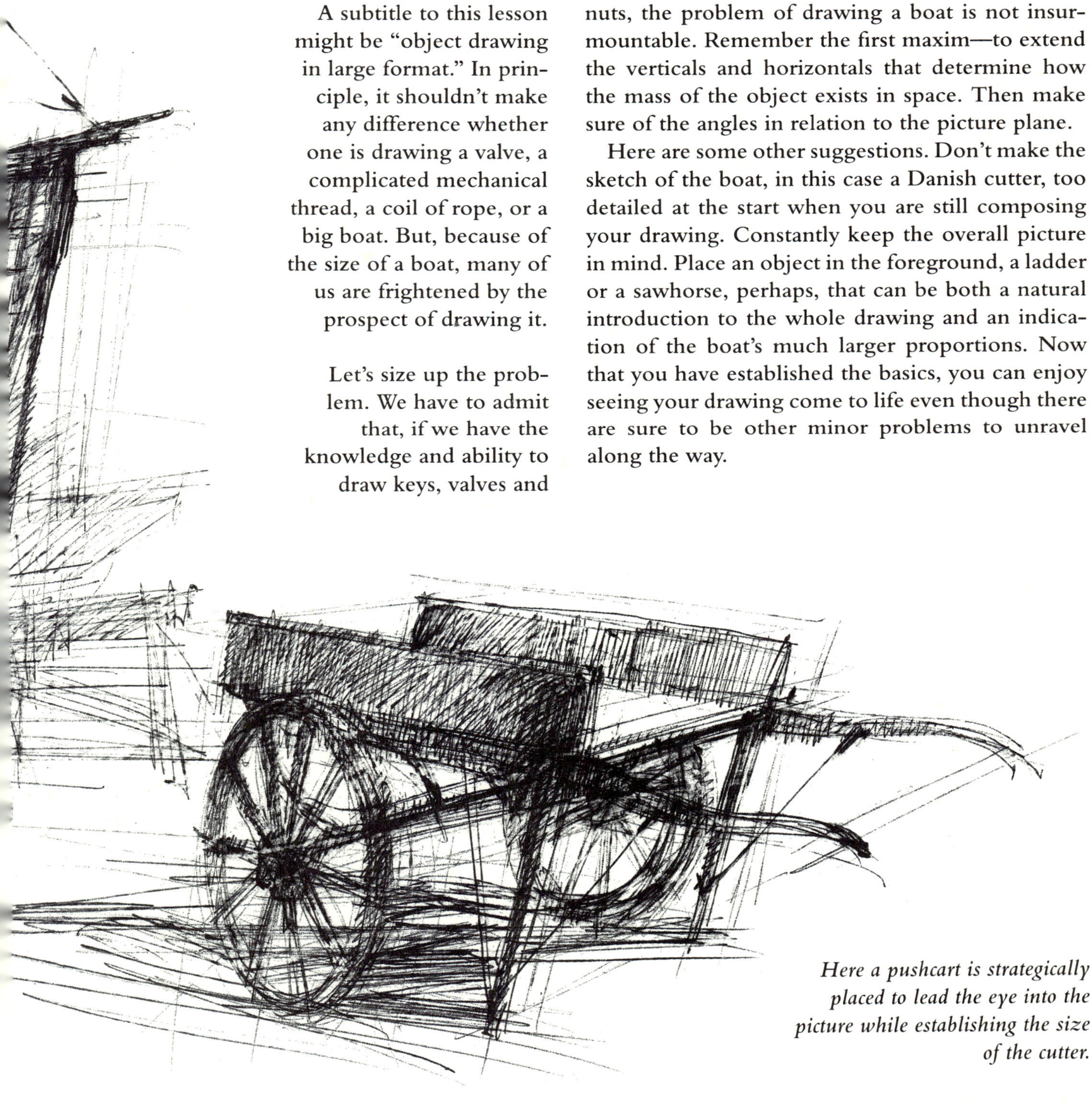

Here a pushcart is strategically placed to lead the eye into the picture while establishing the size of the cutter.

Renault, 1908. The Automobile Museum, Alholm, Denmark.

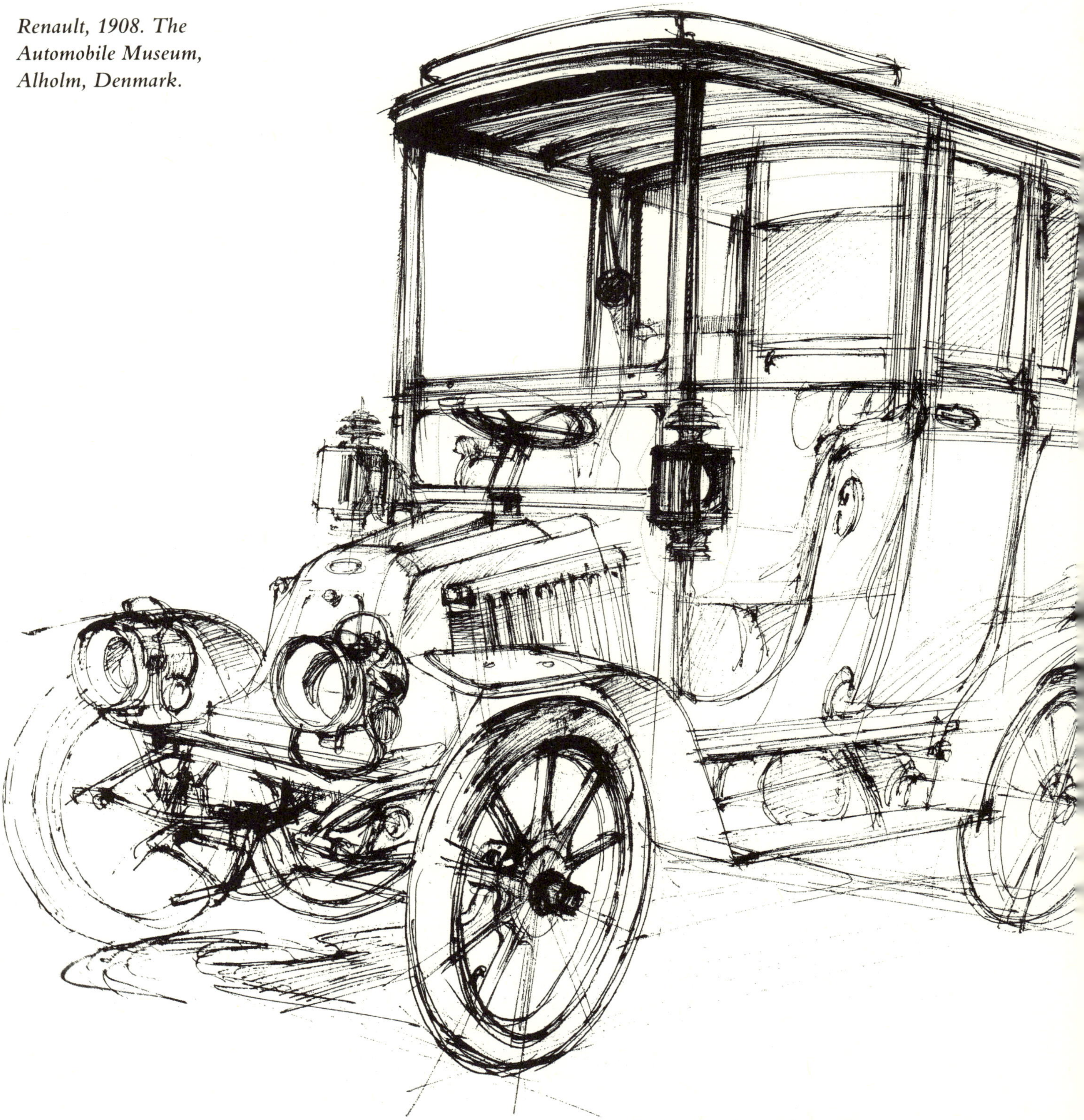

Notice the angles and perspective distortion of both the wheels and lights in my drawing of an antique automobile. Drawings of this kind of subject can be quite successful even if there are small mistakes in proportion, but the wheels and lights must always appear round. If you allow them to be anything but circular, it will ruin your drawing totally.

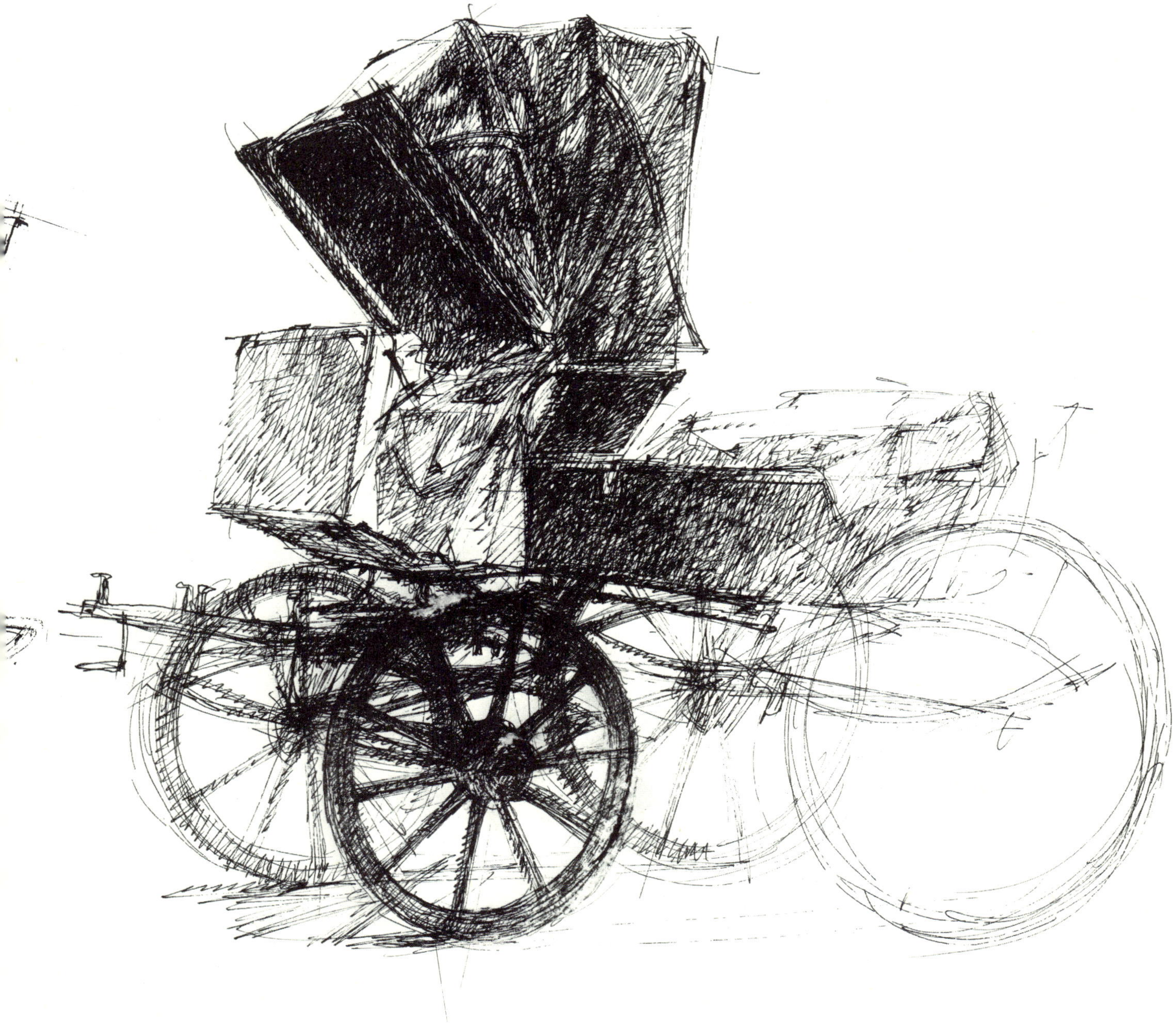

There is a special problem to be aware of in this study of a black lacquered French touring coach from the collection of The Museum of Royal Stables and Coaches, the Riding Course, Christianborg, Denmark. When you represent lacquer or any similar surface with a sheen, you must be very precise in establishing the source of light. As in other situations, you must keep in mind that when you "control light," you must "control shadow" at the same time.

While attempting to be as precise as possible, I have made every effort to capture the lightness and elegance of the coach.

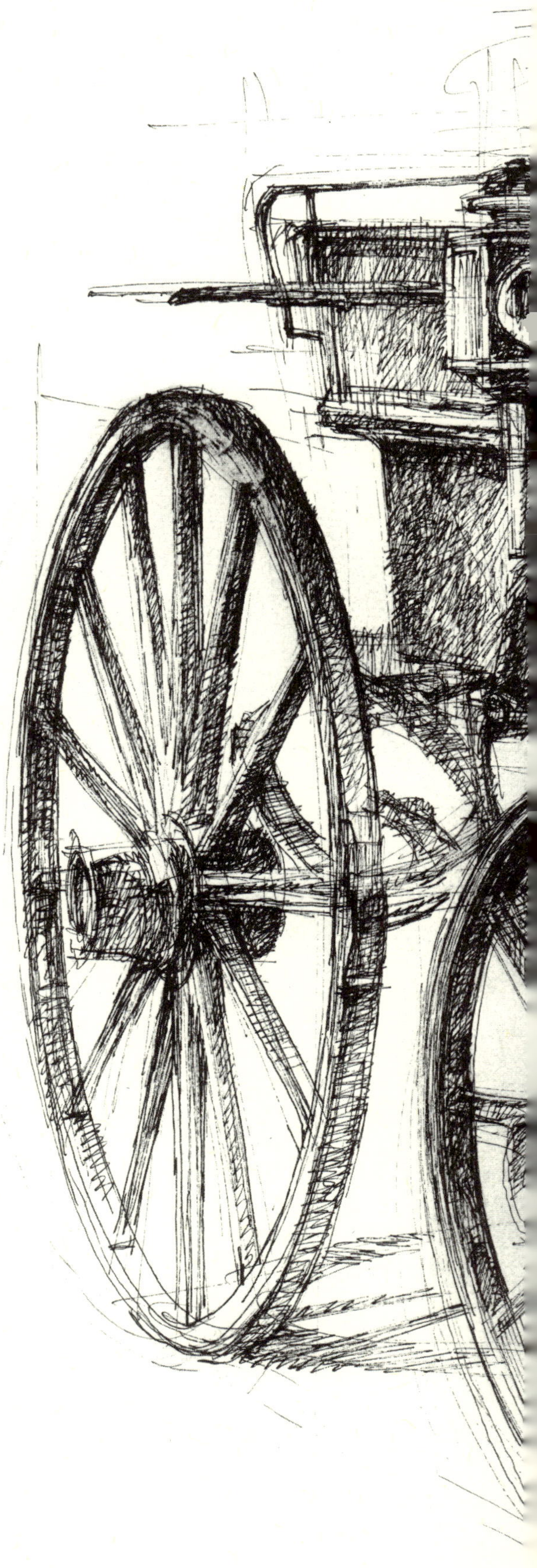

Hunting coach belonging to Queen Alexandra of England. The Museum of Royal Stables and Coaches, Christenborg, Denmark.

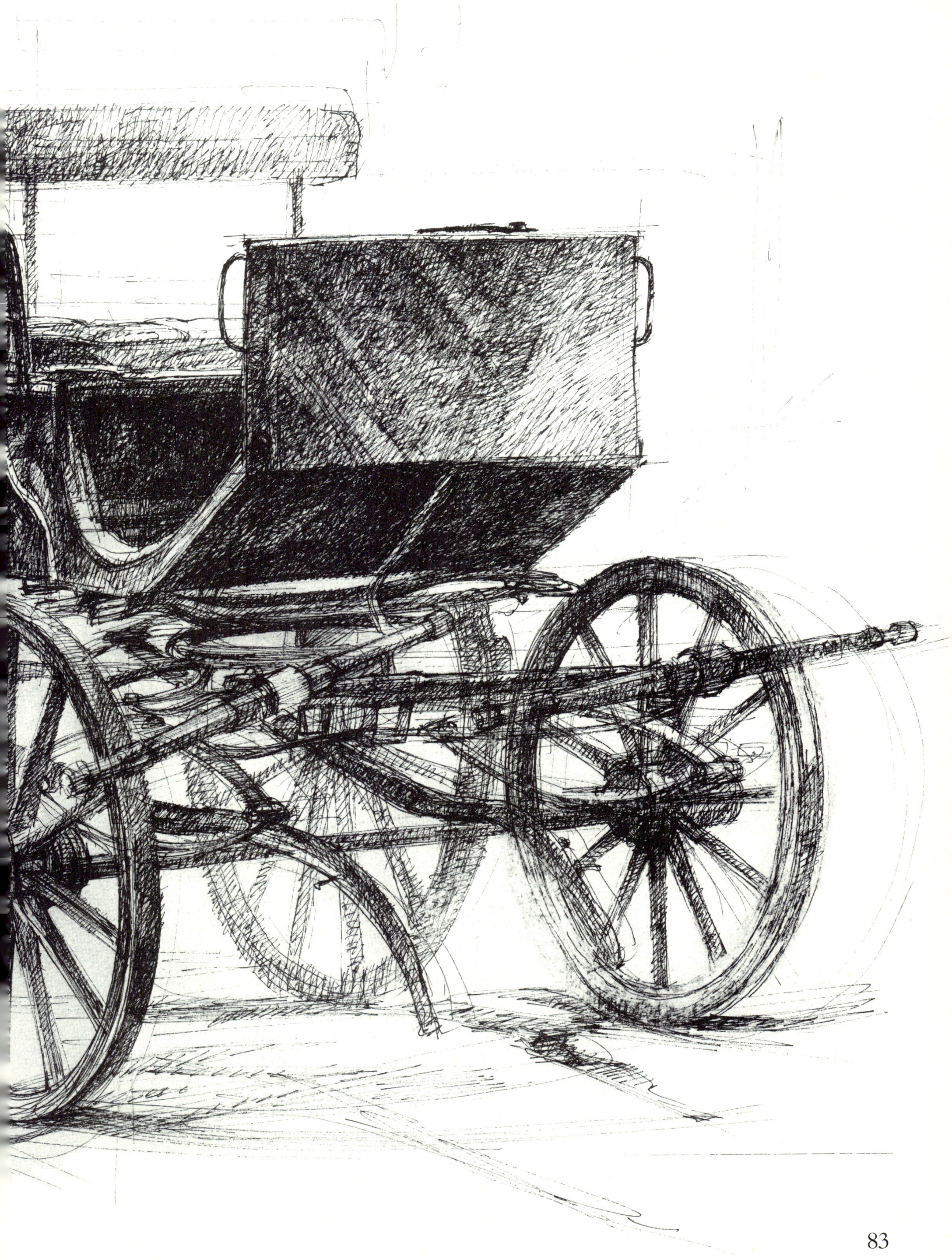

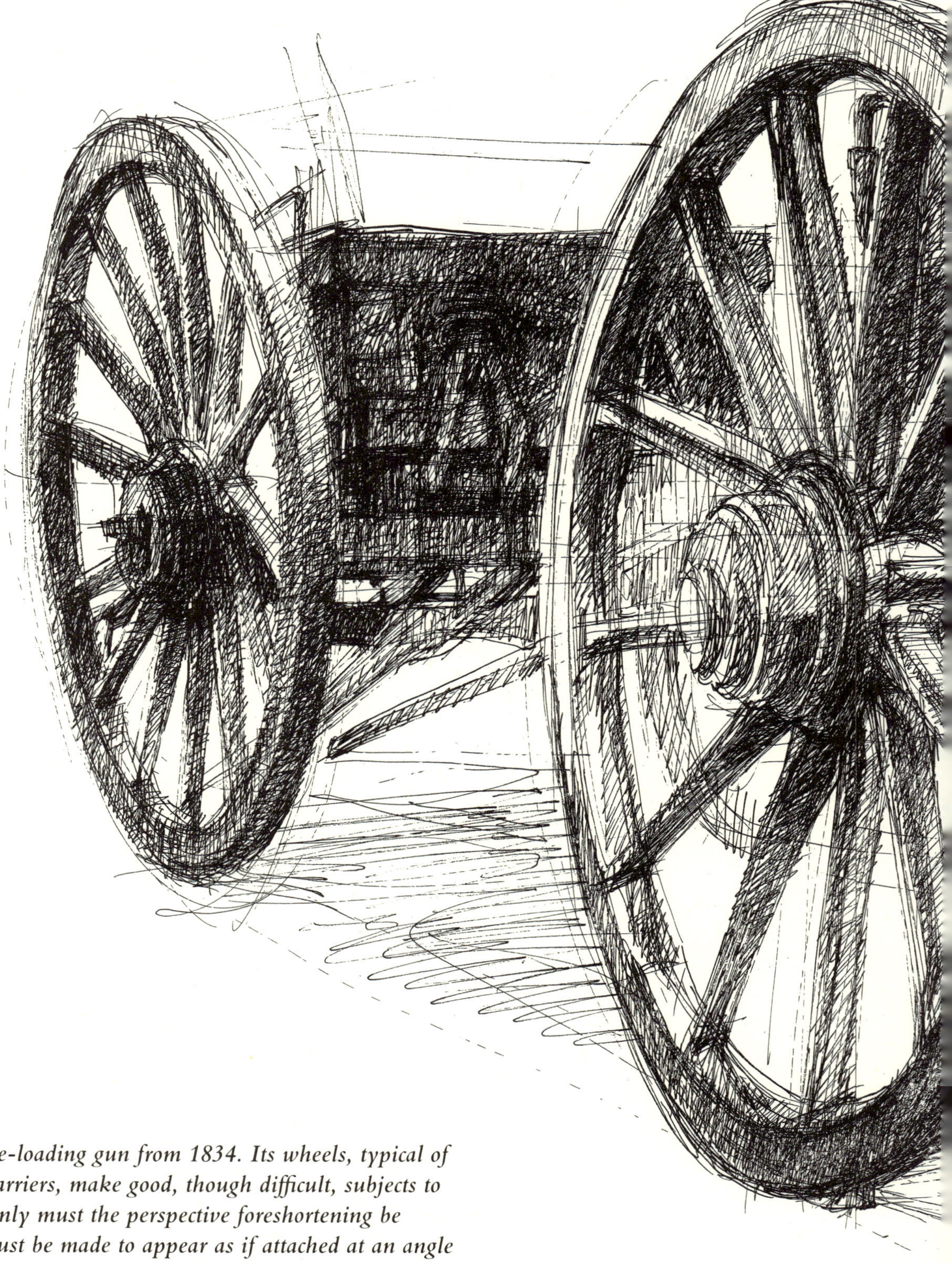

Here is a Danish muzzle-loading gun from 1834. Its wheels, typical of those found on old gun carriers, make good, though difficult, subjects to draw. For instance, not only must the perspective foreshortening be correct, but the wheels must be made to appear as if attached at an angle to the shaft. Start by drawing a square and establishing your verticals and horizontals. I made this drawing and the one on the next page at the Museum of Arms and Uniforms in Copenhagen. The museum is very helpful to those who like to draw as are most such institutions. They even offer stools to sit on!

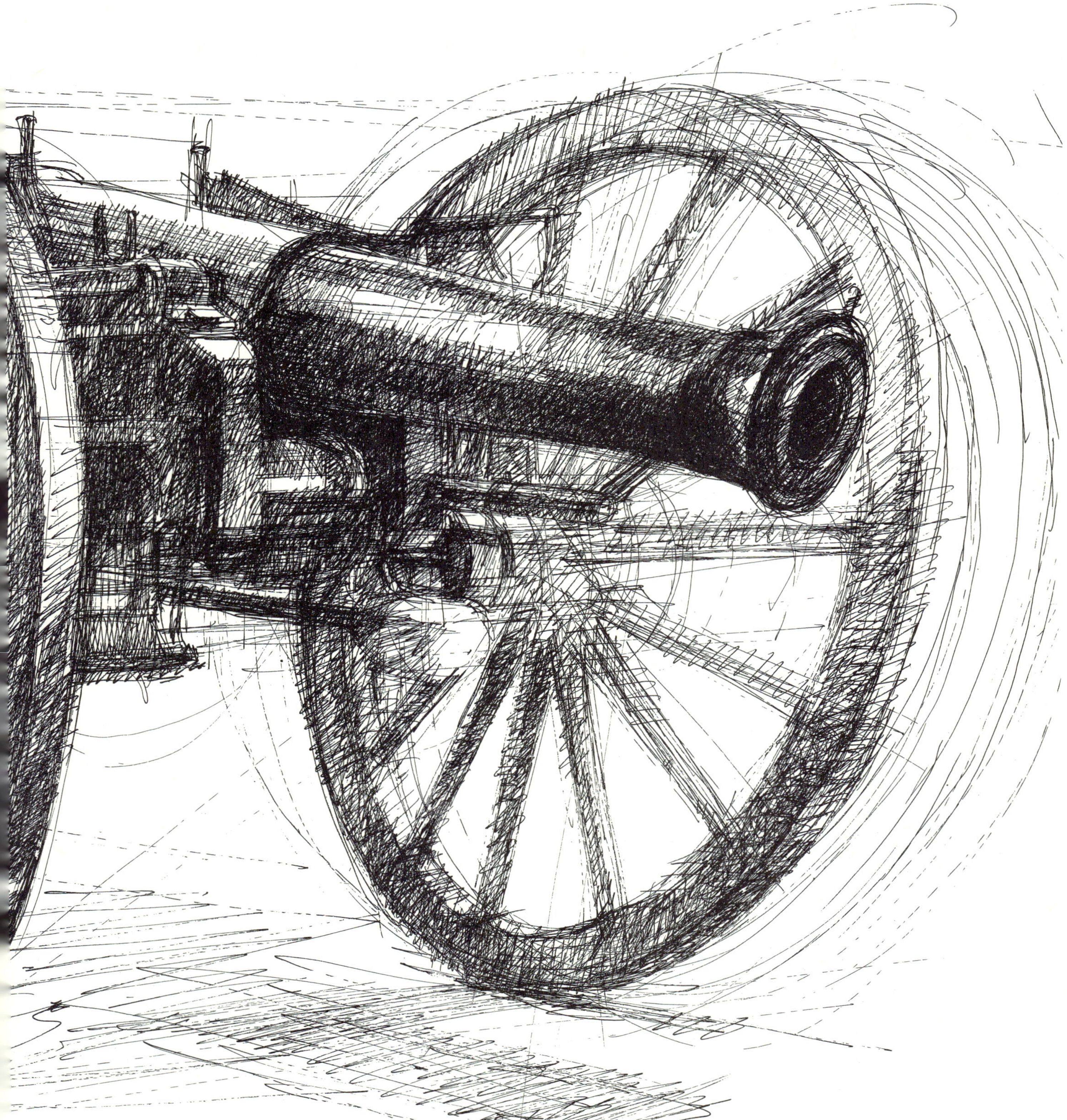

Try to draw rowboats and other small boats. It's worth it if only for the thrill you experience when you get the "curve" of the hull just right. Concentrate first on the total form and end by adding the details.

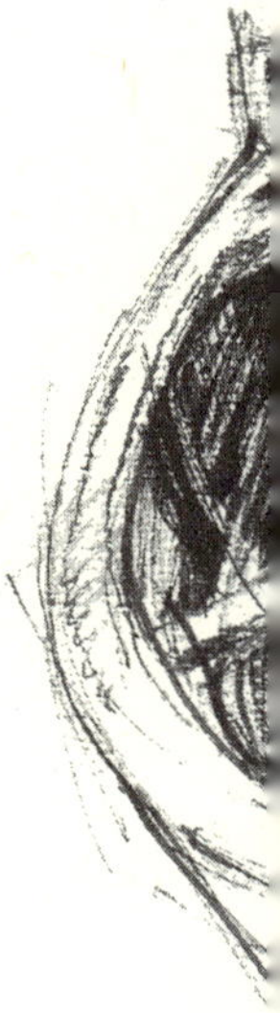

This cannon is one of several saved during the retreat from Dannevirke. I have drawn it in half-profile, varying the surface textures to express how worn and used it is.

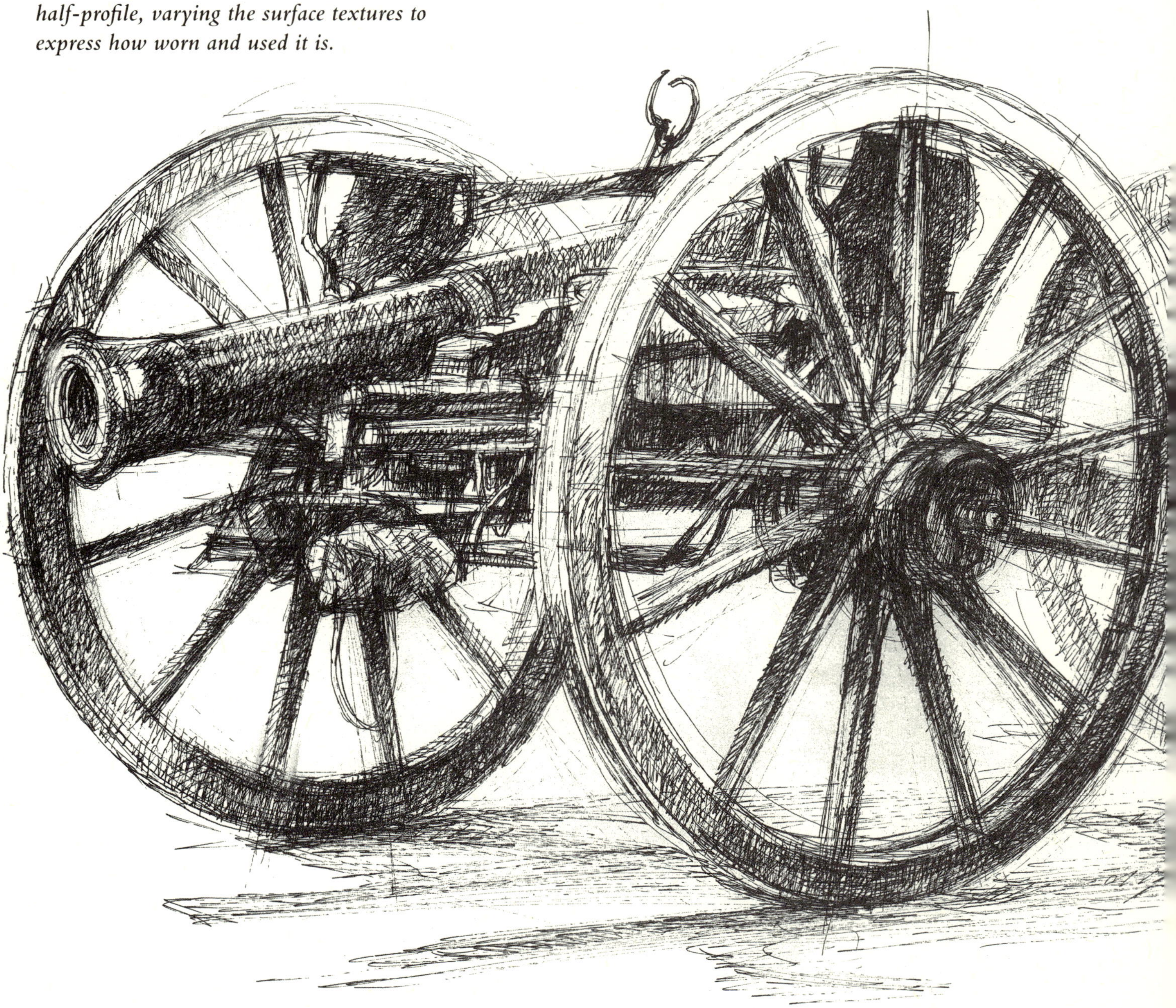

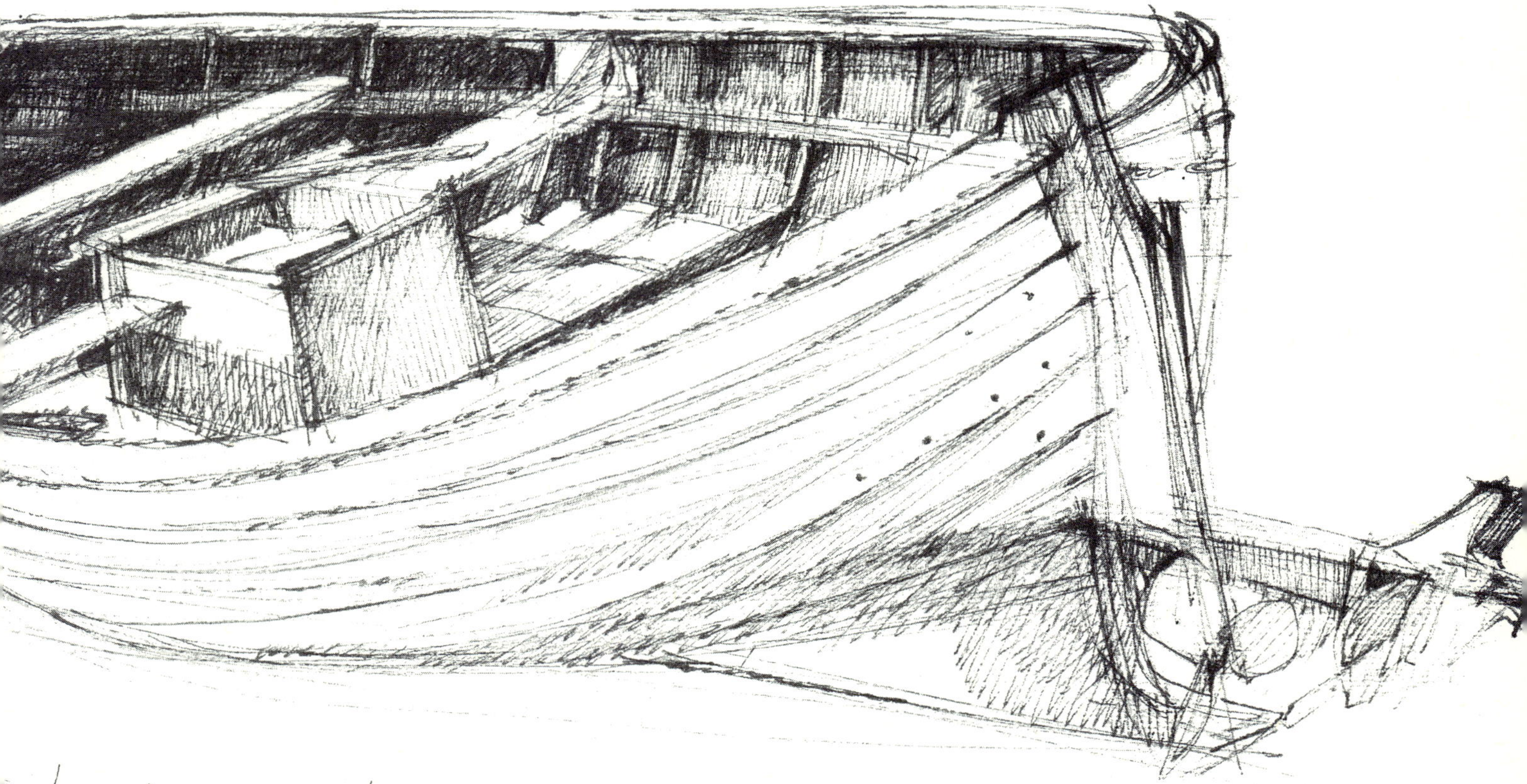

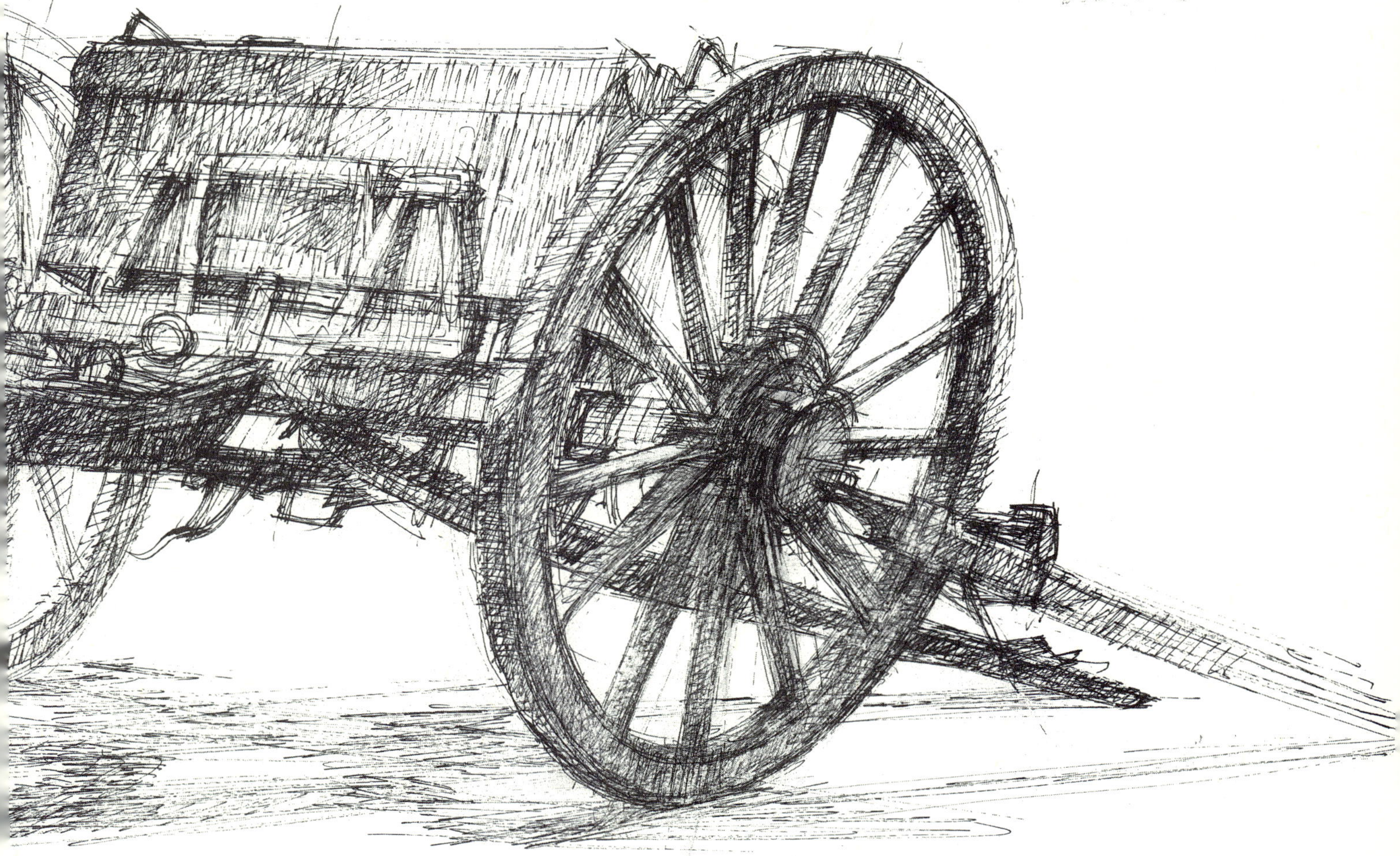

LESSON 9

Mammals

It seems only natural to concentrate on drawing the common mammals we meet in our daily lives. Therefore, this lesson will focus on ways to draw animals we are familiar with, such as horses, dogs and cows. Of course, if there is a zoo near you, it's good practice to sketch the more exotic animals that are always fascinating to draw. But, because the study of mammals in general is such a vast field, we will limit our exploration of animal drawing in this lesson to only a few carefully chosen examples.

The feasibility of this approach becomes obvious when we realize that the animals portrayed on the next few pages have major physical features that are common to most four-legged species. For instance, in drawing any animal, we need to pay particular attention to its bone structure and muscle system. Study the leg muscles and buttocks of a horse as compared to those of a dog or calf. Pay attention to the powerful thigh muscles. Knowledge of these common features in one animal can be readily applied to the study, and subsequent drawing, of another. This kind of close attention to physical attributes demands patience and intense concentration, therefore it can be advantageous to work on several studies concurrently. For instance, the

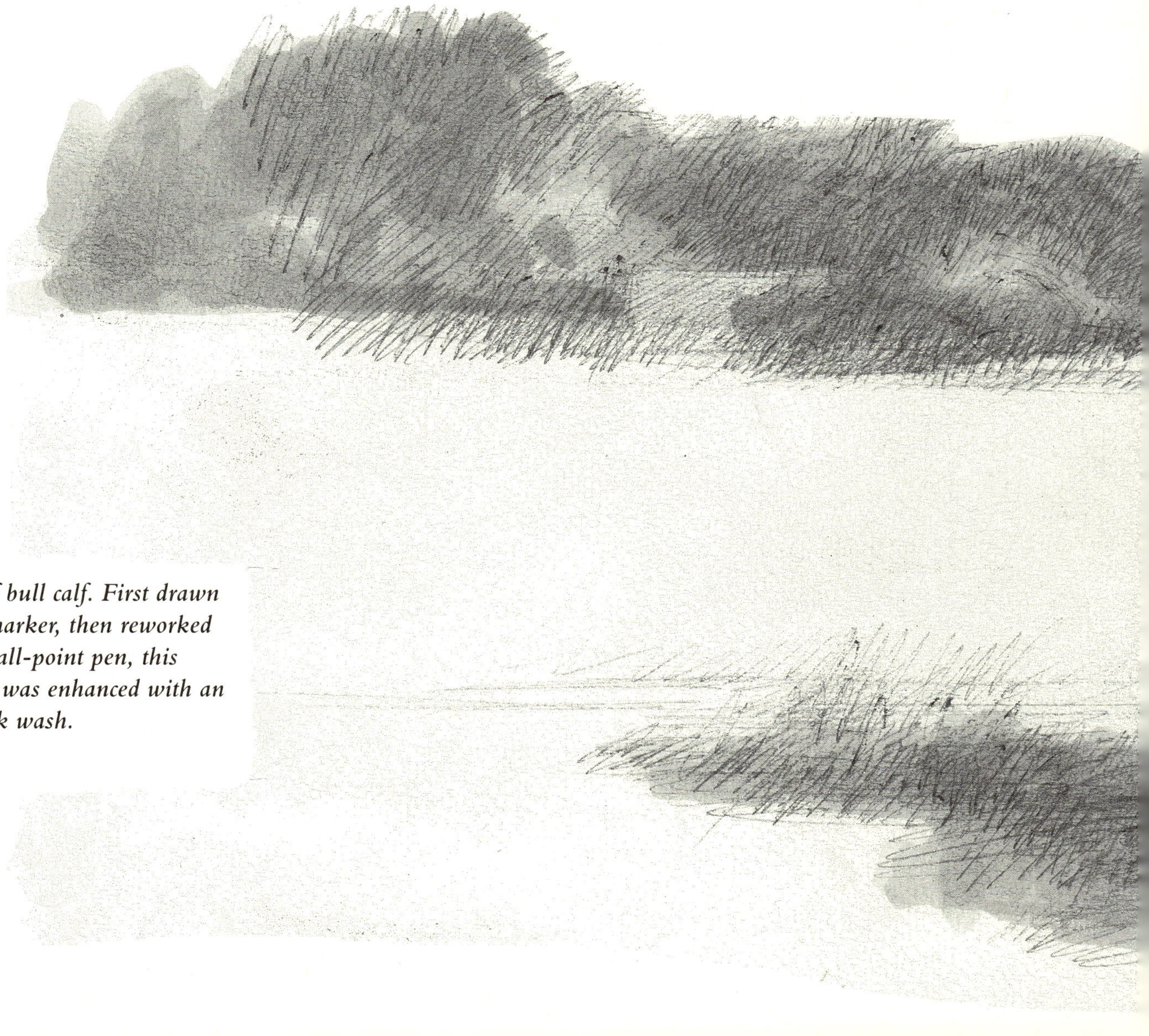

Study of bull calf. First drawn with a marker, then reworked with a ball-point pen, this drawing was enhanced with an India ink wash.

advantage of having more than one sketch of a cow in progress at the same time, from perhaps the front, the side and the back, will be realized the moment the cow changes position, which it is sure to do more often than you might imagine. Rather than wait until it resumes its original pose, you can continue working on the most appropriate of your several studies.

Back in the days when cows were gathered at the milking place and milked individually outdoors, the artist had a chance to sketch an animal while it remained stationary for at least a few minutes. But now, in the era of milking machines, with the cows crowded into stalls, this is no longer possible. The Danish animal painter, Johan Thomas Lundbye, often paid farmers or herdsmen small sums to keep animals in the same position while he sketched them. Now, in the days of modern agriculture, this kind of practice is no longer feasible, making the idea of multiple sketches seem more and more logical.

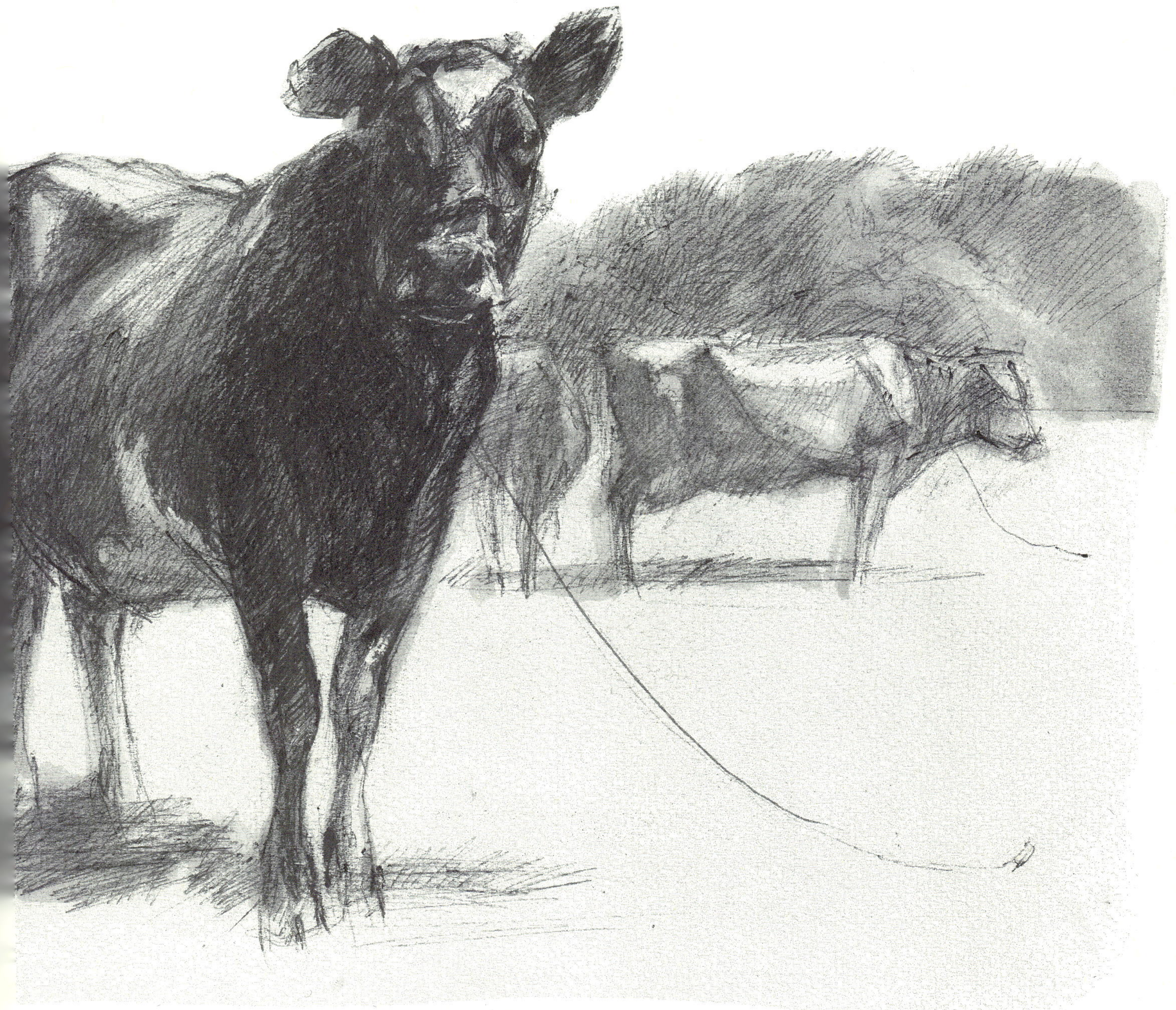

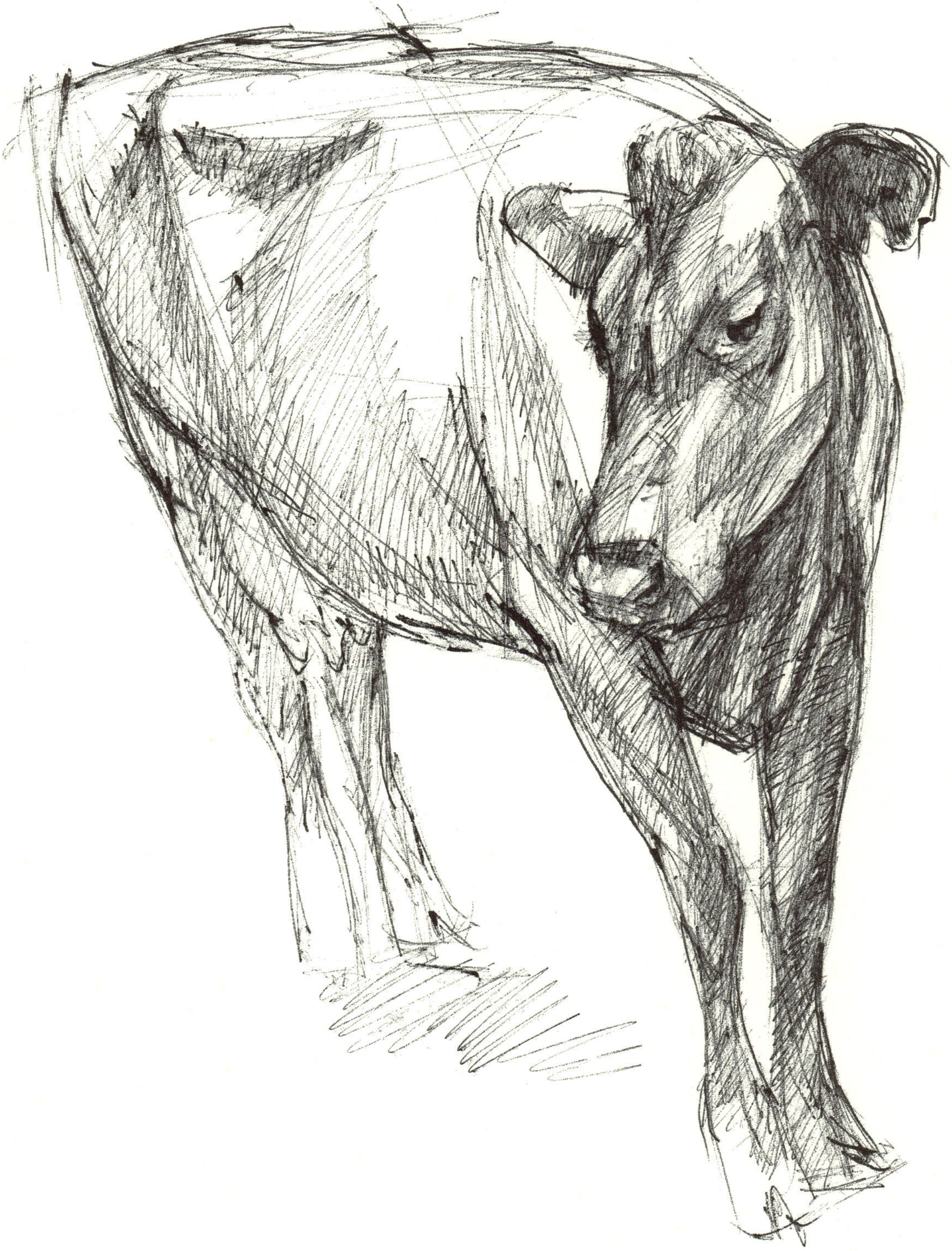

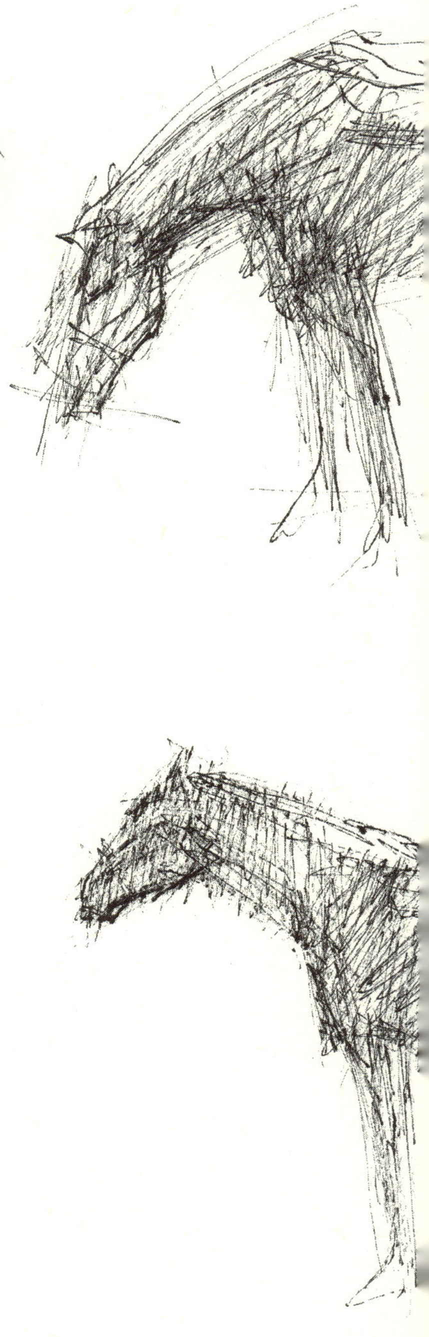

Calf seen mostly from above. This difficult angle is challenging, to say the least. Maintaining the right distances between major body components is essential to getting the proportions right.

Quick sketches (often referred to as "croquis") of horses. Making thumbnail sketches such as these is not only good practice but gives you the opportunity to capture movement and physical attitude more succinctly than you might in your first more studied works.

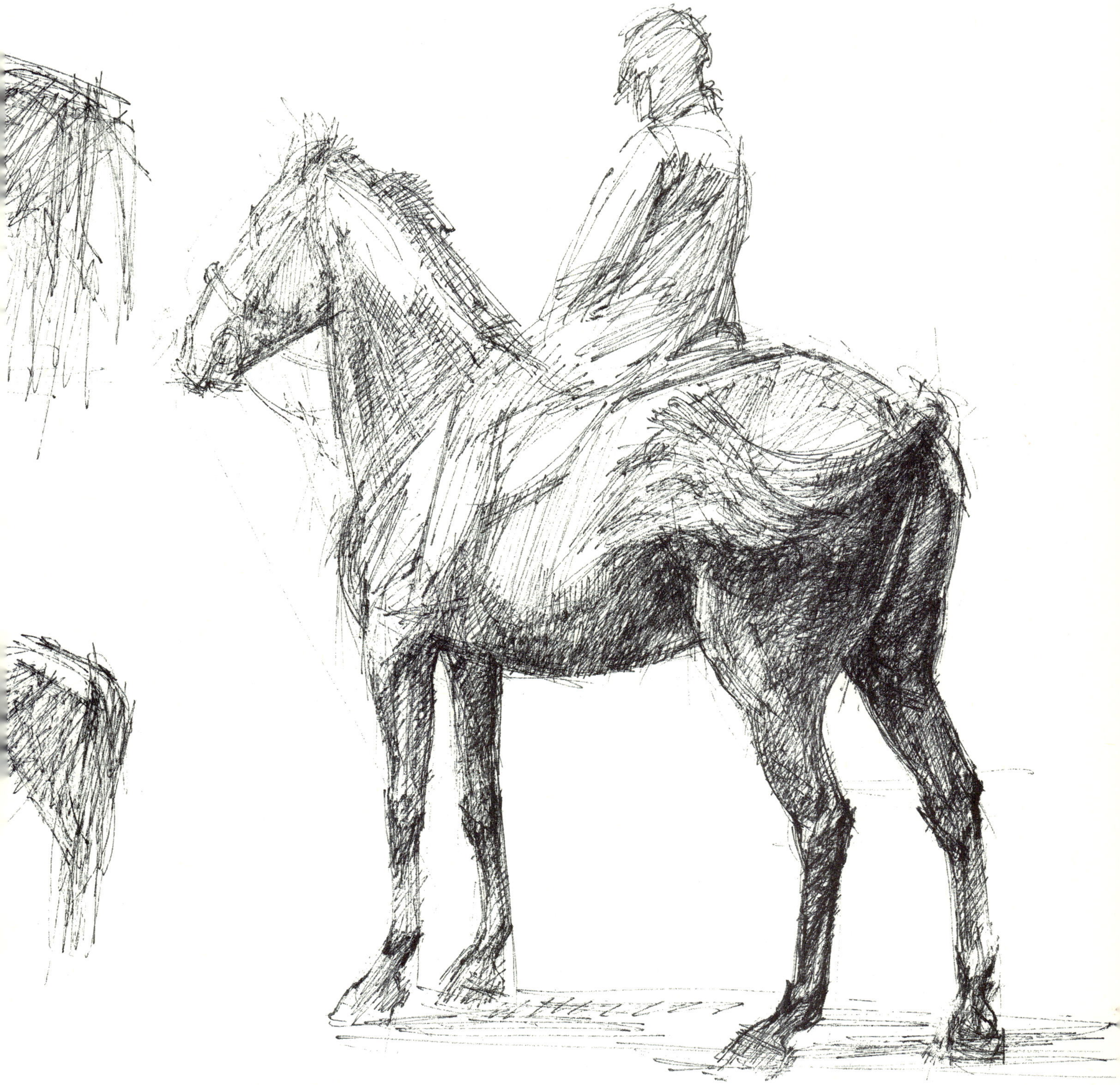

This drawing of a horse and rider is more carefully executed because I felt it was important to picture all the strength and harmony, the fine proportions as well as the pent up energy of this beautiful animal.

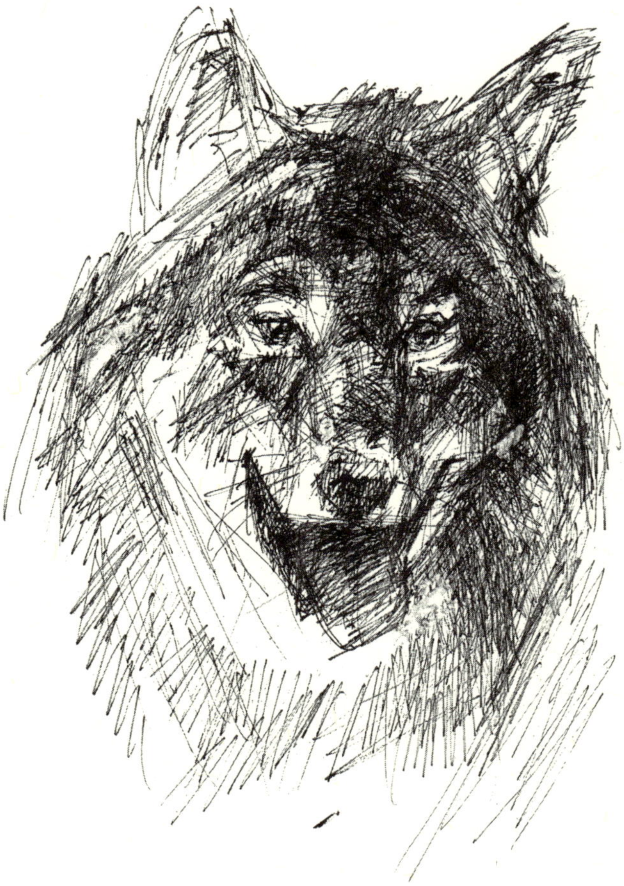

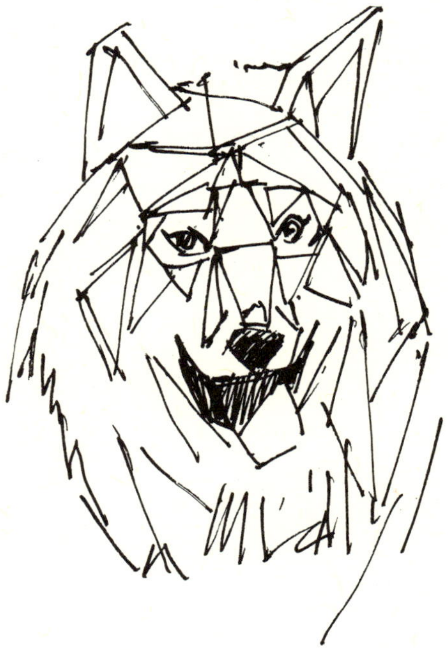

When drawing dogs and related animals (wolves, hyenas, dingos), it's helpful to sketch the different planes as triangles. In illustration, the upturned triangle has long been used to imply aggressiveness and, in the case of dogs, it adds expressiveness to a drawing and suggests ferociousness and danger.

Remember that no matter how longhaired a dog may be, there is always a body underneath. It helps to imagine how a dog looks without all that hair, so that, when you draw what you actually see, the movement of both the dog's body and its coat follow the line of the body.

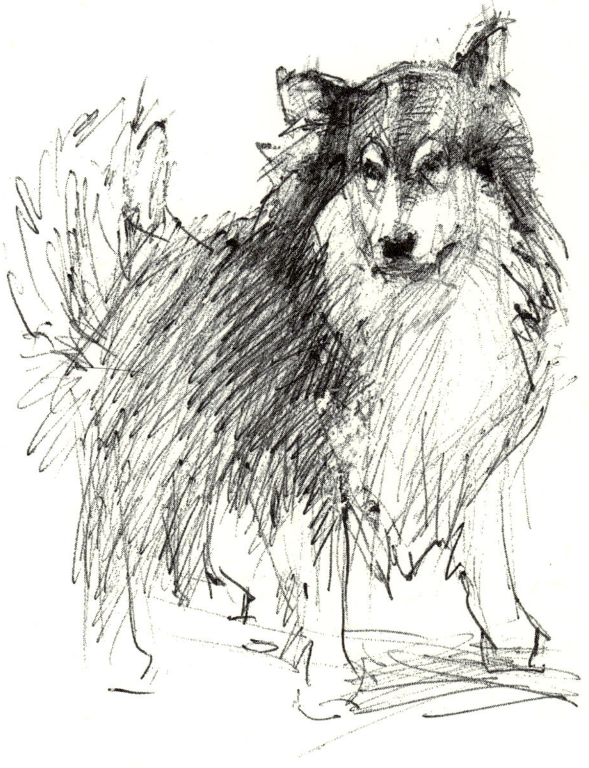

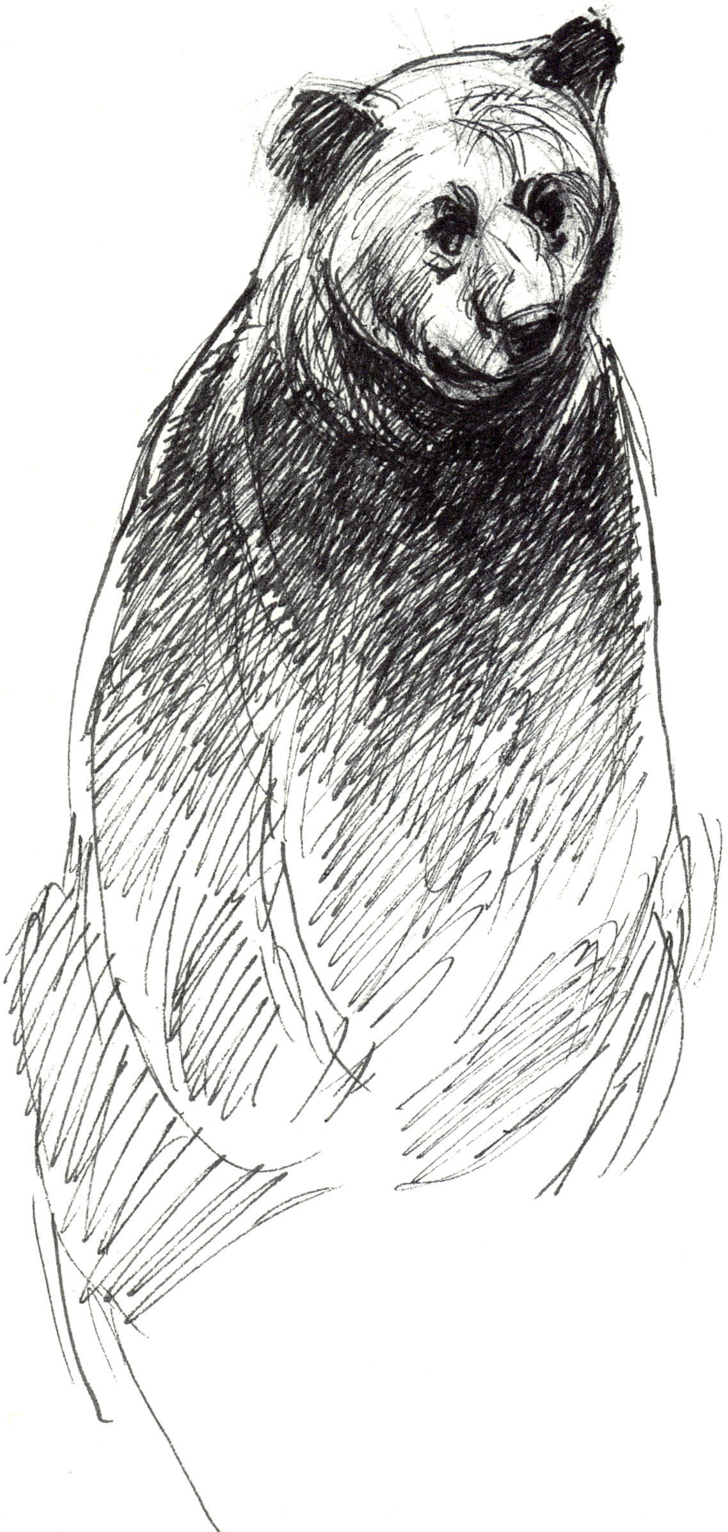

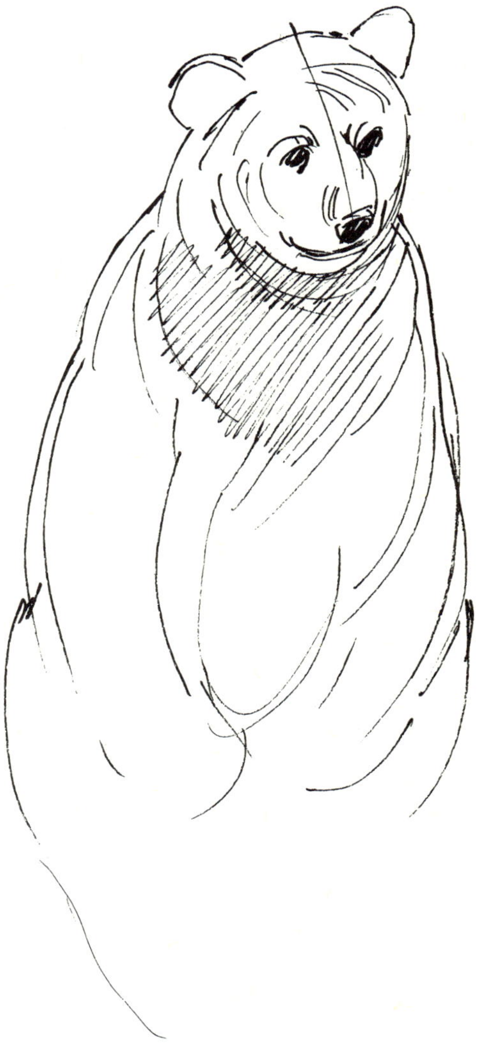

When drawing bears and similar animals, one can use the circle to depict the kind of form that suggests the bear's bulkiness. There is an indication, too, in the bear's sleek coat, of thick, powerful muscles under the skin.

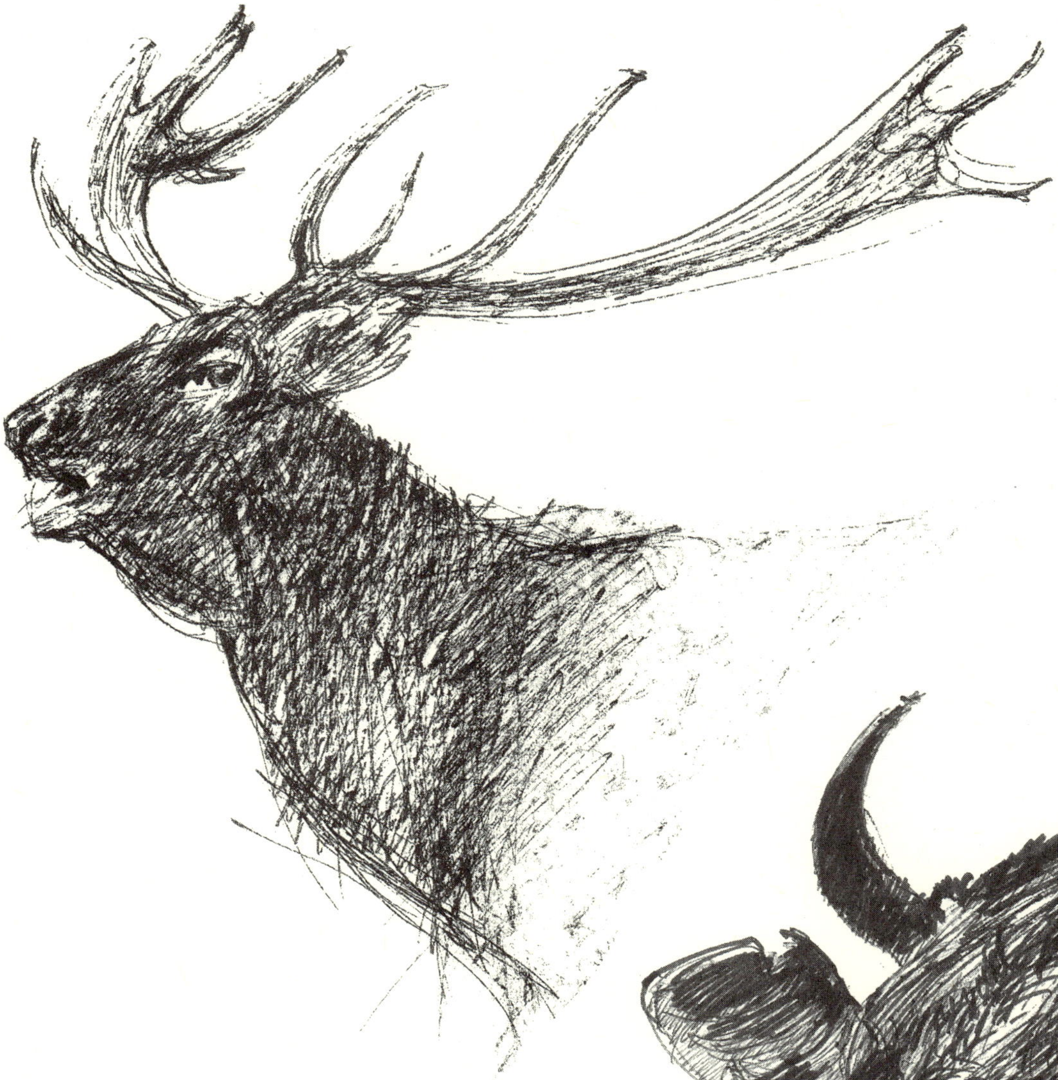

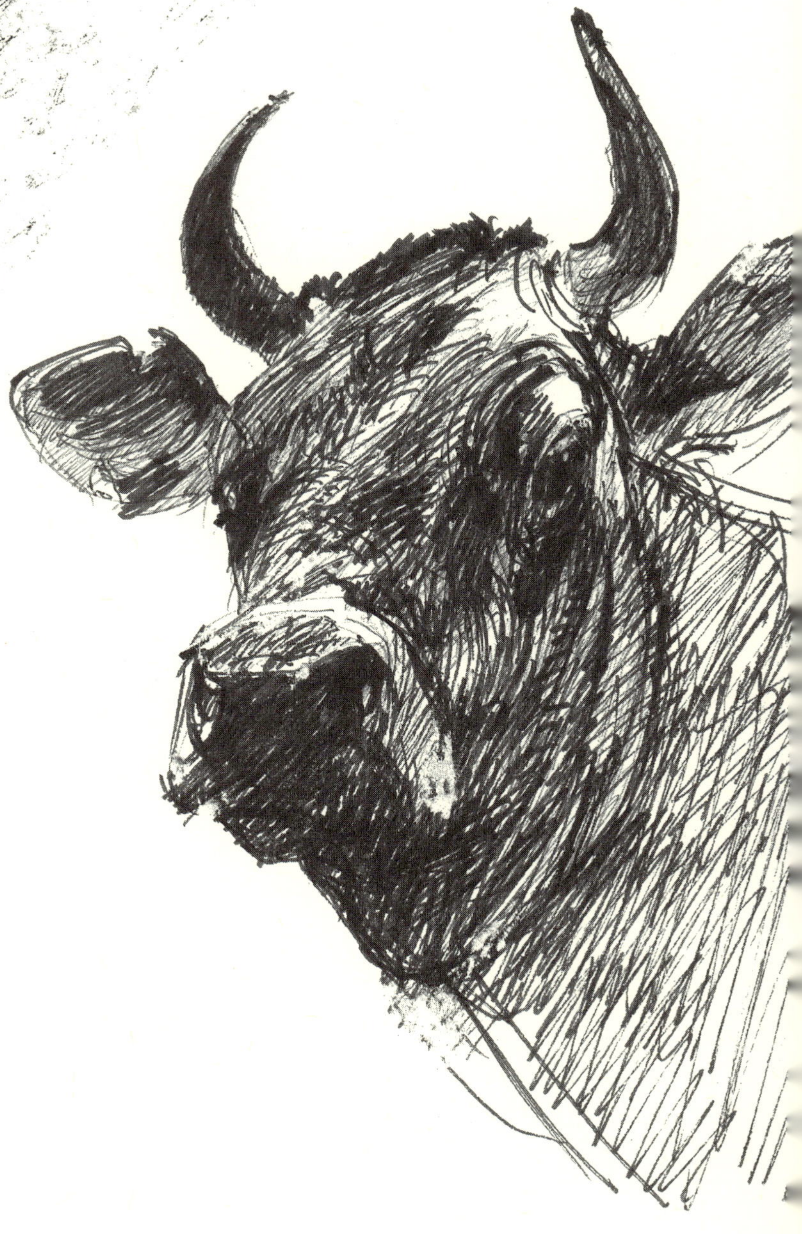

Animals are as individual as people and attempting to demonstrate this in a portrait of a particular animal is a worthwhile exercise. Each kind of animal has certain outstanding characteristics in common, so it pays to devote some care in developing these identifying attributes in your drawing.

This smooth-skinned breed of dog reveals the kind of common features mentioned earlier. Make note of the muscle structure of the back and the build of the forelegs and compare them with those of the horse on page 91.

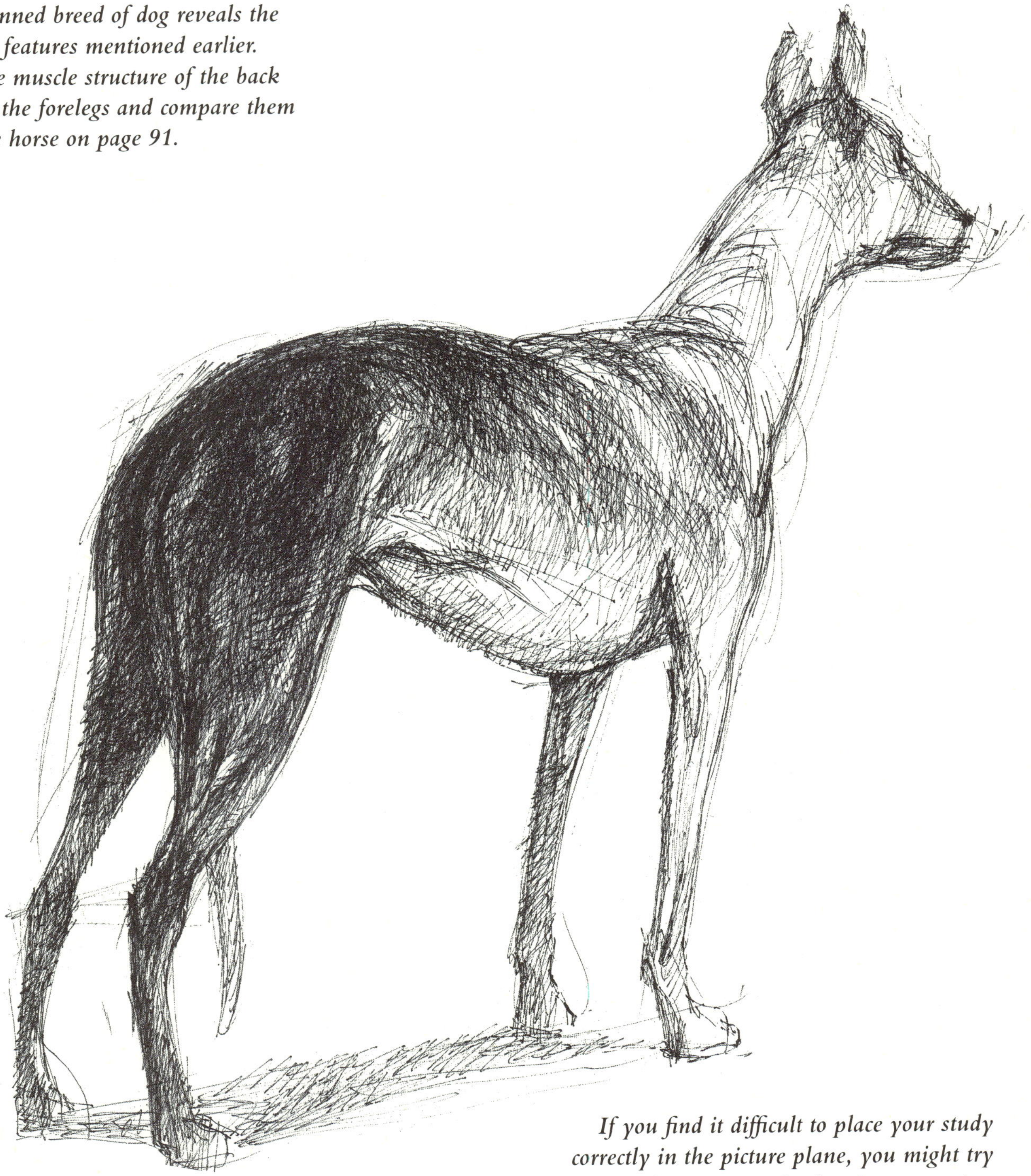

If you find it difficult to place your study correctly in the picture plane, you might try drawing a long rectangular box in perspective. Then sketch the body of the animal within it. This will make your handling of depth and mass (the dog) more credible.

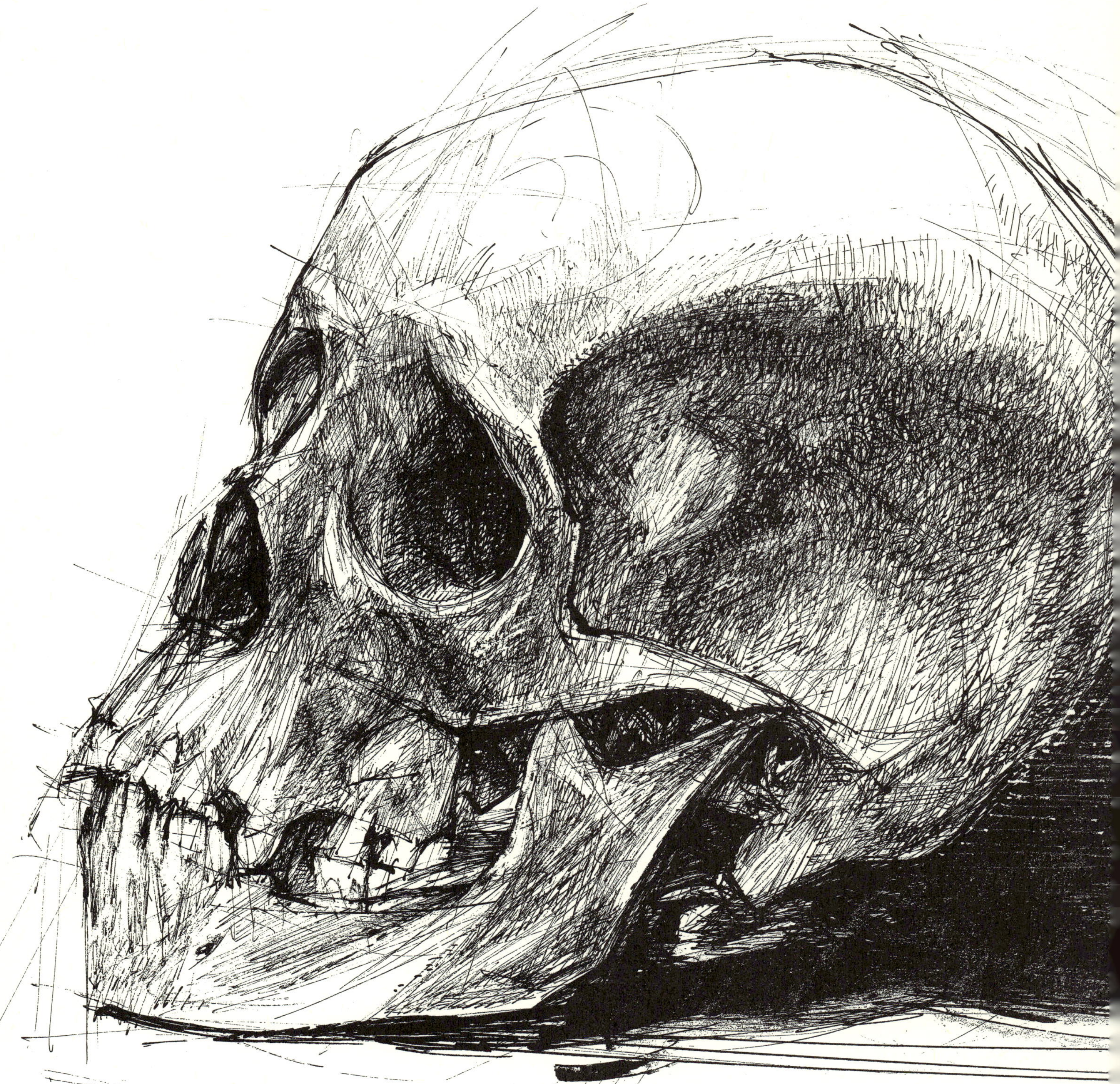

LESSON 10

Studies of the Skeleton

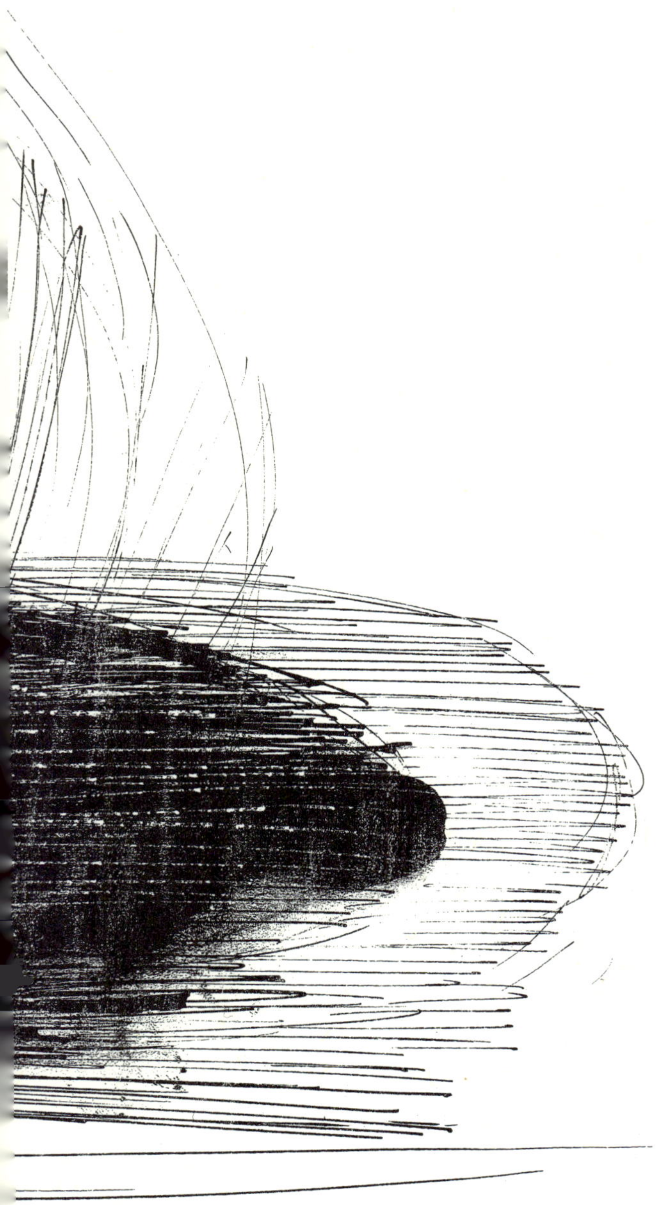

A study in India ink and pen. Much practice is needed before one is capable of producing a convincing rendering of such a complex subject. So, it's best to start your first drawings using a ball-point pen or marker.

The study of the skeleton in all its aspects is extremely important to achieving mastery in drawing. Finding a human skeleton to draw, however, can be difficult. But most schools and zoological collections have animal skeletons you can borrow. If you are lucky enough to get hold of a skull, you will quickly discover that, besides its value for future portrait studies, it is in itself a challenging and worthwhile object for you to draw.

In my own classes, I often have students draw the skull from different angles in the morning and then draw portraits after lunch. This helps students understand the planes that guide us in drawing the head; those that parallel the picture edge and those that are perpendicular to the picture plane. Even though the large facial muscles are no longer attached, studying the skull also helps us to visualize and thus better understand their function and positioning.

It is important when drawing the skull to measure it. When teaching, it soon becomes apparent that students have some deep-seated misconceptions about the spatial relationship of the eye sockets to the nasal cavity and size of the cheeks. Consequently, both the forehead and the skull itself often appear too small in their drawings. Besides working with the human skull from different angles, I have drawn the forearm, the hands, the pelvic region, and some skulls of wild and domestic animals to indicate the wide scope of this area of drawing and to demonstrate the many ways in which the nature of skeletal form can be expressed on paper.

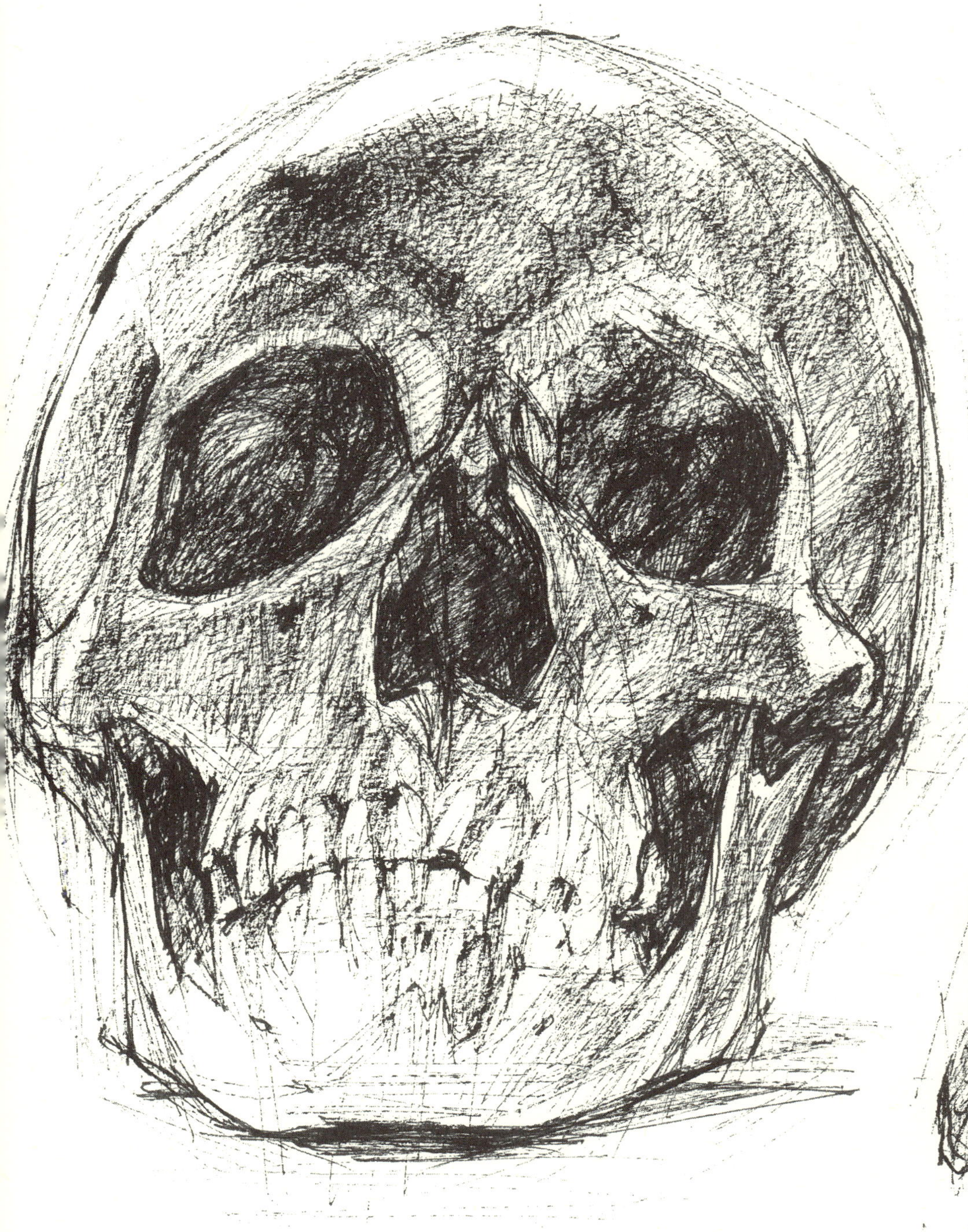

The box-shaped cranium can, at certain angles, give the impression of being surprisingly large.

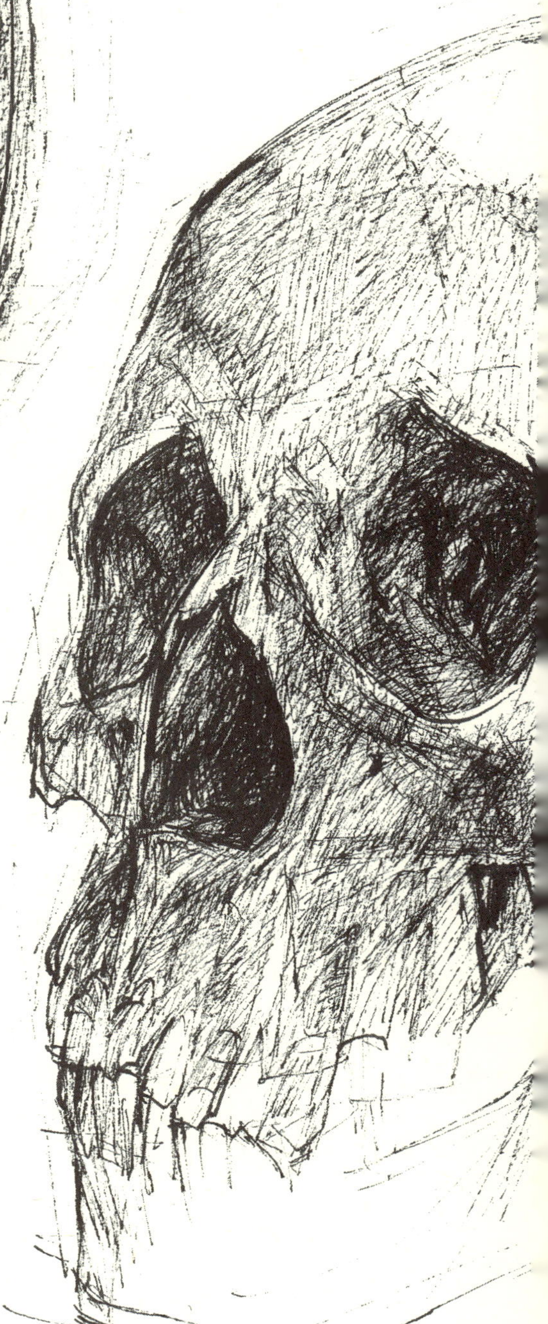

Size up the proportions of the skull. Don't underestimate its bulk. Doublecheck your measurements. You can express the skull's character with textural effects but be careful not to confuse your shaded areas with the natural discoloring that often appears on skulls. Before you begin, select a permanent light source and decide on how it will affect the play of light and shade.

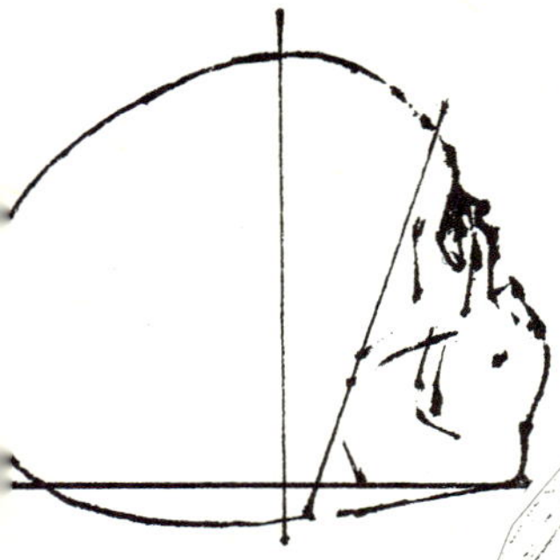

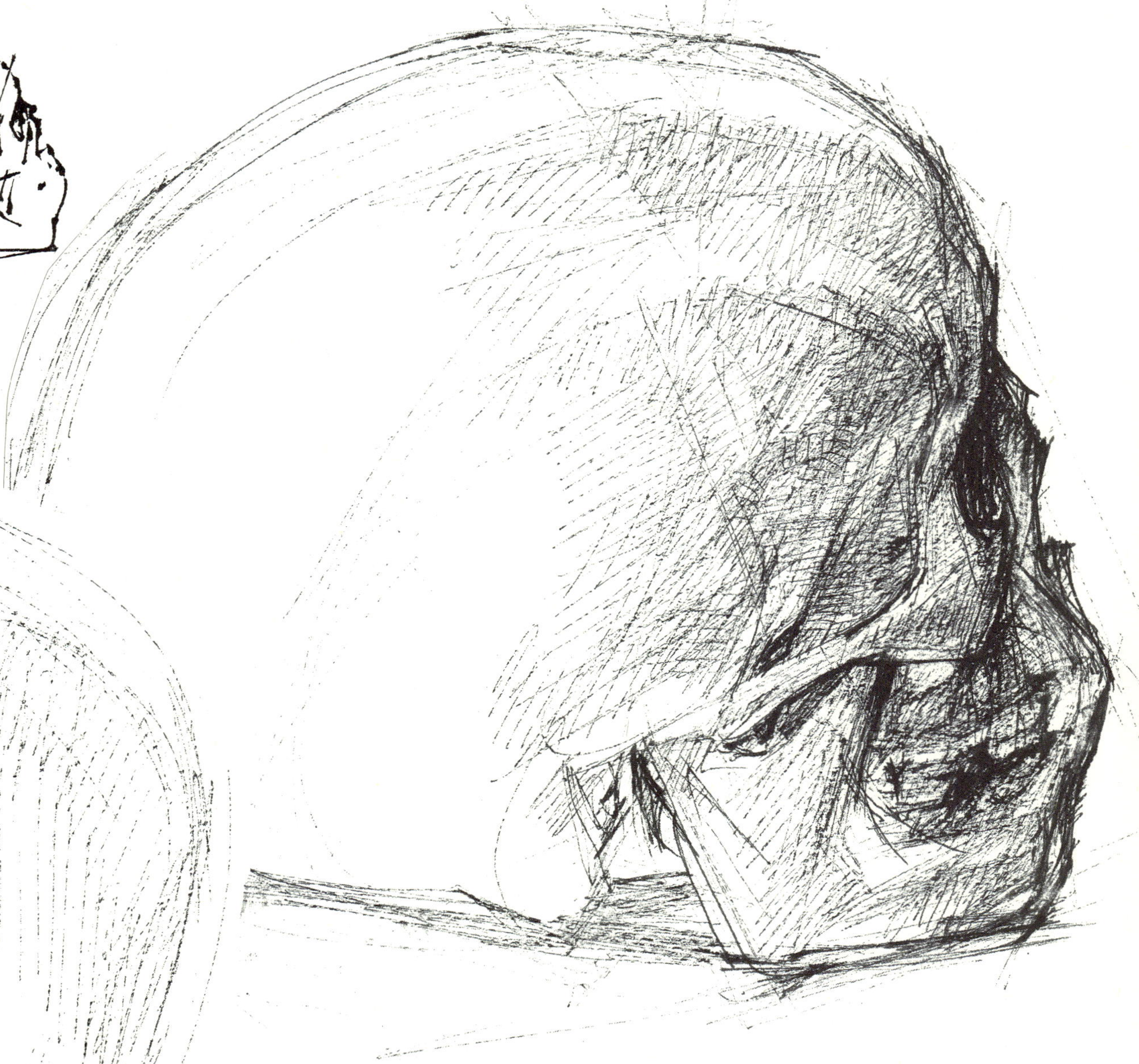

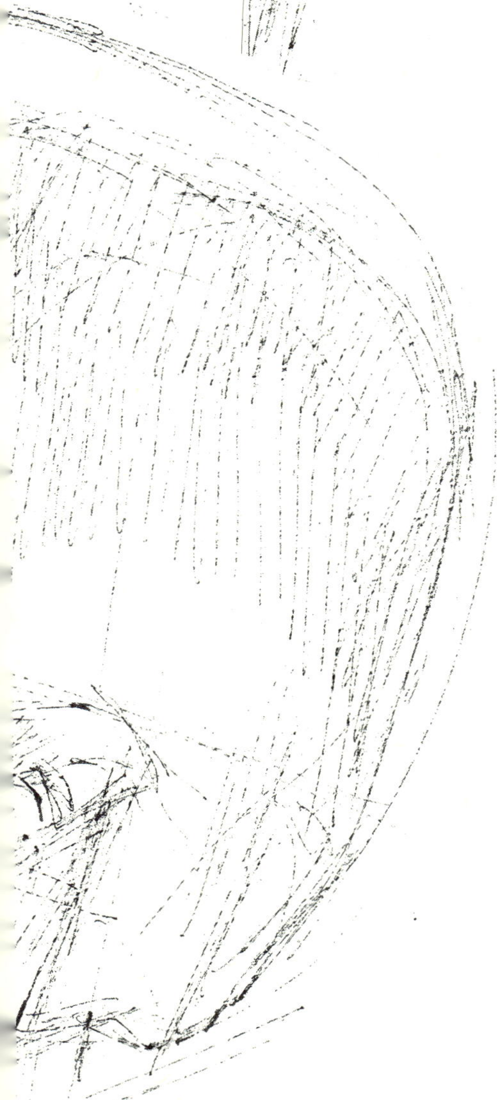

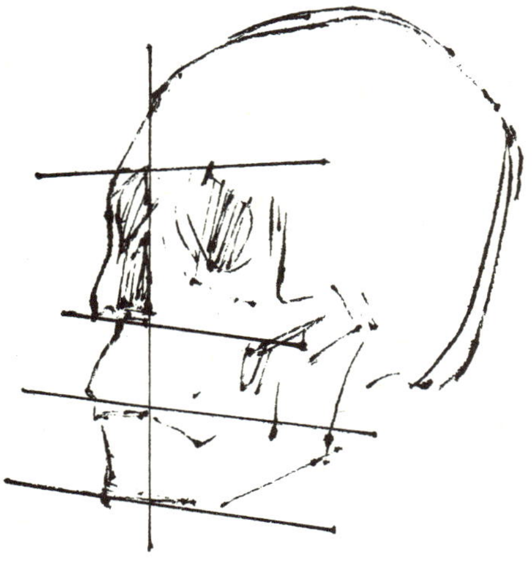

As mentioned earlier, measuring is important and must be systematic starting with the main lines.

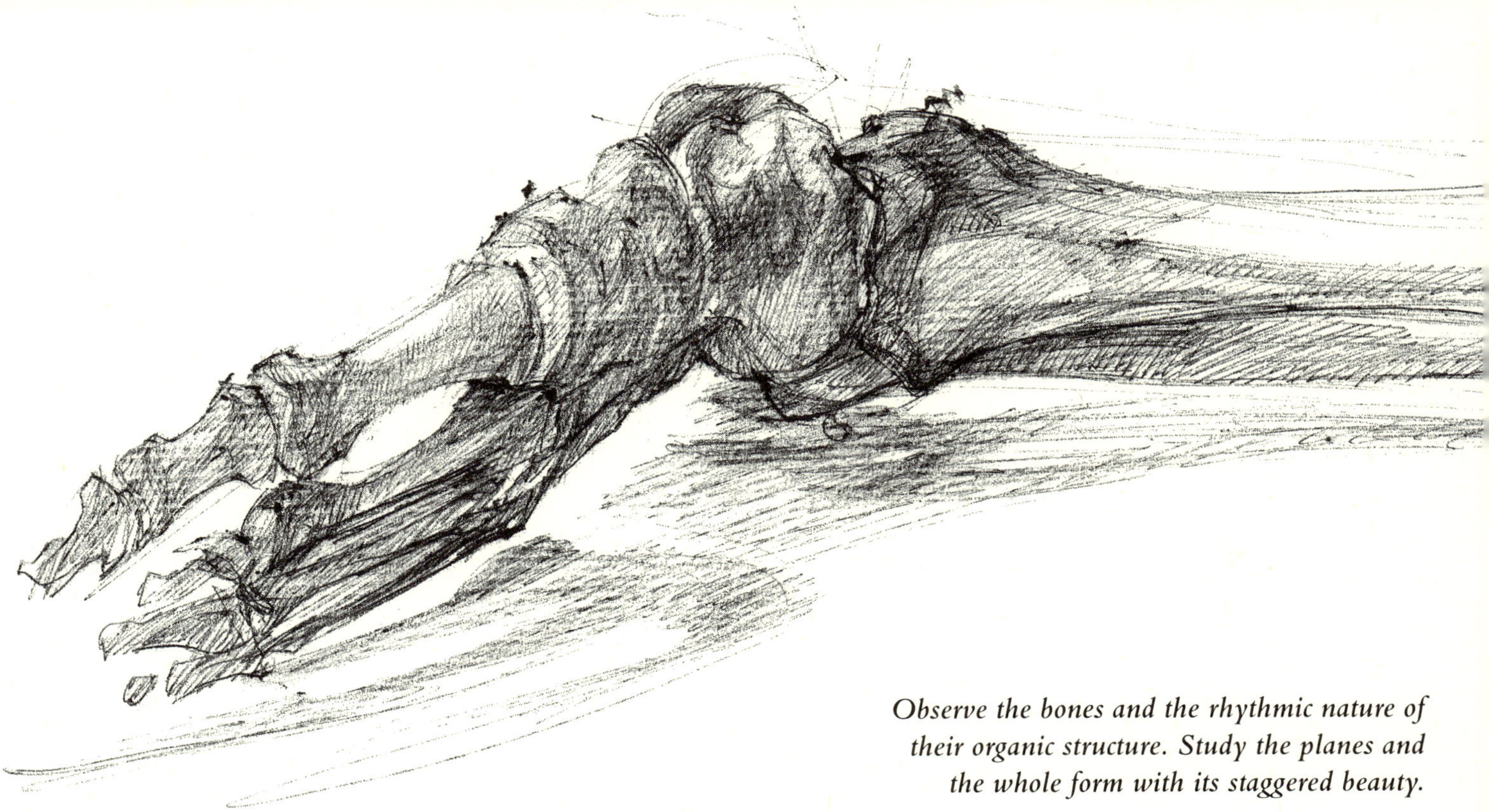

Observe the bones and the rhythmic nature of their organic structure. Study the planes and the whole form with its staggered beauty.

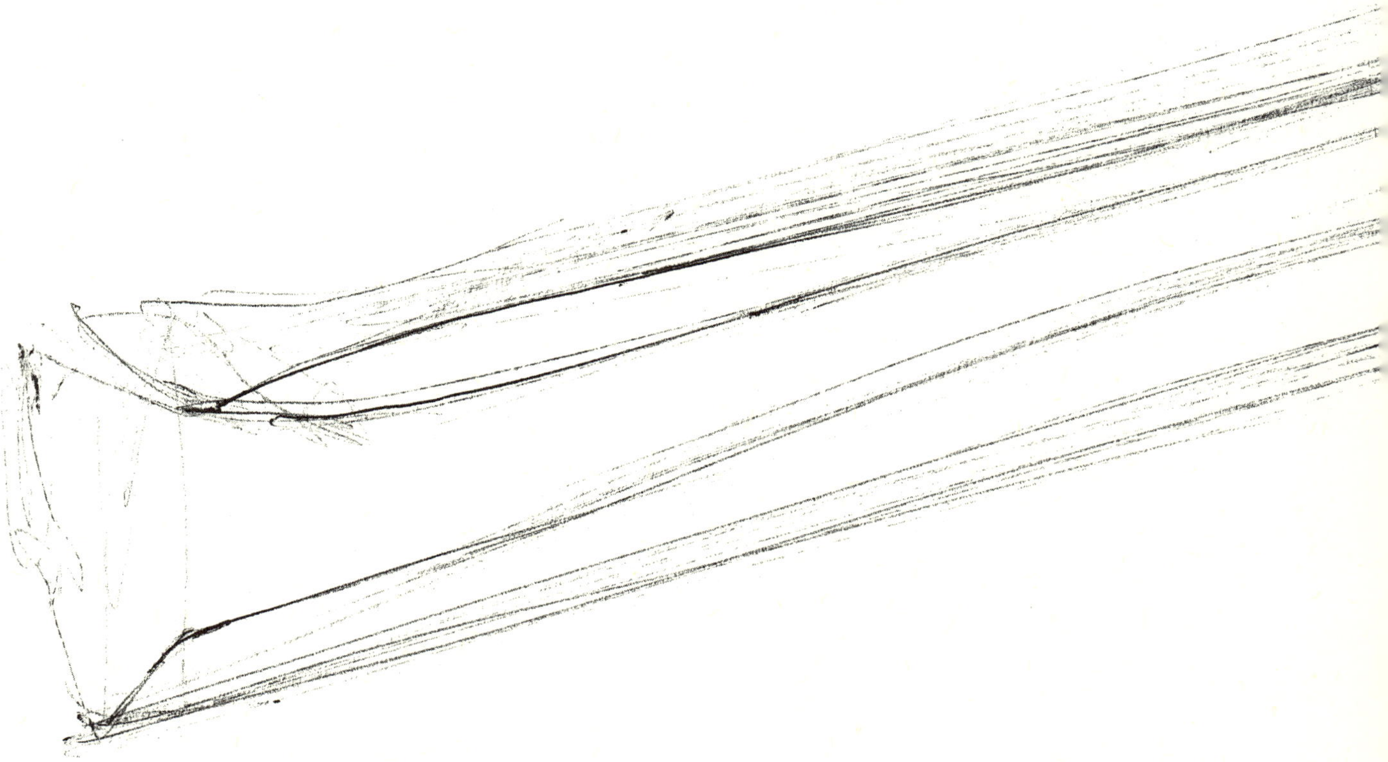

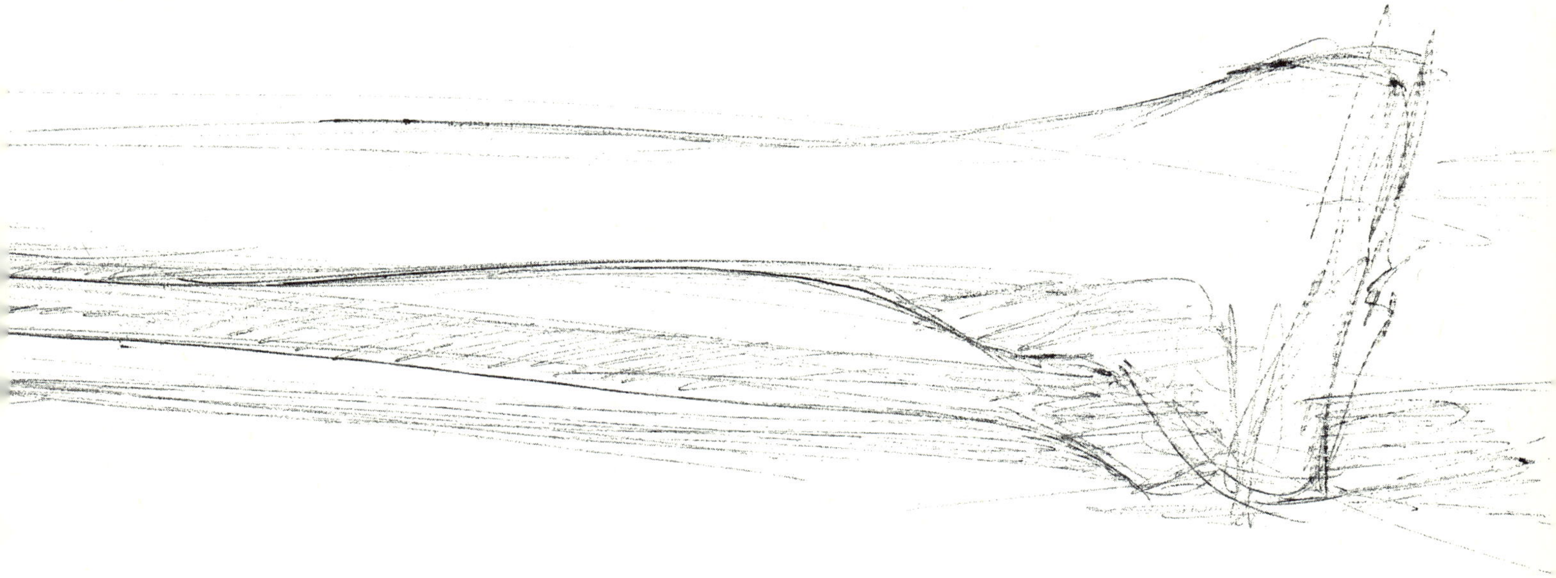

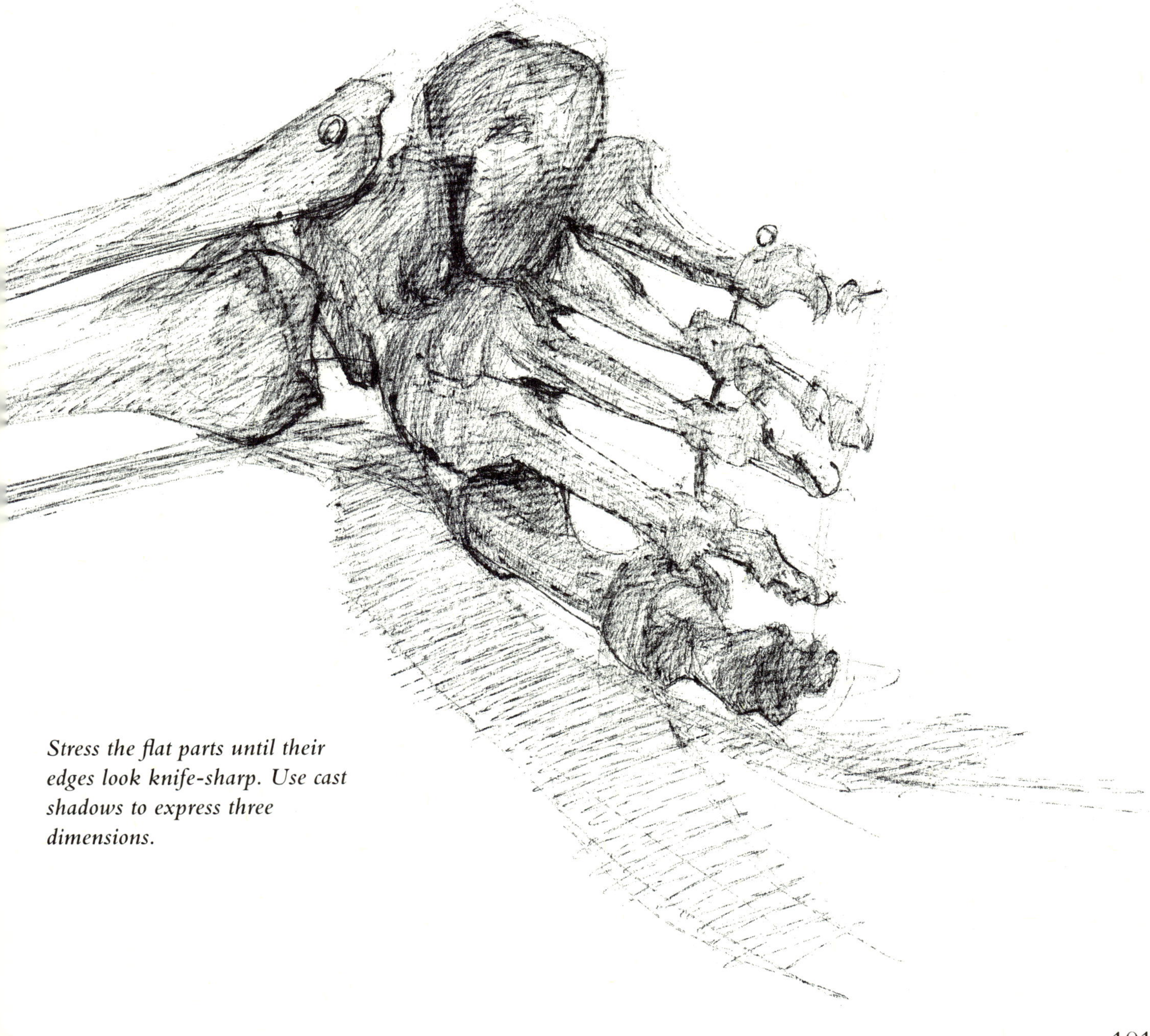

Stress the flat parts until their edges look knife-sharp. Use cast shadows to express three dimensions.

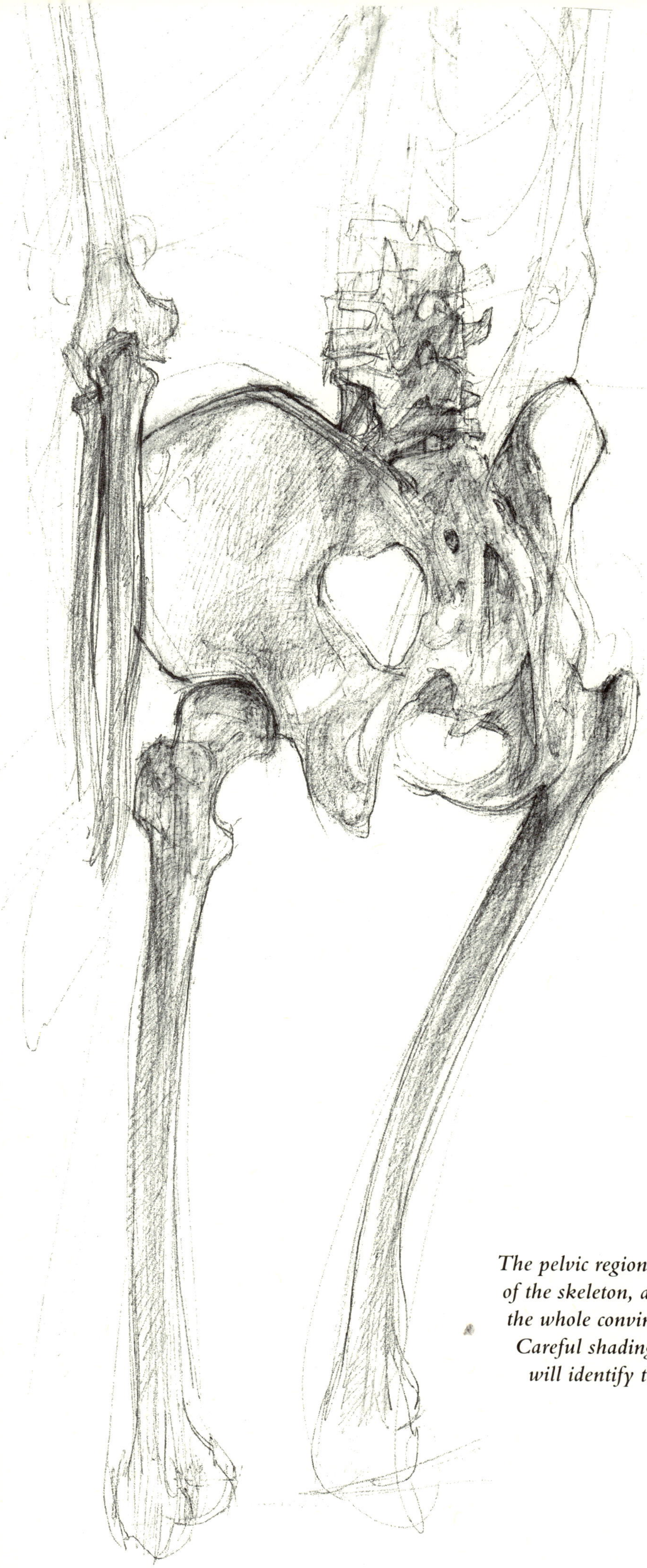

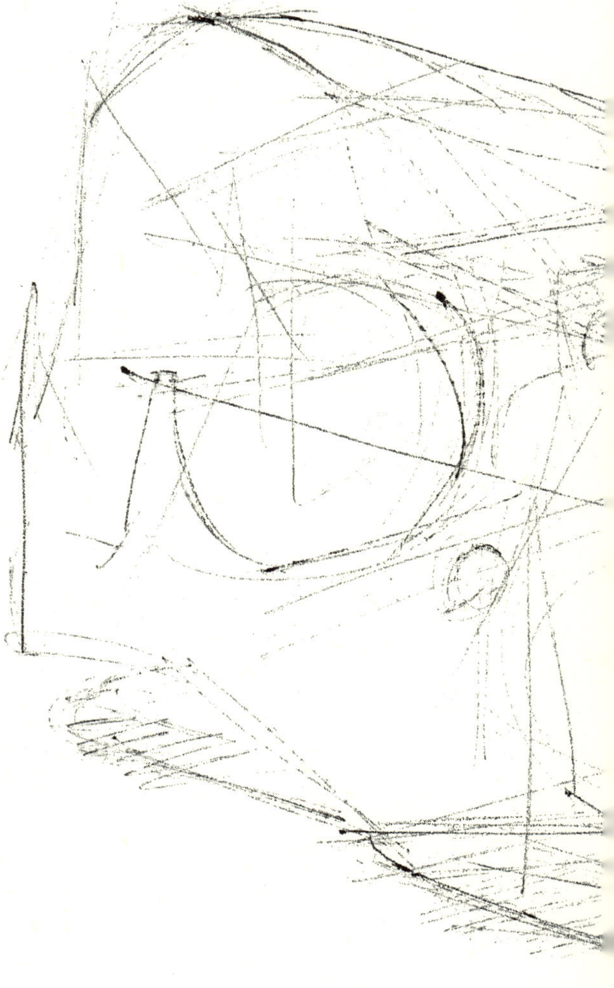

The importance of a systematic sketch cannot be emphasized too often. Look at all the triangles that appear. They can be used to place the skull correctly and gauge the right proportions.

The pelvic region and the thighbones must, like all the other bones of the skeleton, appear as parts of a whole. To make the parts and the whole convincingly real, a concentration of shadows is needed. Careful shading to equate "common light with common shadow" will identify the flats and the rounds giving a sense of reality to your drawing.

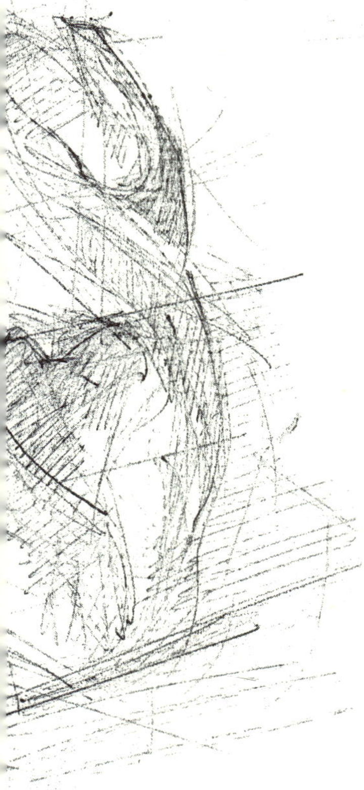

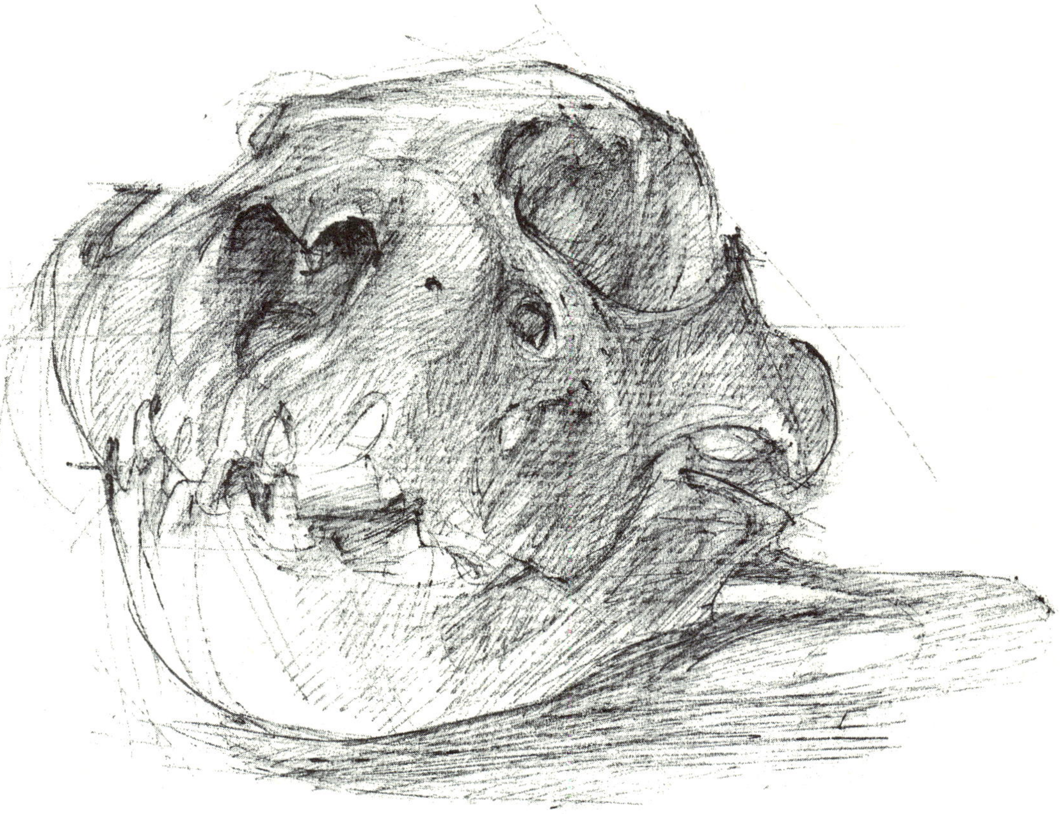

A study of a lion skull and jaw. Here's an example of how shading that follows the form tightens and models both drawings so that, with the help of cast shadows, they achieve a feeling of three dimensions.

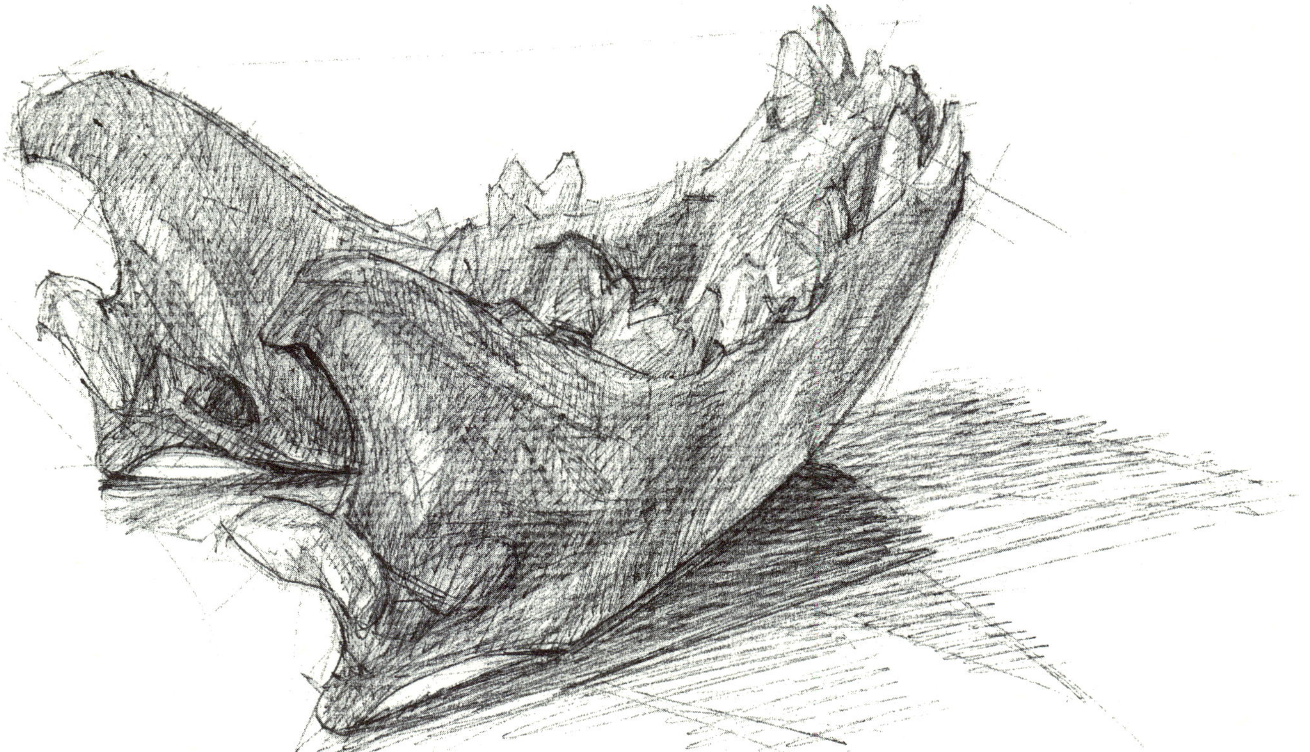

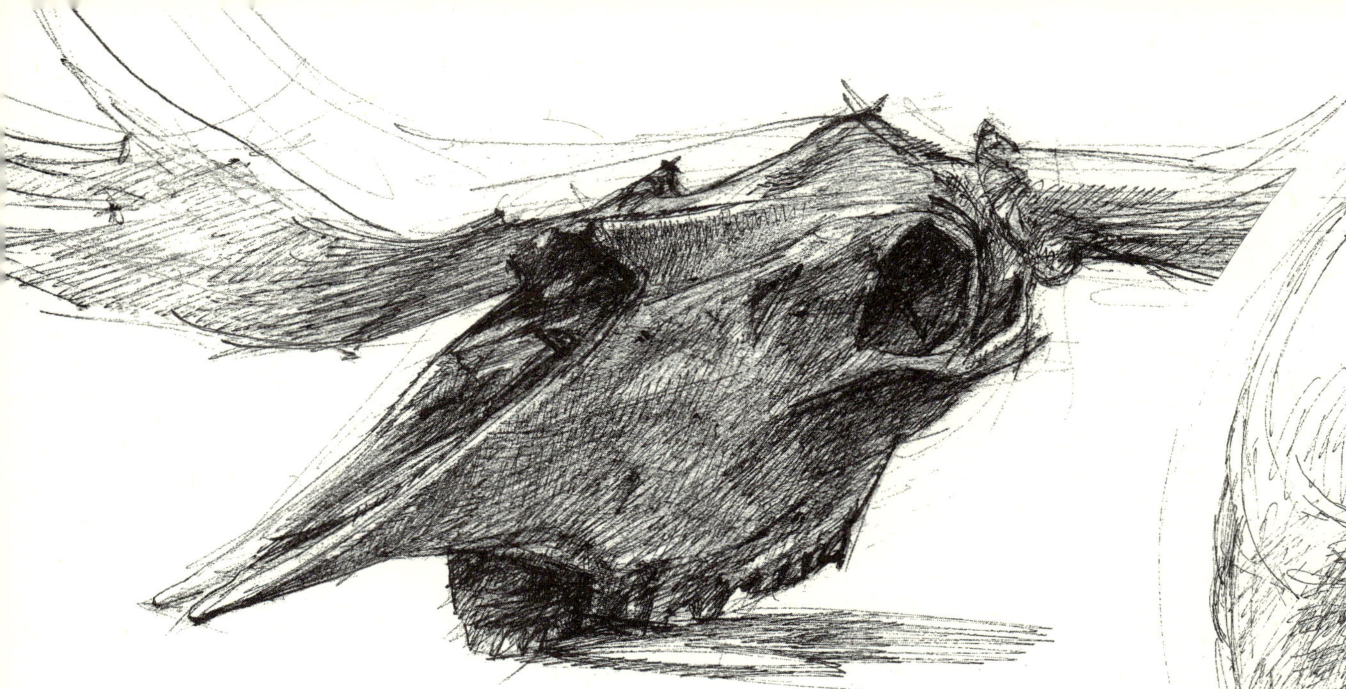

This sketch of the skull of a prehistoric deer was made at Copenhagen's Zoological Museum where there is an excellent collection open to the public.

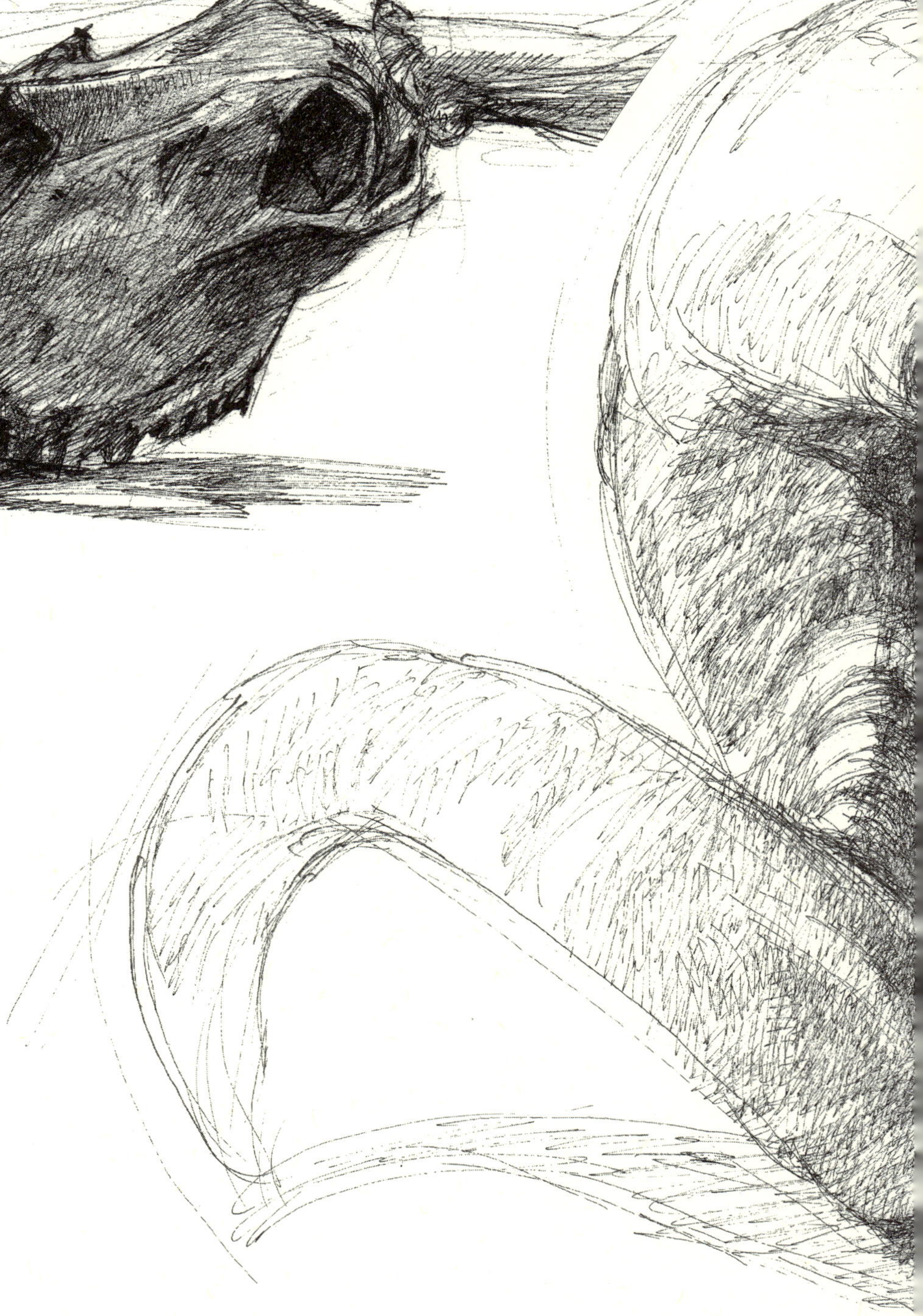

This skull of a ram emphasizes the importance of precisely delineating the planes in a drawing. Here, such attention to structure has endowed the drawing with the kind of spatial "bigness" that we associate with the curled horns of this noble but aggressive animal.

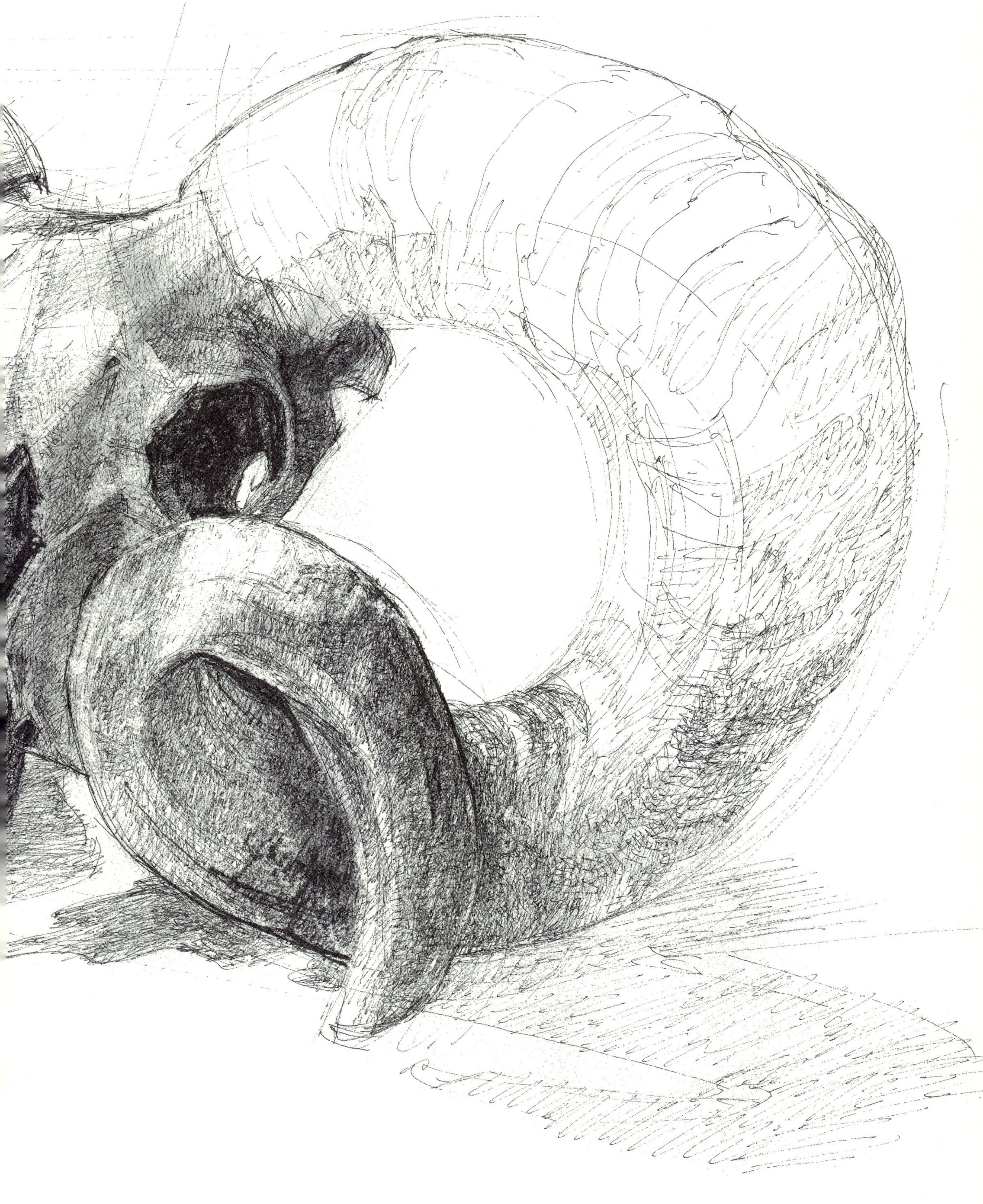

A correct use of shading and shadows cannot help but clarify form. Incorrect applications of shading and shadowing techniques blur the form and should be avoided.

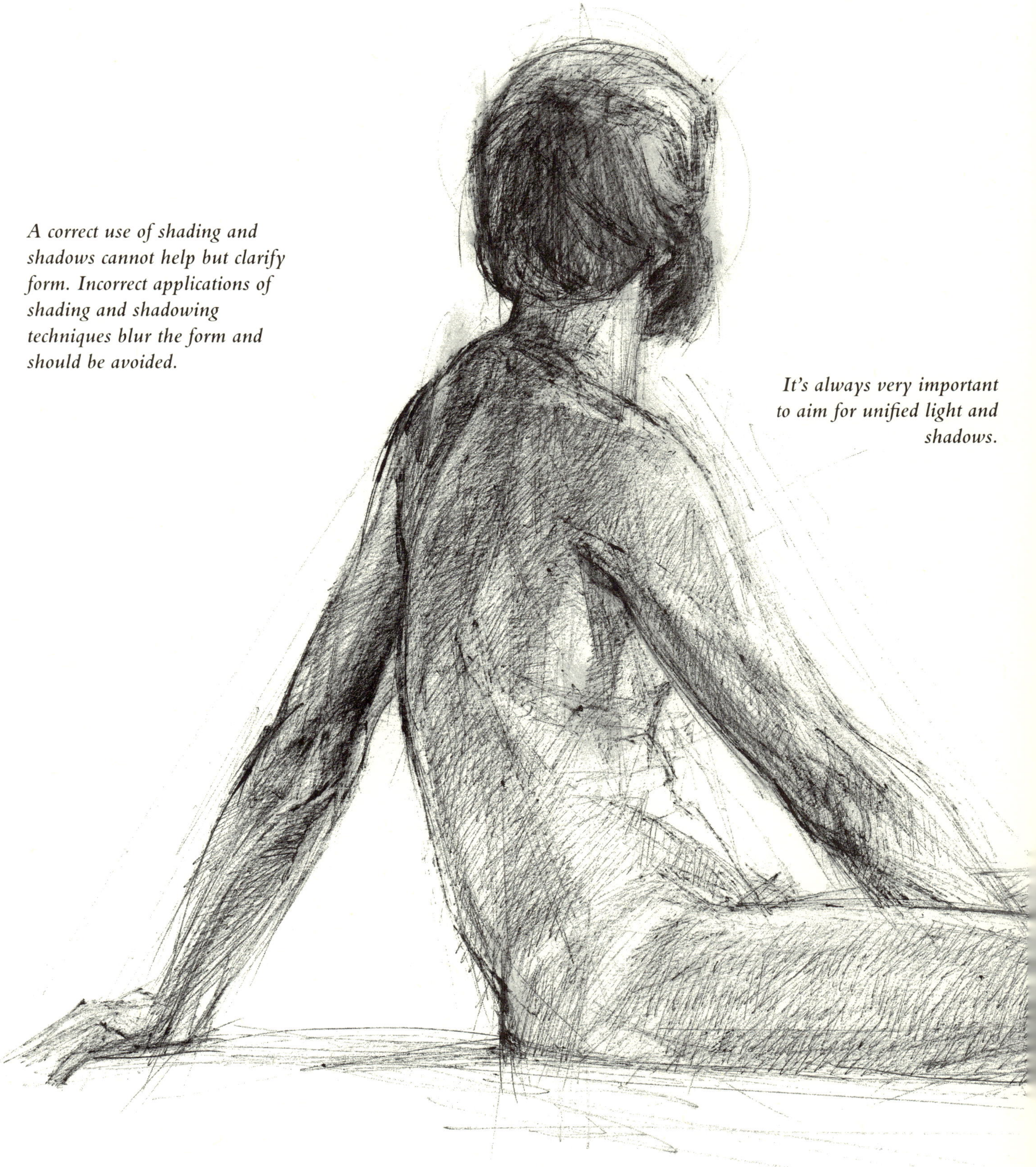

It's always very important to aim for unified light and shadows.

LESSON 11

Nudes

The study of the human body has been considered a key element in the teaching of drawing ever since the early Renaissance when, at the beginning of the fifteenth century, Antonio Pisano, more popularly known as Pisanello (1397–1455), defied the church and for the first time, after centuries of denunciation and suppression of figure drawing, began to sketch from the nude.

Now the study of the naked figure is so extensive that there are several distinct ways in which instruction is presented. Movement studies, for instance, call on the student to make quick sketches (croquis) of the model posing in a series of different positions with each pose lasting no more than 2 to 20 minutes. But the method of instruction we will use here calls for much longer poses of from 2½ to 3 hours. The purpose of "life drawing" is to organize learning around "studies from life" in which the student concentrates on such elements of drawing as form and proportion. Although poses are held for long periods, they are interrupted by pauses every 20 minutes or so and the model is only asked to assume positions that do not cause physical strain or become too tiring.

In life drawing, it's important that each pose, sitting, standing or lying, be satisfactory to both artist and model. To begin a figure study, quickly sketch the full dimensions or "bulk" of the body and head just as a sculptor sizes up how much moist clay he or she needs. At this stage, it's better to forget the details but discover the big lines of the figure, size up the diagonals, and take a close look at the spaces created by the way the arms and legs relate to the body—hands on hips or a hand resting on a knee, for example.

We have talked more than once about planes (surfaces) and how important they are in drawing. This is especially true when drawing people. Look carefully at the figure and observe which planes are receding in space (think of the picture plane) and which run parallel to the edge of the drawing board. Once you have these considerations firmly in mind and have established the bulk of the figure, you should be able to build up your drawing. Using plumb lines or a pencil held against the thumb at arm's length are popular ways to check measurements. But be careful. I have had long discussions with students using such techniques who insist they have measured up and down and sideways, yet the drawing on the board had very little to do with the figure on the platform. Using such mechanical methods without careful observation gets us nowhere. Better to forget them and rely on your eyes.

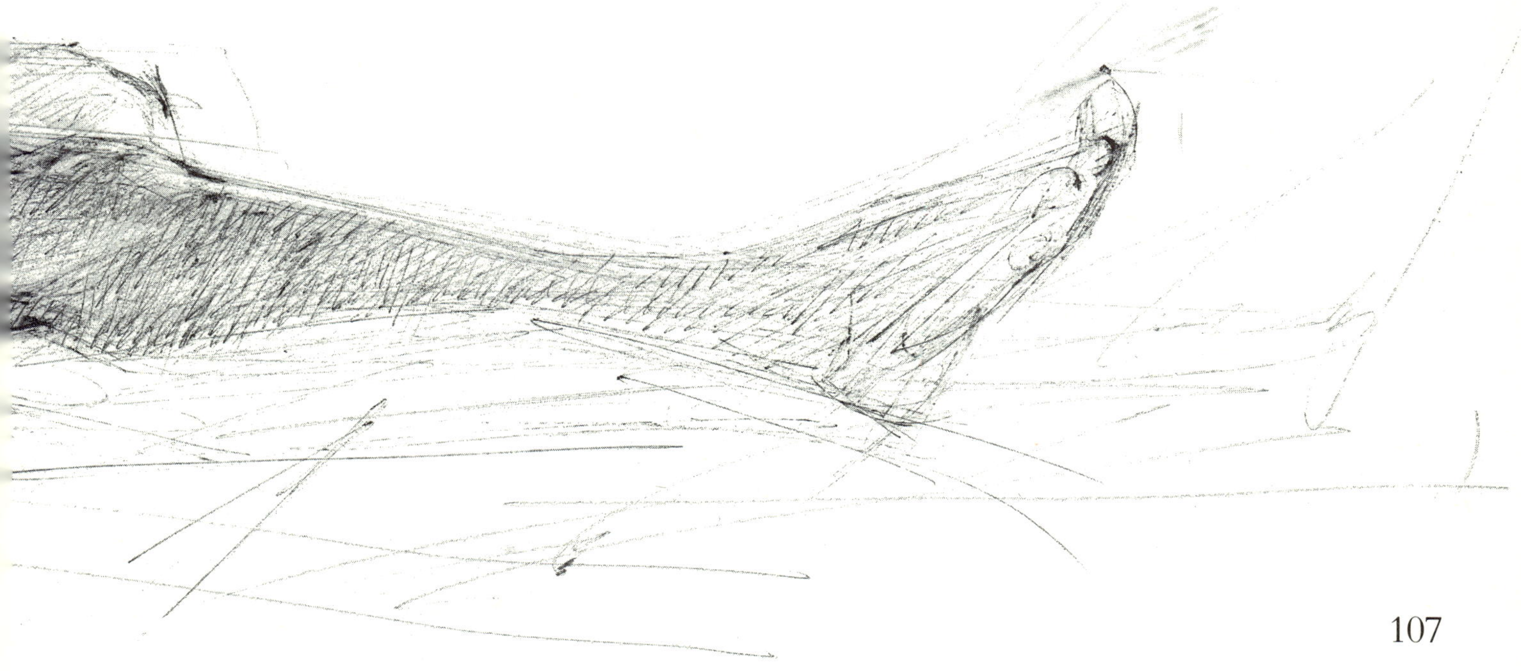

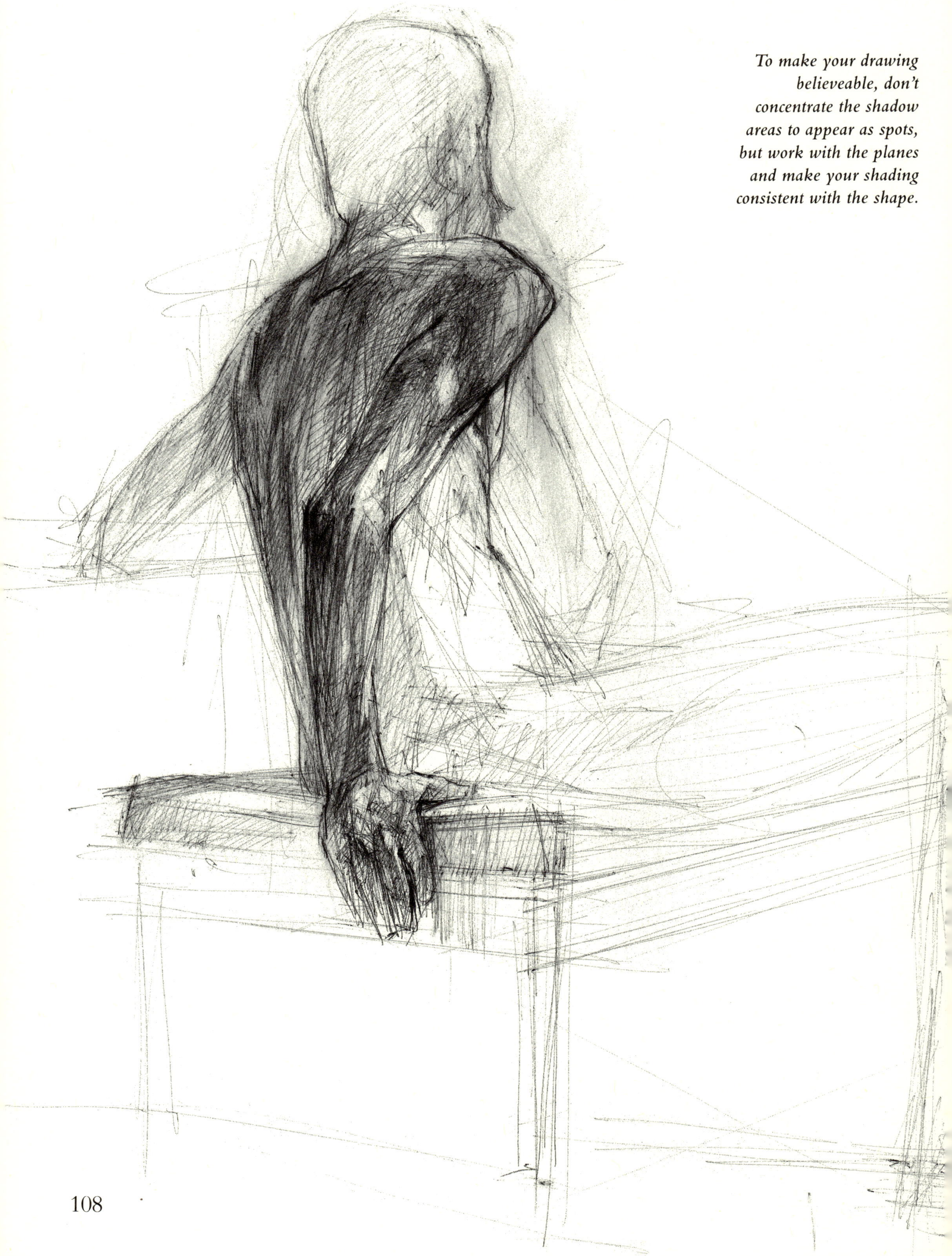

To make your drawing believeable, don't concentrate the shadow areas to appear as spots, but work with the planes and make your shading consistent with the shape.

Show the head, but first concentrate on getting the body correct. I have often seen students waste time fiddling with the head and completely forgetting the larger shape.

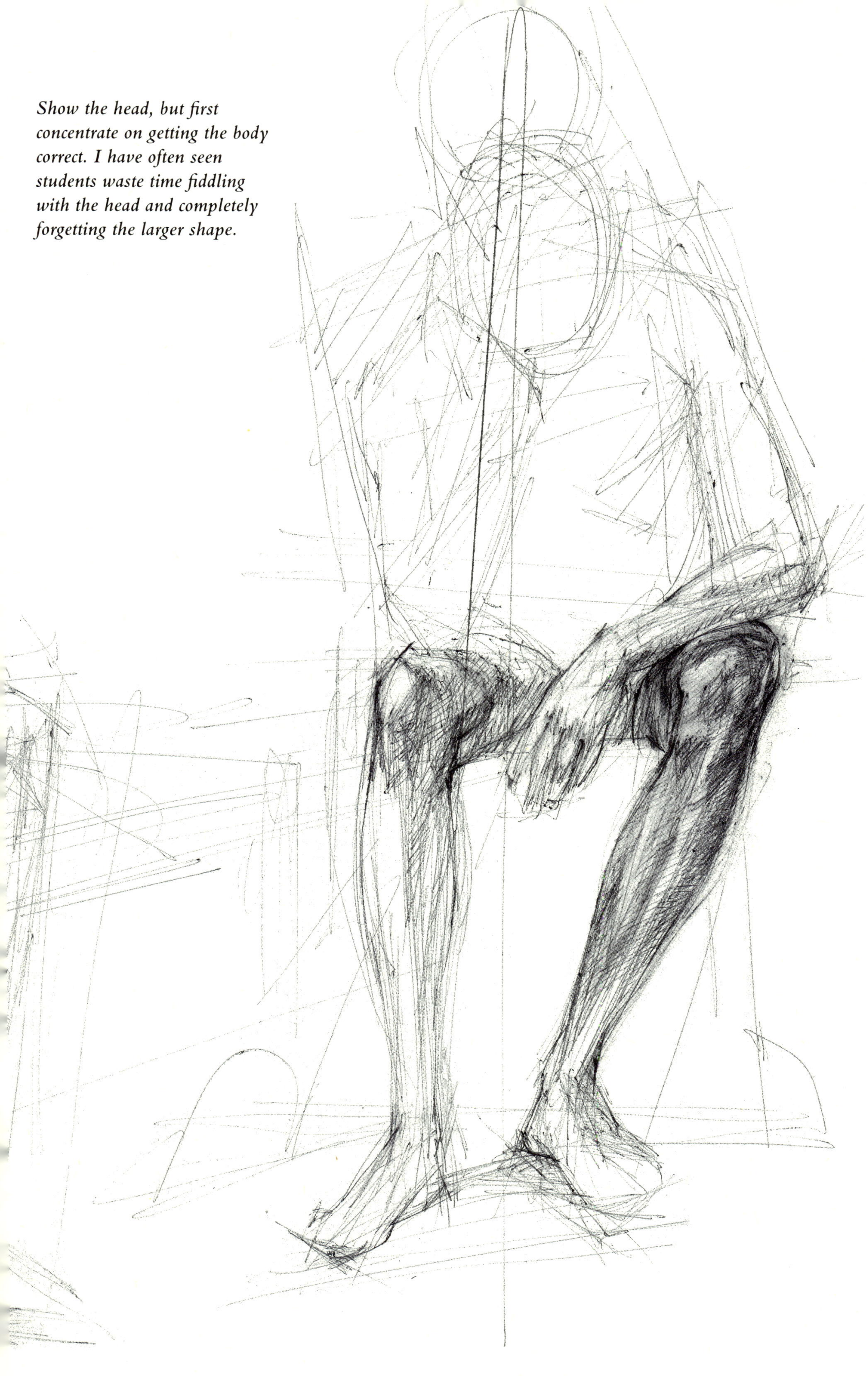

Besides a ball-point pen you can also use a Rapidograph or similar pen or marker that makes a fine line. Refrain from using an eraser. Instead let your corrected mistakes stand in the hope that they will encourage you not to make them again.

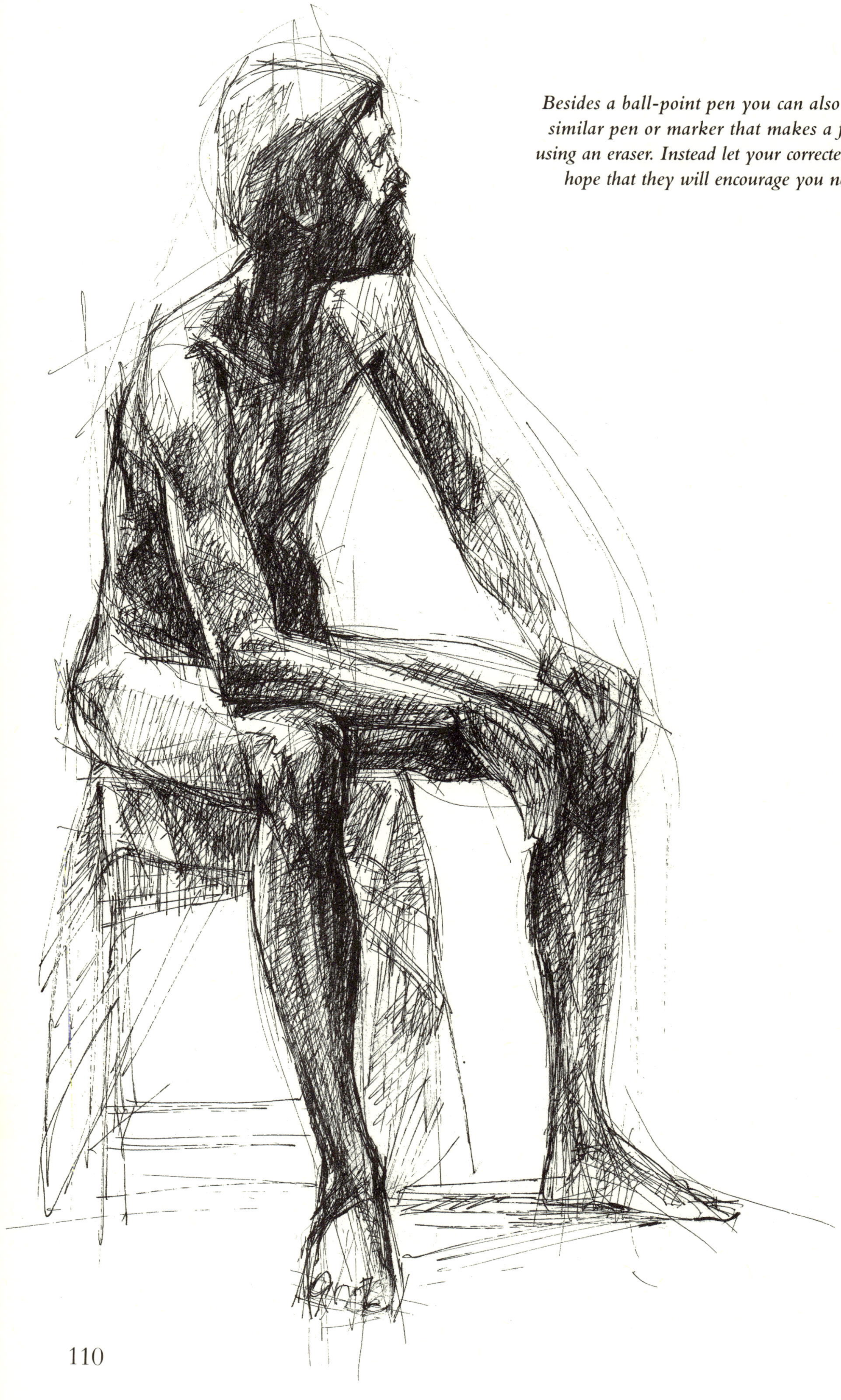

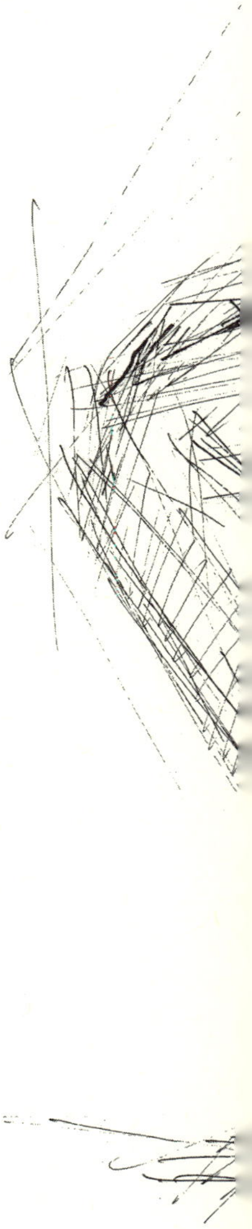

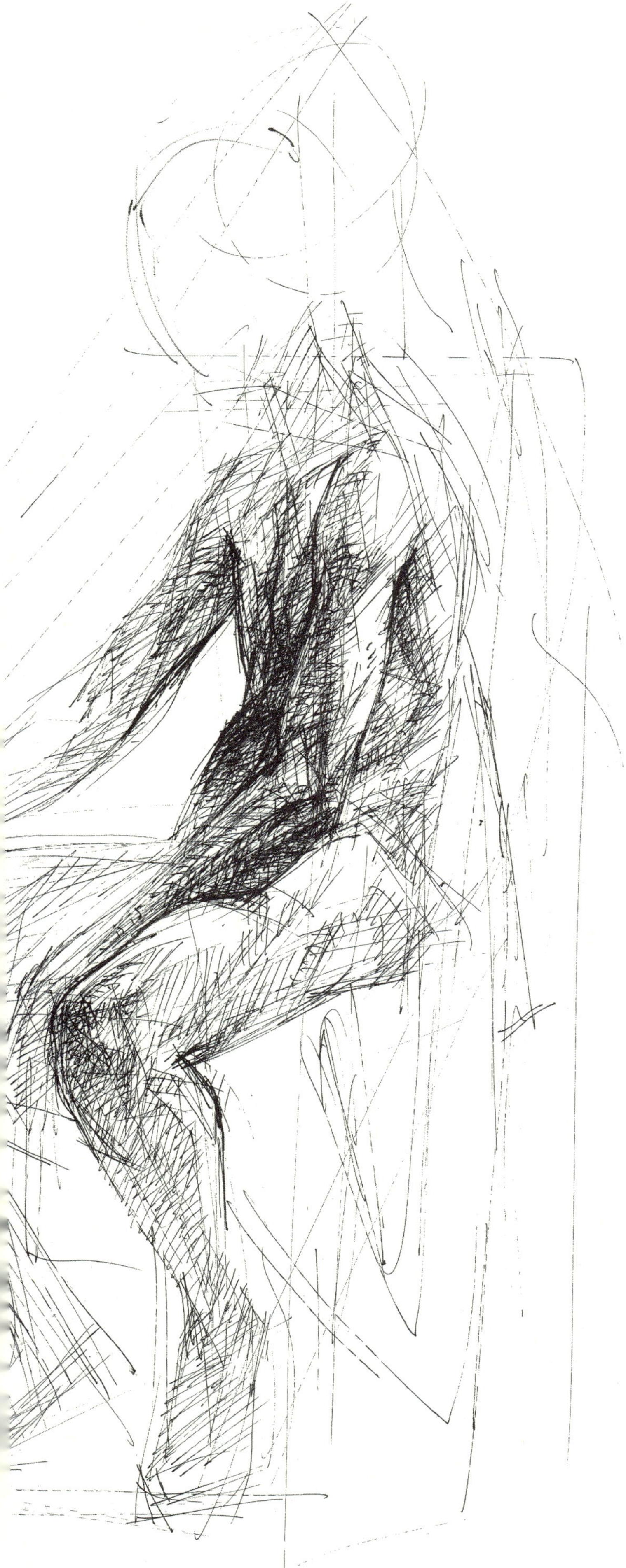

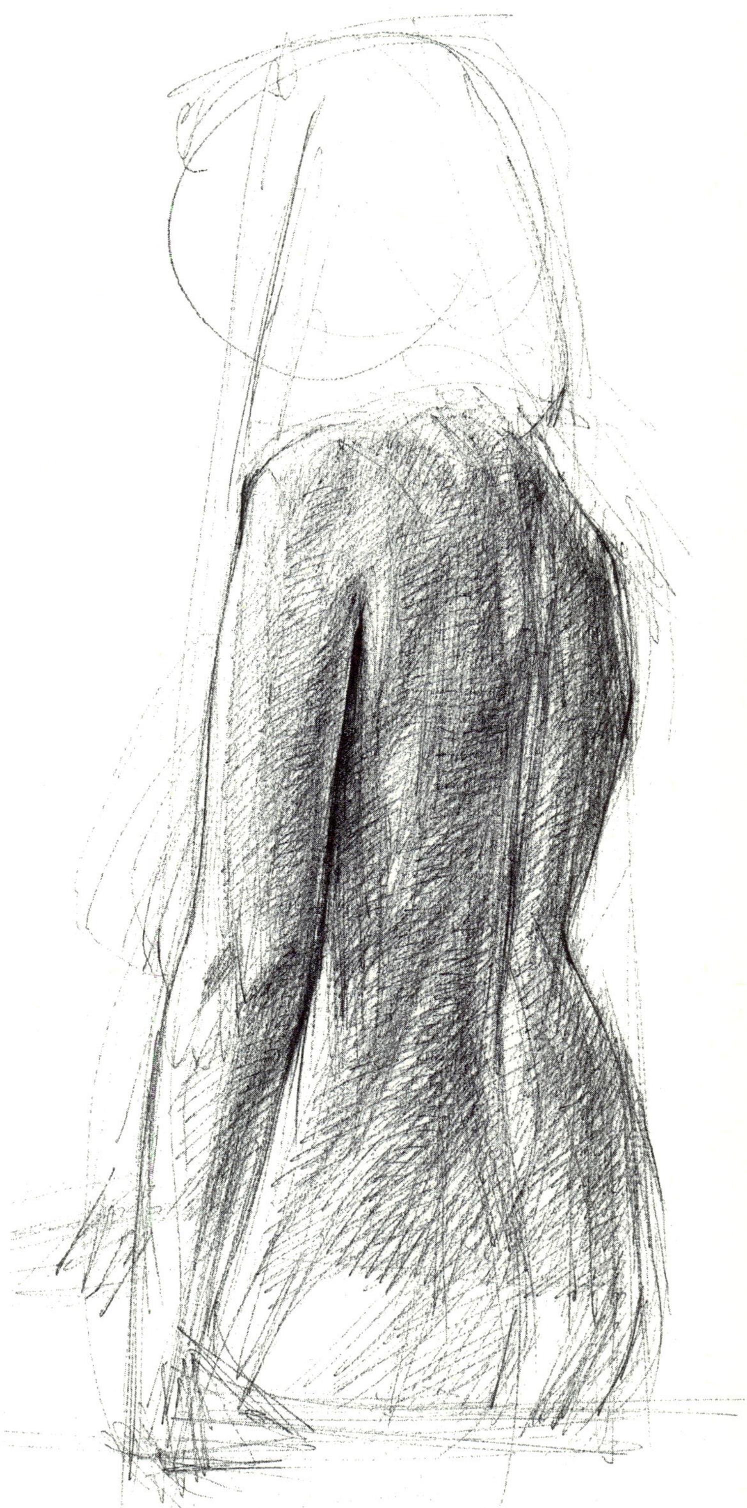

Alternate male and female models so that you can distinguish between the characteristics of the female body as compared to those of the male.

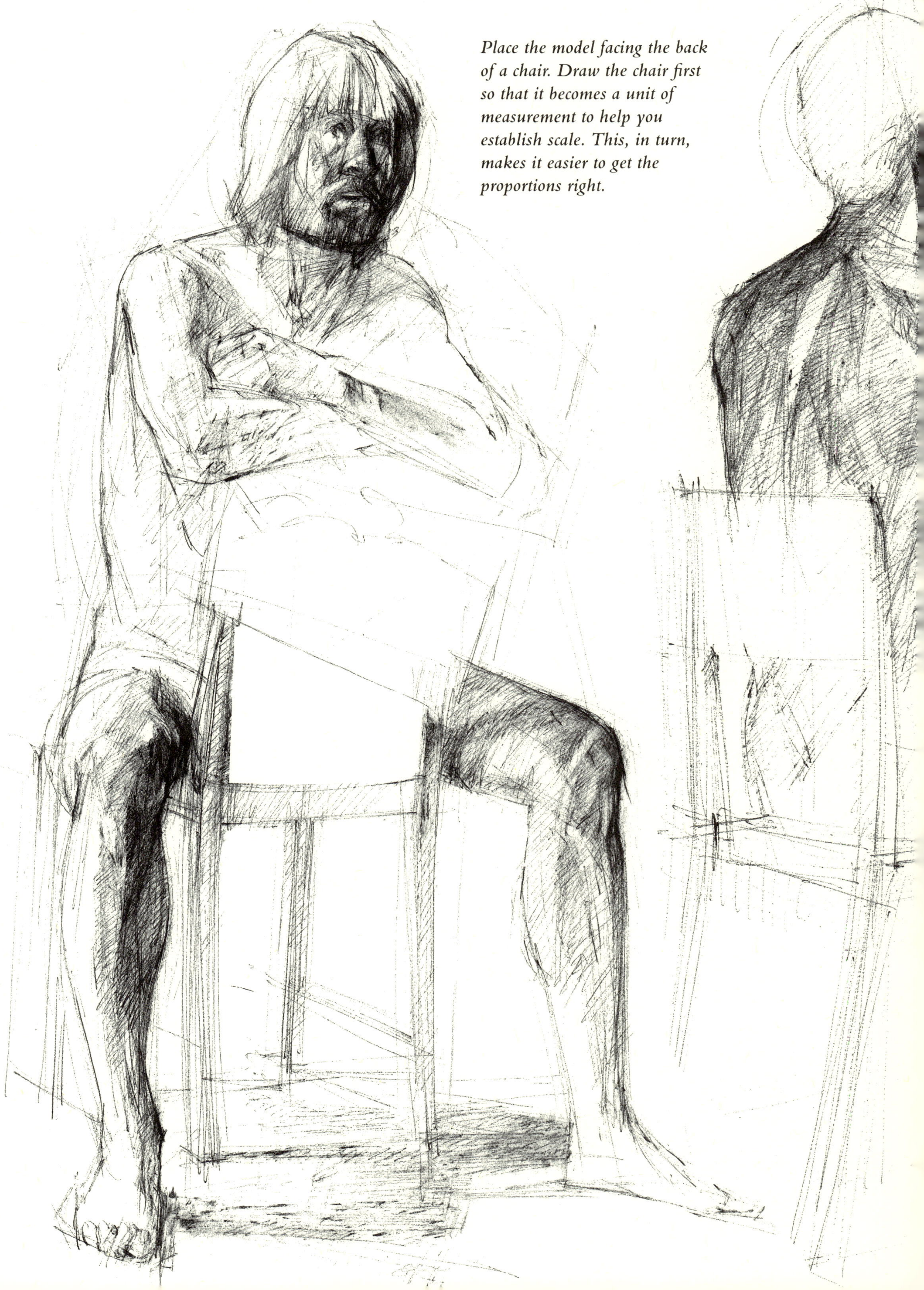

Place the model facing the back of a chair. Draw the chair first so that it becomes a unit of measurement to help you establish scale. This, in turn, makes it easier to get the proportions right.

This study of a young man's back is not distinguished by a striking division of space but it does show how important it is to map the planes.

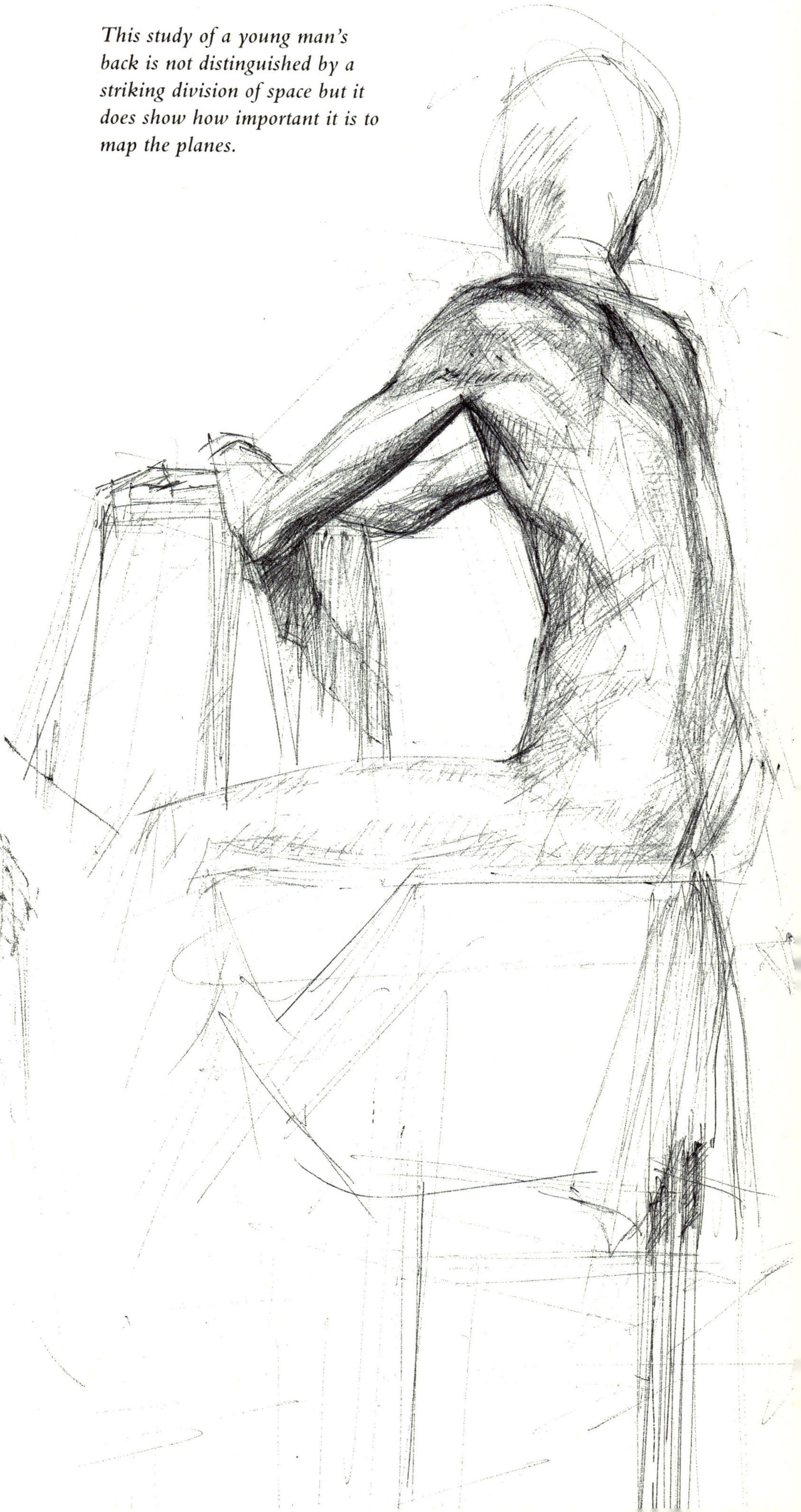

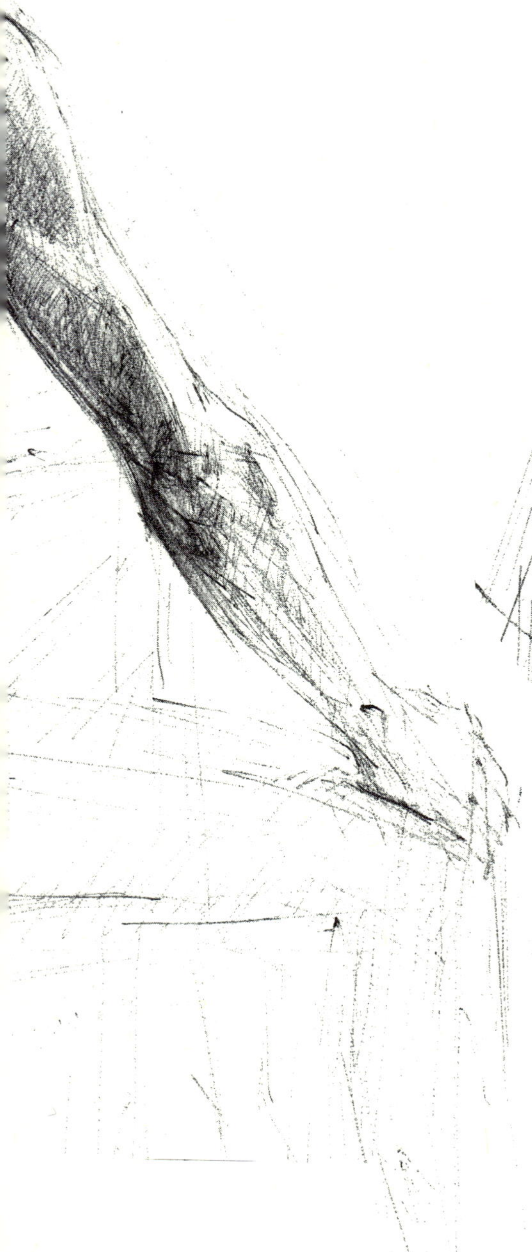

In this drawing of the back, the planes are clearly rendered while shading following the drawn line reveals the shape.

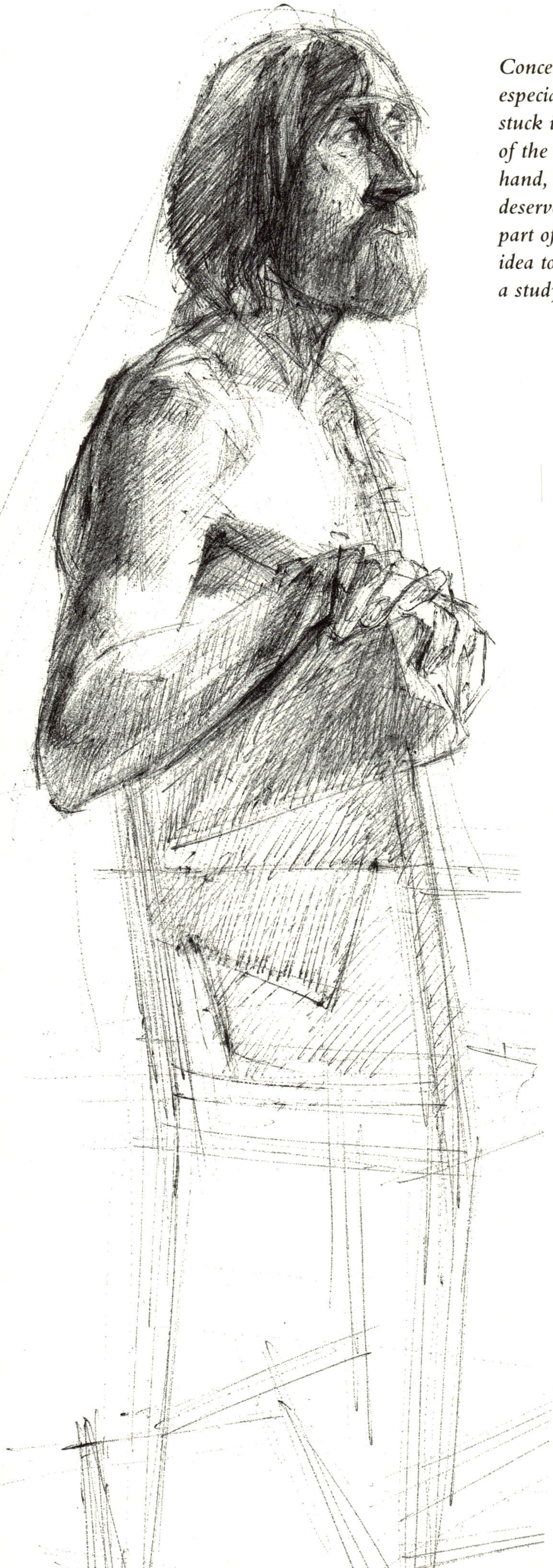

Concentrating too much on details, especially those of the head, one can get stuck in an attempt to represent the bulk of the whole body. But, on the other hand, the head is important and deserves as much attention as any other part of your drawing. So, it's a good idea to draw an occasional portrait with a study of the upper torso.

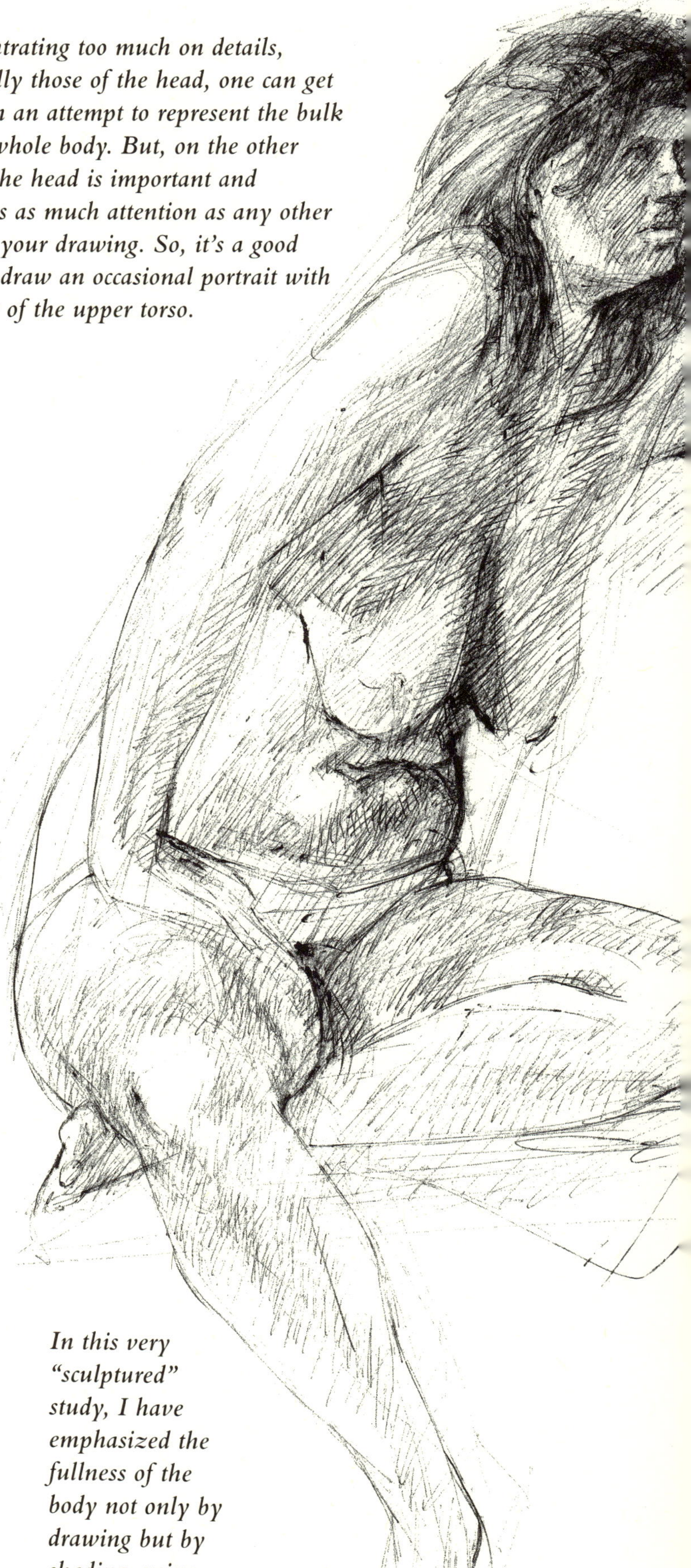

In this very "sculptured" study, I have emphasized the fullness of the body not only by drawing but by shading, using a light uniform shadowing in those areas not important to the main idea.

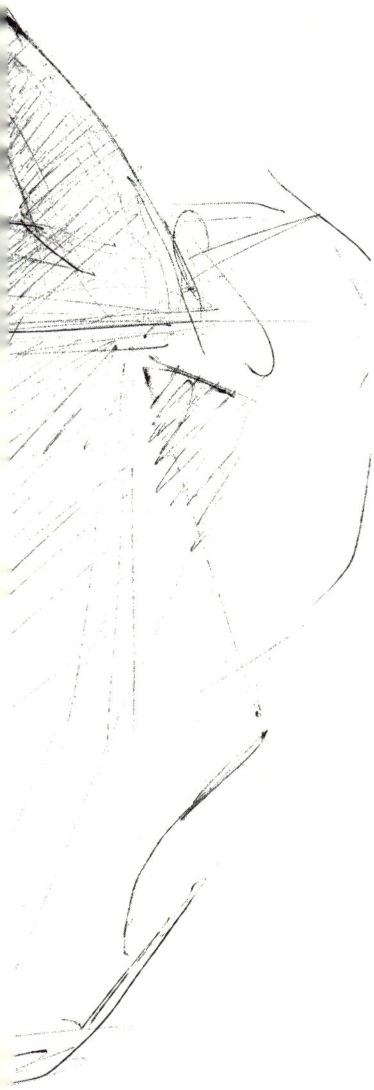

Grey cartridge paper (or any other grey drawing paper) gives us an opportunity to use white to show the highlights in a figure study. Use this effect sparingly, however, since it can very quickly become merely a mannerism empty of true expression.

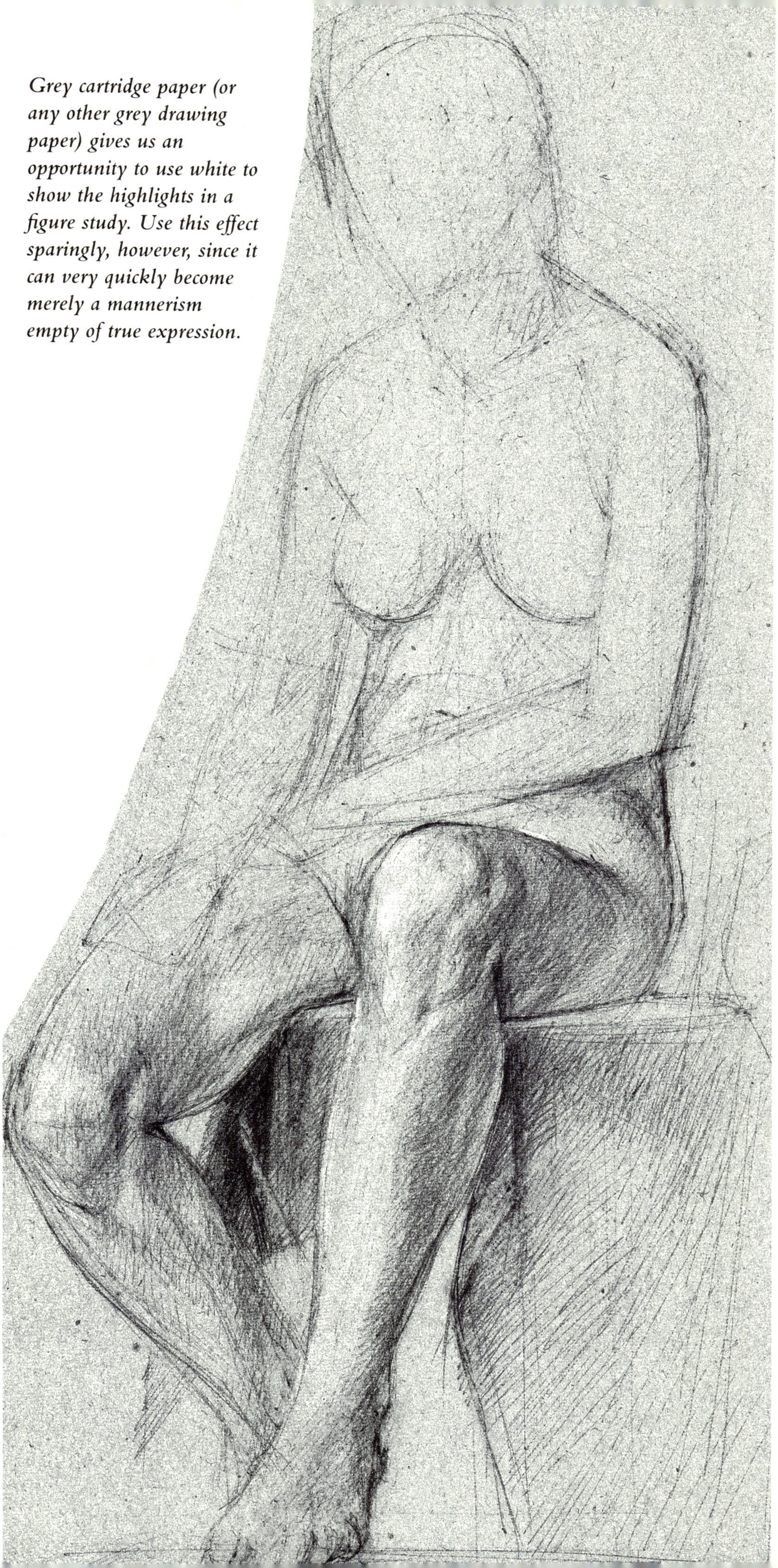

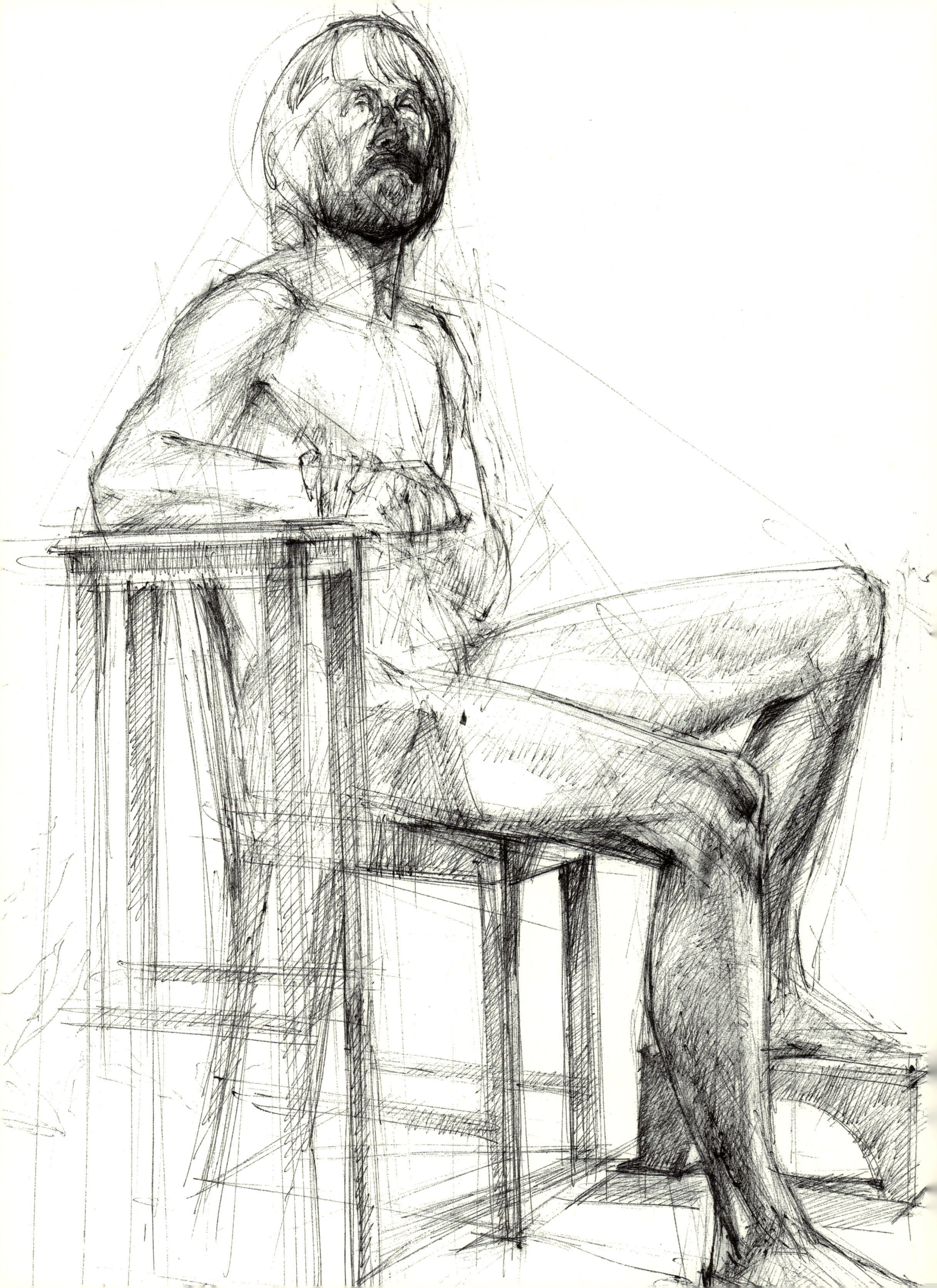

Once the model is posed, it's important to make sketches from all sides. A three-hour pose allows ample time for this. It's a good idea to make use of chairs and stools because they can prove helpful in establishing verticals and horizontals as you work on your study.

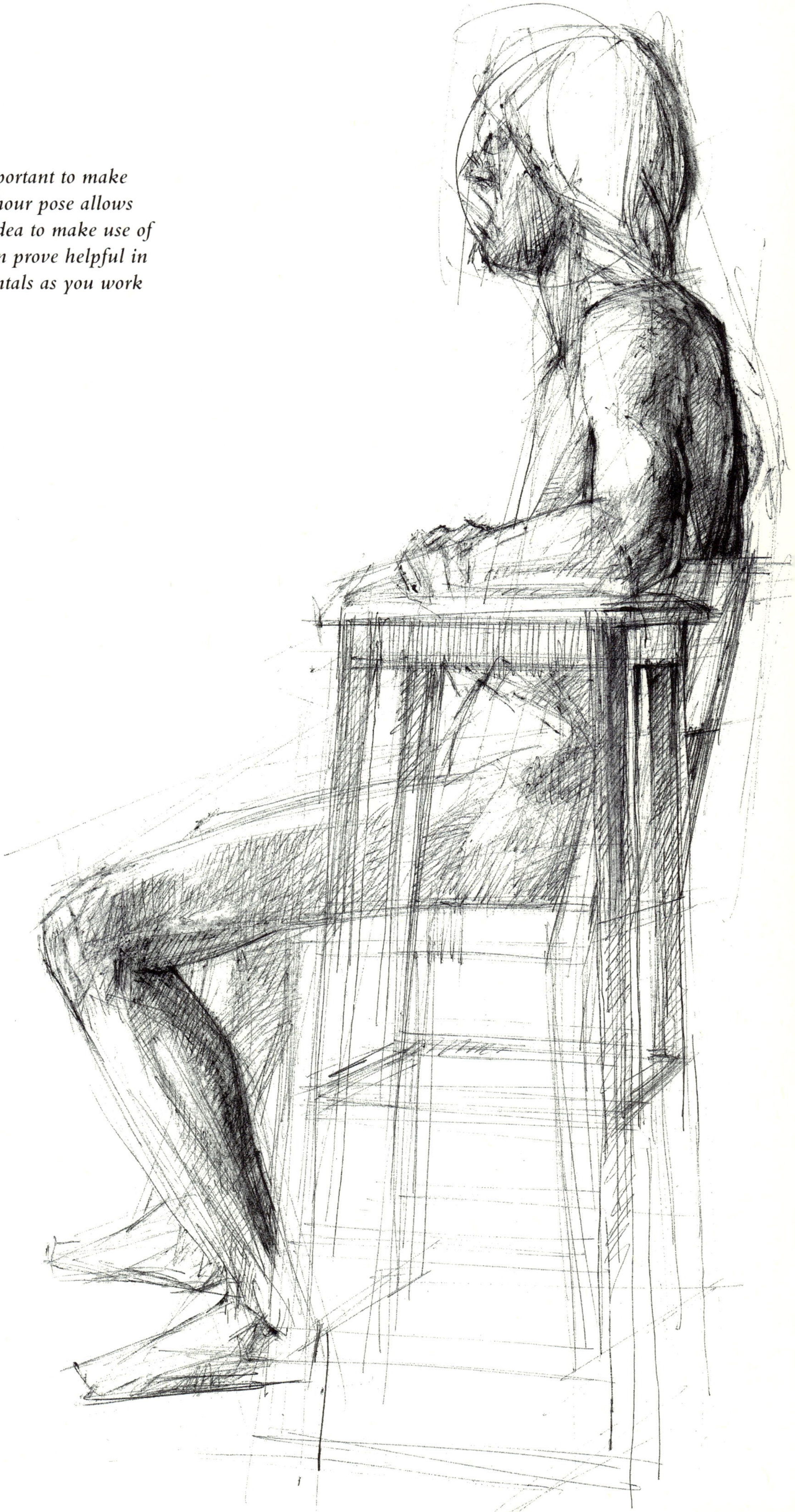

LESSON 12

People Dressed

After a thorough study of animal and human anatomy, including skulls and bone fragments as well as the nude figure, we can finally turn our attention to the clothed person.

Some rules that have served us well in solving previous problems can be just as effective here: size up the total mass of the figure you want to draw; disregard details at first; explore the volume; pay attention to the spaces; and tighten up your drawing of the figure from the inside.

Fabrics now become important. We need to study their characteristics and how folds and creases develop as a result of the way fabrics are draped. As you work, you will realize that "drape studies" can be as important as "figure studies." Pin a piece of cloth to the wall. Let the larger part of it fall freely. Observe the way it drapes, pay attention to the line of its folds, then render it carefully in large format. Select a chair at home and hang a coat on it (see page 122). Sketch the chair in the way demonstrated earlier and then turn your attention to the coat and note how its material has arranged itself as a consequence of the way it was hung. Try to capture the total image and, before you continue your sketch, note how the weight of the material determines how it will hang. How you succeed in capturing the feel of the material will depend in large part on how you handle shading and cast shadows. Artists of the last century could indicate whether the portrayed person was wearing a linen or a woolen shirt solely by their skillful rendering of these same two elements.

Mastery of drawing the clothed person does not come easily. You should repeat exercises similar to the ones outlined here as a regular part of your future drawing activities. Also, spend some time working with the drape studies (see pages 120 through 122) before you attempt drawing the clothed figure.

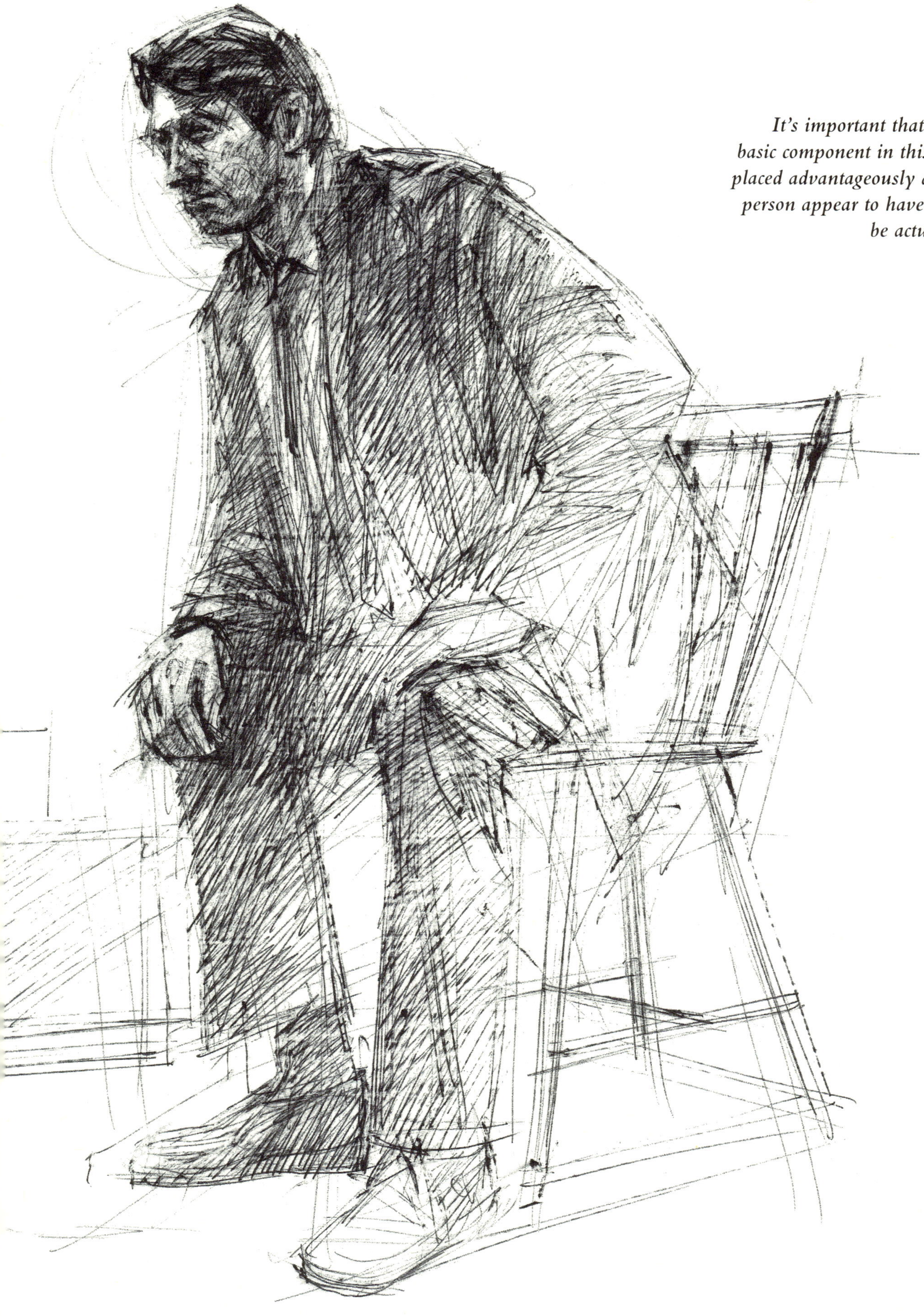

It's important that the chair, a basic component in this picture, be placed advantageously and that the person appear to have weight and be actually sitting.

To project the idea of real fabric, one must practise rendering its form and texture. To create the best circumstances for this, hang a sheet on the wall, illuminate with artificial light (don't use sunlight) and arrange the material so that it falls in an interesting way. Study it carefully, paying attention to the way it drapes and, using a ball-point pen or India ink, attempt to transfer what you see onto paper in large format.

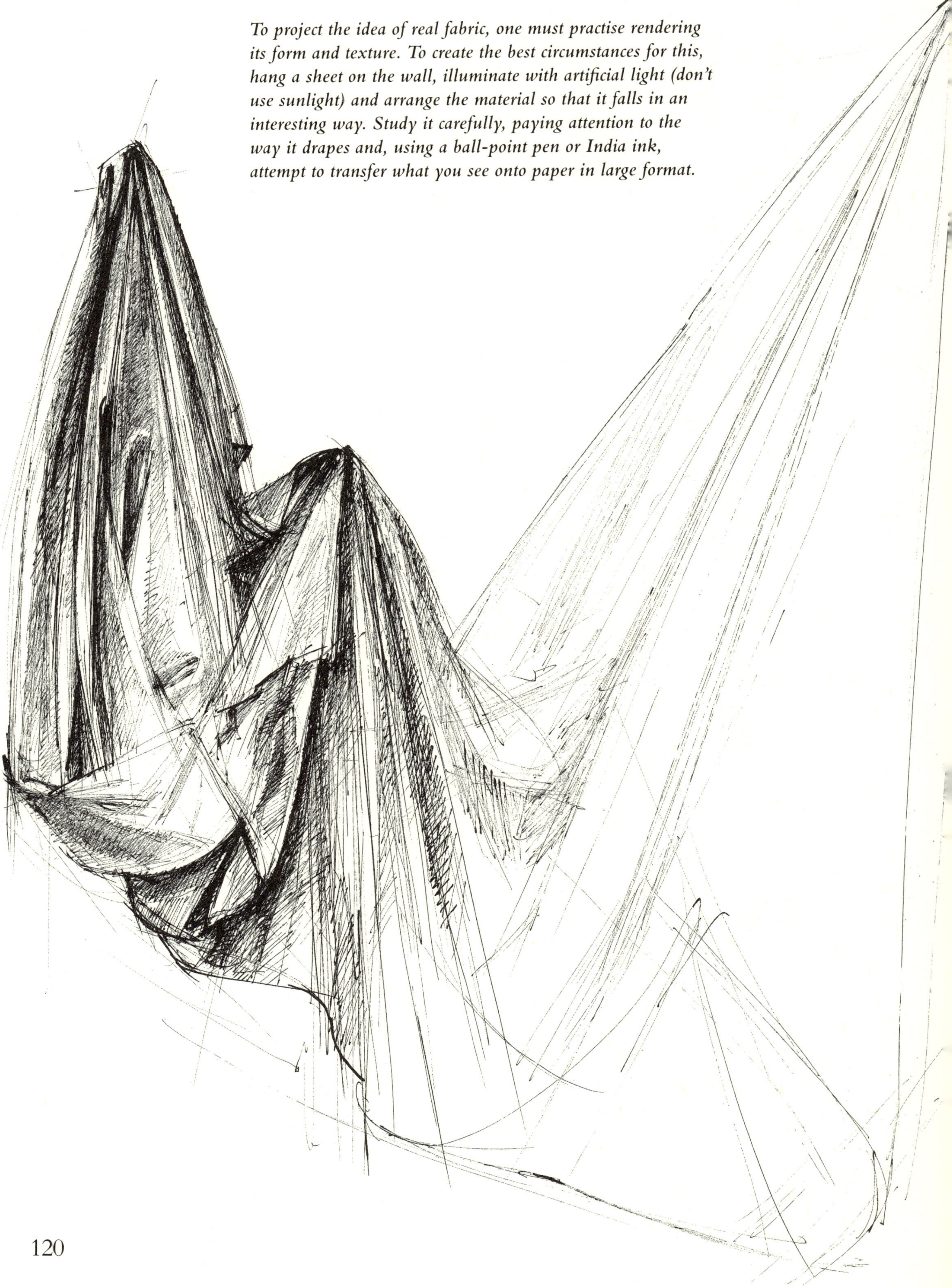

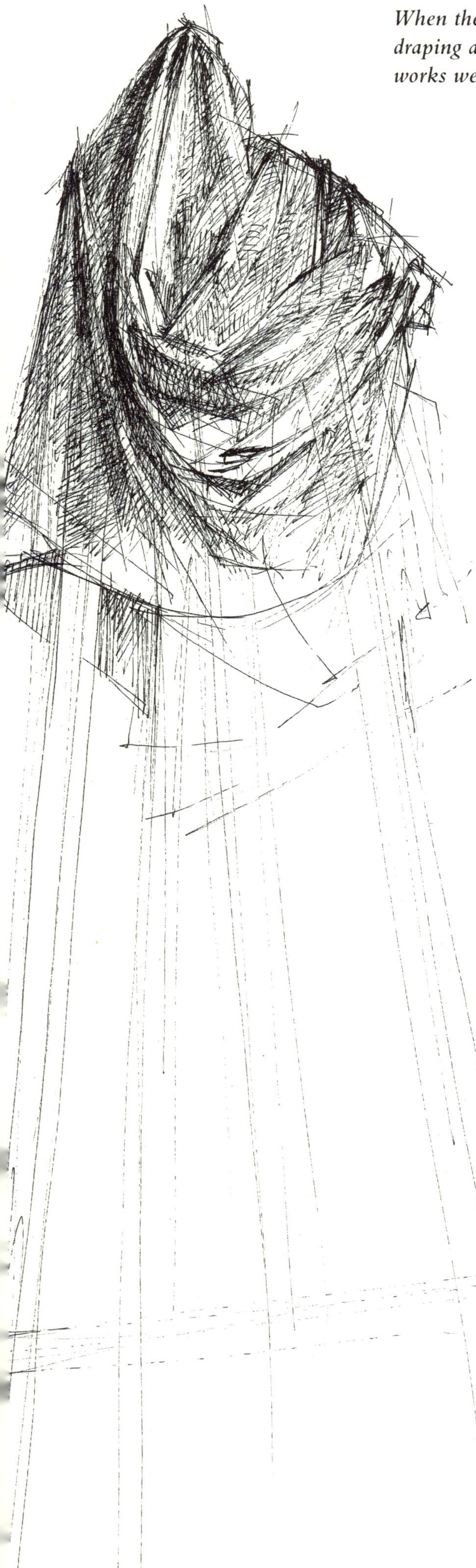

When there is not much wall space, draping a sheet over a studio easel works well.

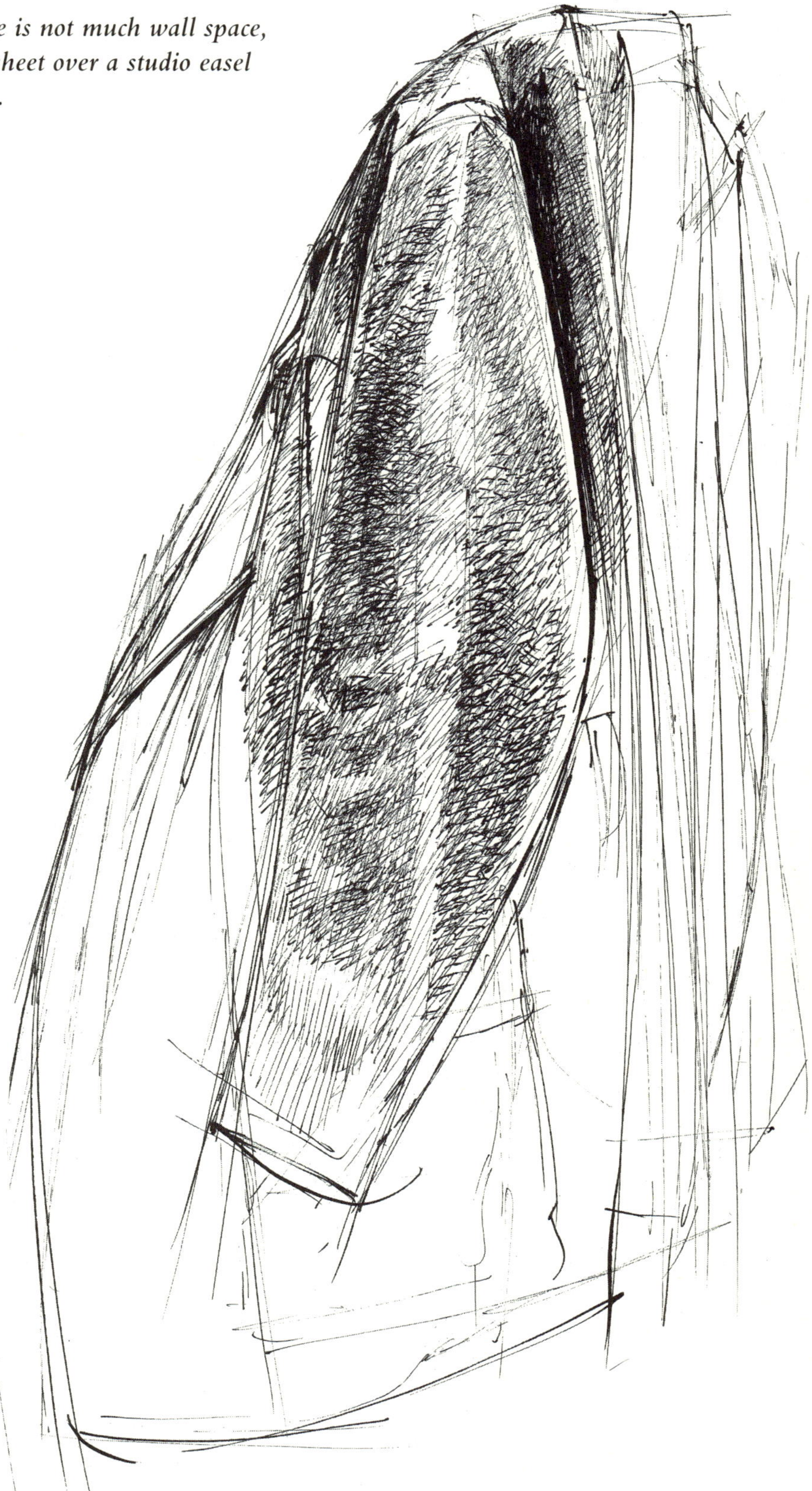

Hang a wool coat over a chair. Notice how the heavier material falls in quite a different way from the sheet's much lighter cotton material. The cut of the coat dictates the final form, while the creases reflect daily use.

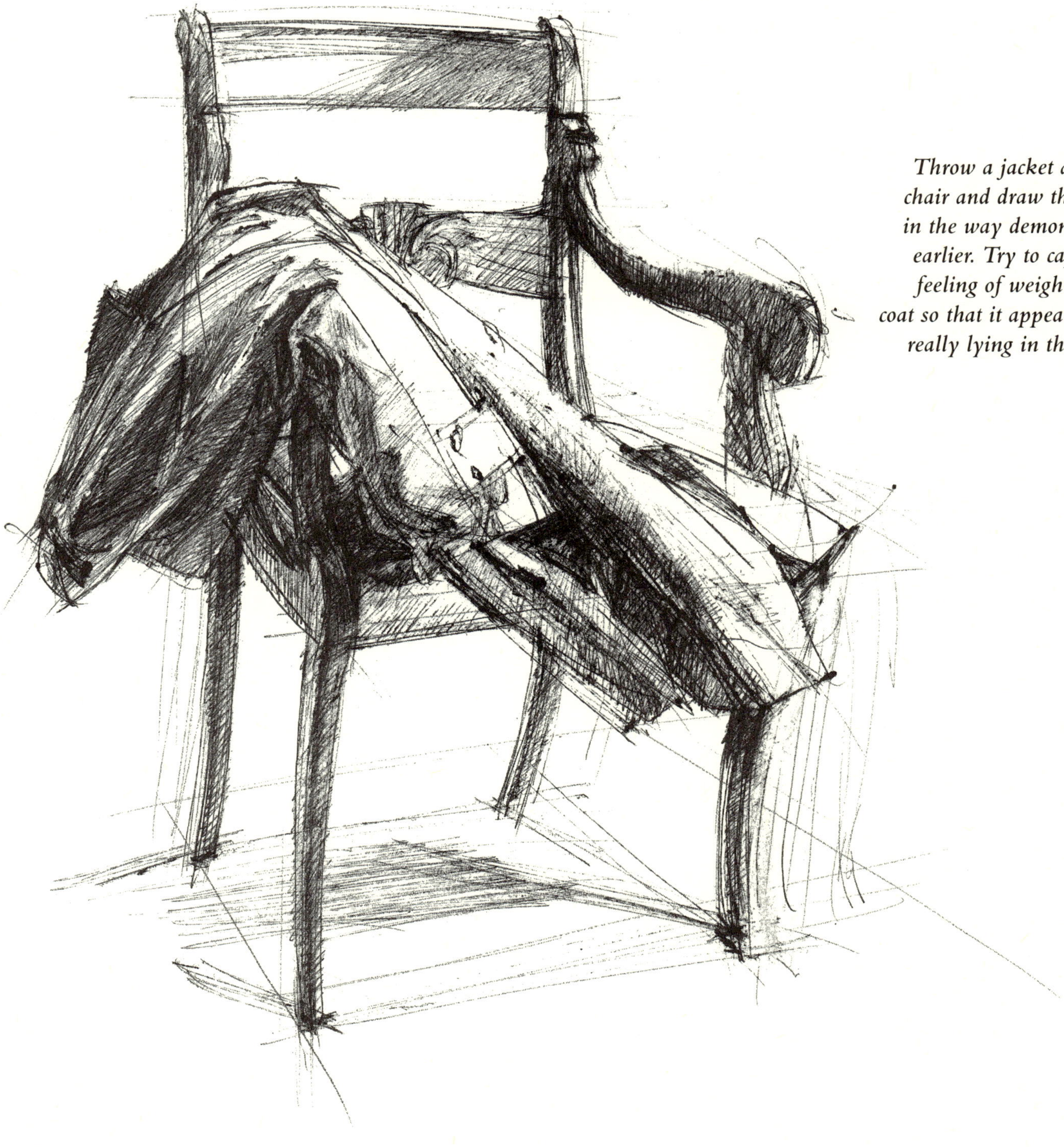

Throw a jacket across a chair and draw the chair in the way demonstrated earlier. Try to capture a feeling of weight in the coat so that it appears to be really lying in the chair.

Now that we have spent considerable time working with drapery, let's turn to the dressed model. Try to get a member of your family to sit for you and then put to use those principles demonstrated in the section on working with the figure.

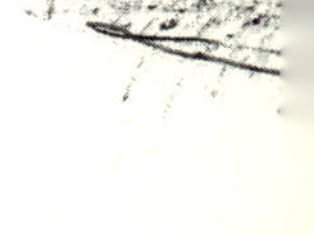

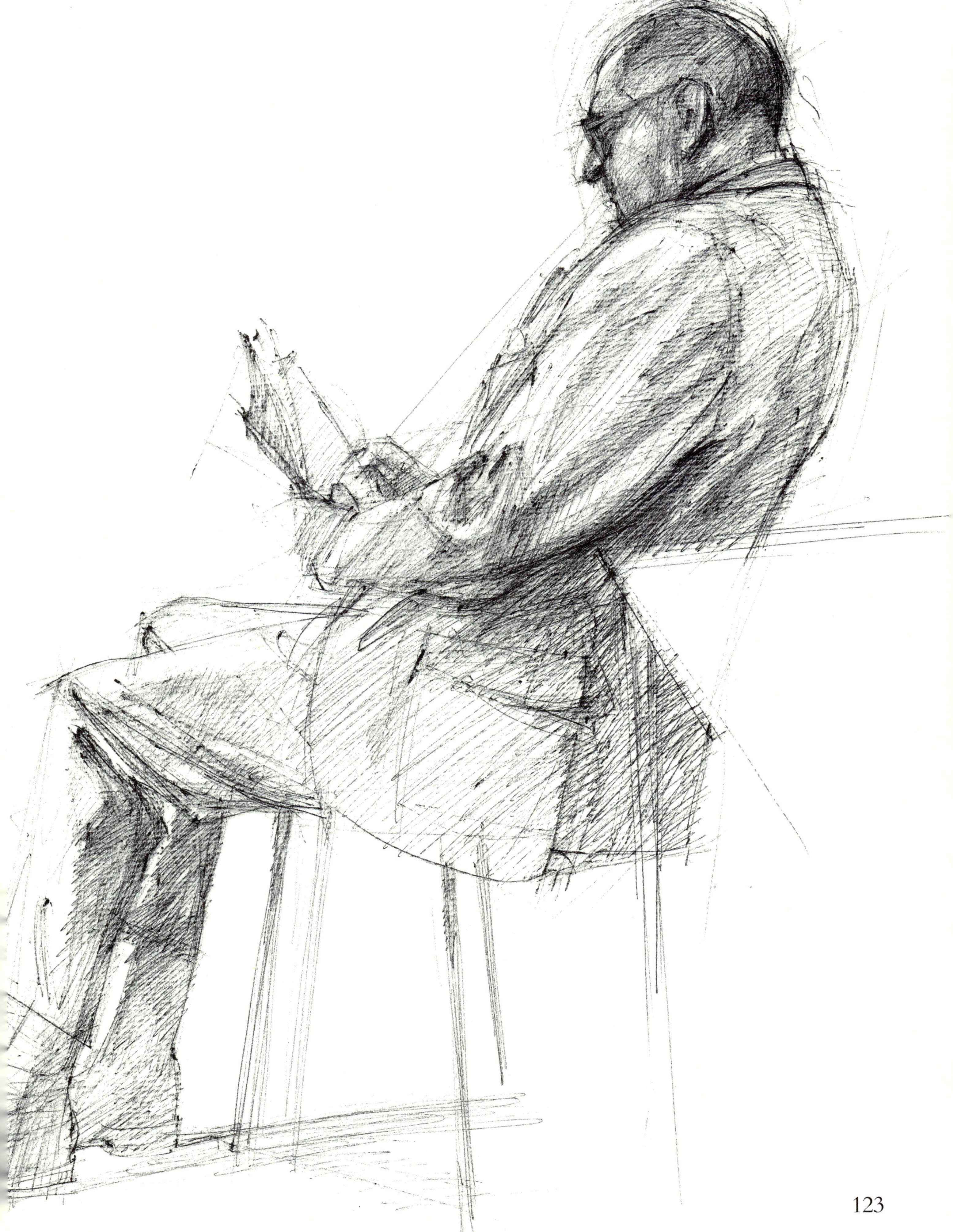

Sketch the model in different poses, letting him or her help decide on the various positions. This creates a warm relationship and more natural poses.

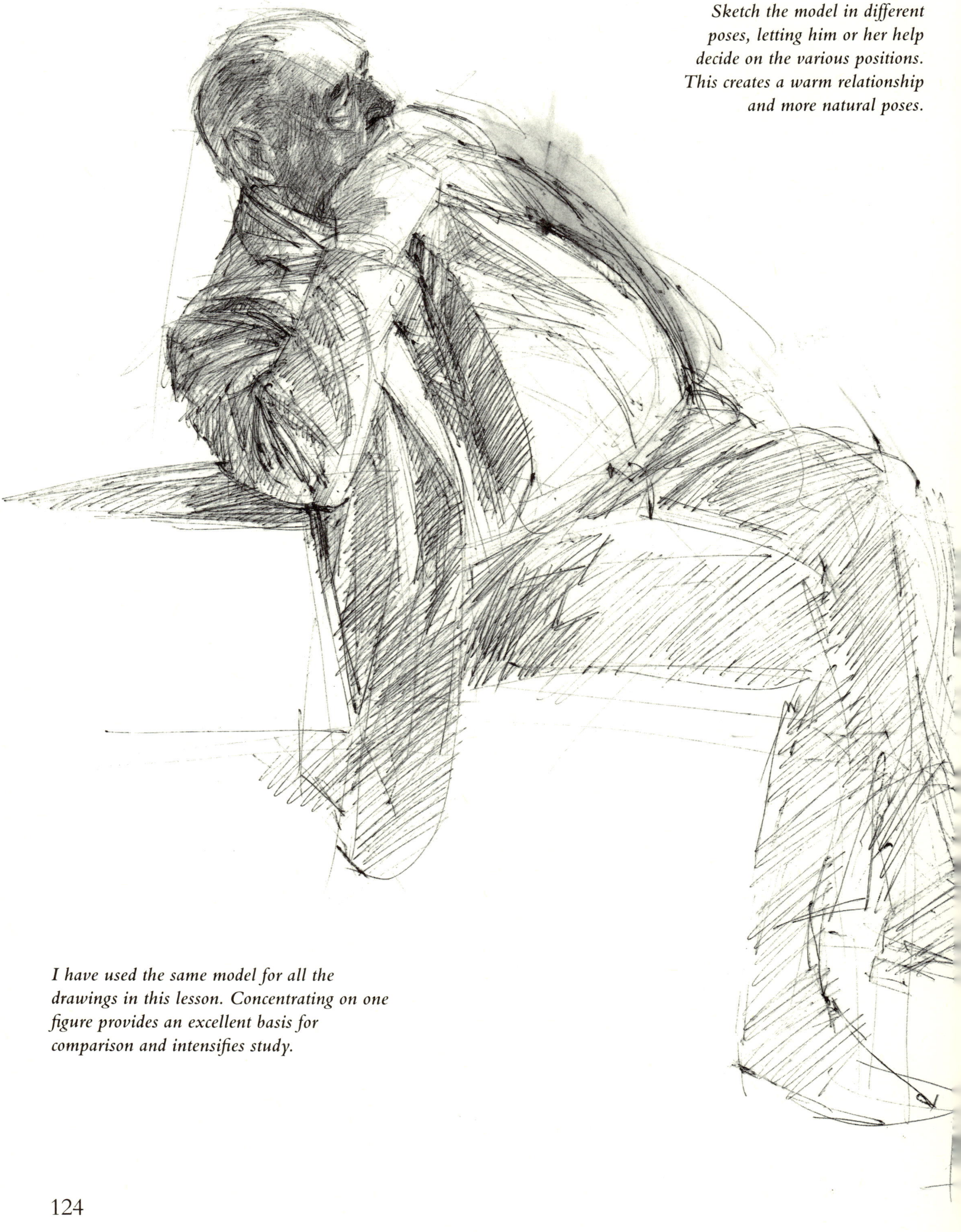

I have used the same model for all the drawings in this lesson. Concentrating on one figure provides an excellent basis for comparison and intensifies study.

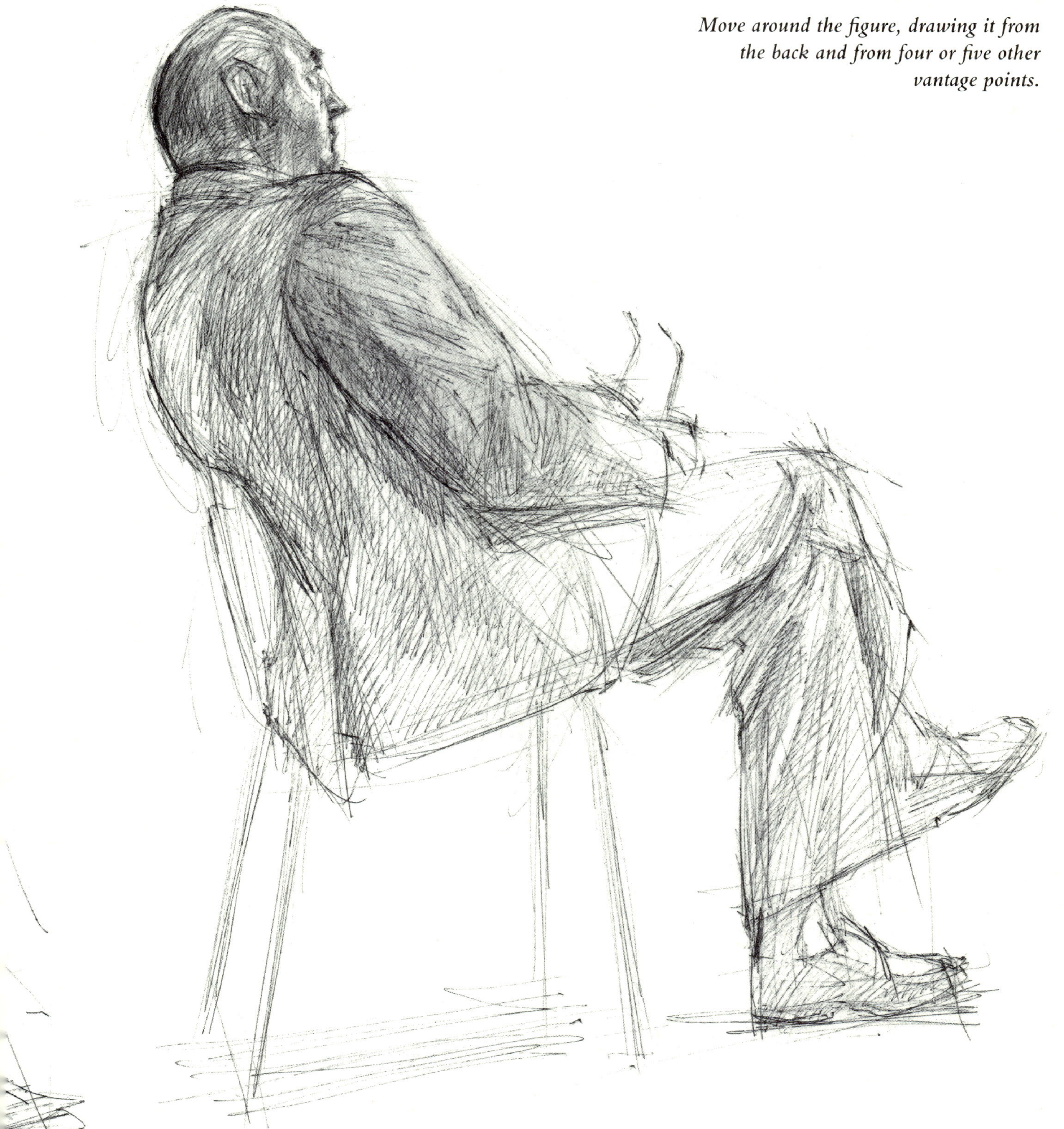

Move around the figure, drawing it from the back and from four or five other vantage points.

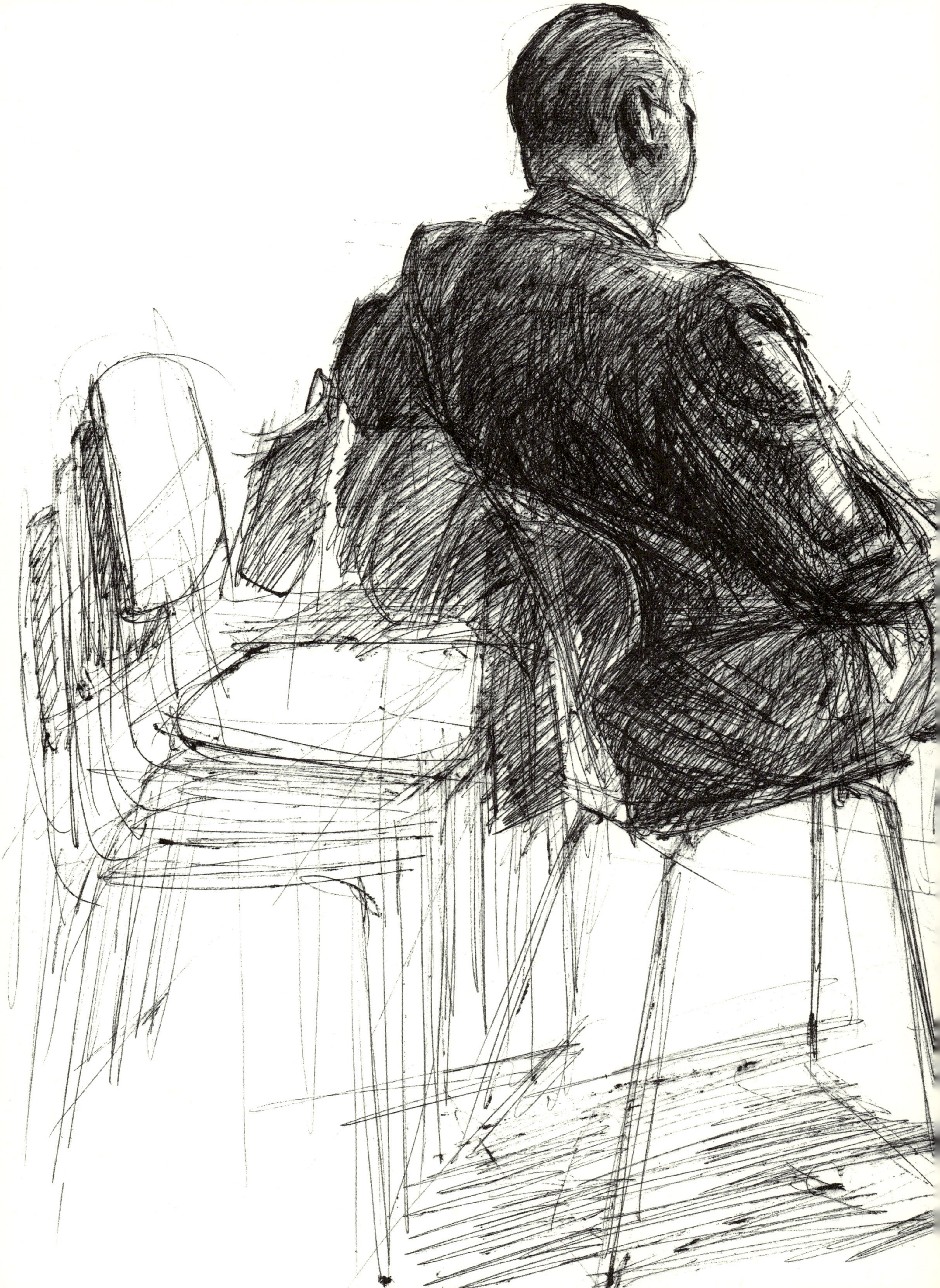

After rendering the figure from several sides, it's time to include the room in a drawing. It's not necessary to include the actual room in which the model sits but only to suggest a feeling of occupied space. Here some stacked chairs and one chair placed further back does the trick.

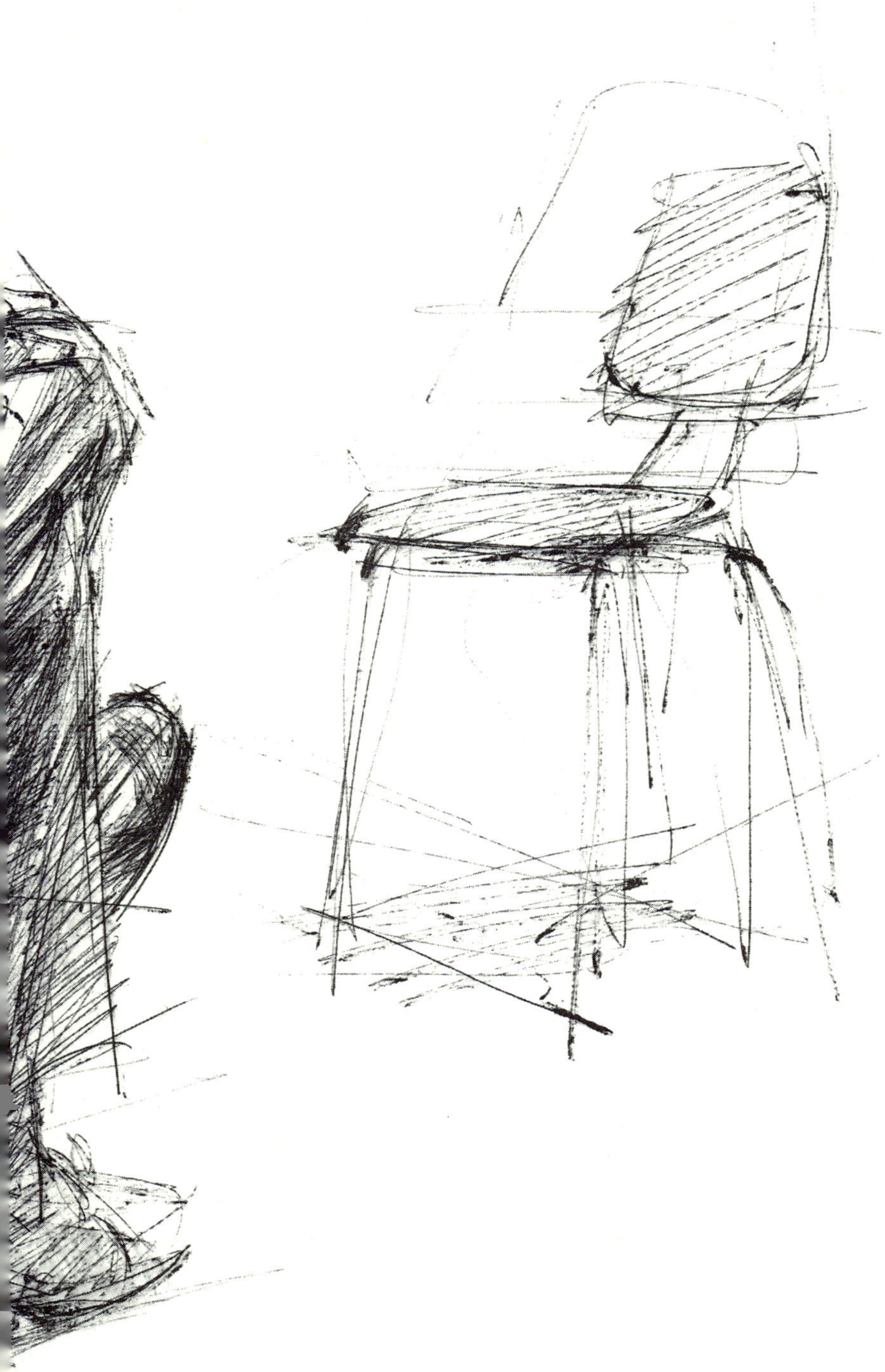

LESSON 13

Arms and Hands, Legs and Feet

The hands are our most important working tools. Besides employing them to help with physical tasks, we also use the hands to express emotion. It's natural for some people to depict both sorrow and contempt with their hands. Enriching spoken language by gesture is closely connected with the emotional nature of a people—we might think of a certain friend, for instance, as "speaking" as much with his hands as with his mouth. The hands become a sort of antenna by which to communicate literally or figuratively. The hands also are used symbolically in religious rituals, particularly those concerning prayer and the bestowing of a blessing.

Throughout the centuries, the appearance of a person's hands has been thought to indicate some special characteristic about that individual. While we may doubt the credibility of such a belief, we have to admit that one person's hands can be very different from another's. We speak of sensitive, delicate hands, for instance, as opposed to rough, coarse hands. Observation indicates that, more often than not, short, compact hands complement a stocky human form while the hands of a slender person often tend to appear more elongated and fragile.

Even though the hands are strong enough to function as gripping tools, they are so delicately put together that they are difficult to draw. I've found that students can become so involved in trying to master the drawing of a hand that they lose their sense of proportion. The result is that the hands become too large or too small in relation to the figure. This is easy to remedy by drawing hands and feet simultaneously with the arms and legs whenever possible. Even in your early sketches, keep checking the size of both hands and feet while constantly evaluating the scale of the various parts of the body to the whole. And, of course, as I've pointed out many times, don't start working on details and shading too soon. As the well-known Danish painter, Harald Giersing, once said: "Those who love details will never experience wholeness!"

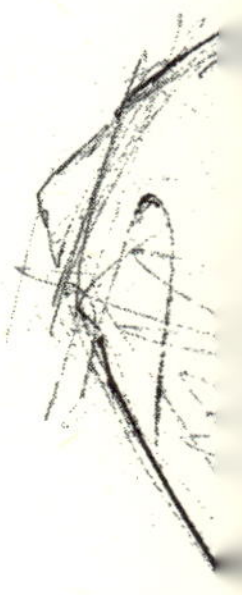

In these two studies of a model, it's important to notice how the hands are rhythmically connected to the arms forming a natural unit.

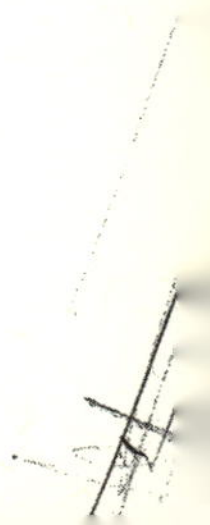

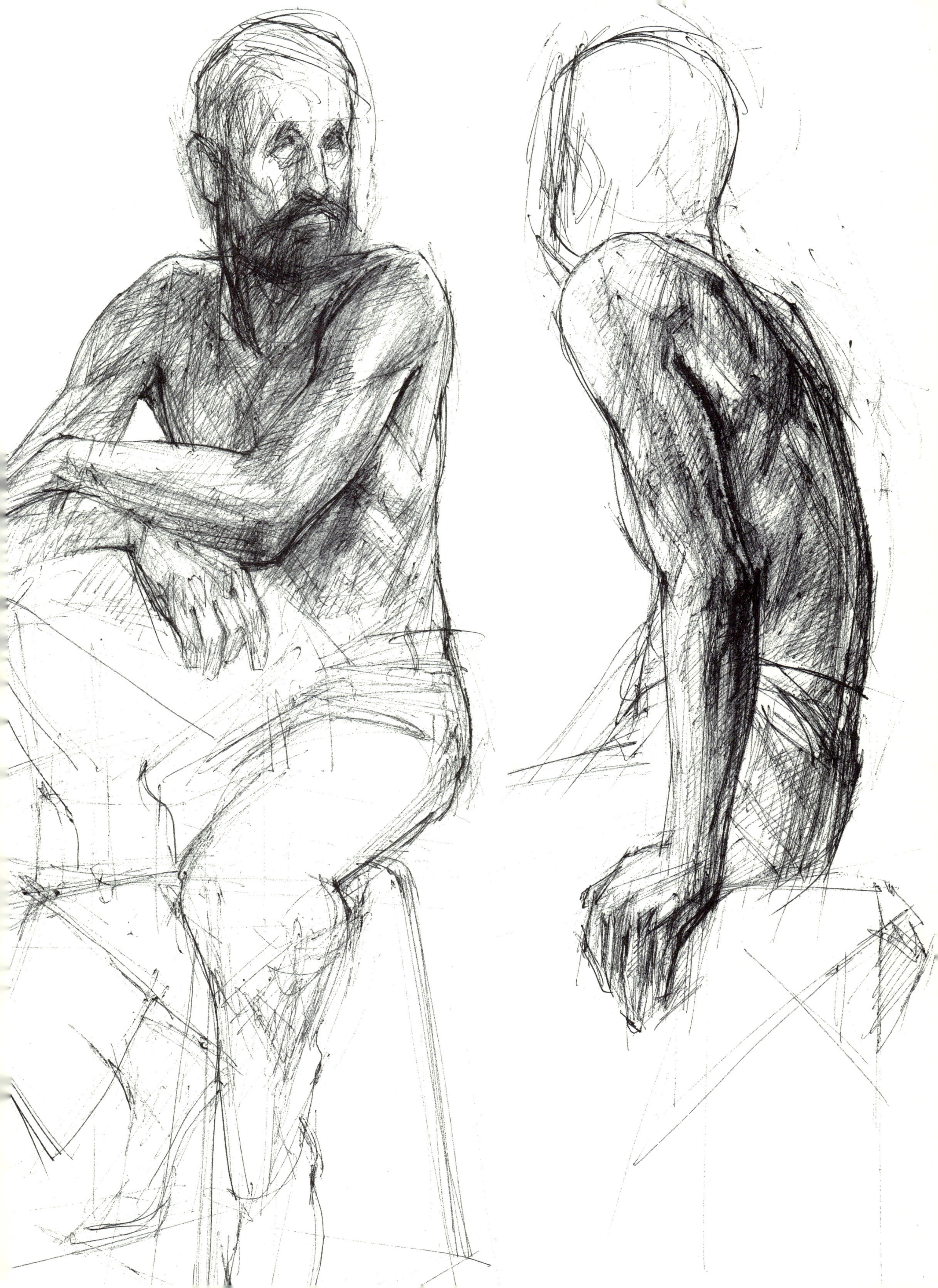

Don't feel you always have to draw hands and feet with arms and legs, although it's a good idea much of the time. It also pays to practise drawing your own left or right hand. Locate a steady light source to illuminate the hand and try drawing it in different positions.

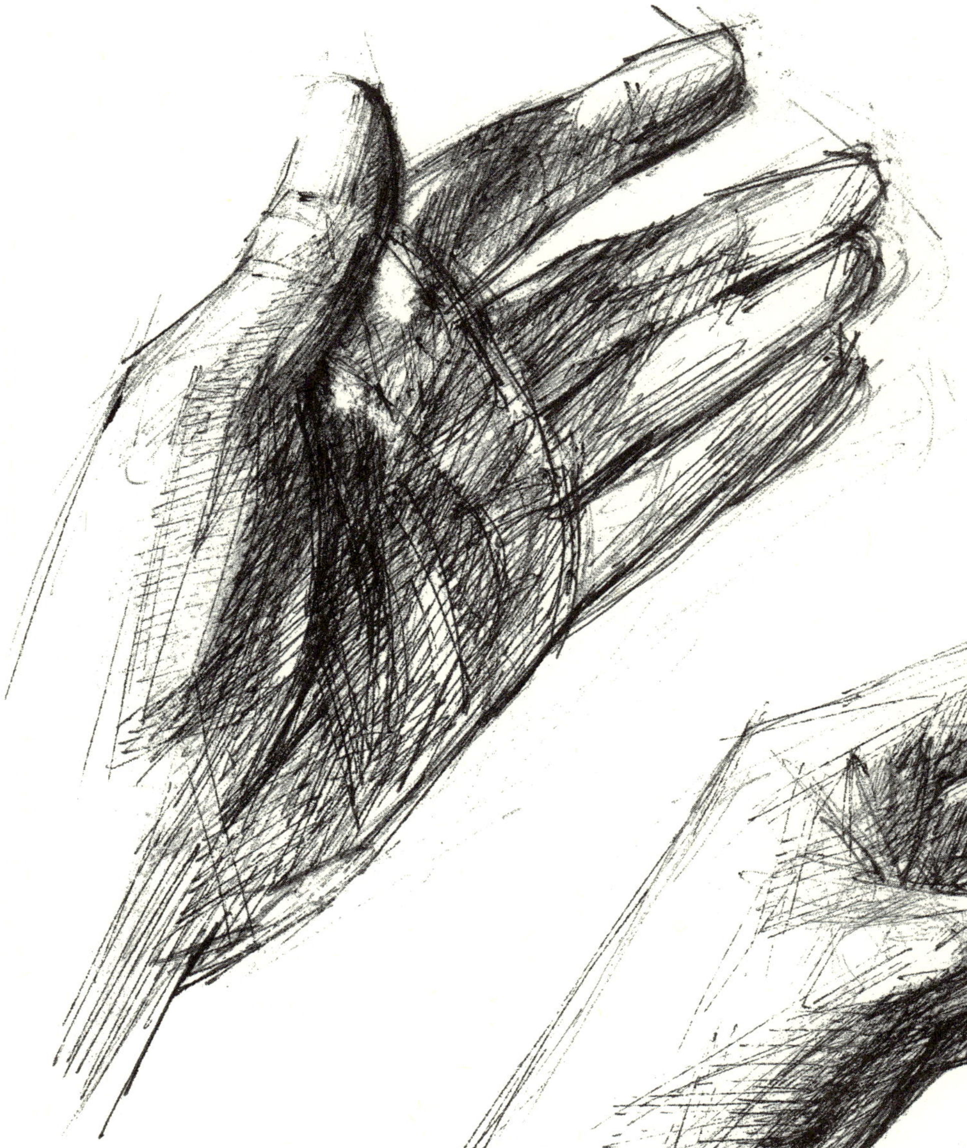

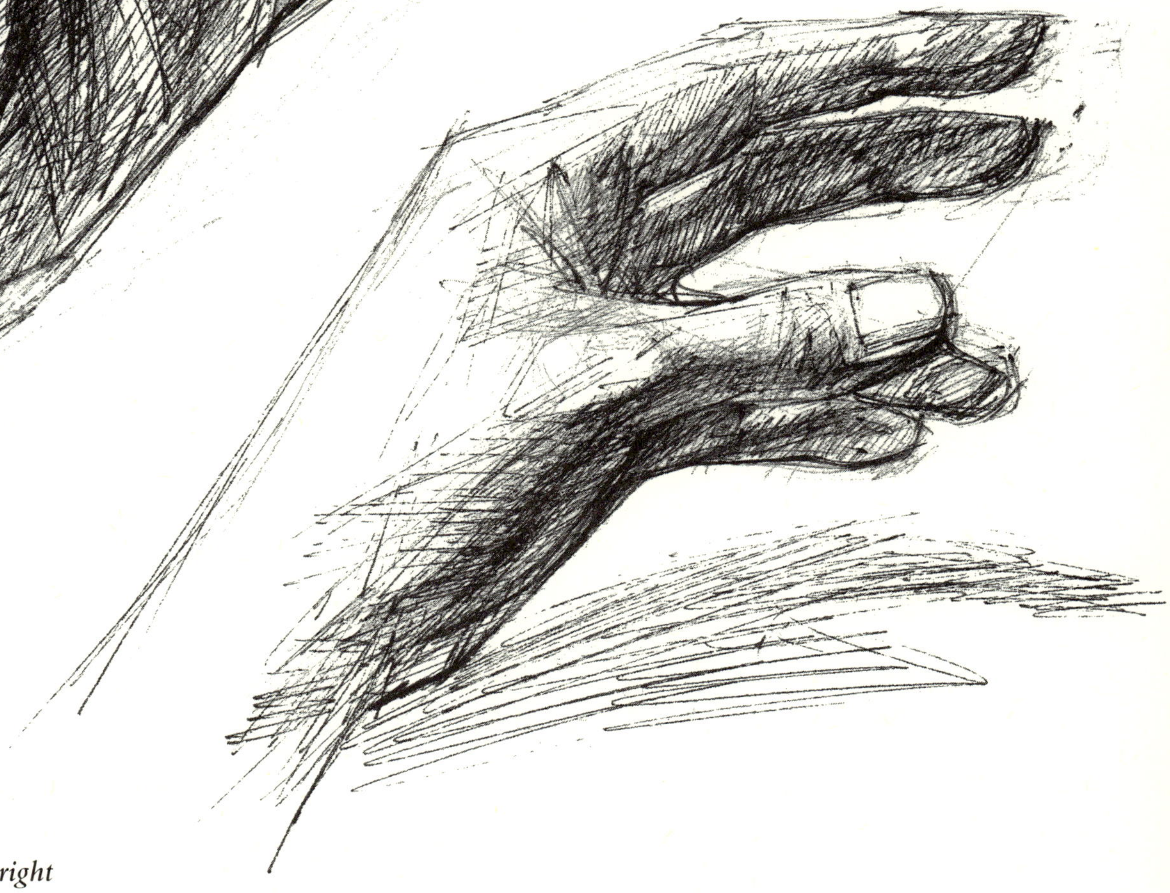

It's well to remember right from the start that the planes of the hand must form an organic whole. Make use of light and shadow to help you.

Draw different-sized hands both open and closed.

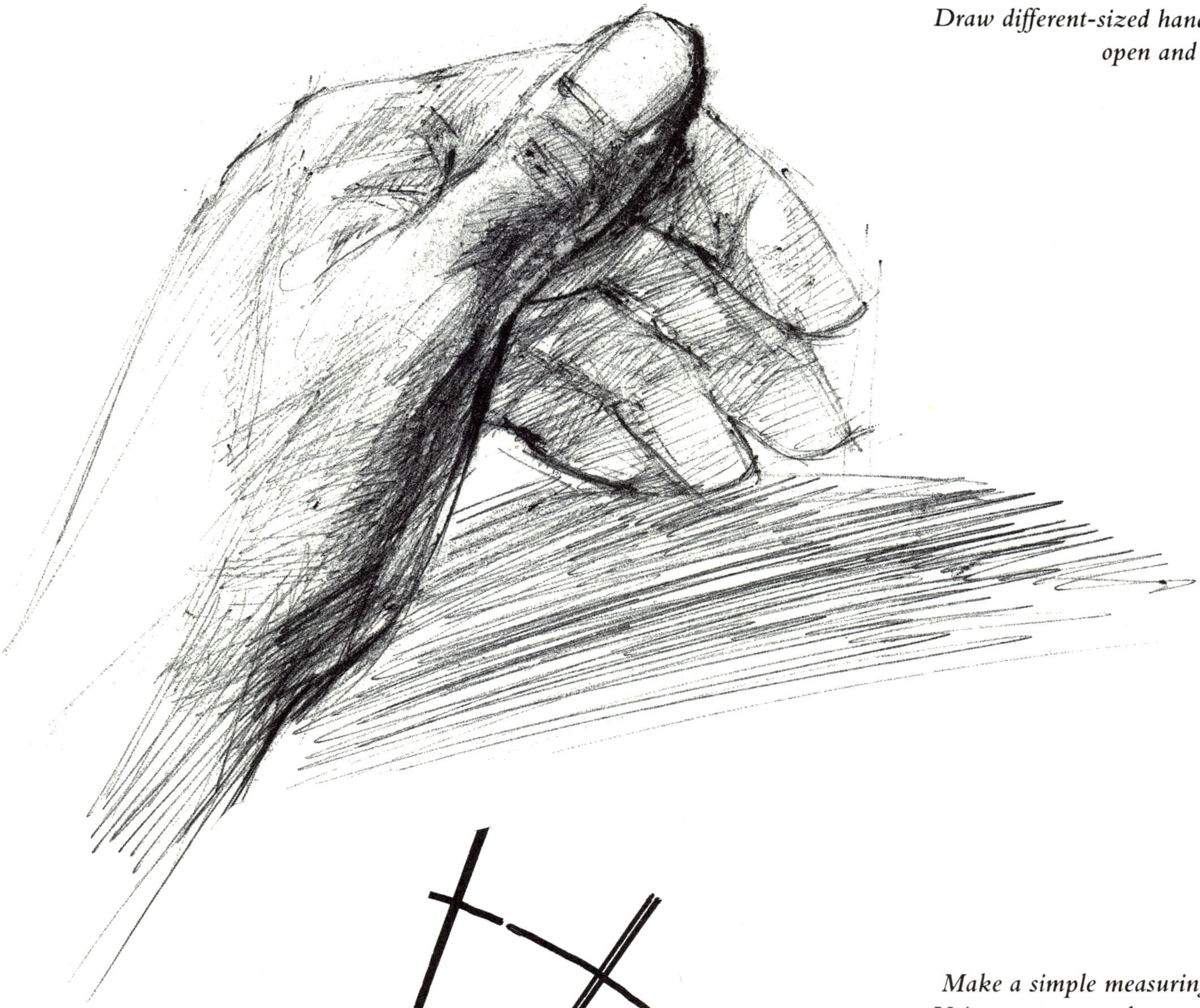

Make a simple measuring unit. Using a compass place one point where you imagine the wrist to be and draw two circles. The first circle will represent the maximum spread of the palm of the hand, the second indicates the arc made by the fingertips. Measure the length of each finger and then draw it. This will give you a better feeling about the proportions of the hand as related to the wrist.

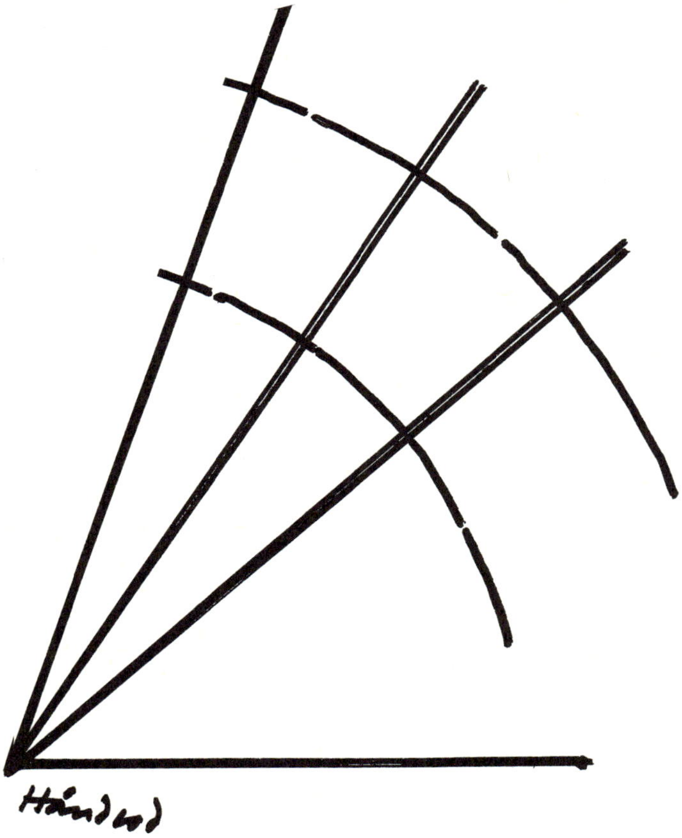

Even when the emphasis is on the study of clothes, it's still necessary to draw the hands carefully to make them an integral part of the total image.

In a study drawing, no one area is given first or second priority. Everything must be of equal importance. However, certain areas can be drawn in detail and others only indicated, as long as everything contributes to the unity of the composition.

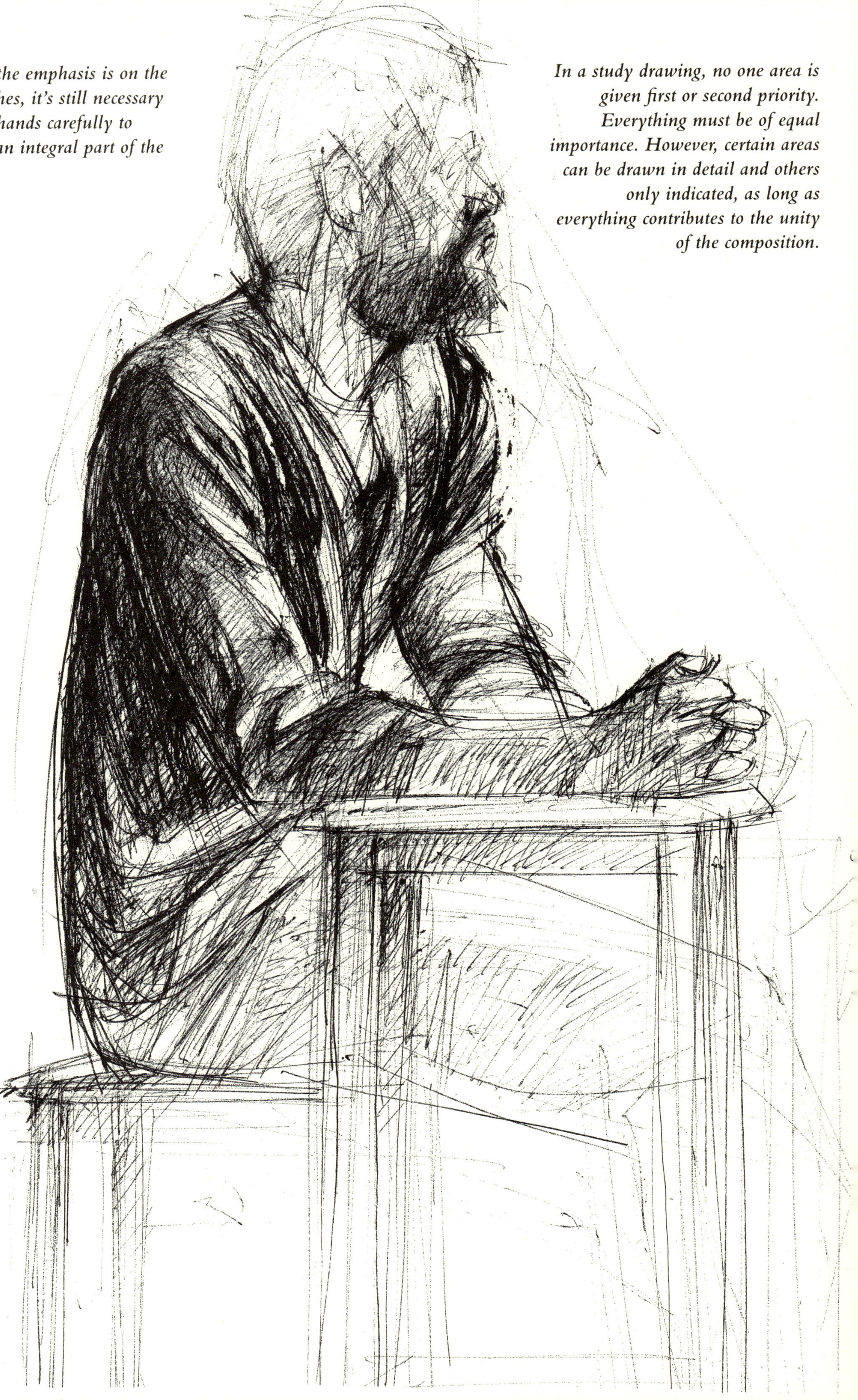

Because of my interest in this model's frail and nervous hands, I have concentrated mostly on them. But I have not neglected the arms, legs and body, knowing that it is the unity of the drawing that is visually satisfying and makes you want to take a second look.

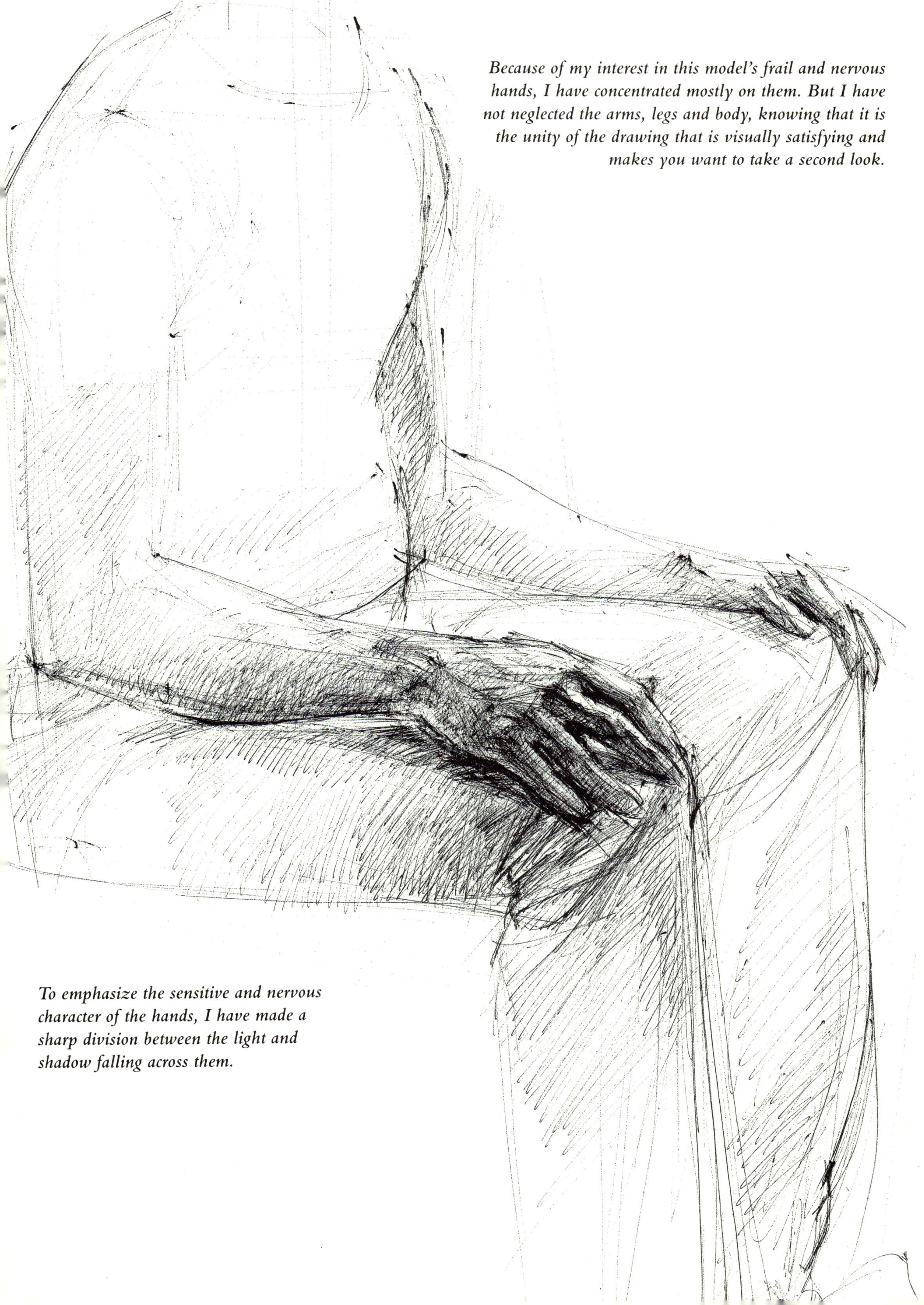

To emphasize the sensitive and nervous character of the hands, I have made a sharp division between the light and shadow falling across them.

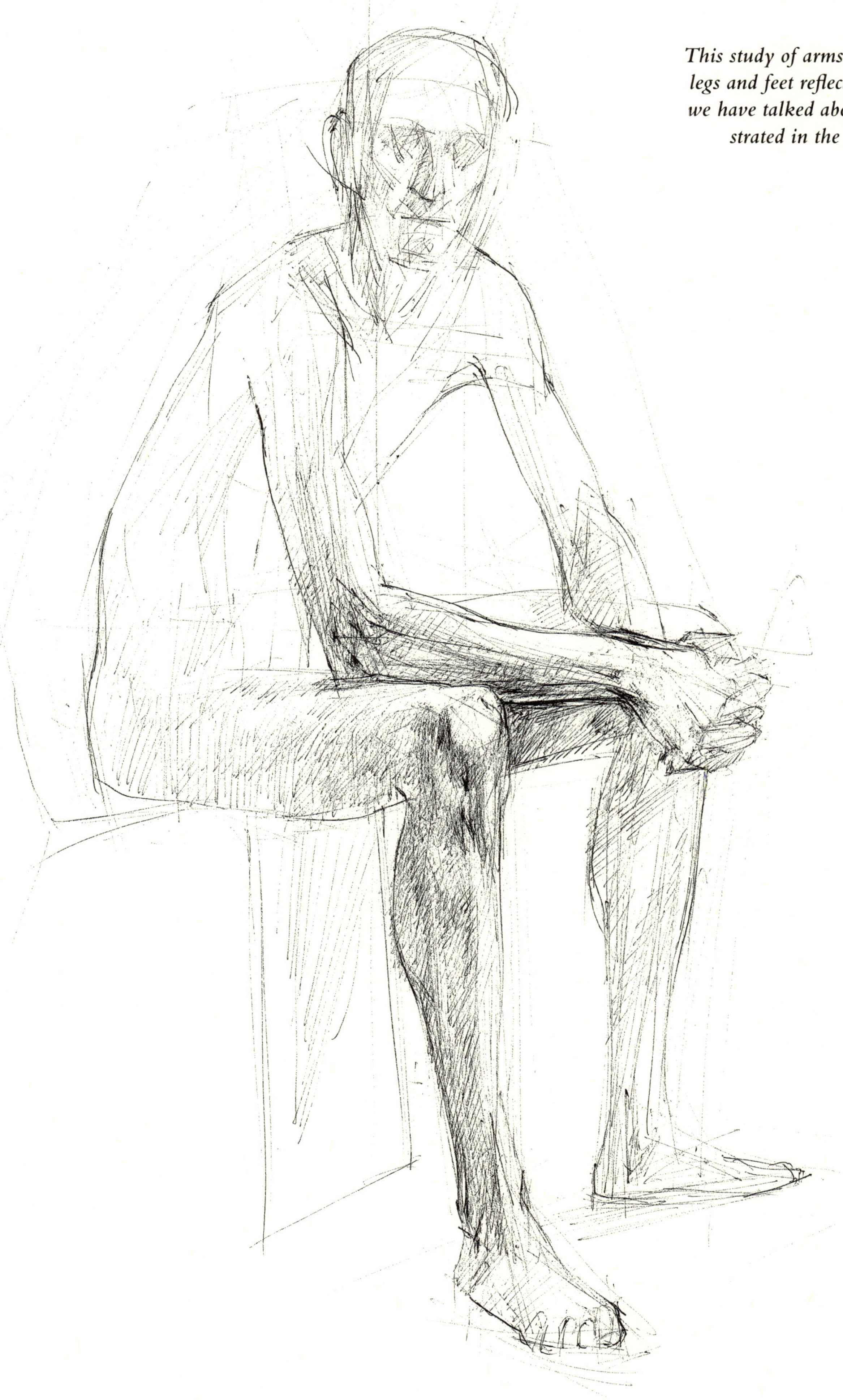

This study of arms and hands and legs and feet reflects the principles we have talked about and demonstrated in the previous pages.

When looking at the drawn clothed figure one must get the impression that there is a body underneath the clothes. This is especially true of the hands, legs and feet. They cannot appear to be "stuck on" to the shirtsleeve or the pant leg, but must be seen as natural extensions of the body.

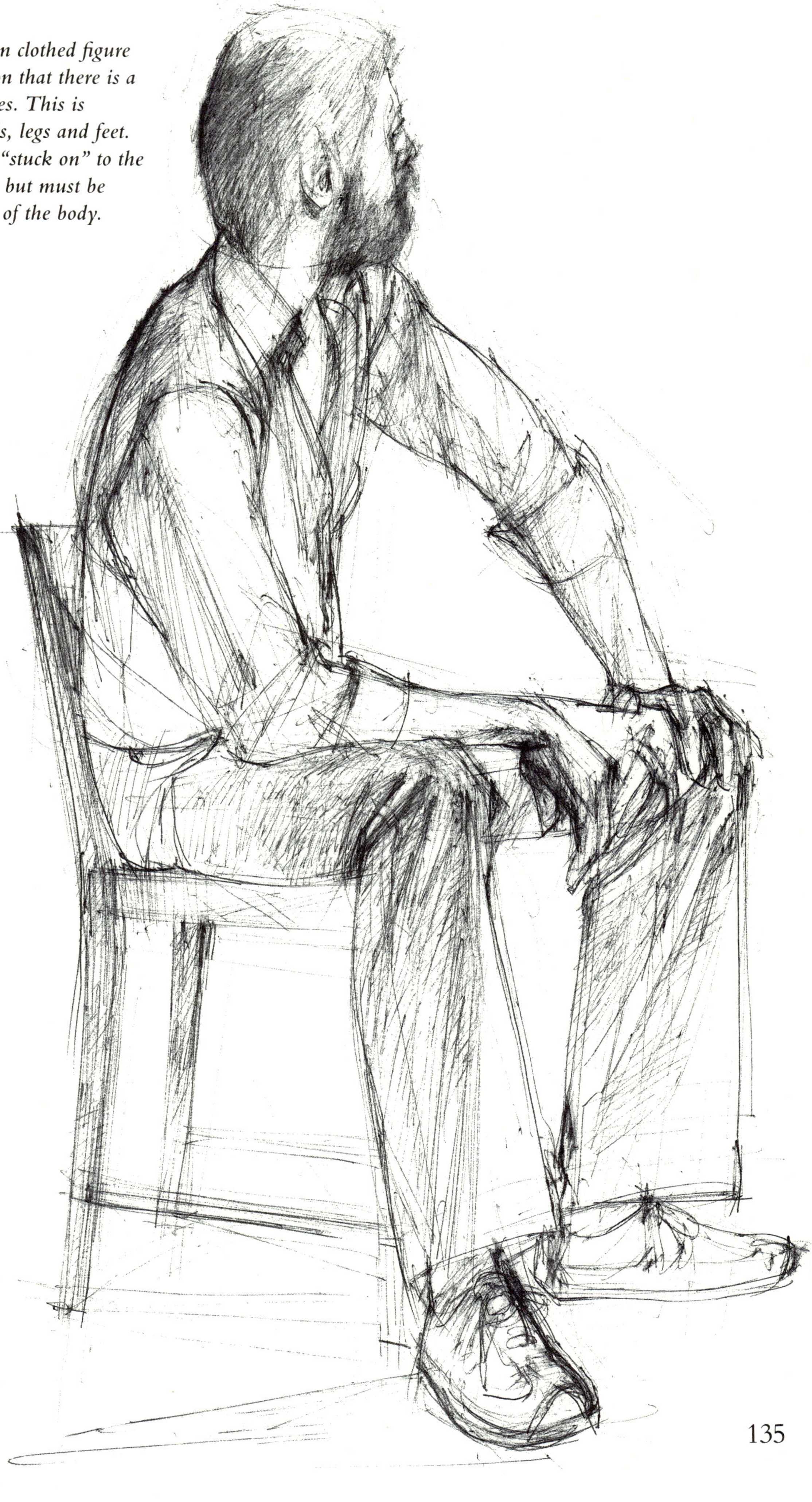

In this quick study of the slim legs of a girl, I have emphasized the "falling" movement by shading with downward strokes.

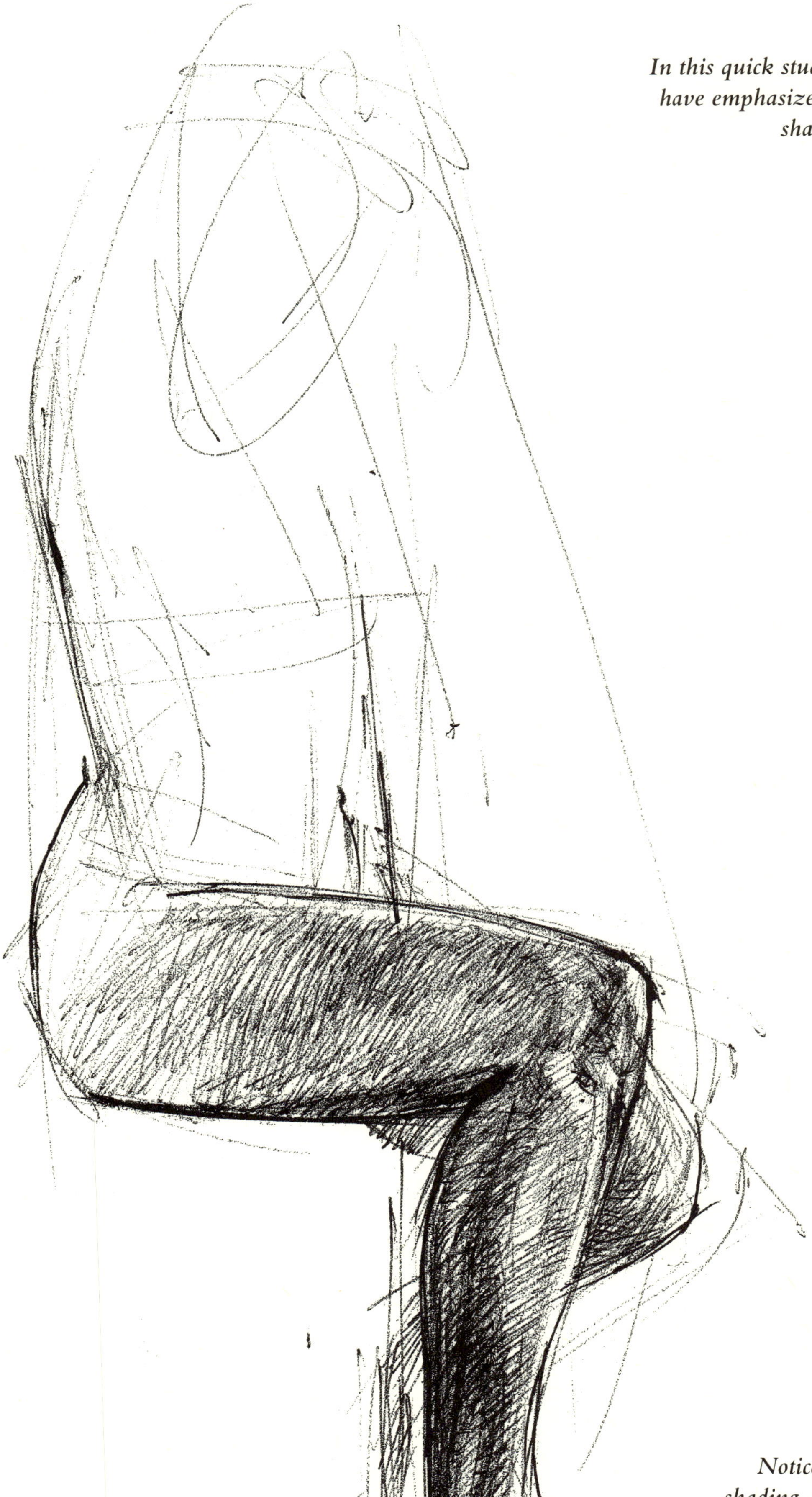

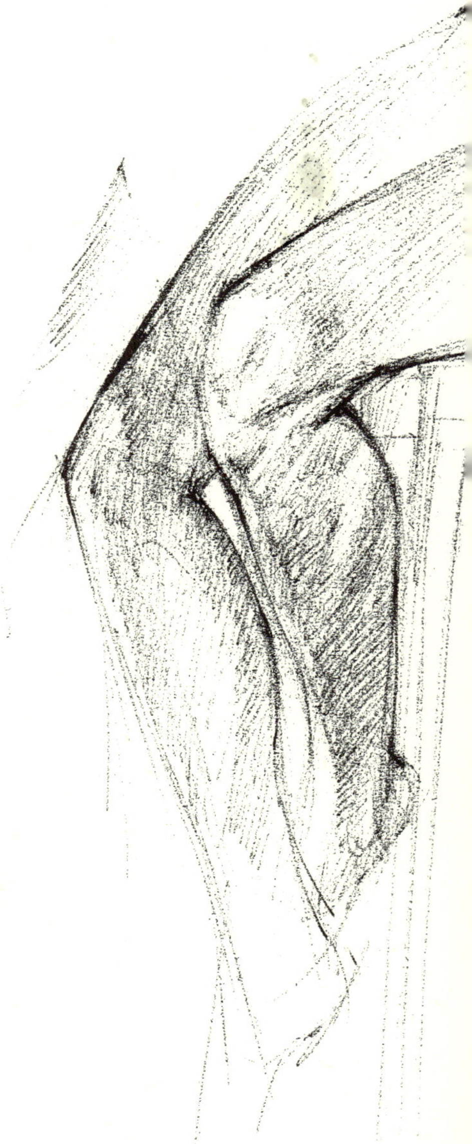

Notice how, by changing the direction of the shading, the shadow falling on these strong legs makes them appear heavy—an effect, incidentally, useful in drawing the legs of older people.

I have taken some care in rendering the torso and upper arms of this sturdy woman. However, even though I have only indicated the hands and feet, they are very much a part of the drawing.

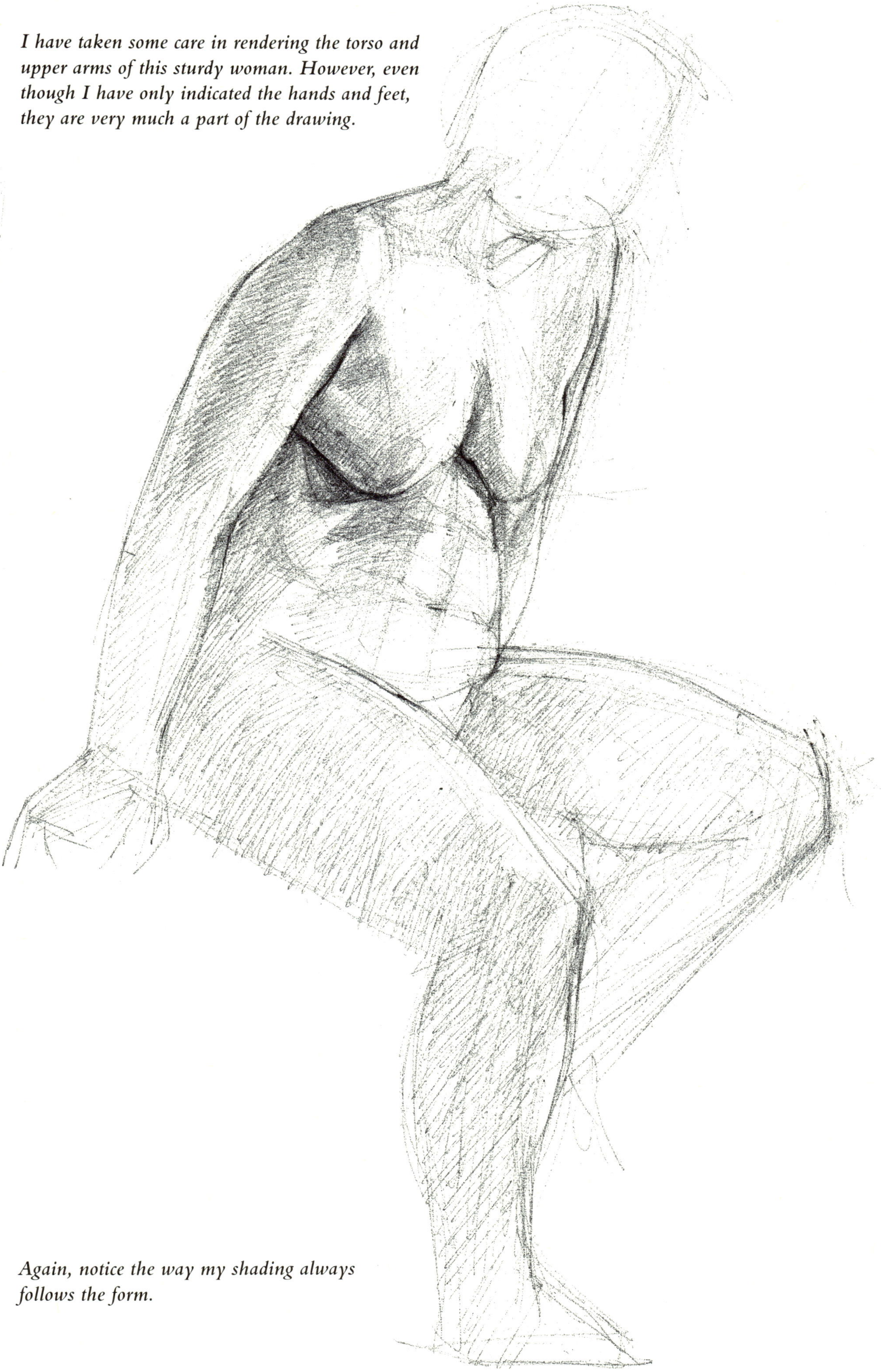

Again, notice the way my shading always follows the form.

When drawing a portrait, try to include the entire person pictured in his or her own environment.

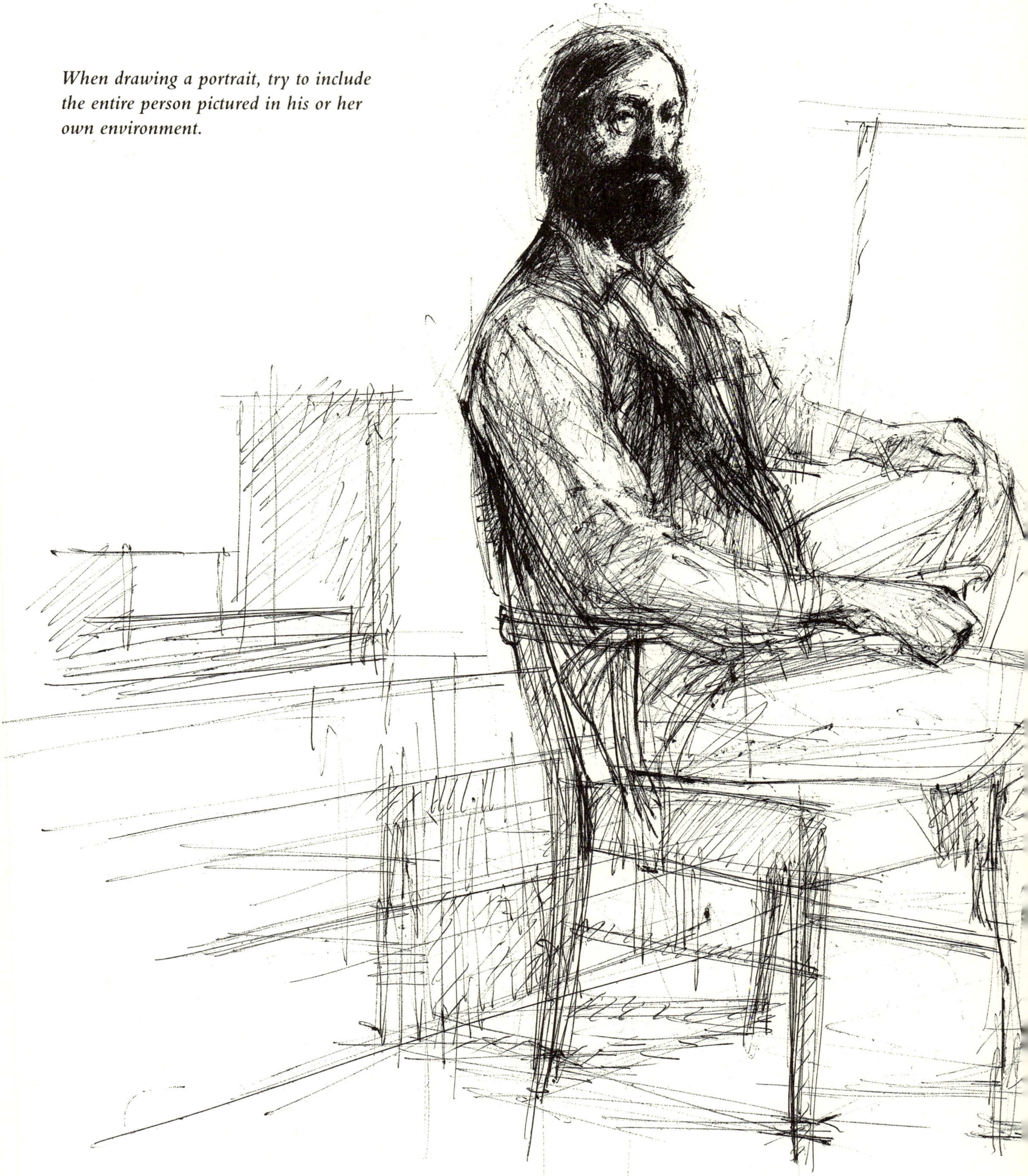

LESSON 14

Portrait Drawing

It is said that the famous Swedish painter and graphic artist, Anders Zorn, was interrupted while executing the portrait of a middle-aged lady of the Swedish bourgeois by his model crying, "It doesn't look like me at all!" "That," Zorn replied dryly, "is a hypothetical question that could only interest you, my dear lady. Your family and your descendants will be completely indifferent as to whether it looks like you or not. They will, on the other hand, be delighted to own a genuine Zorn." It sounds arrogant and unnecessarily cruel, but there is no doubt that Zorn was at least partially right. In fact, one could say that whether a portrait is or is not a true likeness has more to do with the vanity of the sitter than with art. One portrait can be true to life and, at the same time, be a poor drawing, while another can fail to capture a likeness but be brilliantly drawn.

When drawing a portrait one must get the proportions of the face as accurate as possible with the planes placed correctly. The expression is important, too, and the rendering must be both distinctive and dynamic. Exploring the varied expressions that the face is capable of and noting how the proportions of one face differ widely from another is exciting and can be the basis for remarkable drawings. Such approaches to portraiture suggest that merely seeking a likeness is of secondary importance.

So, don't be intimidated when someone asks you to draw their portrait. Make it clear to the person who insists on a perfect likeness that this is not your primary interest, that your goal is to bring out the sitter's personality. After all, in the final analysis, it is capturing the inner spirit of a person that brings a portrait to life.

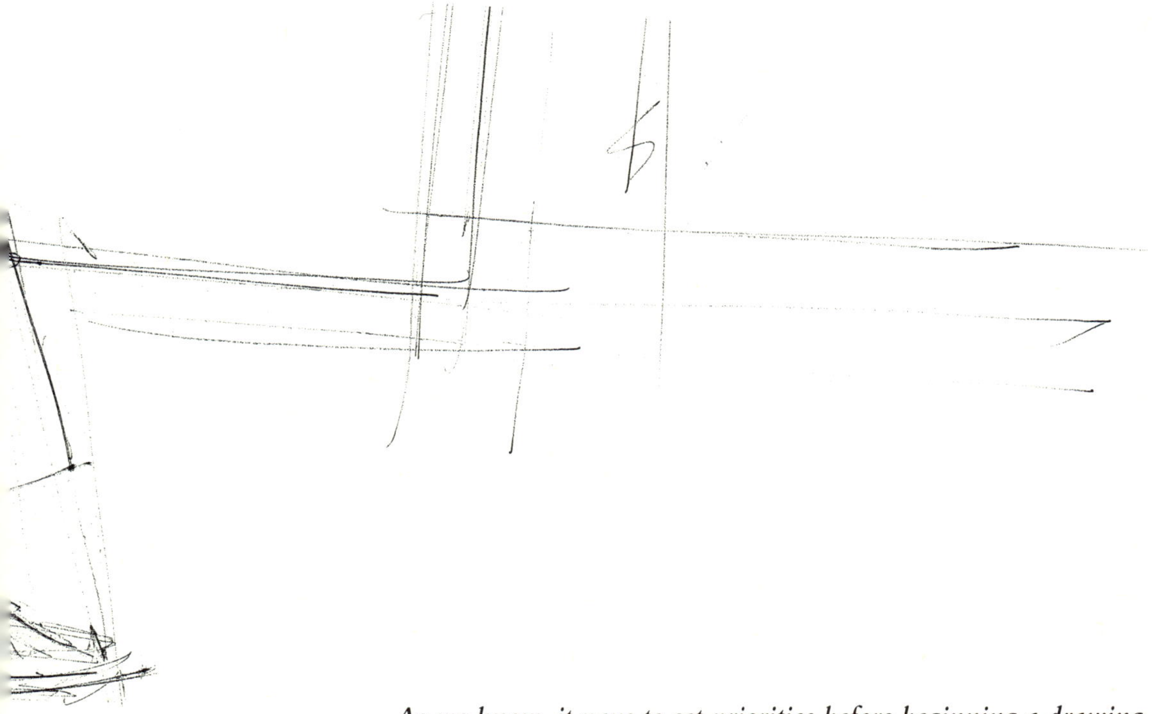

As we know, it pays to set priorities before beginning a drawing. Here my priority was to picture the artist, Anders Zorn, so I concentrated on rendering his face and torso in detail, and merely suggested the setting.

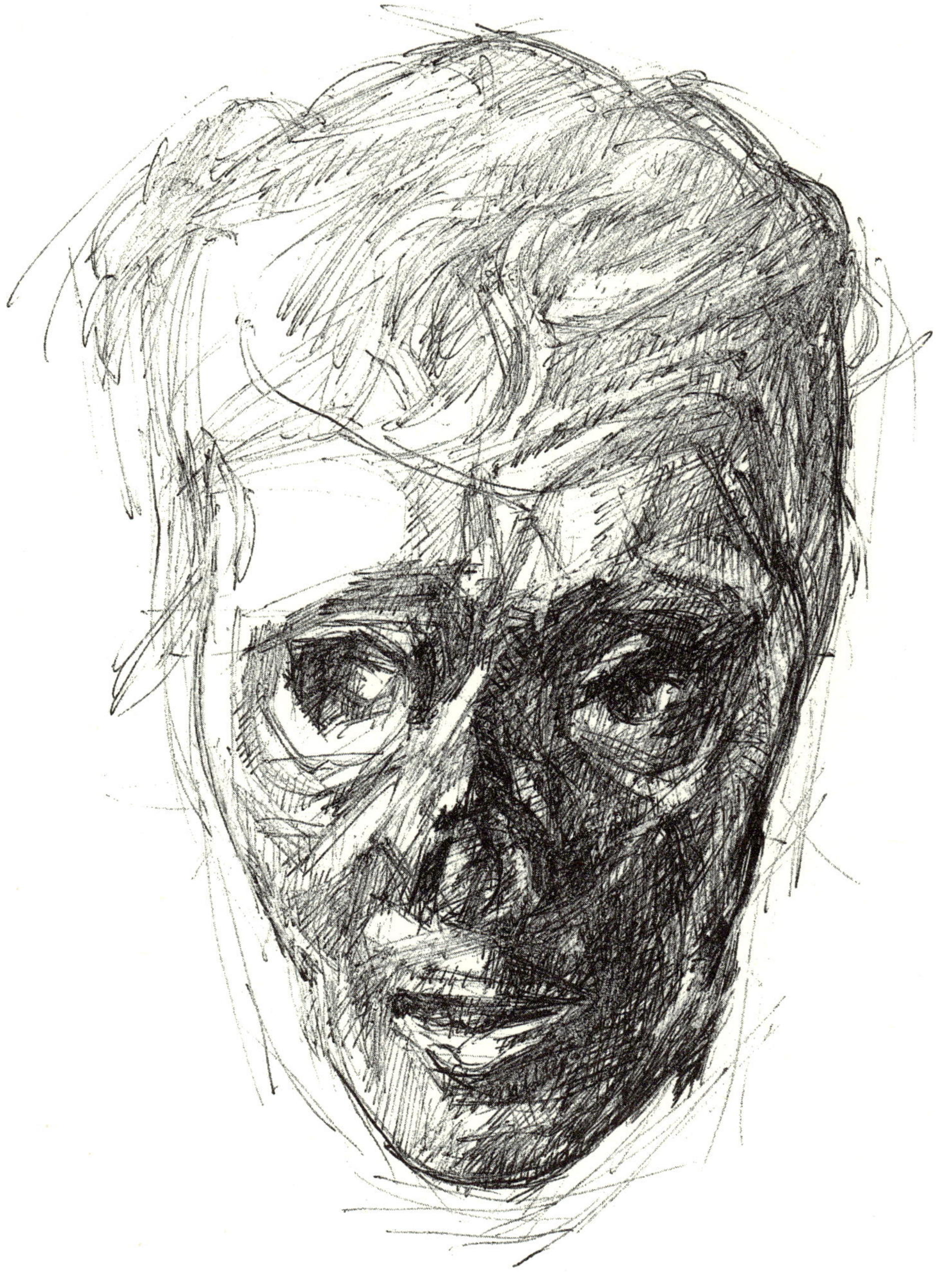

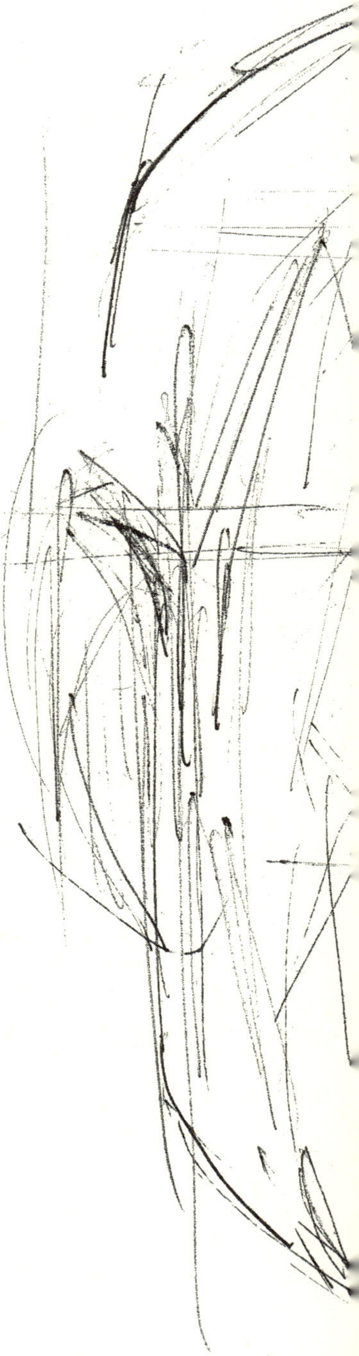

Mummies are always intriguing to draw, especially if you've had a chance to study skulls. In this mummy, the muscles, skin and hair appear here and there to give a better understanding of the anatomy of the head.

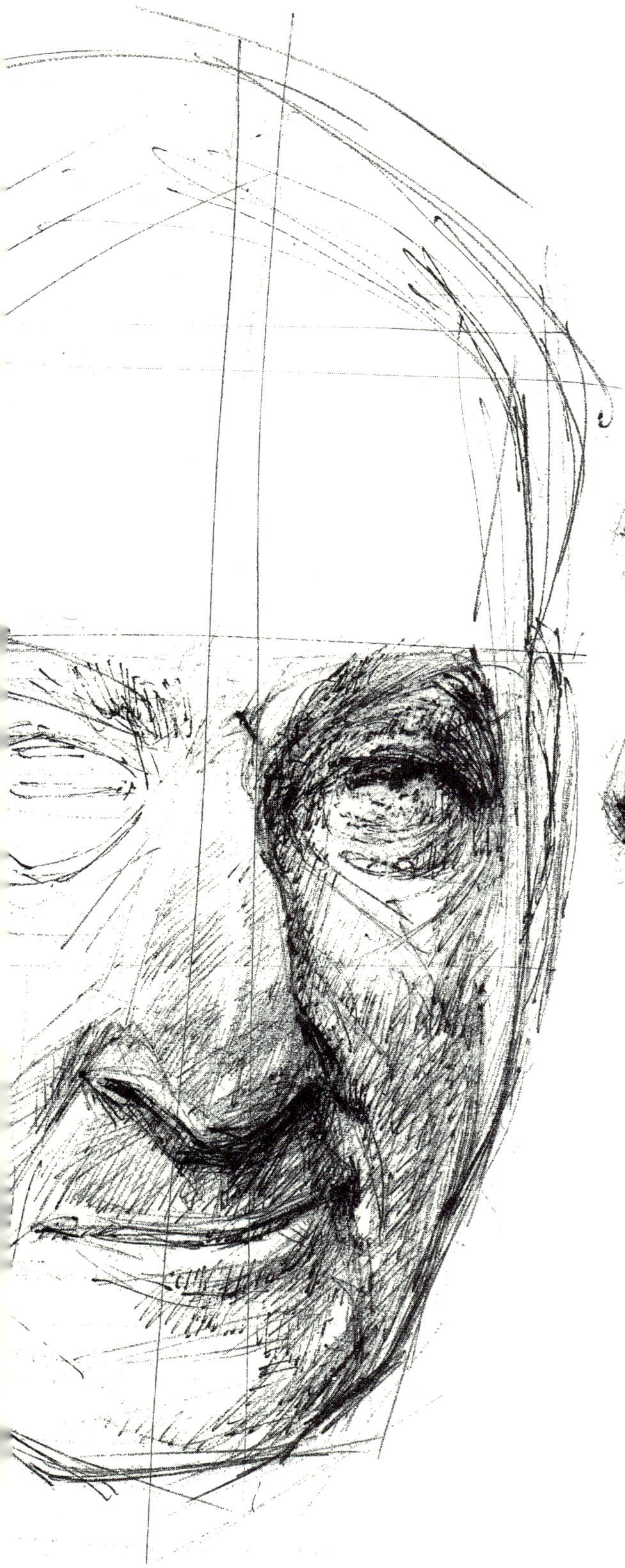

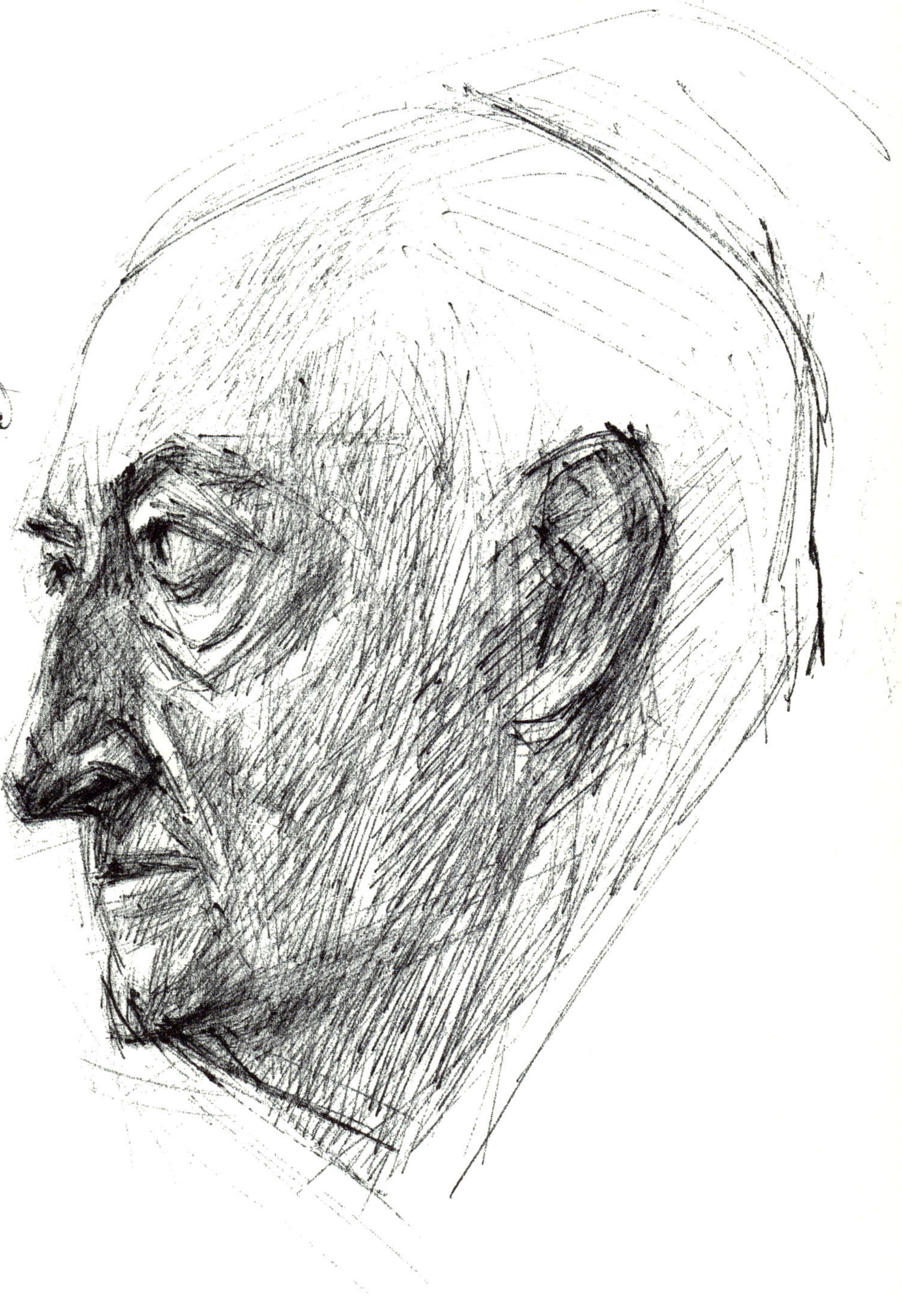

When you begin a portrait it's important to capture a sense of the whole mass of the head. It can be compared to the lump of clay the sculptor slaps on the modelling stand. It's just as ludicrous to see a drawing student begin a portrait without paying any attention to the total form as it would be to observe a sculptor start with an eye or a nose.

Notice how I begin by drawing the basic form—the "lump"—then the middle line and on to the placement of the eyes before I even think of starting on the finished drawing.

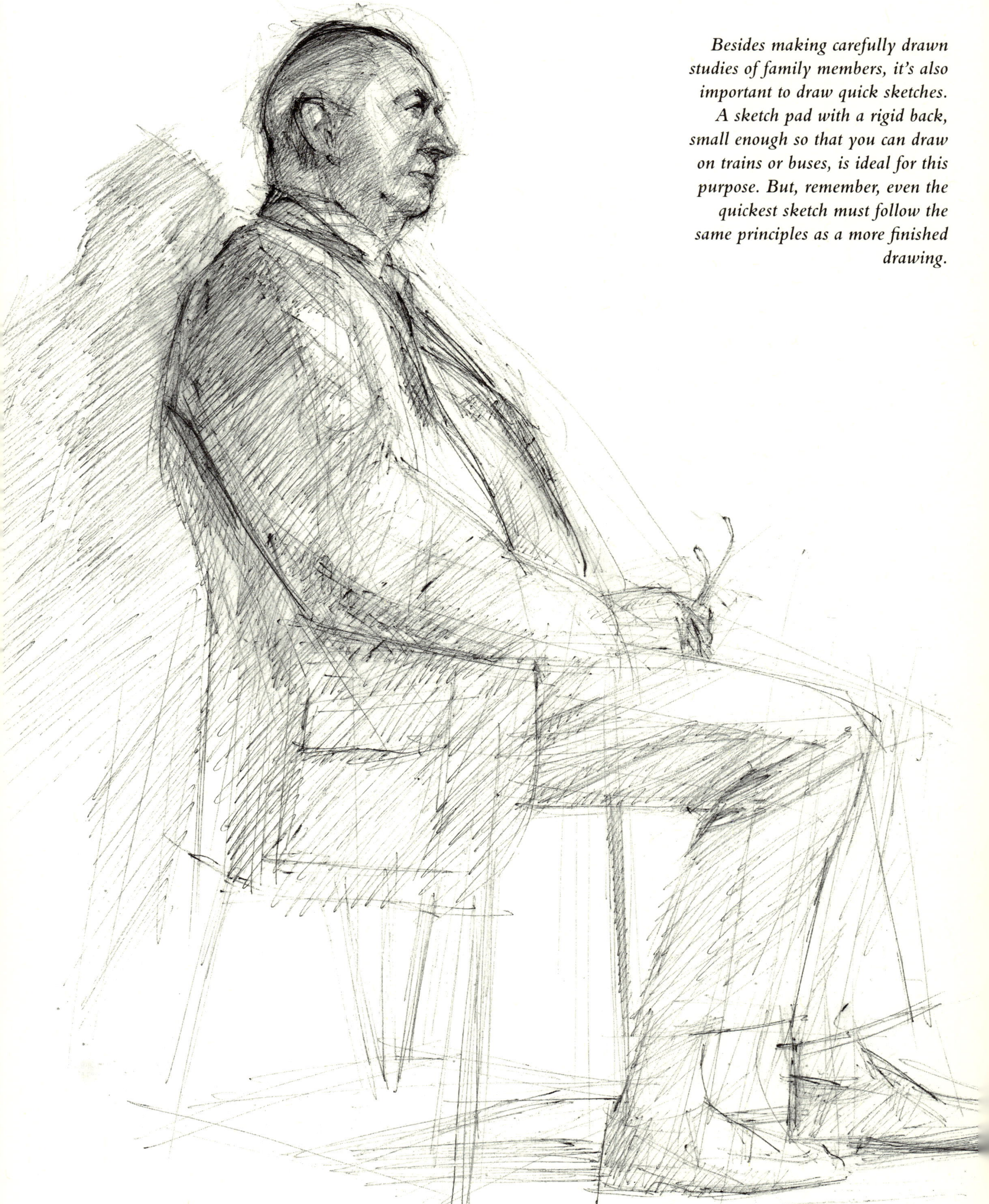

Besides making carefully drawn studies of family members, it's also important to draw quick sketches. A sketch pad with a rigid back, small enough so that you can draw on trains or buses, is ideal for this purpose. But, remember, even the quickest sketch must follow the same principles as a more finished drawing.

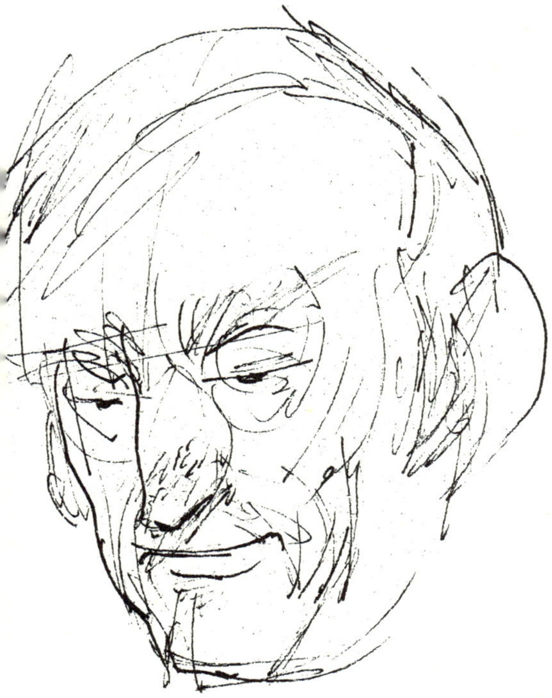

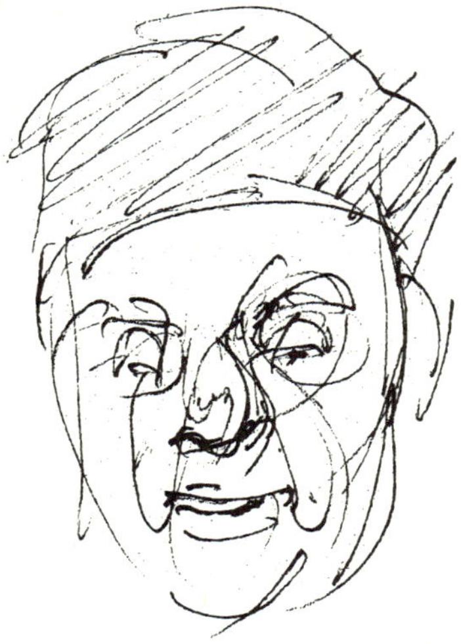

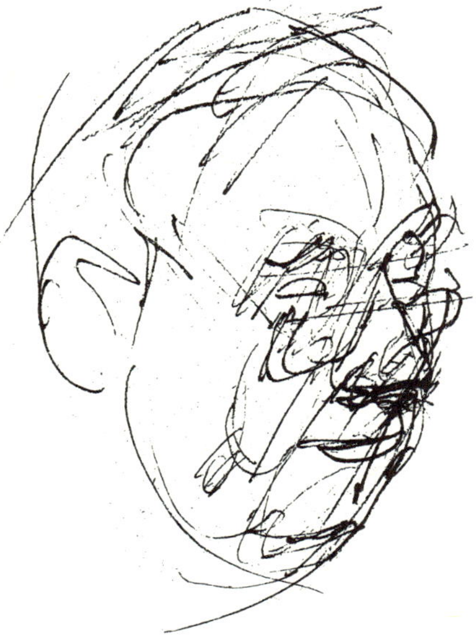

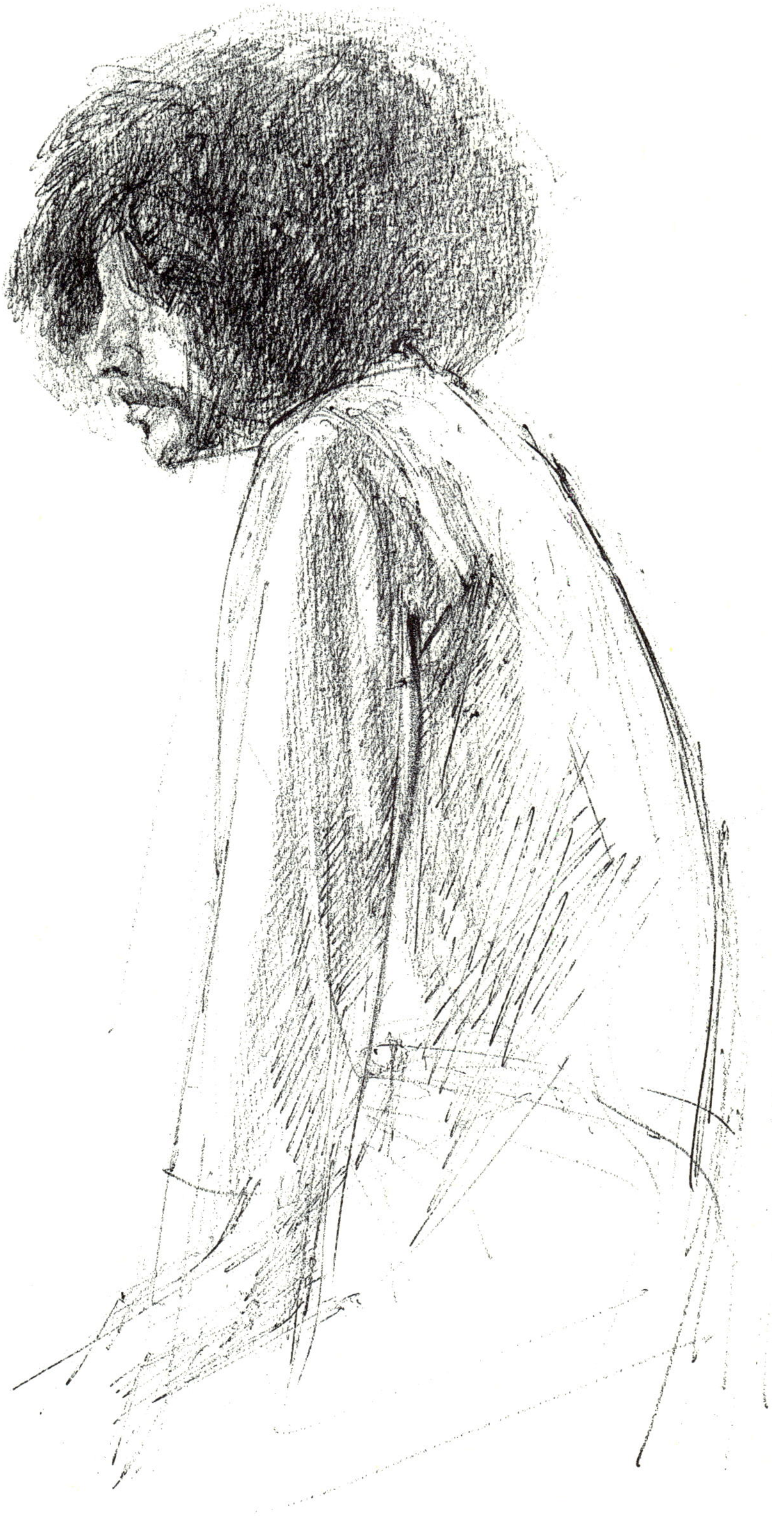

In this study, it is the big mop of hair that brings character to the drawing. Notice how the profile is carefully drawn and how a feeling of aggression is created by the way the arm, head and back form a triangle. This type of triangular composition was in use as long ago as the beginning of the Middle Ages and is still employed to suggest an aggressive or menacing situation.

Elderly people make sympathetic models. There is a certain satisfaction in rendering the character that many years of living have brought to an older face. It's easier, too, to capture the form in a head like this.

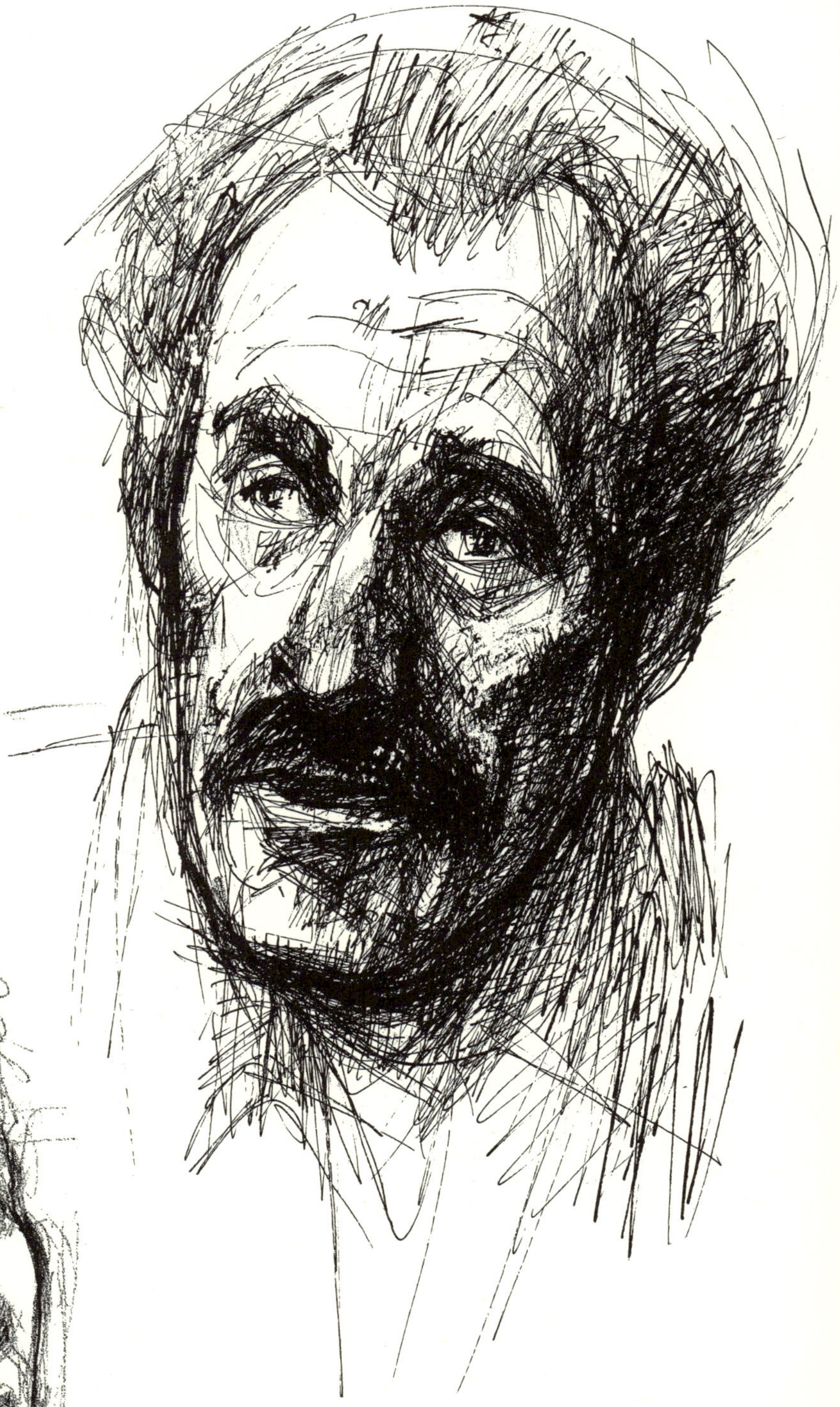

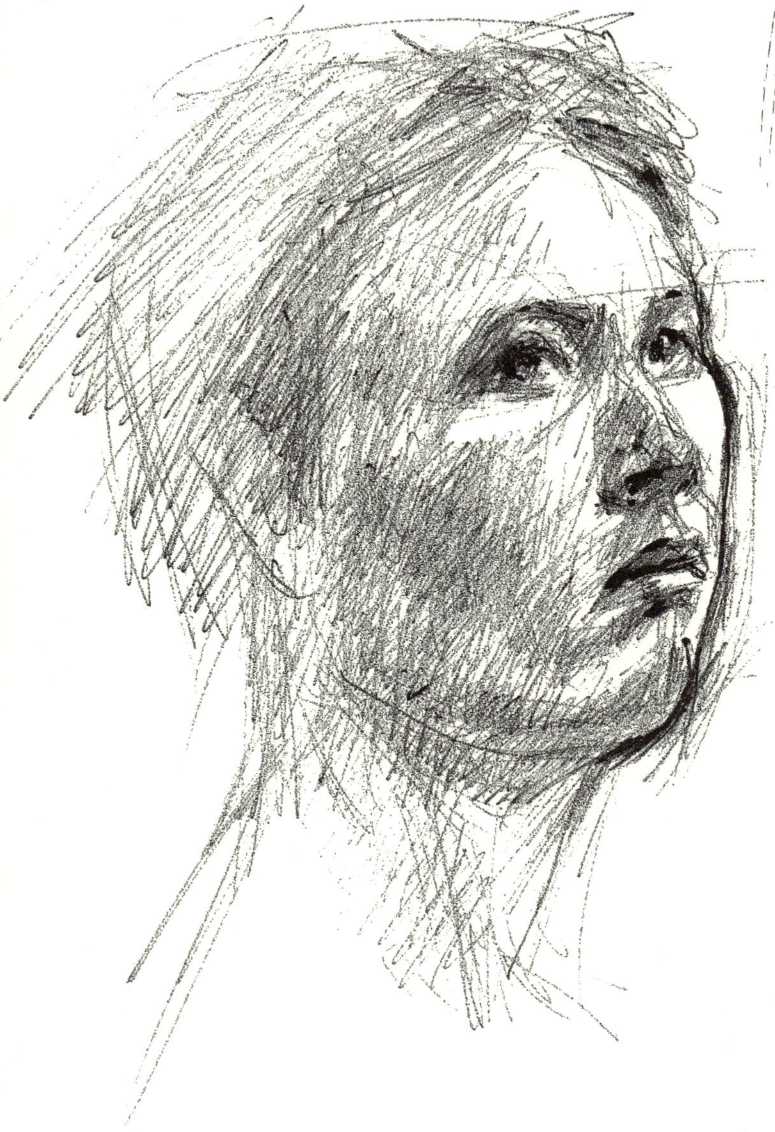

You should also draw young people. The smooth features of an immature face can be difficult to grasp. Try your hand at both male and female heads, noting the distinguishing features that identify each sex.

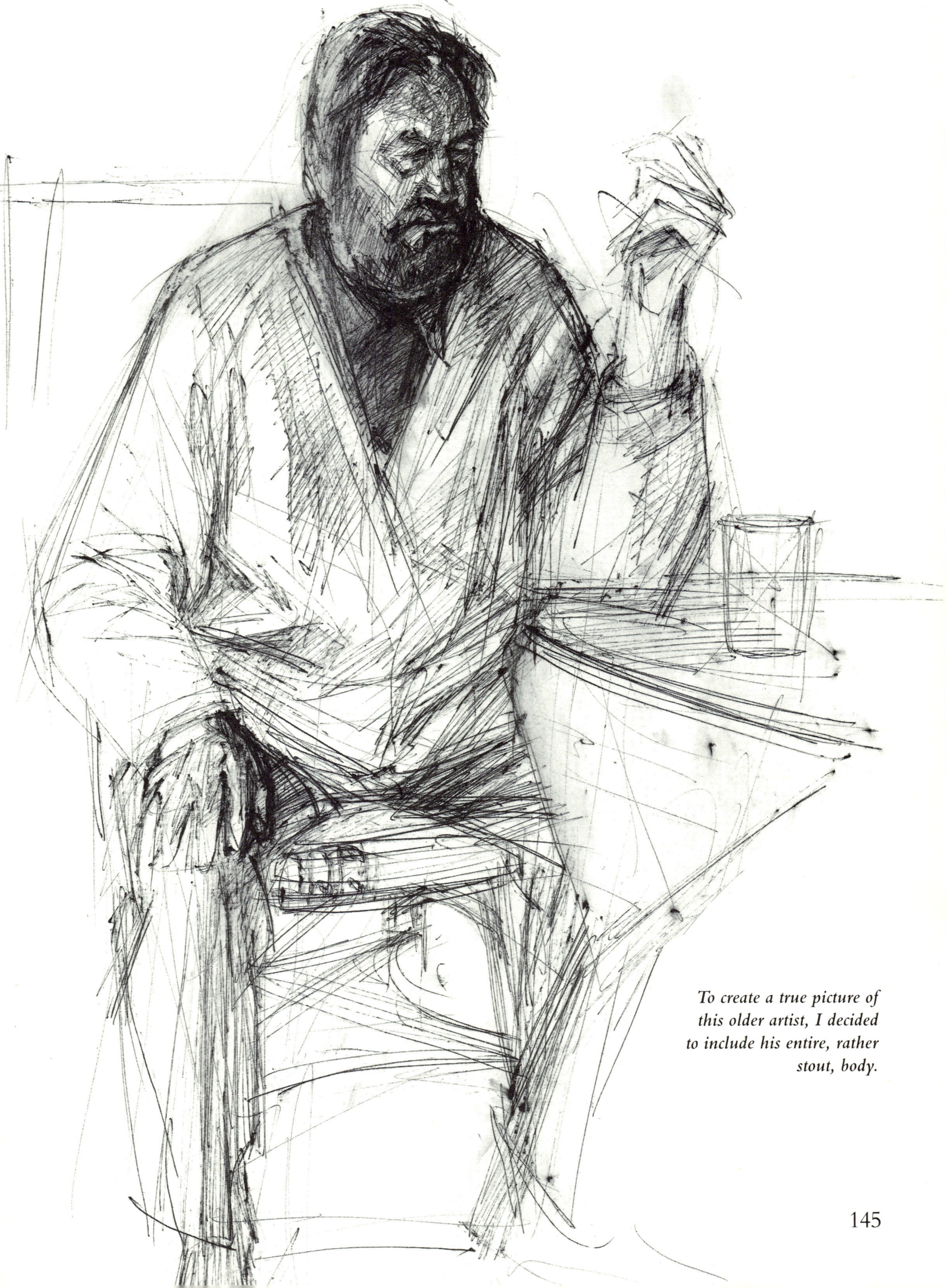

To create a true picture of this older artist, I decided to include his entire, rather stout, body.

A very full and distinctive head of hair inspired me to make this portrait. It's interesting how the position of the arms both finishes and repeats the form of the head.

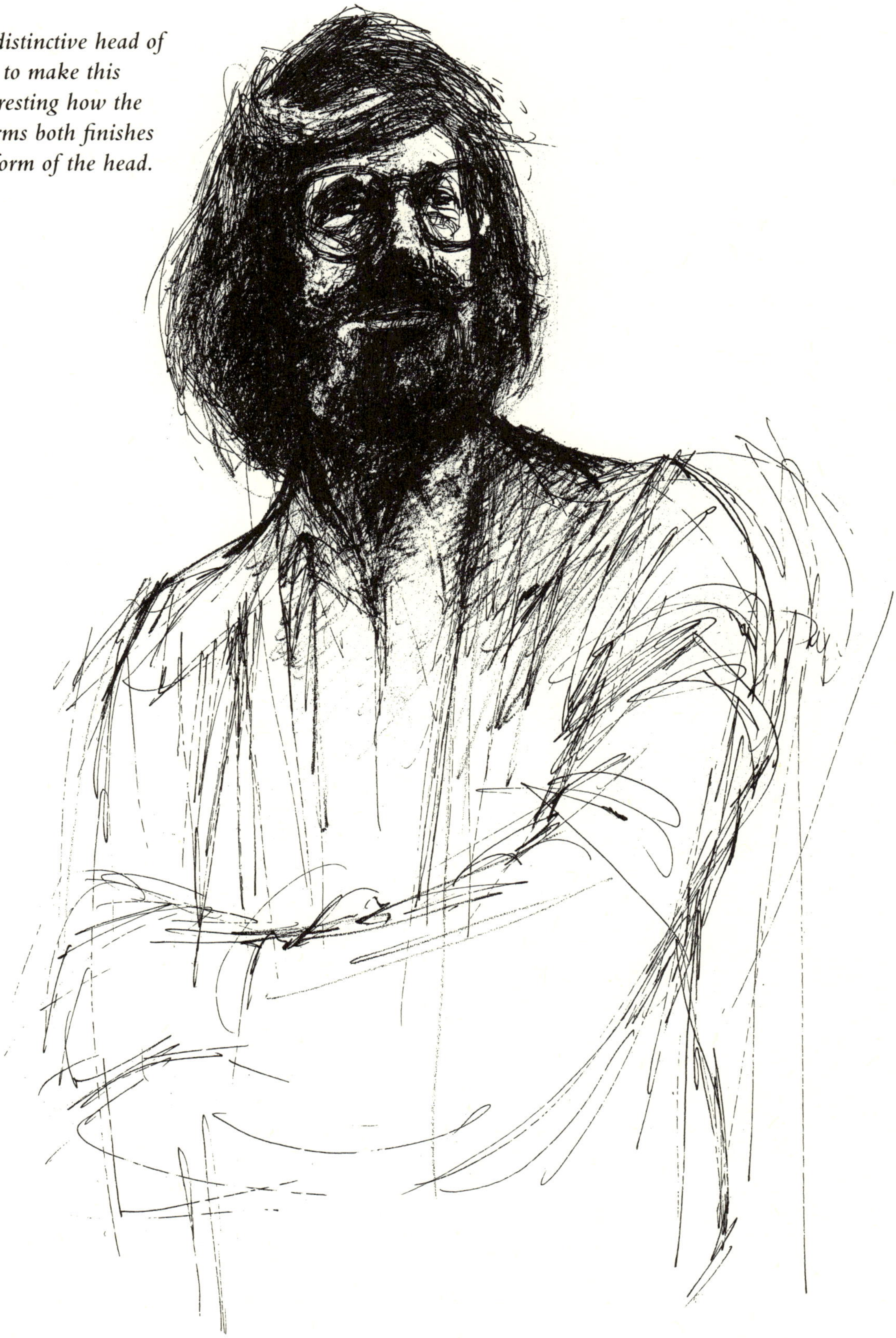

Thinking of the mass of the head as having the shape of an egg and then scribing it with measuring lines that correspond to the placement of various features, such as the nose or the eyes, will make it easier for you to understand the placement of the planes.

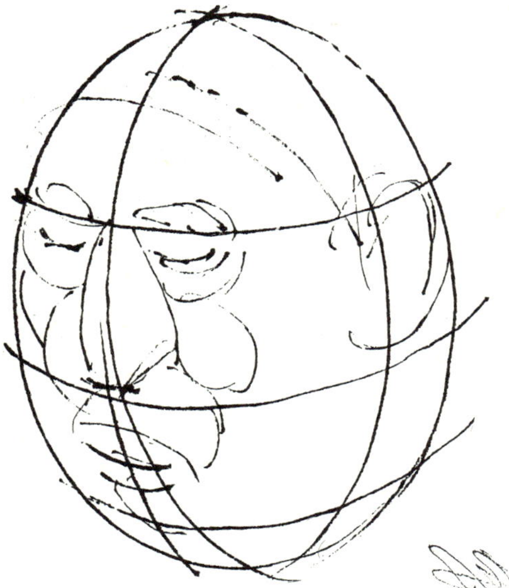

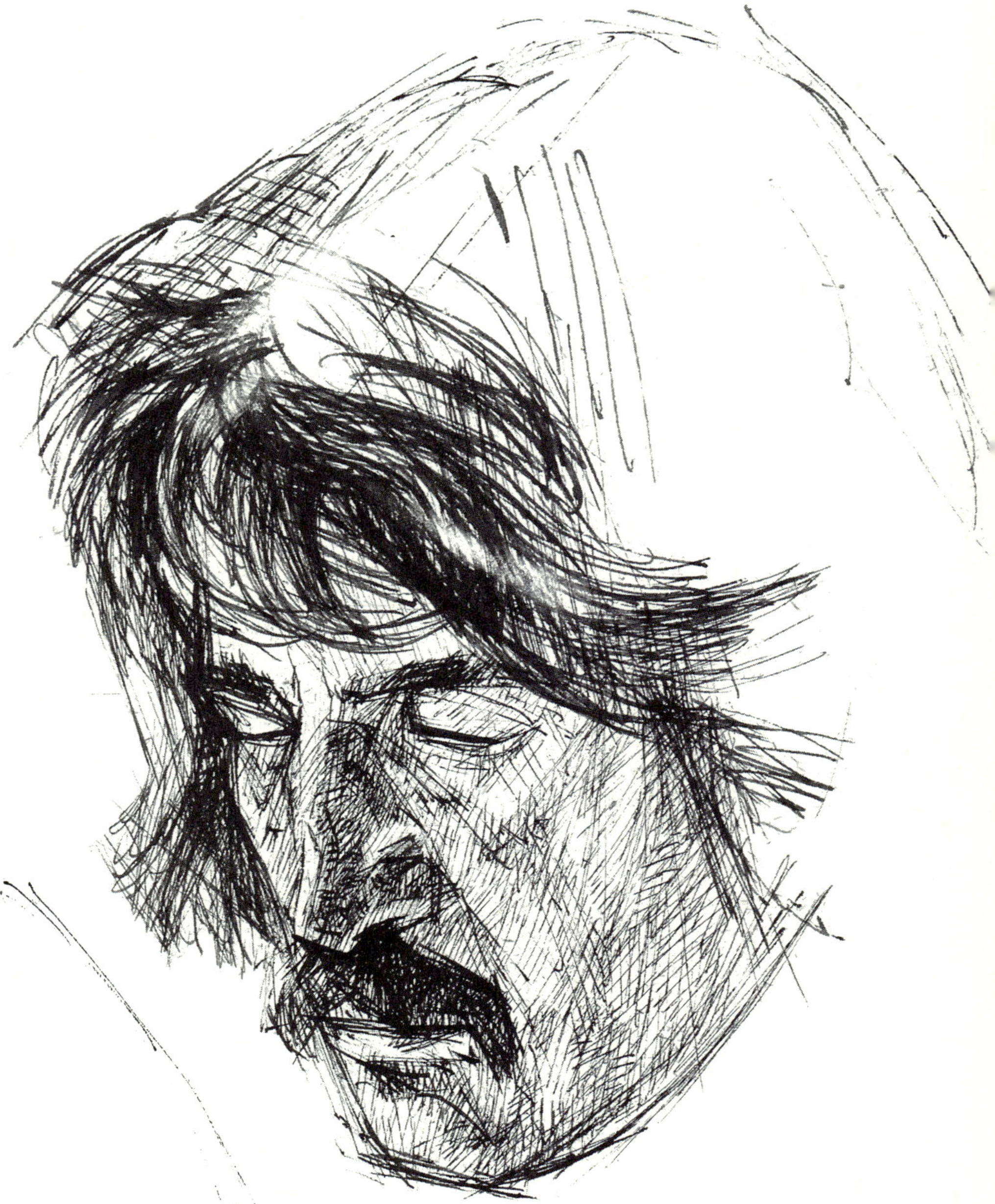

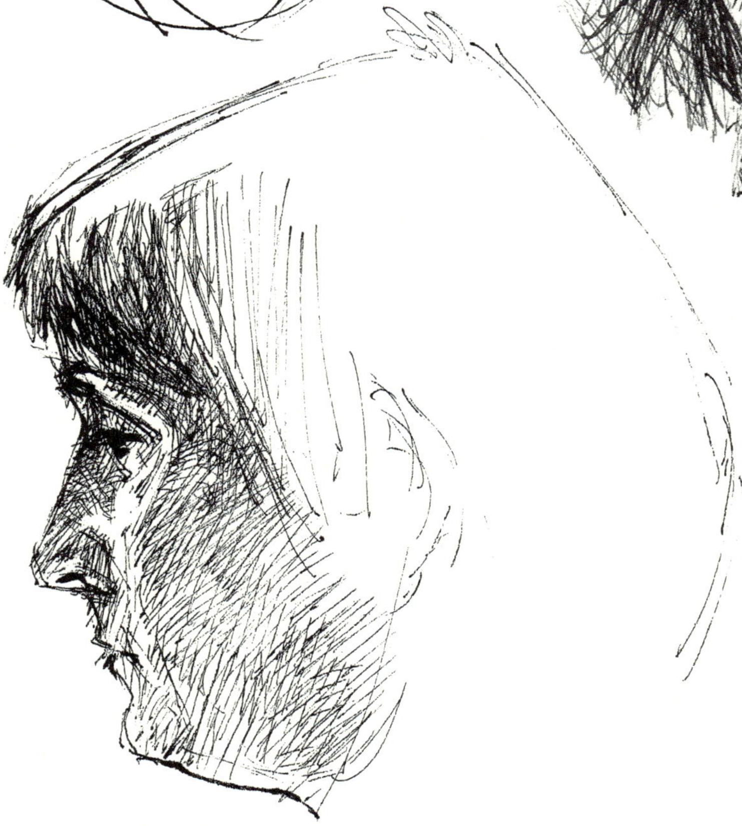

Drawing even straightforward profiles is not as easy as it looks but it's good practice and helps you to understand the form of the head from another angle.

Afterword

I hope this book demonstrates how observation and subject drawing are two very significant ways of recording one's surroundings. They are very different, for example, from photography by which we also see and record, not with our own eyes, but by means of technical aids.

Having sat by the roadside on a warm summer's day and sketched the surroundings or attempted a portrait of Aunt Anna, you begin to understand that the personal effort you put into such drawing activities yields experiences that widen your perception.

The experience of sitting with a piece of paper and a few simple tools to create a personal impression is a pleasure one would like to grant every human. To draw is to learn to see! When one's eyes are opened and trained to notice things around one, then one is not so easily deceived.

Drawing ought to be a way of life and a daily pleasure both in itself and as preparation for enjoying the work of others. Drawings are being created every minute of every day wherever people live and work and, for some, drawing is everything. Adolf Menzel, when asked why he drew everyday, succinctly answered, "I can't find anything I enjoy as much!" He was then 82 years old and had been drawing since childhood.

Let me end by saying that it would please me very much if this book shows you the way to a life made rich by the experience of drawing.

Karl V. Larsen, graphic artist and teacher.

Summer, 1988.

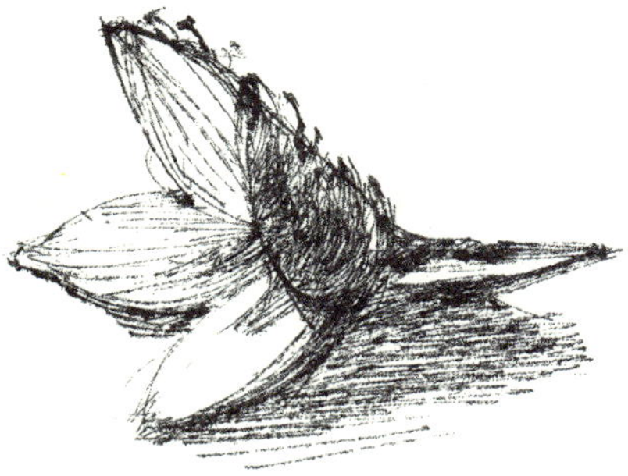